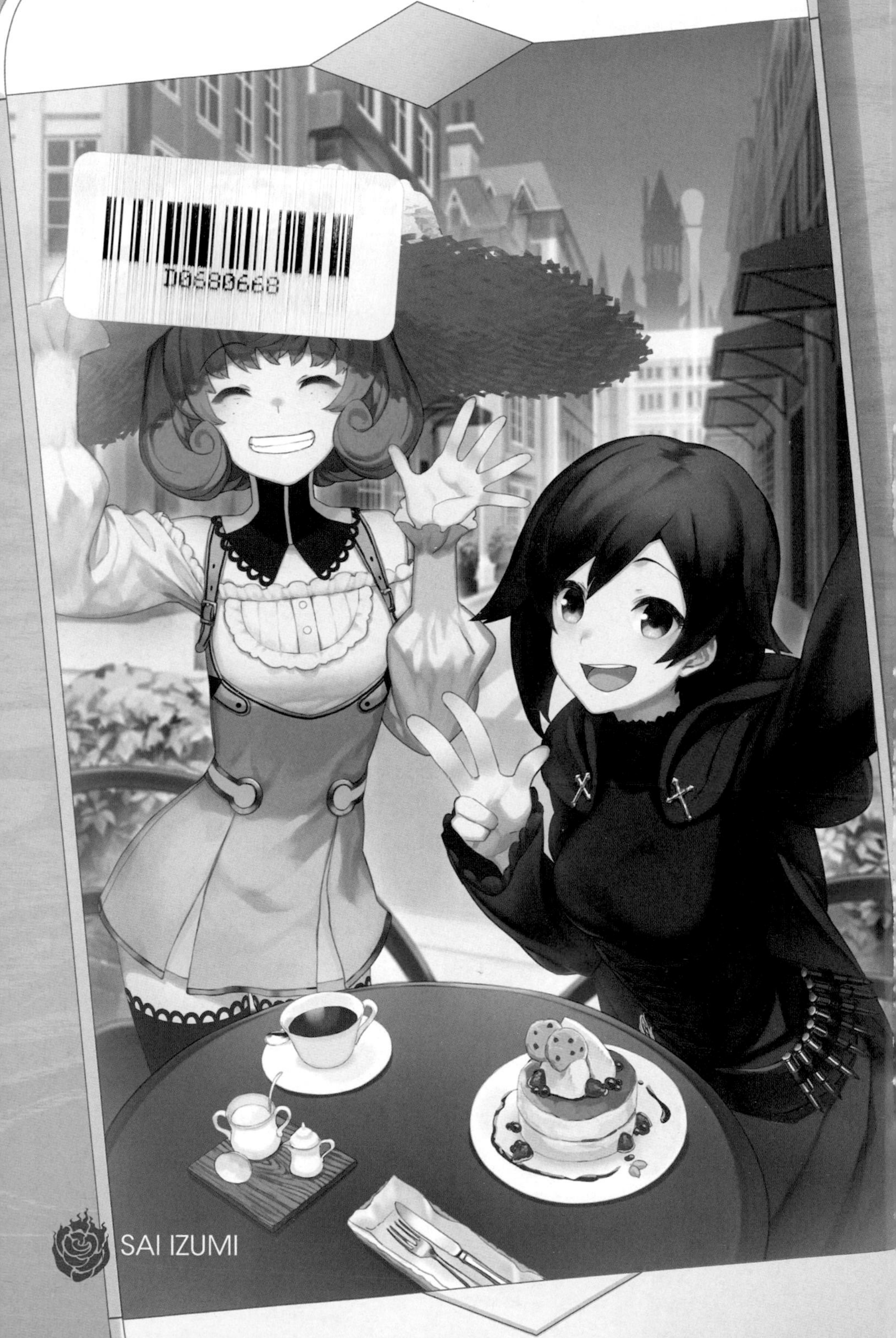
SAI IZUMI

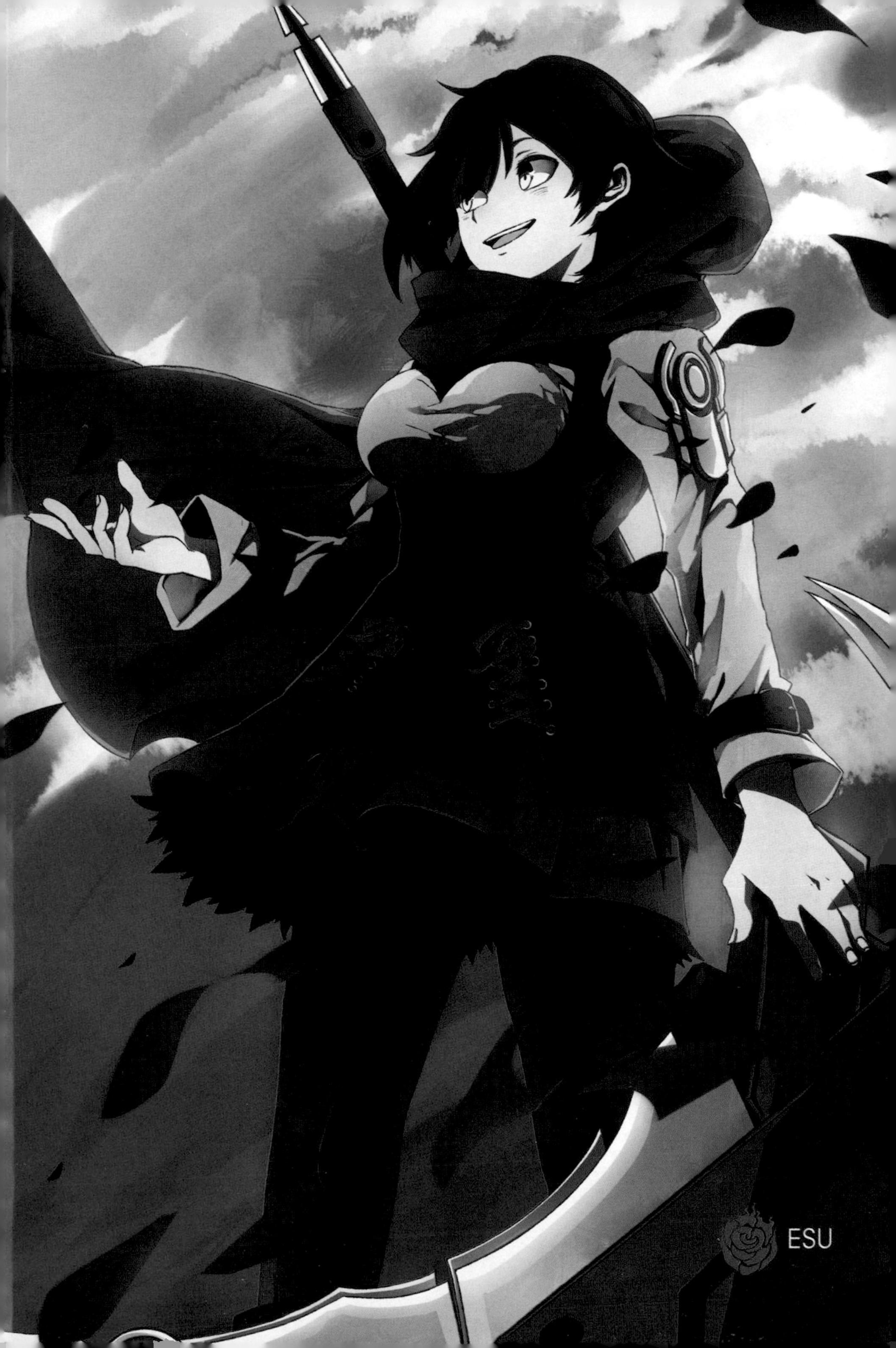
ESU

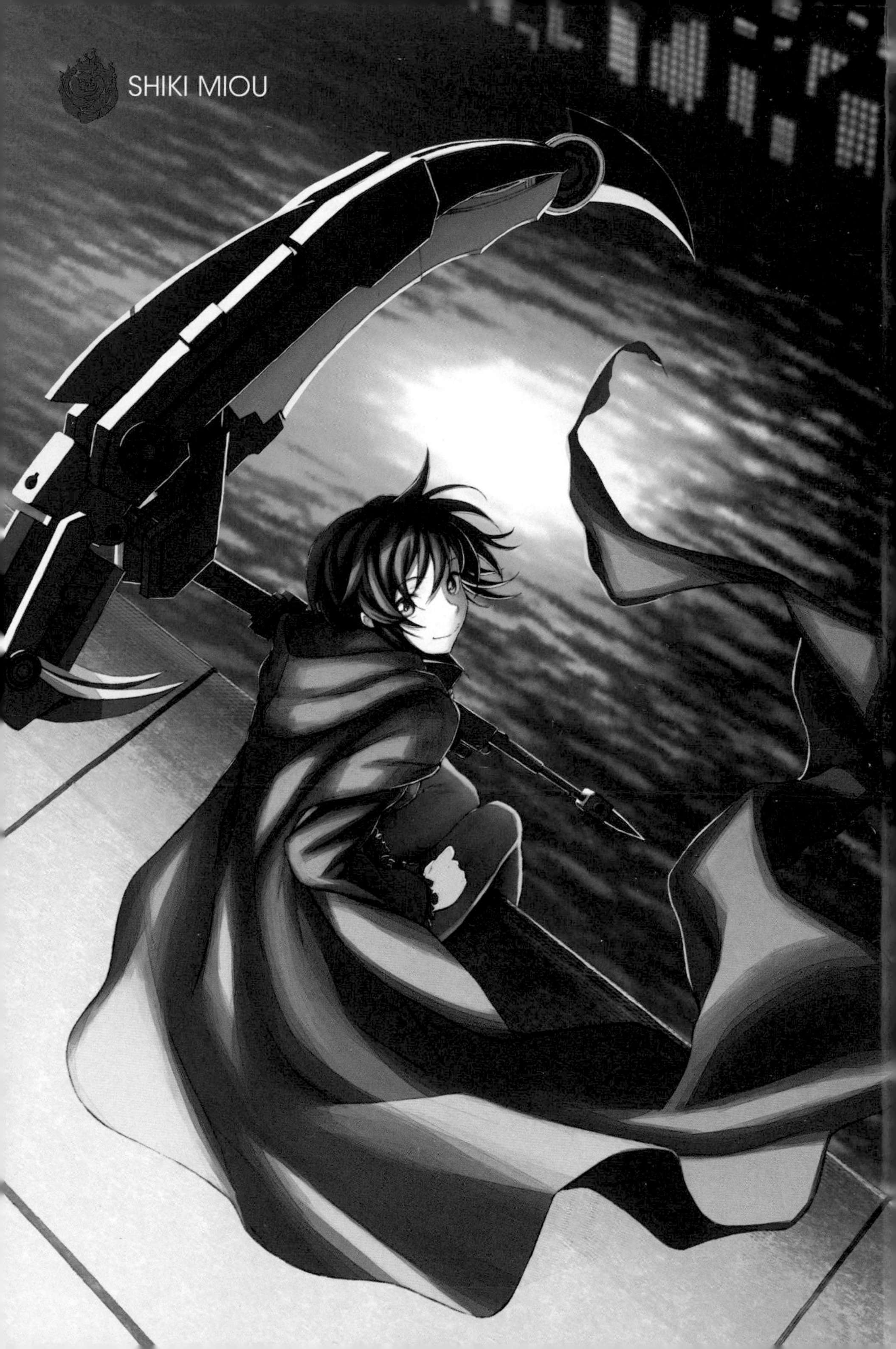
SHIKI MIOU

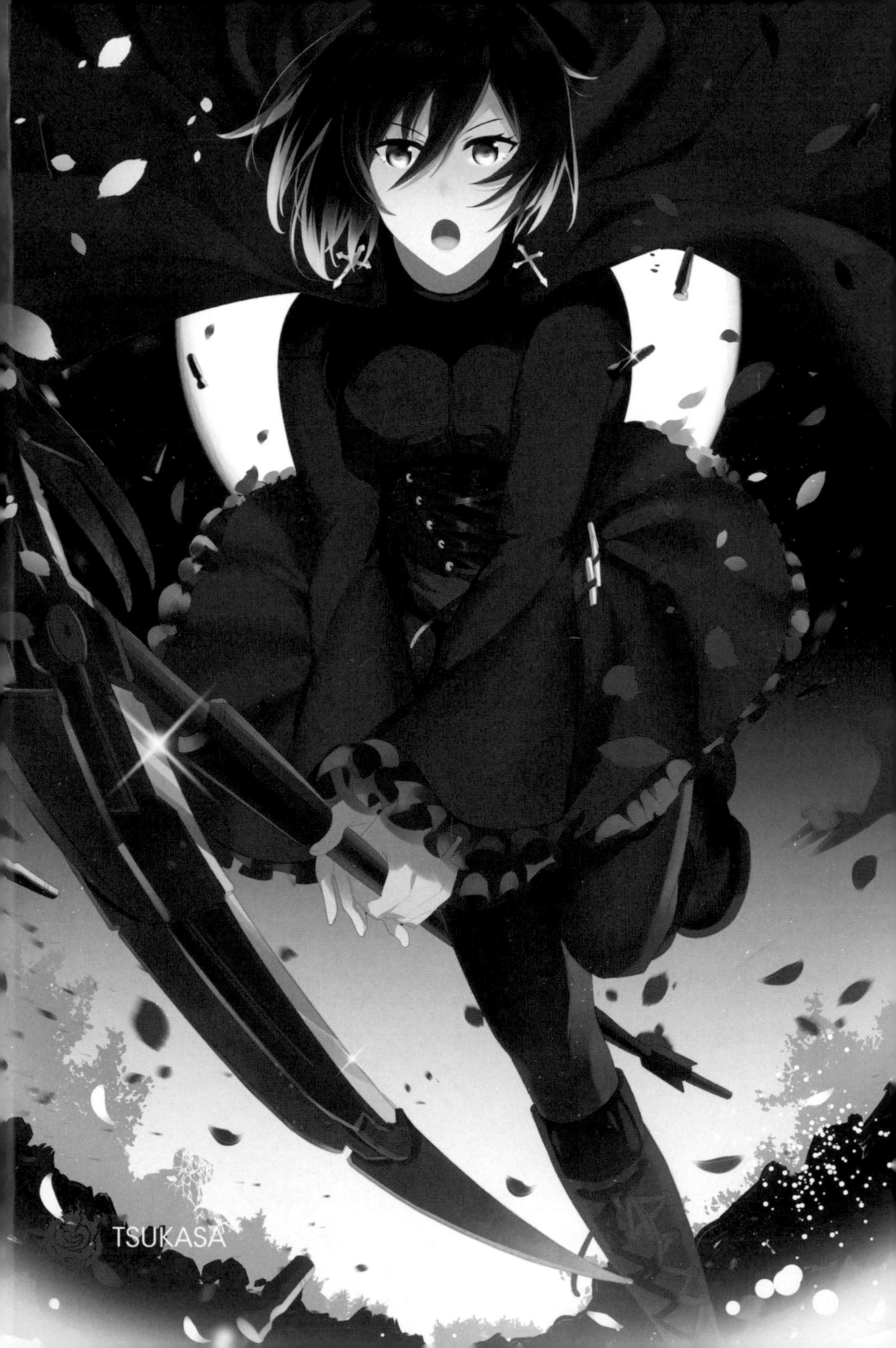
TSUKASA

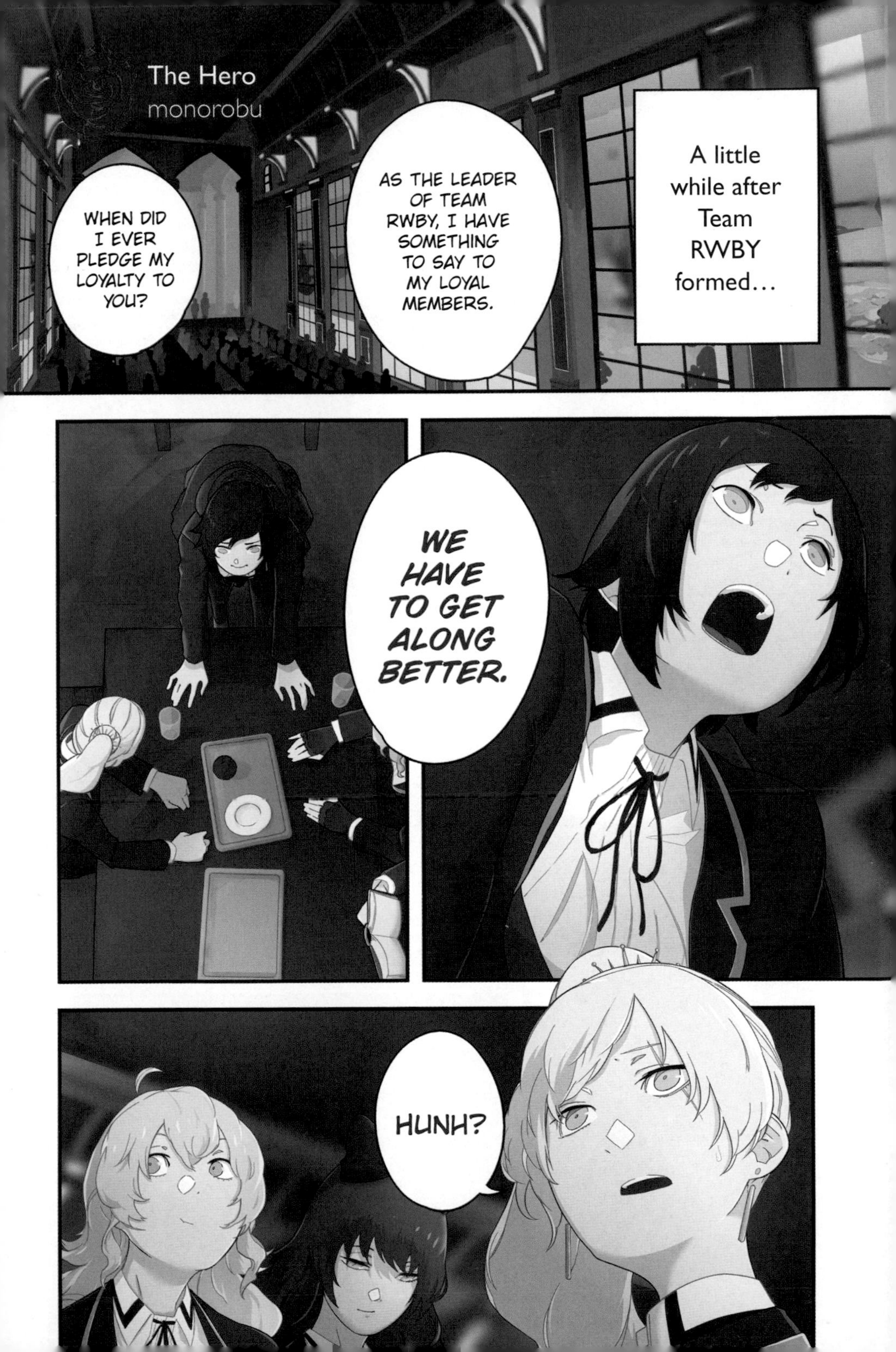
The Hero
monorobu
A little while after Team RWBY formed…
AS THE LEADER OF TEAM RWBY, I HAVE SOMETHING TO SAY TO MY LOYAL MEMBERS.
WHEN DID I EVER PLEDGE MY LOYALTY TO YOU?
WE HAVE TO GET ALONG BETTER.
HUNH?

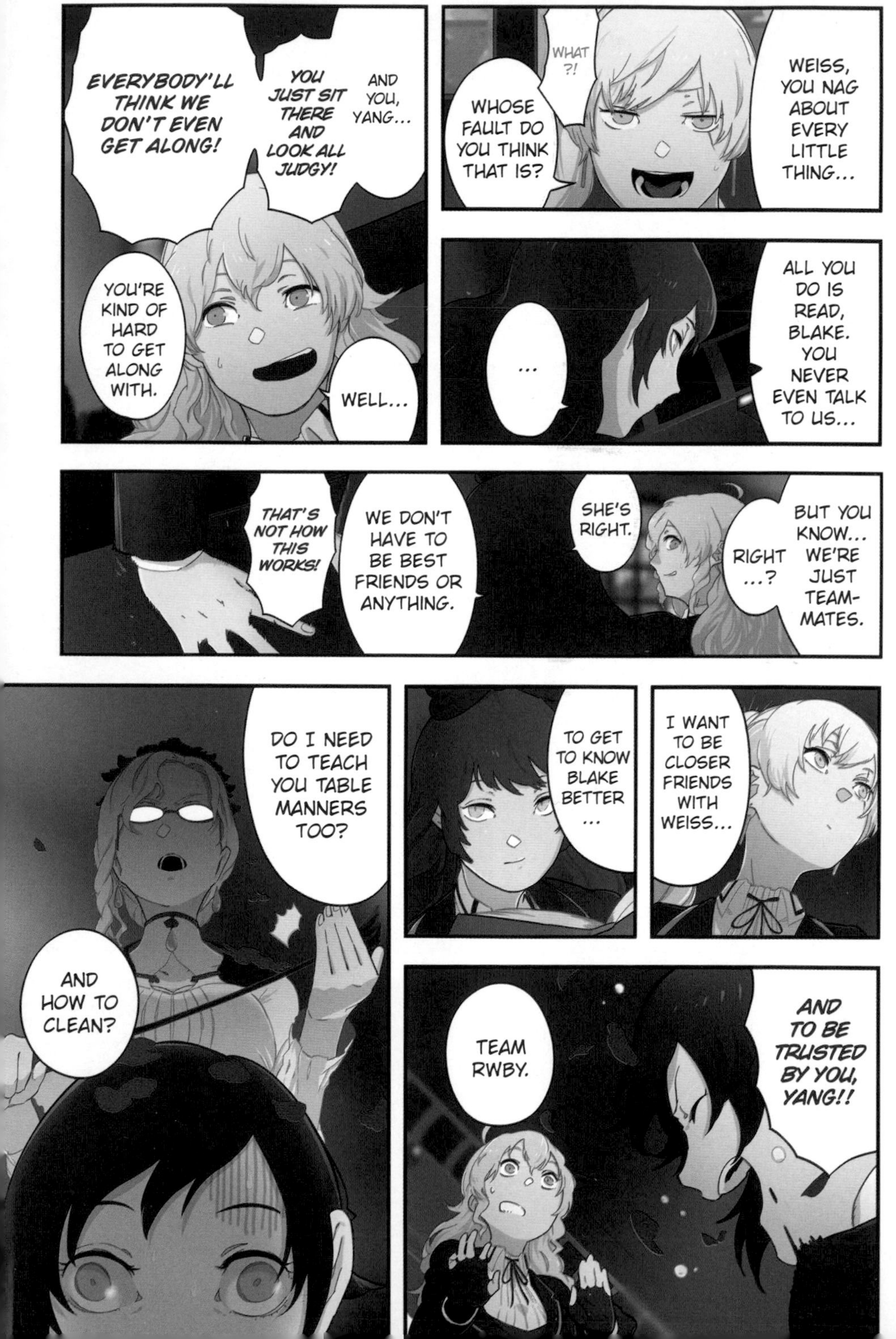
WEISS, YOU NAG ABOUT EVERY LITTLE THING...
WHAT ?!
WHOSE FAULT DO YOU THINK THAT IS?
ALL YOU DO IS READ, BLAKE. YOU NEVER EVEN TALK TO US...
...
AND YOU, YANG...
YOU JUST SIT THERE AND LOOK ALL JUDGY!
EVERYBODY'LL THINK WE DON'T EVEN GET ALONG!
WELL...
YOU'RE KIND OF HARD TO GET ALONG WITH.
BUT YOU KNOW... WE'RE JUST TEAM-MATES.
RIGHT ...?
SHE'S RIGHT.
WE DON'T HAVE TO BE BEST FRIENDS OR ANYTHING.
THAT'S NOT HOW THIS WORKS!
I WANT TO BE CLOSER FRIENDS WITH WEISS...
TO GET TO KNOW BLAKE BETTER ...
AND TO BE TRUSTED BY YOU, YANG!!
TEAM RWBY.
DO I NEED TO TEACH YOU TABLE MANNERS TOO?
AND HOW TO CLEAN?

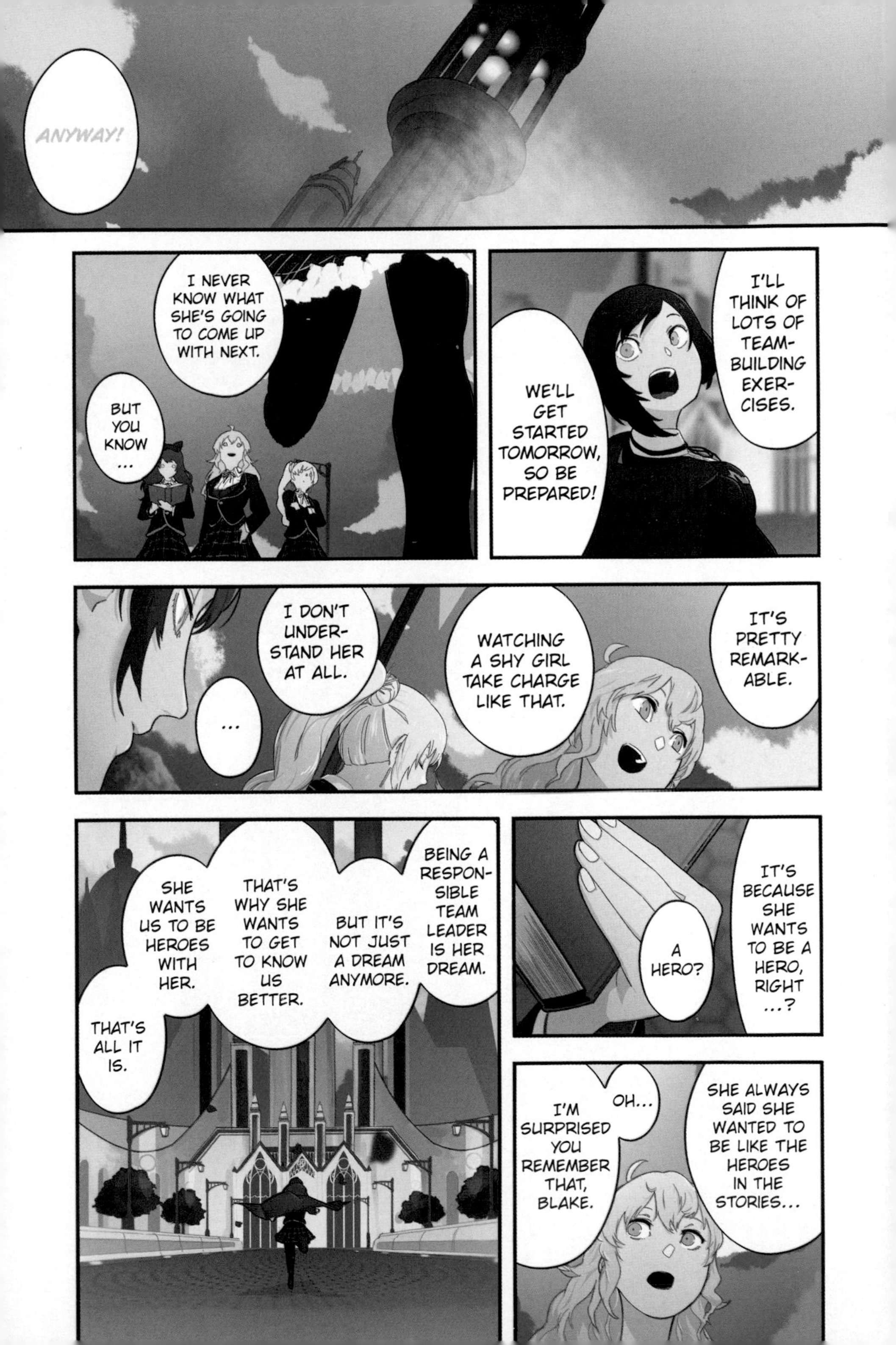
ANYWAY!
I'LL THINK OF LOTS OF TEAM-BUILDING EXERCISES.
WE'LL GET STARTED TOMORROW, SO BE PREPARED!
I NEVER KNOW WHAT SHE'S GOING TO COME UP WITH NEXT.
BUT YOU KNOW ...
IT'S PRETTY REMARKABLE.
WATCHING A SHY GIRL TAKE CHARGE LIKE THAT.
I DON'T UNDERSTAND HER AT ALL.
...
IT'S BECAUSE SHE WANTS TO BE A HERO, RIGHT ...?
A HERO?
SHE ALWAYS SAID SHE WANTED TO BE LIKE THE HEROES IN THE STORIES...
OH... I'M SURPRISED YOU REMEMBER THAT, BLAKE.
BEING A RESPONSIBLE TEAM LEADER IS HER DREAM.
BUT IT'S NOT JUST A DREAM ANYMORE.
THAT'S WHY SHE WANTS TO GET TO KNOW US BETTER.
SHE WANTS US TO BE HEROES WITH HER.
THAT'S ALL IT IS.

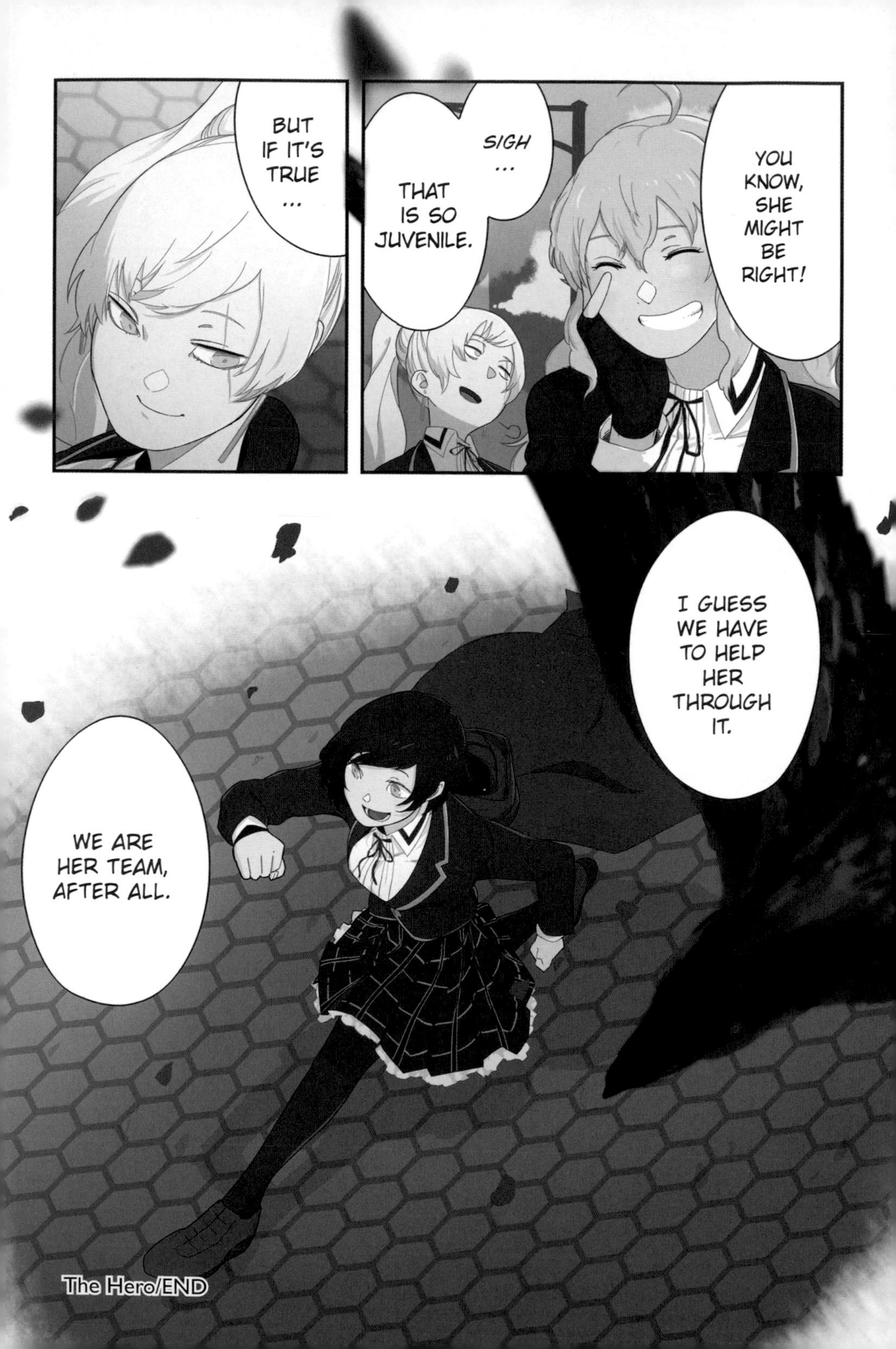
YOU KNOW, SHE MIGHT BE RIGHT!
SIGH ...
THAT IS SO JUVENILE.
BUT IF IT'S TRUE ...
I GUESS WE HAVE TO HELP HER THROUGH IT.
WE ARE HER TEAM, AFTER ALL.
The Hero/END

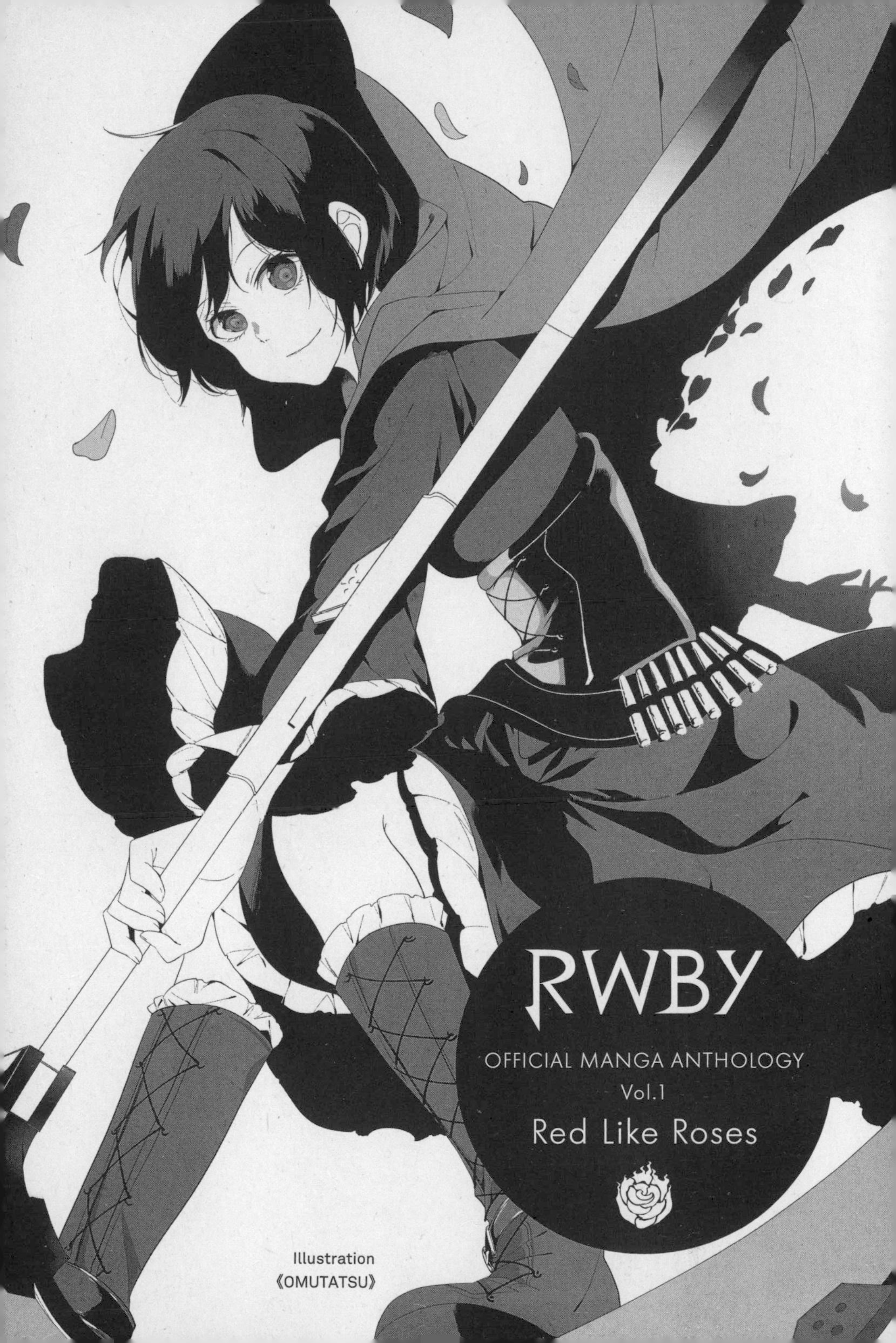
RWBY
OFFICIAL MANGA ANTHOLOGY
Vol.1
Red Like Roses
Illustration
《OMUTATSU》

RWBY OFFICIAL MANGA ANTHOLOGY 1

Red Like Roses

CONTENTS

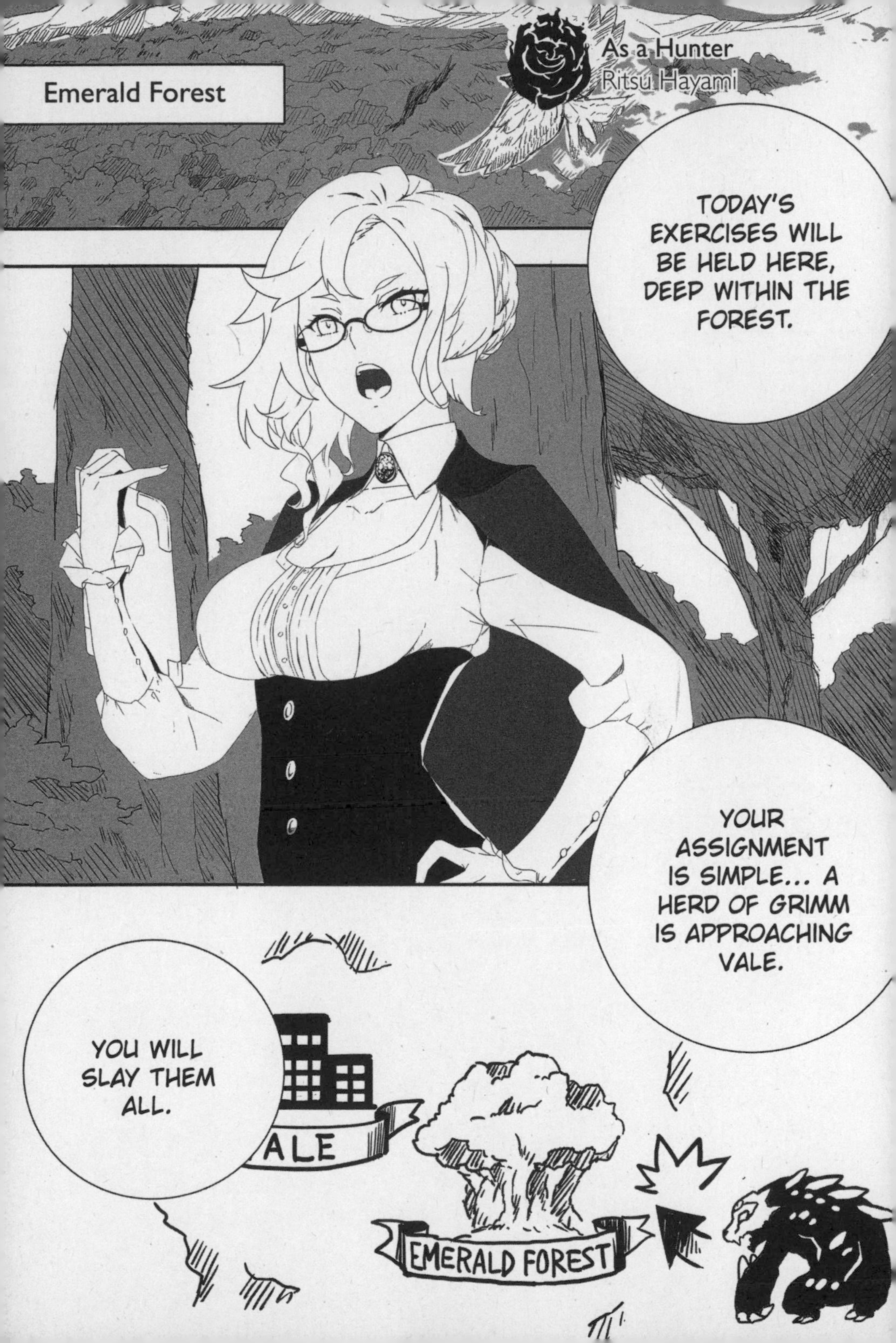
As a Hunter
Ritsu Hayami
Emerald Forest
TODAY'S EXERCISES WILL BE HELD HERE, DEEP WITHIN THE FOREST.
YOUR ASSIGNMENT IS SIMPLE... A HERD OF GRIMM IS APPROACHING VALE.
YOU WILL SLAY THEM ALL.
ALE
EMERALD FOREST

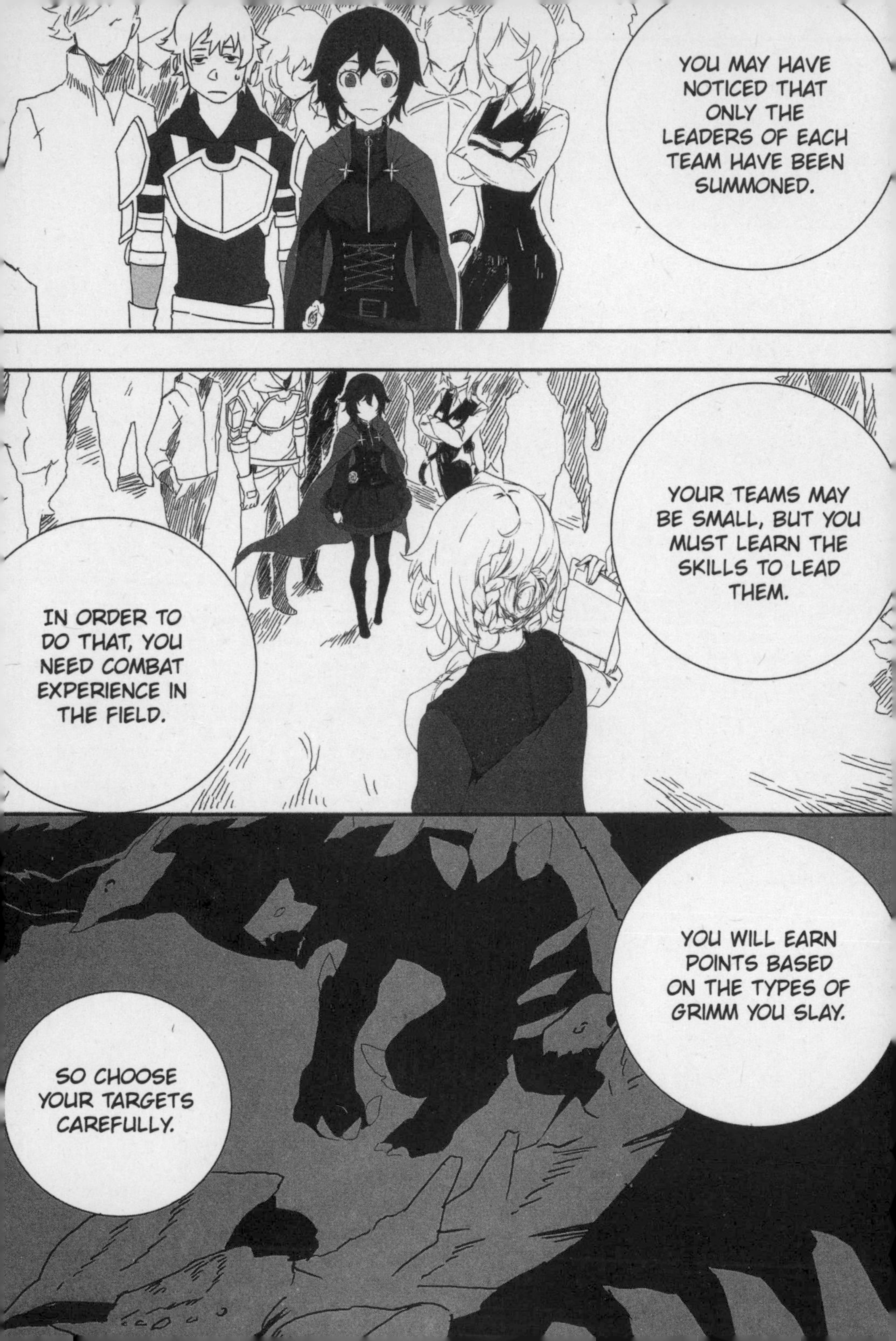
YOU MAY HAVE NOTICED THAT ONLY THE LEADERS OF EACH TEAM HAVE BEEN SUMMONED.
YOUR TEAMS MAY BE SMALL, BUT YOU MUST LEARN THE SKILLS TO LEAD THEM.
IN ORDER TO DO THAT, YOU NEED COMBAT EXPERIENCE IN THE FIELD.
YOU WILL EARN POINTS BASED ON THE TYPES OF GRIMM YOU SLAY.
SO CHOOSE YOUR TARGETS CAREFULLY.

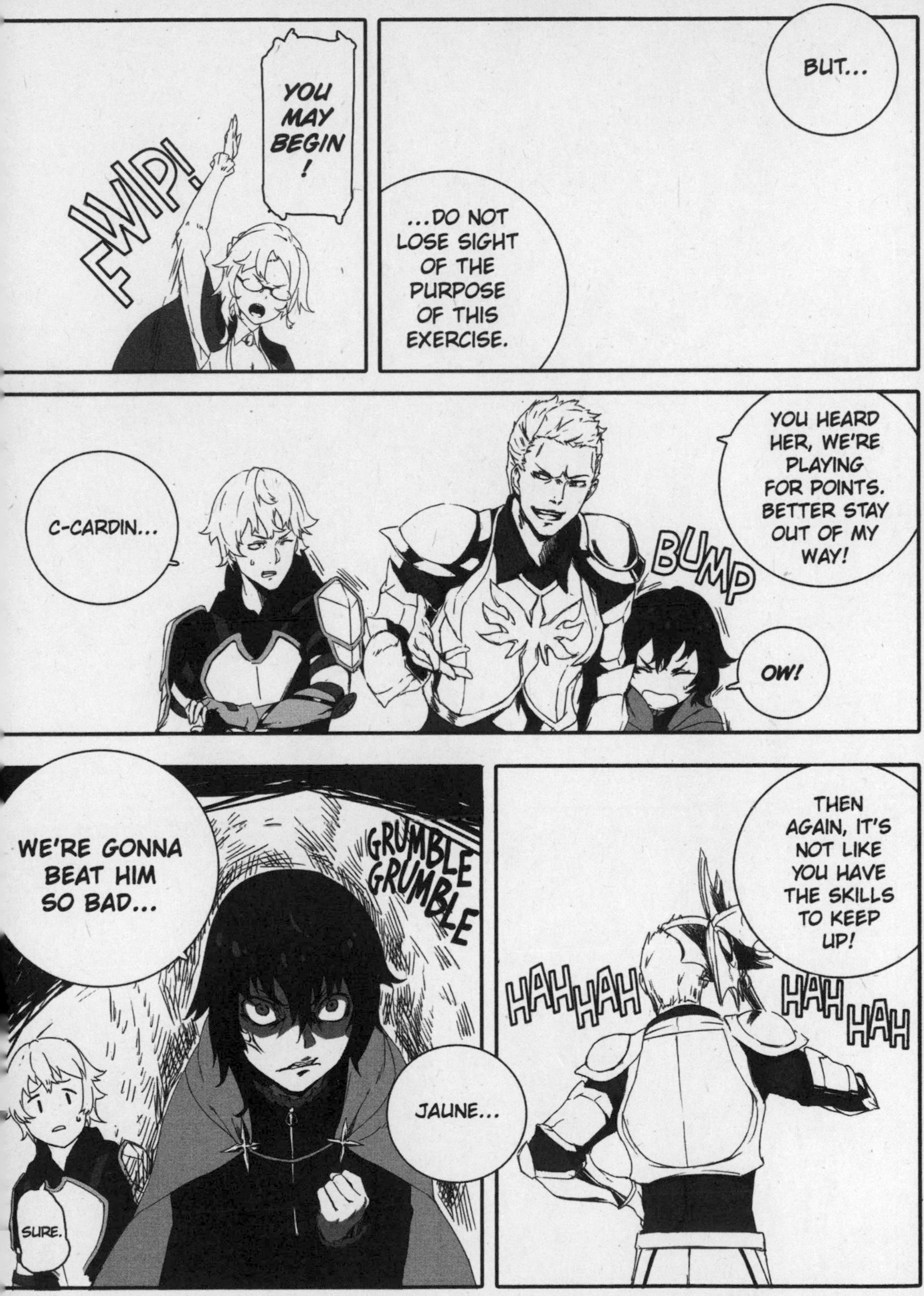
BUT...
...DO NOT LOSE SIGHT OF THE PURPOSE OF THIS EXERCISE.
YOU MAY BEGIN!
FWIP!
YOU HEARD HER, WE'RE PLAYING FOR POINTS. BETTER STAY OUT OF MY WAY!
BUMP
OW!
C-CARDIN...
THEN AGAIN, IT'S NOT LIKE YOU HAVE THE SKILLS TO KEEP UP!
HAH HAH
HAH HAH
GRUMBLE GRUMBLE
WE'RE GONNA BEAT HIM SO BAD...
JAUNE...
SURE.

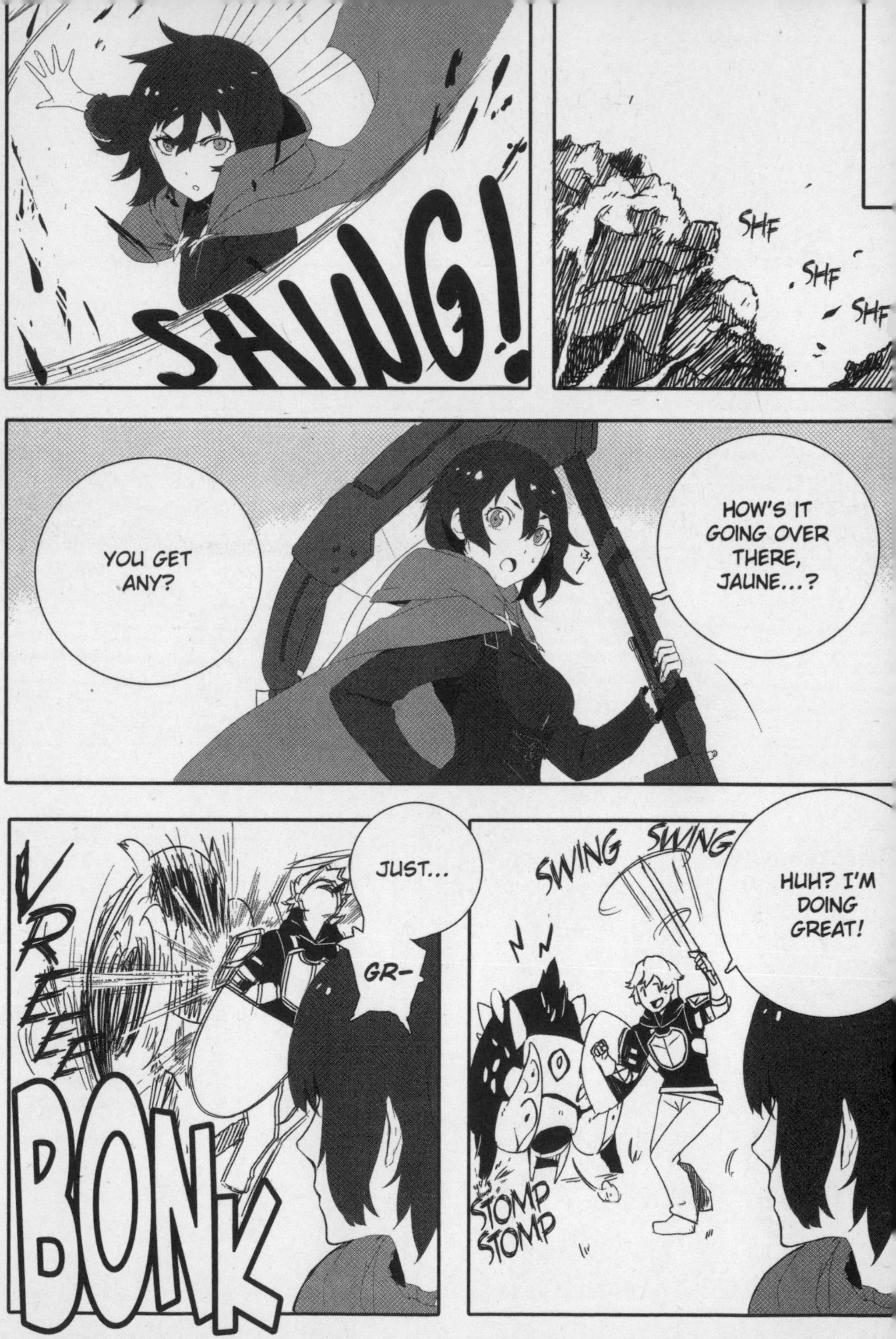
SHF
SHF
SHF
SHING!
HOW'S IT GOING OVER THERE, JAUNE...?
YOU GET ANY?
SWING SWING
HUH? I'M DOING GREAT!
STOMP STOMP
JUST...
GR-
VREEEE
BONK

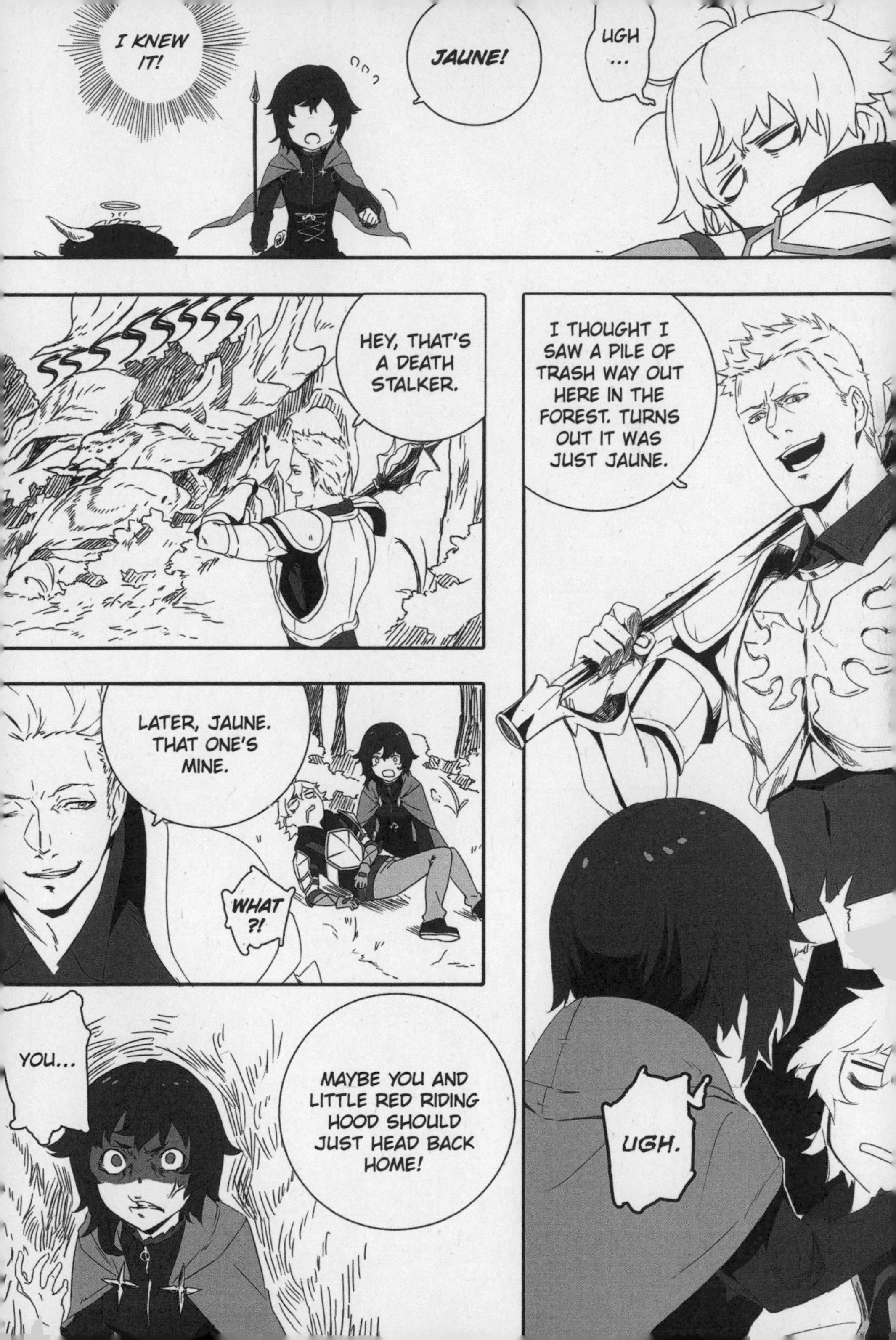
UGH ...
JAUNE!
I KNEW IT!
I THOUGHT I SAW A PILE OF TRASH WAY OUT HERE IN THE FOREST. TURNS OUT IT WAS JUST JAUNE.
UGH.
HEY, THAT'S A DEATH STALKER.
LATER, JAUNE. THAT ONE'S MINE.
WHAT ?!
MAYBE YOU AND LITTLE RED RIDING HOOD SHOULD JUST HEAD BACK HOME!
YOU...

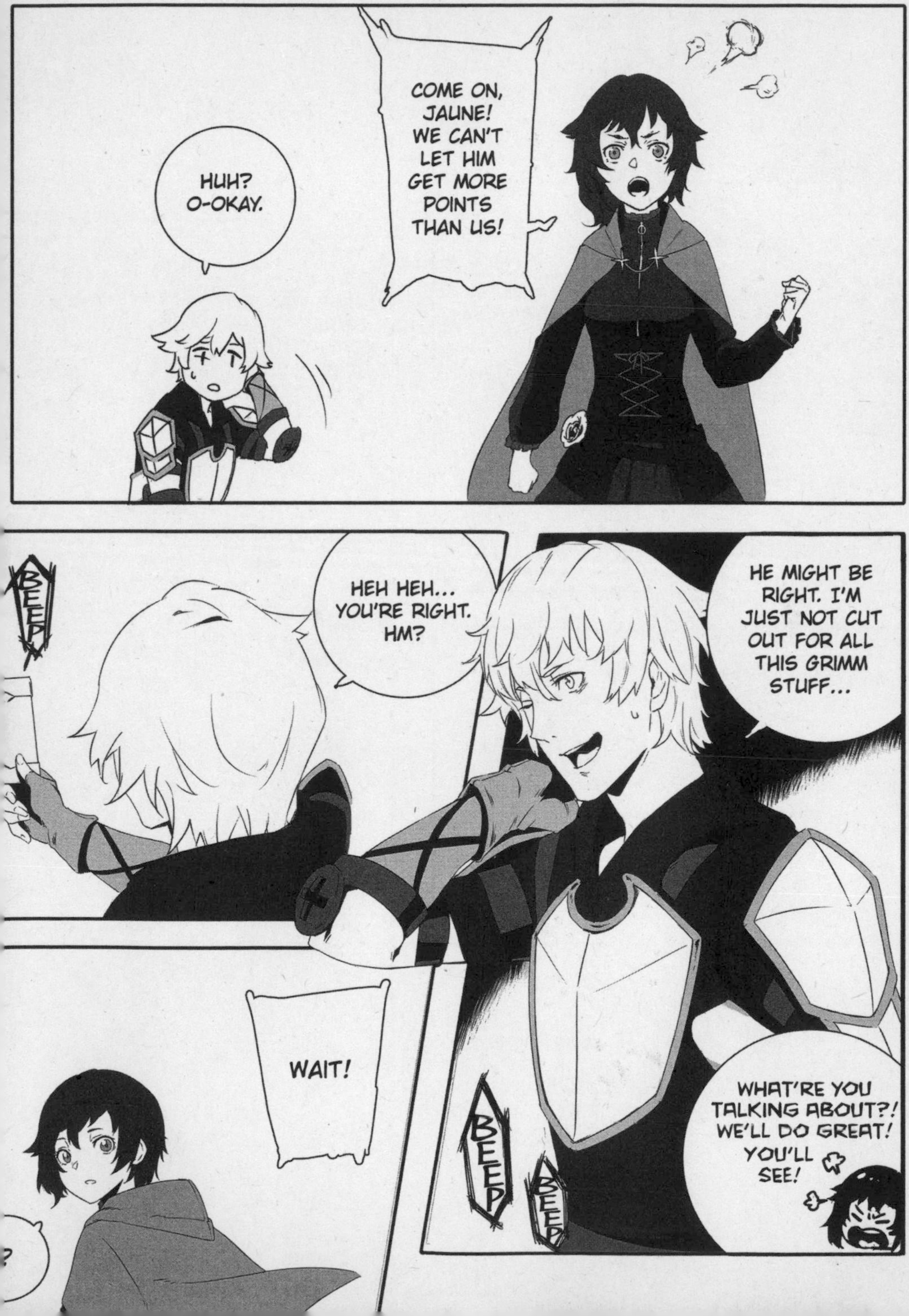
COME ON, JAUNE! WE CAN'T LET HIM GET MORE POINTS THAN US!
HUH? O-OKAY.
HE MIGHT BE RIGHT. I'M JUST NOT CUT OUT FOR ALL THIS GRIMM STUFF...
WHAT'RE YOU TALKING ABOUT?! WE'LL DO GREAT! YOU'LL SEE!
BEEP
BEEP
HEH HEH... YOU'RE RIGHT. HM?
BEEP
WAIT!

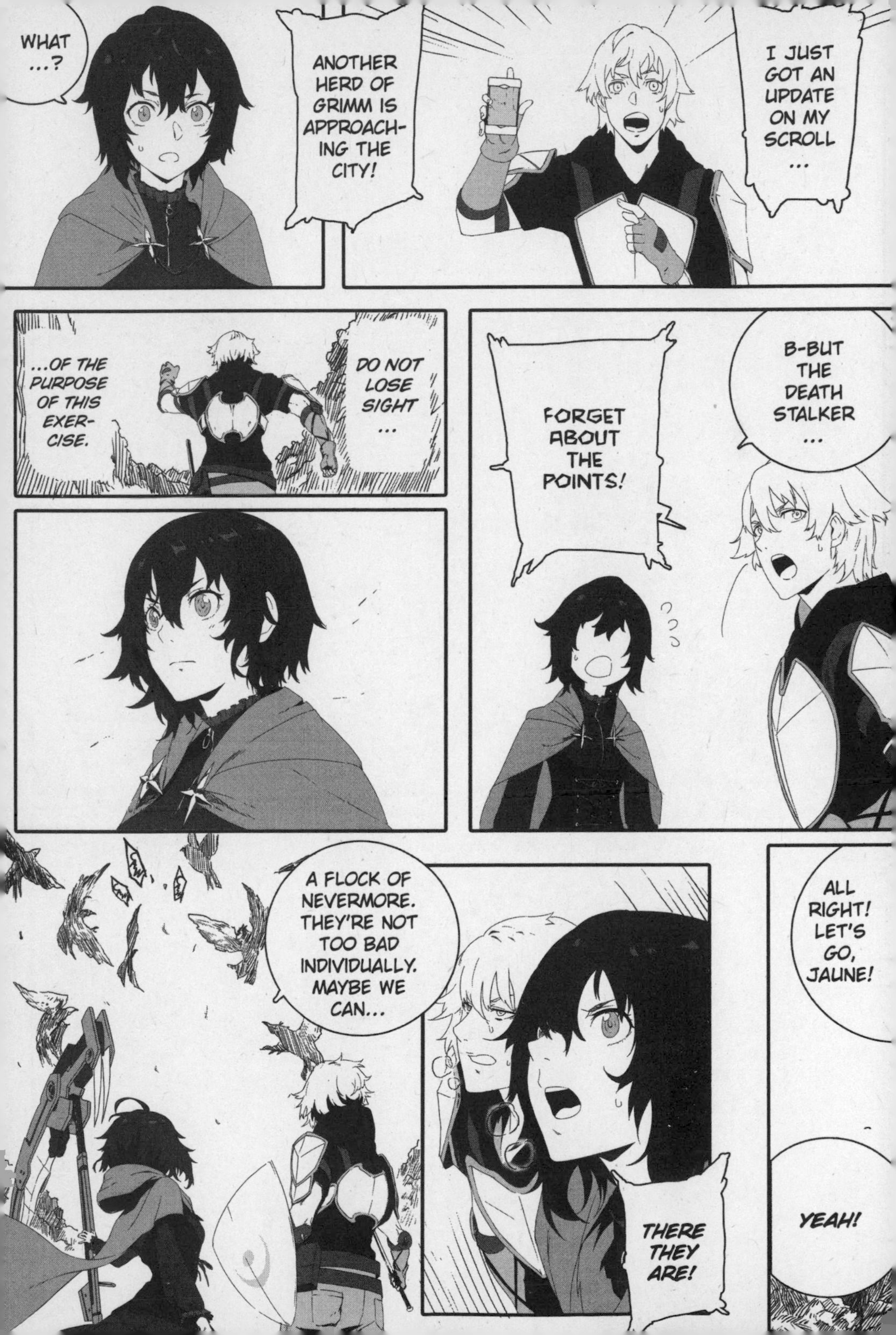
I JUST GOT AN UPDATE ON MY SCROLL ...
ANOTHER HERD OF GRIMM IS APPROACHING THE CITY!
WHAT ...?
B-BUT THE DEATH STALKER ...
FORGET ABOUT THE POINTS!
DO NOT LOSE SIGHT ...
...OF THE PURPOSE OF THIS EXERCISE.
ALL RIGHT! LET'S GO, JAUNE!
YEAH!
THERE THEY ARE!
A FLOCK OF NEVERMORE. THEY'RE NOT TOO BAD INDIVIDUALLY. MAYBE WE CAN...

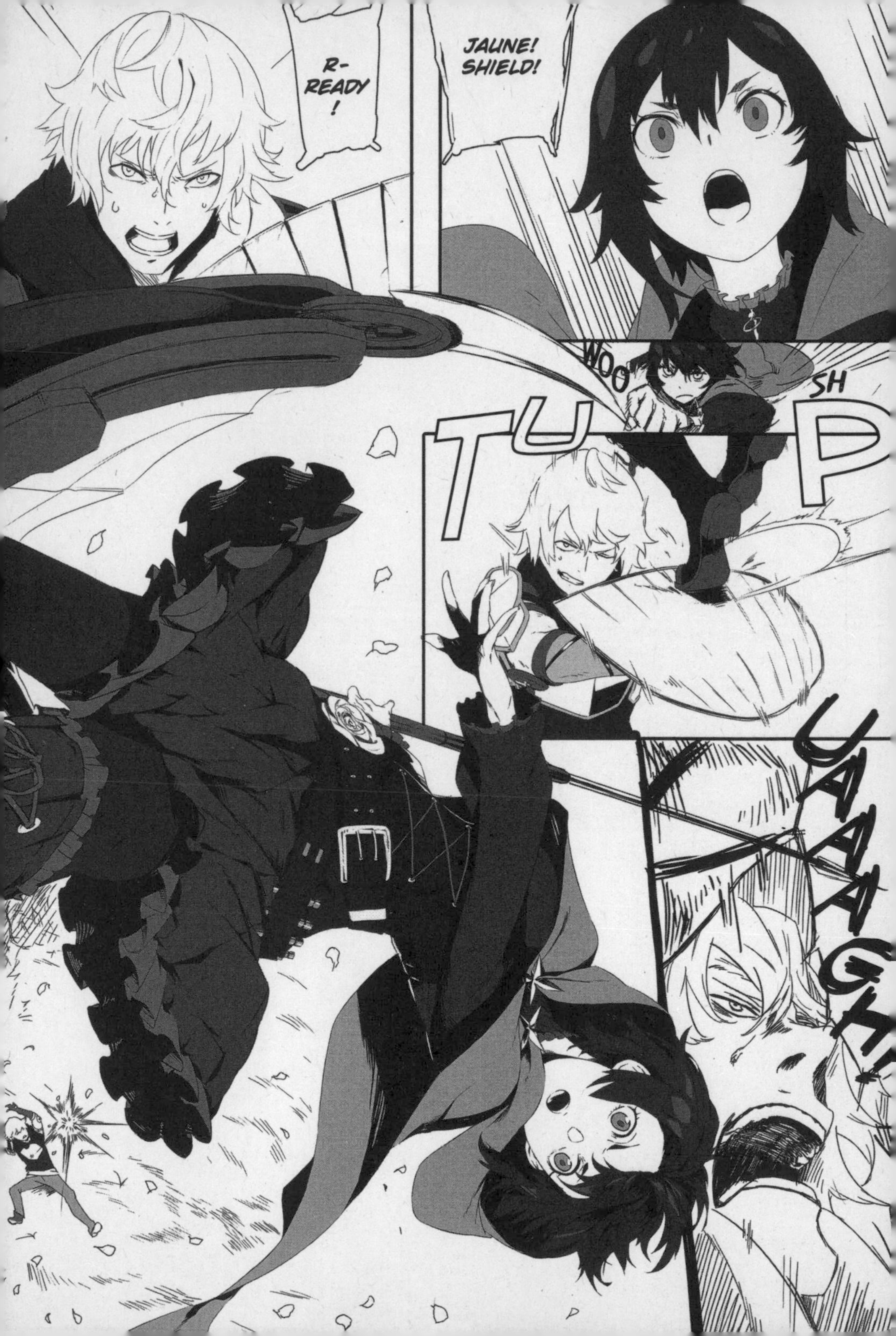
JAUNE! SHIELD!
R-READY!
WOO
SH
TU
P
UAAAGH!

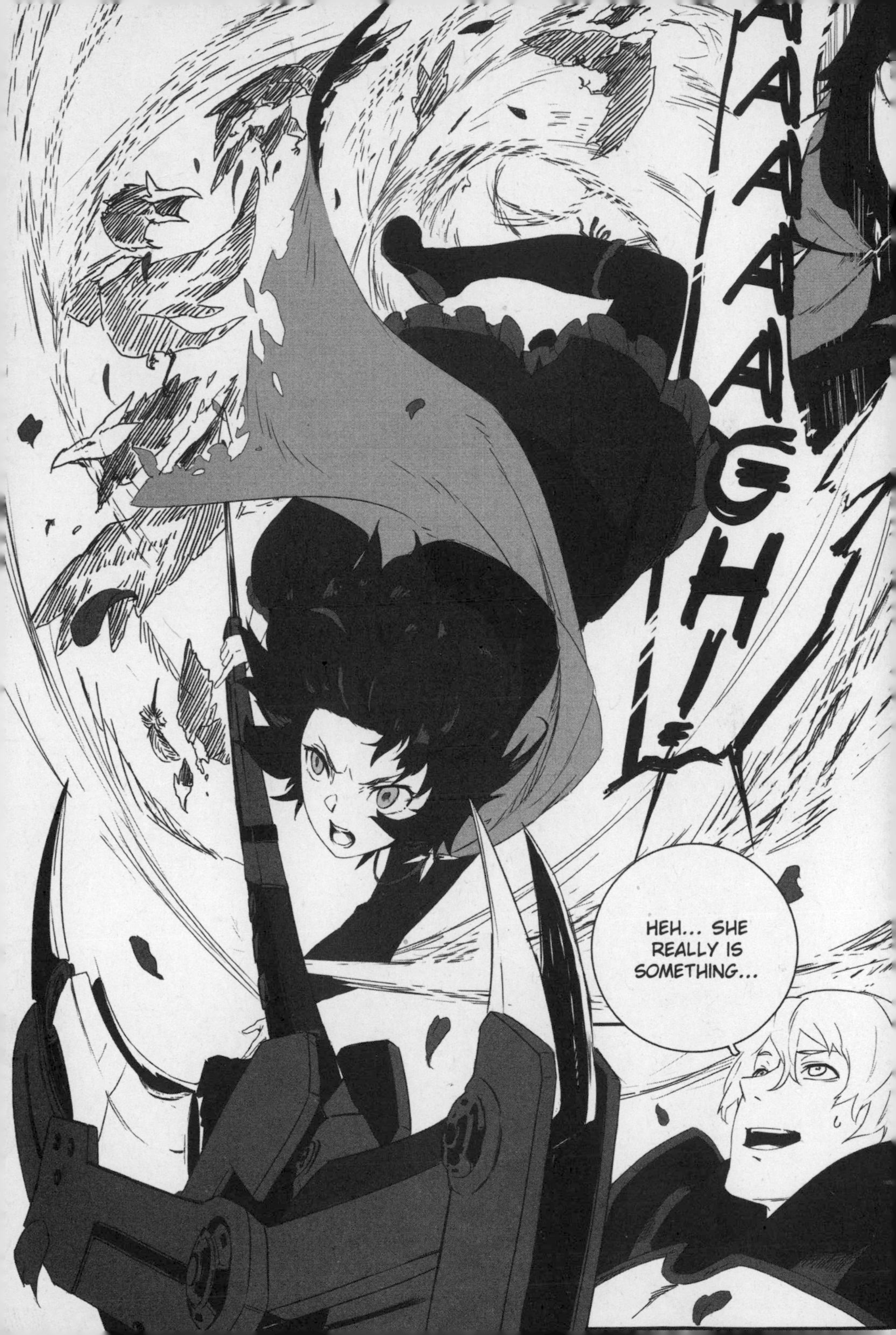
AAAAAAGH!!
HEH... SHE REALLY IS SOMETHING...

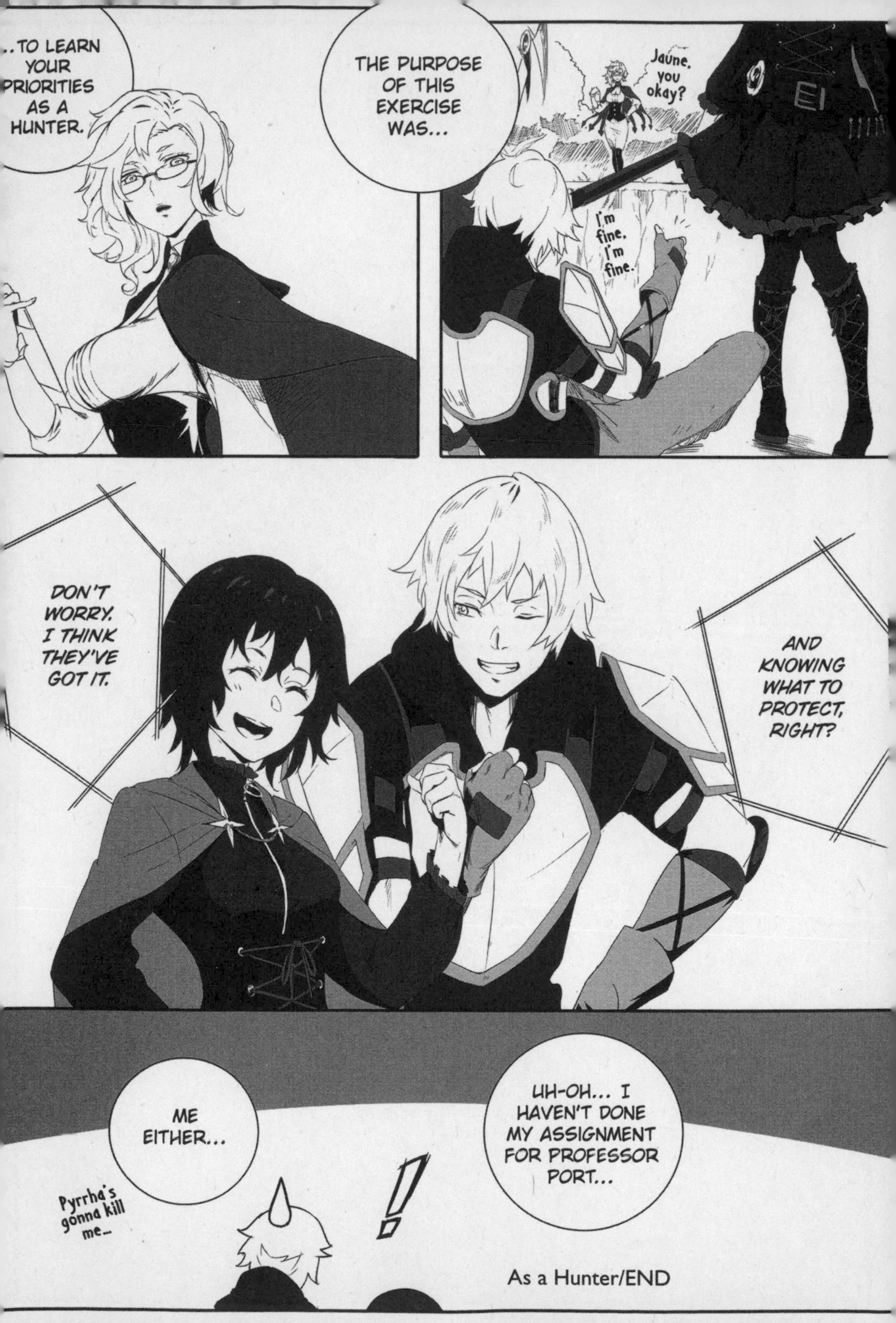
Jaune, you okay?
I'm fine, I'm fine.
THE PURPOSE OF THIS EXERCISE WAS...
...TO LEARN YOUR PRIORITIES AS A HUNTER.
AND KNOWING WHAT TO PROTECT, RIGHT?
DON'T WORRY. I THINK THEY'VE GOT IT.
UH-OH... I HAVEN'T DONE MY ASSIGNMENT FOR PROFESSOR PORT...
ME EITHER...
Pyrrha's gonna kill me...
As a Hunter/END

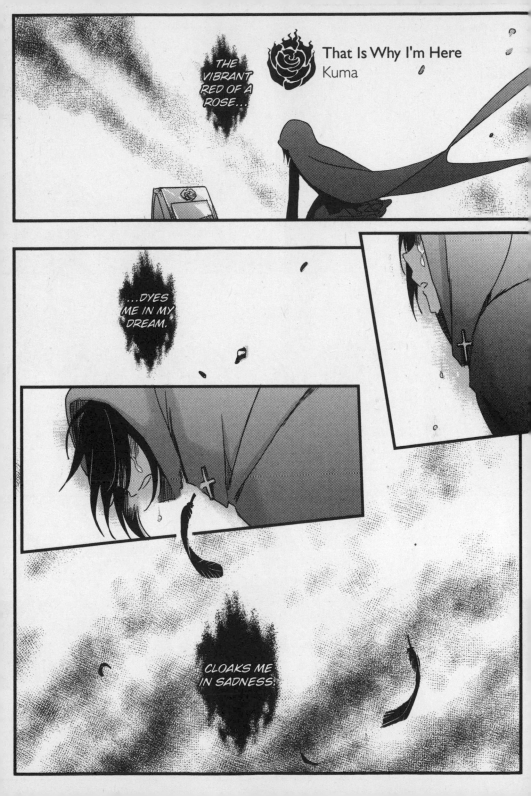

That Is Why I'm Here
Kuma

THE VIBRANT RED OF A ROSE...

...DYES ME IN MY DREAM.

CLOAKS ME IN SADNESS.

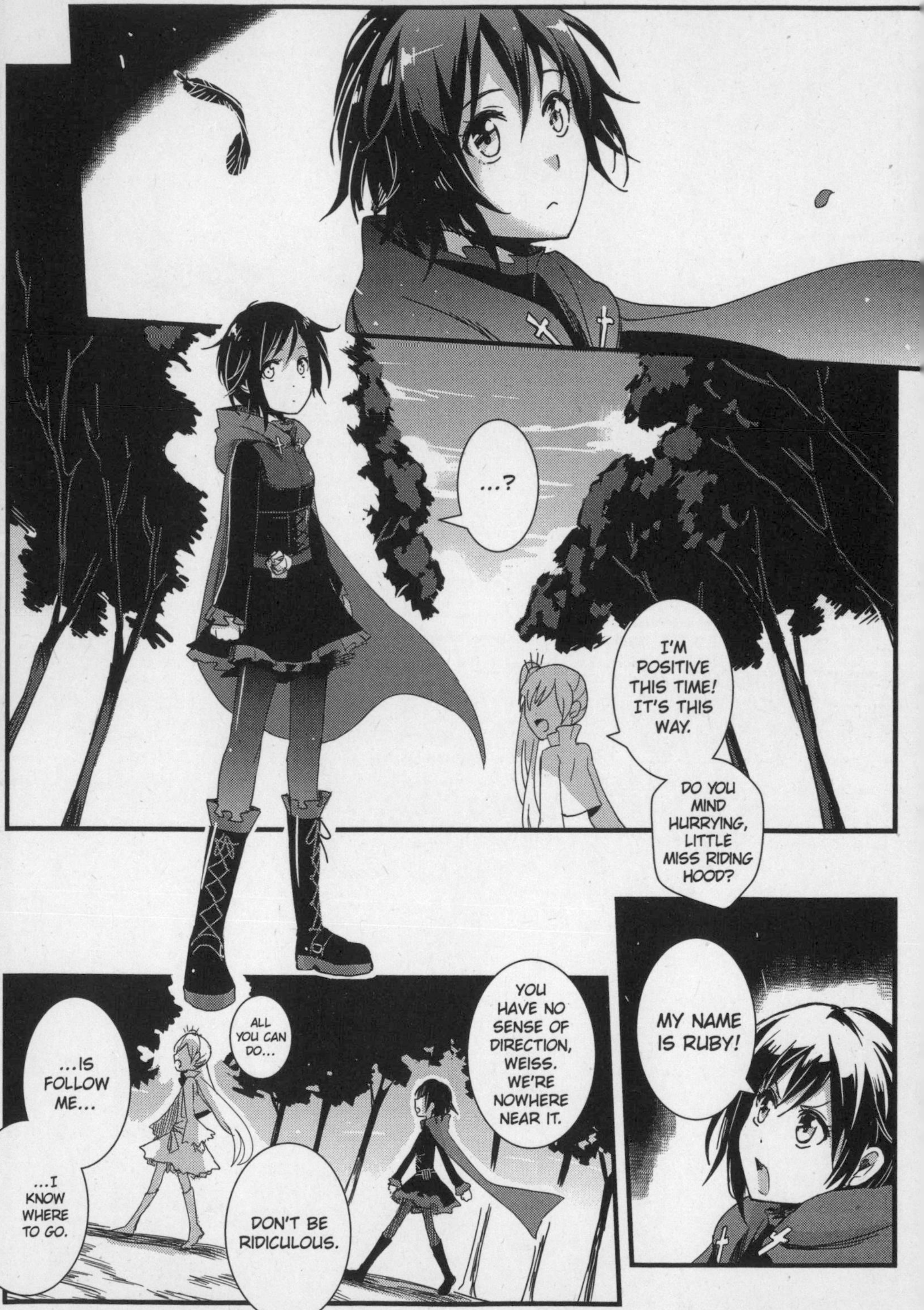
...?
I'M POSITIVE THIS TIME! IT'S THIS WAY.
DO YOU MIND HURRYING, LITTLE MISS RIDING HOOD?
MY NAME IS RUBY!
YOU HAVE NO SENSE OF DIRECTION, WEISS. WE'RE NOWHERE NEAR IT.
DON'T BE RIDICULOUS.
ALL YOU CAN DO...
...IS FOLLOW ME...
...I KNOW WHERE TO GO.

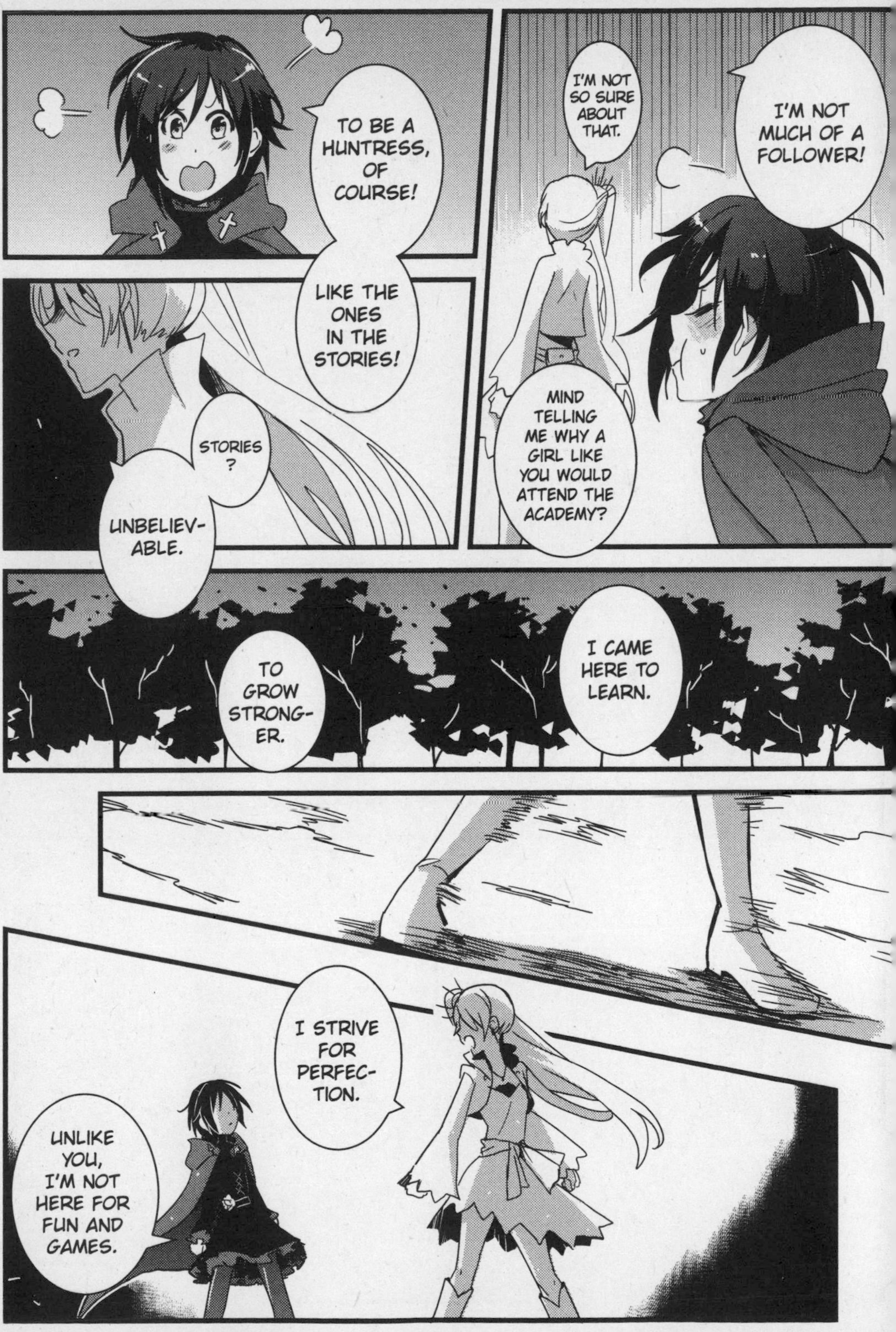
I'M NOT MUCH OF A FOLLOWER!
I'M NOT SO SURE ABOUT THAT.
MIND TELLING ME WHY A GIRL LIKE YOU WOULD ATTEND THE ACADEMY?
TO BE A HUNTRESS, OF COURSE!
LIKE THE ONES IN THE STORIES!
STORIES?
UNBELIEVABLE.
I CAME HERE TO LEARN.
TO GROW STRONGER.
I STRIVE FOR PERFECTION.
UNLIKE YOU, I'M NOT HERE FOR FUN AND GAMES.

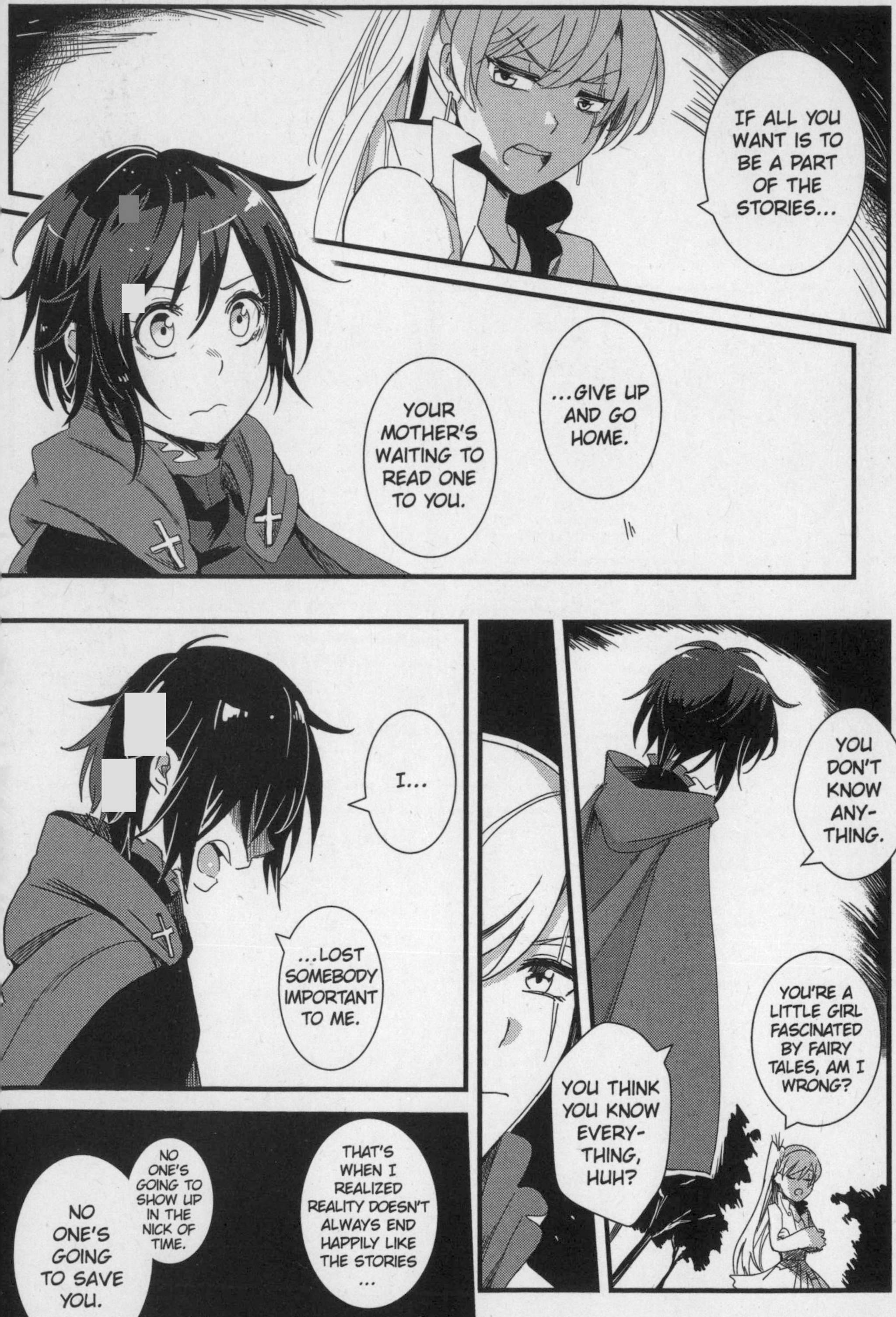
IF ALL YOU WANT IS TO BE A PART OF THE STORIES...
...GIVE UP AND GO HOME.
YOUR MOTHER'S WAITING TO READ ONE TO YOU.
YOU DON'T KNOW ANY-THING.
YOU'RE A LITTLE GIRL FASCINATED BY FAIRY TALES, AM I WRONG?
YOU THINK YOU KNOW EVERY-THING, HUH?
I...
...LOST SOMEBODY IMPORTANT TO ME.
THAT'S WHEN I REALIZED REALITY DOESN'T ALWAYS END HAPPILY LIKE THE STORIES ...
NO ONE'S GOING TO SHOW UP IN THE NICK OF TIME.
NO ONE'S GOING TO SAVE YOU.

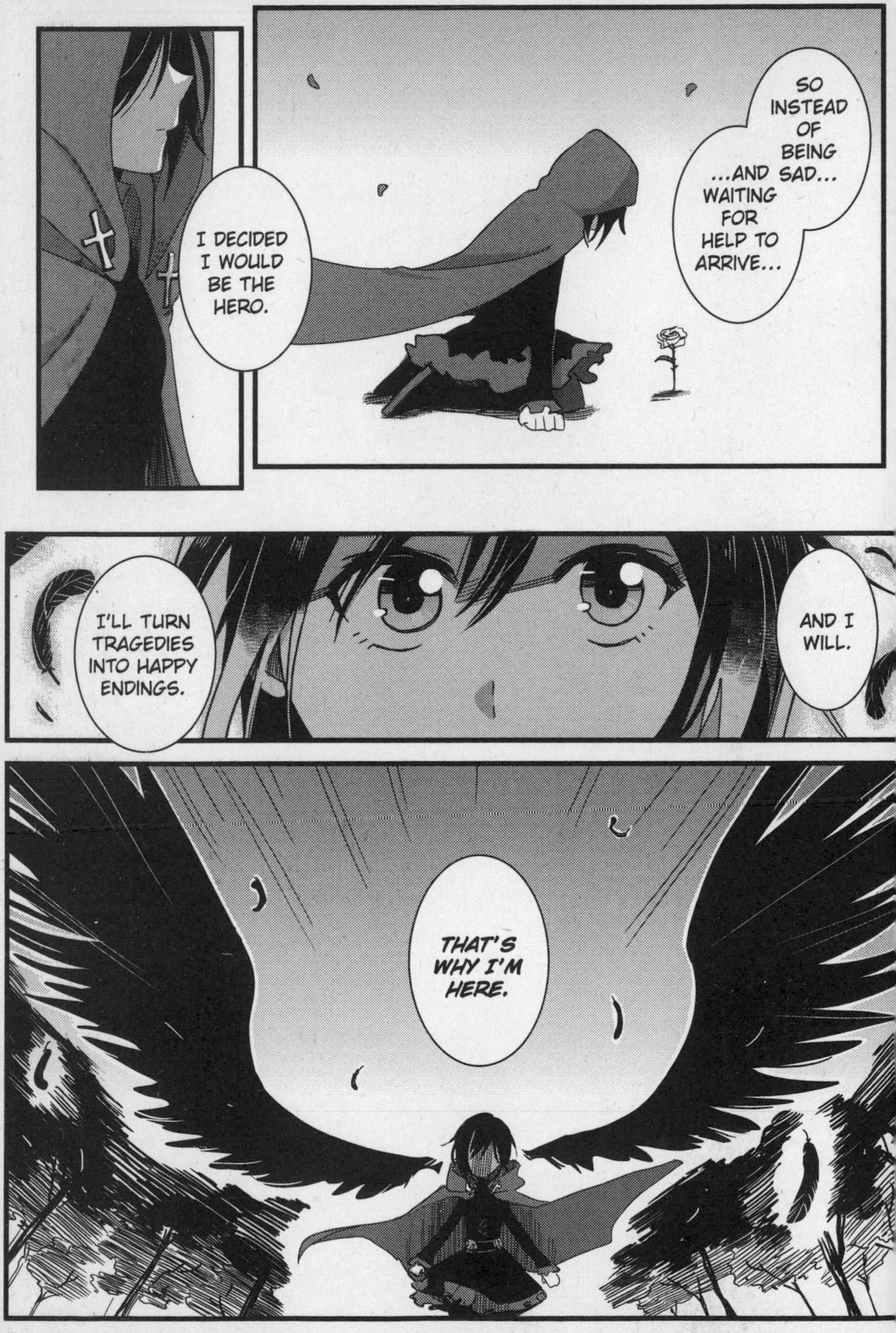
SO INSTEAD OF BEING SAD...
...AND WAITING FOR HELP TO ARRIVE...
I DECIDED I WOULD BE THE HERO.
AND I WILL.
I'LL TURN TRAGEDIES INTO HAPPY ENDINGS.
THAT'S WHY I'M HERE.

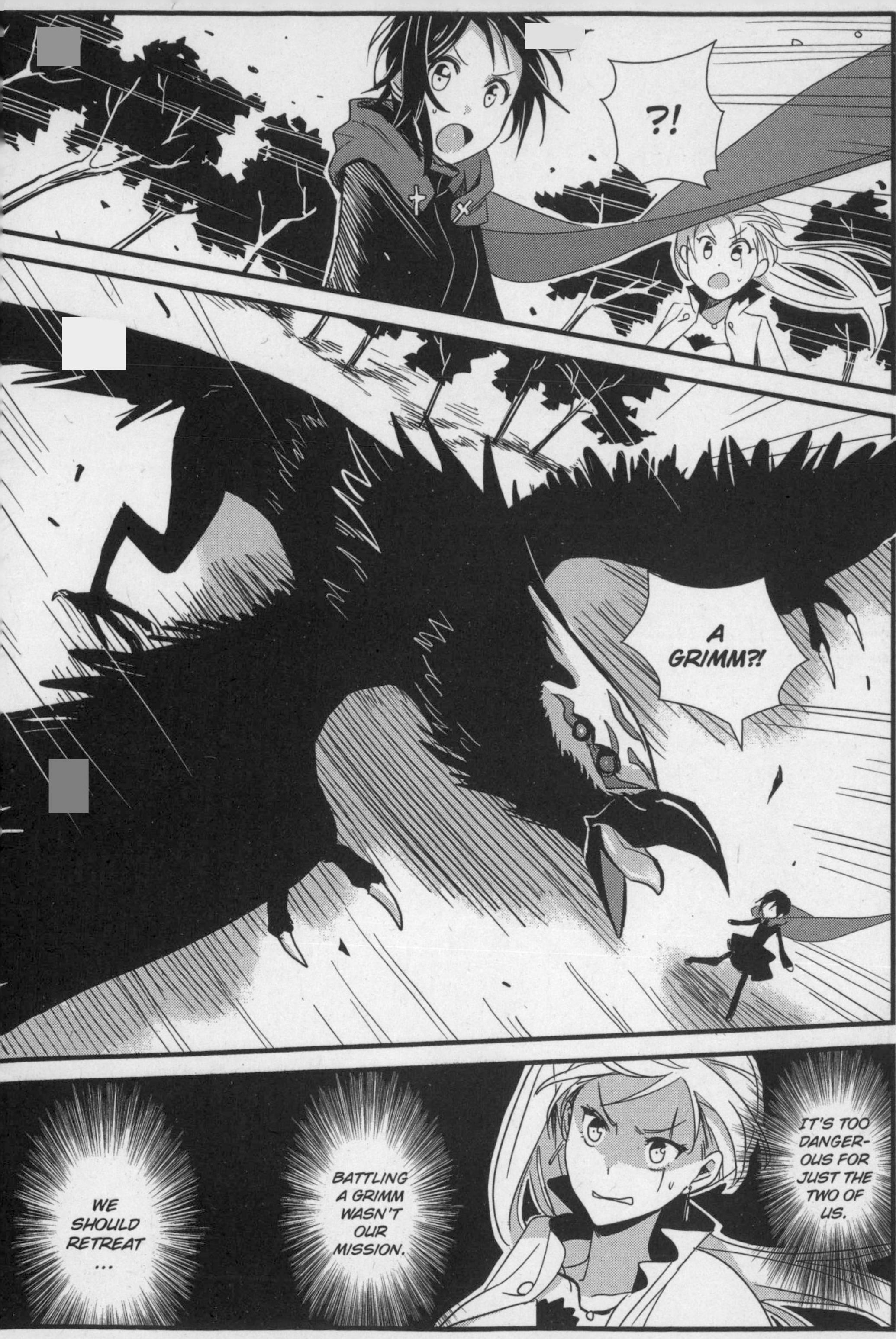
?!
A GRIMM?!
IT'S TOO DANGER-OUS FOR JUST THE TWO OF US.
BATTLING A GRIMM WASN'T OUR MISSION.
WE SHOULD RETREAT ...

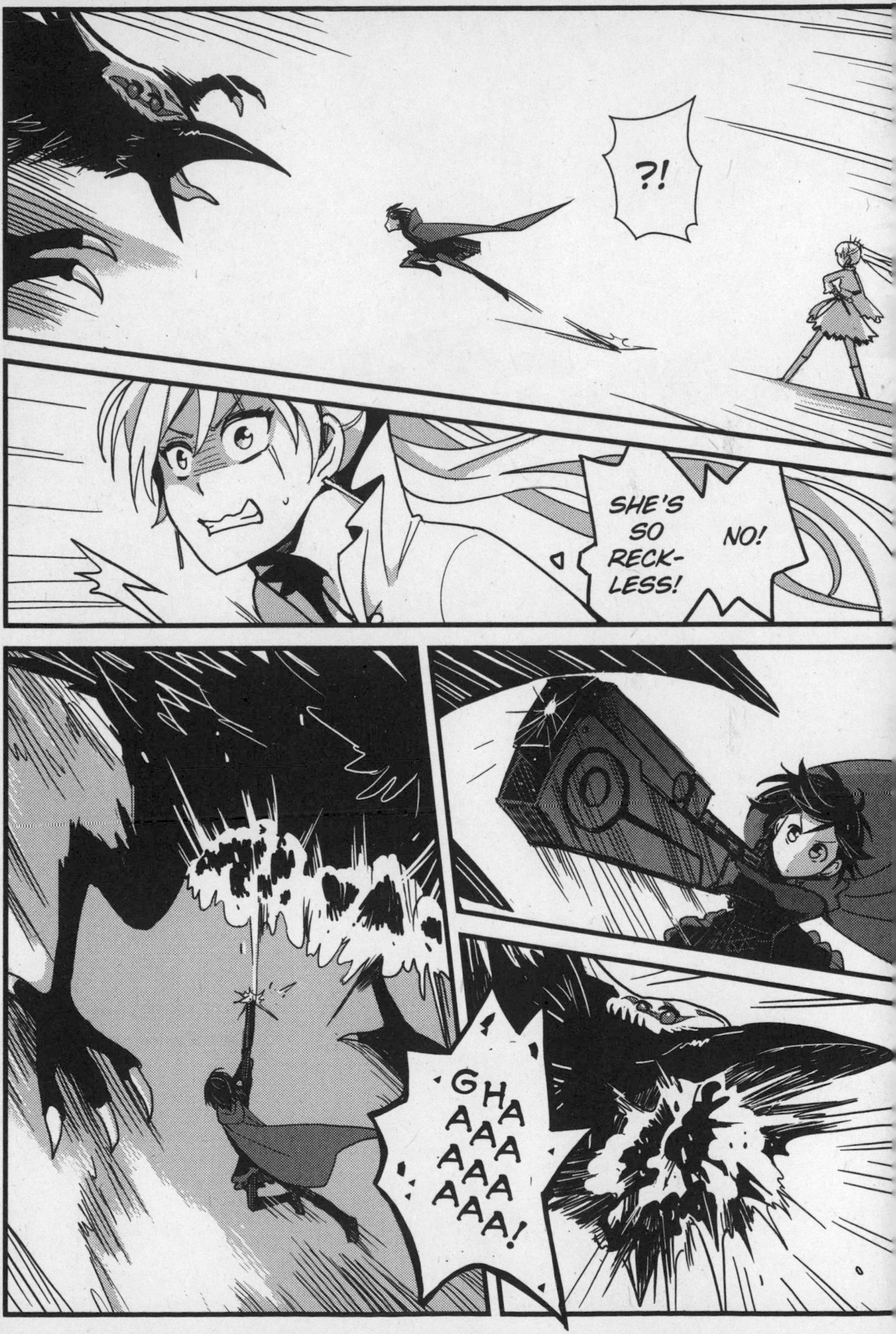
?!
NO!
SHE'S SO RECK-LESS!
GHAAAAAAAAAAAAA!

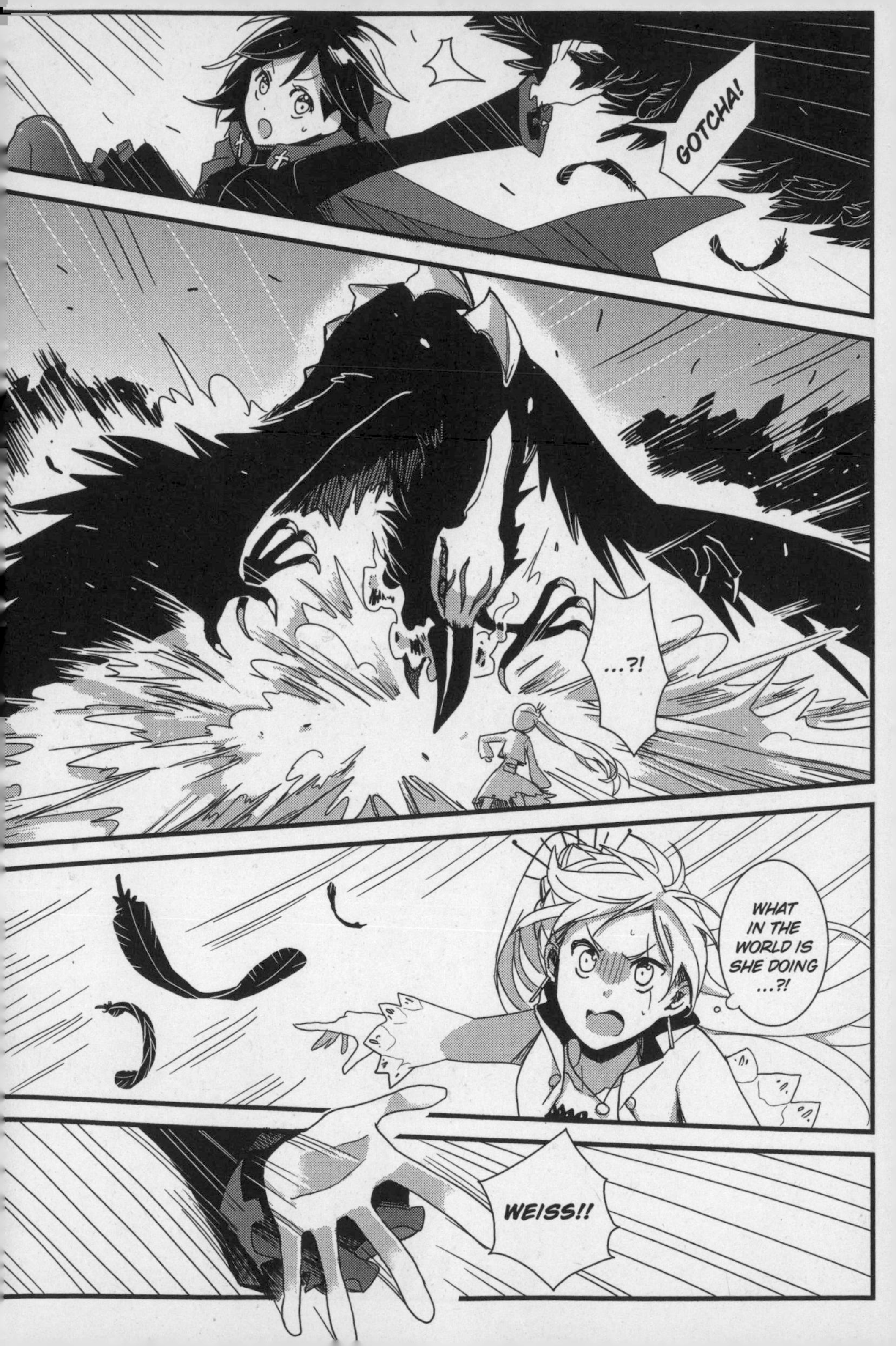
GOTCHA!
...?!
WHAT IN THE WORLD IS SHE DOING ...?!
WEISS!!

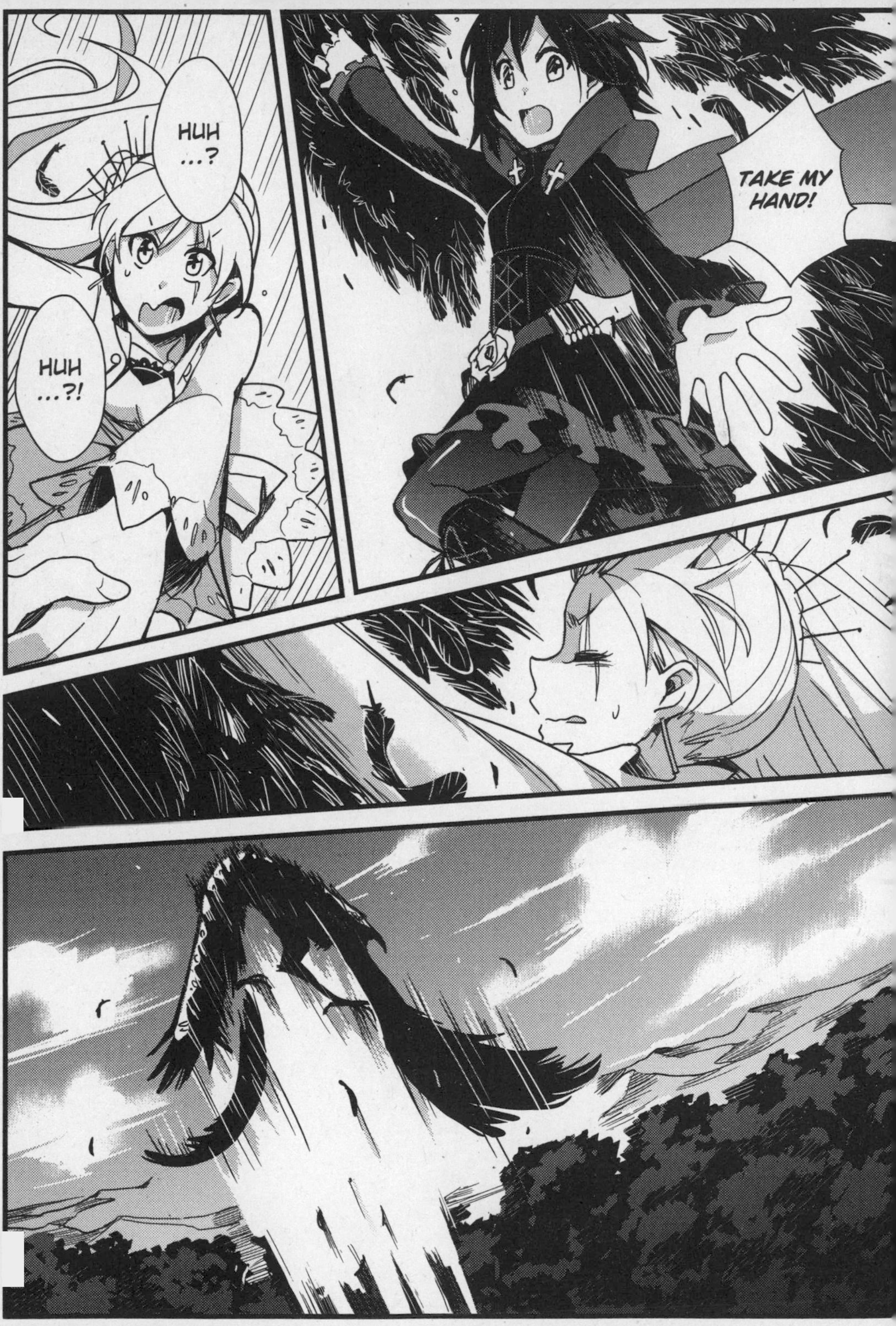
TAKE MY HAND!
HUH ...?
HUH ...?!

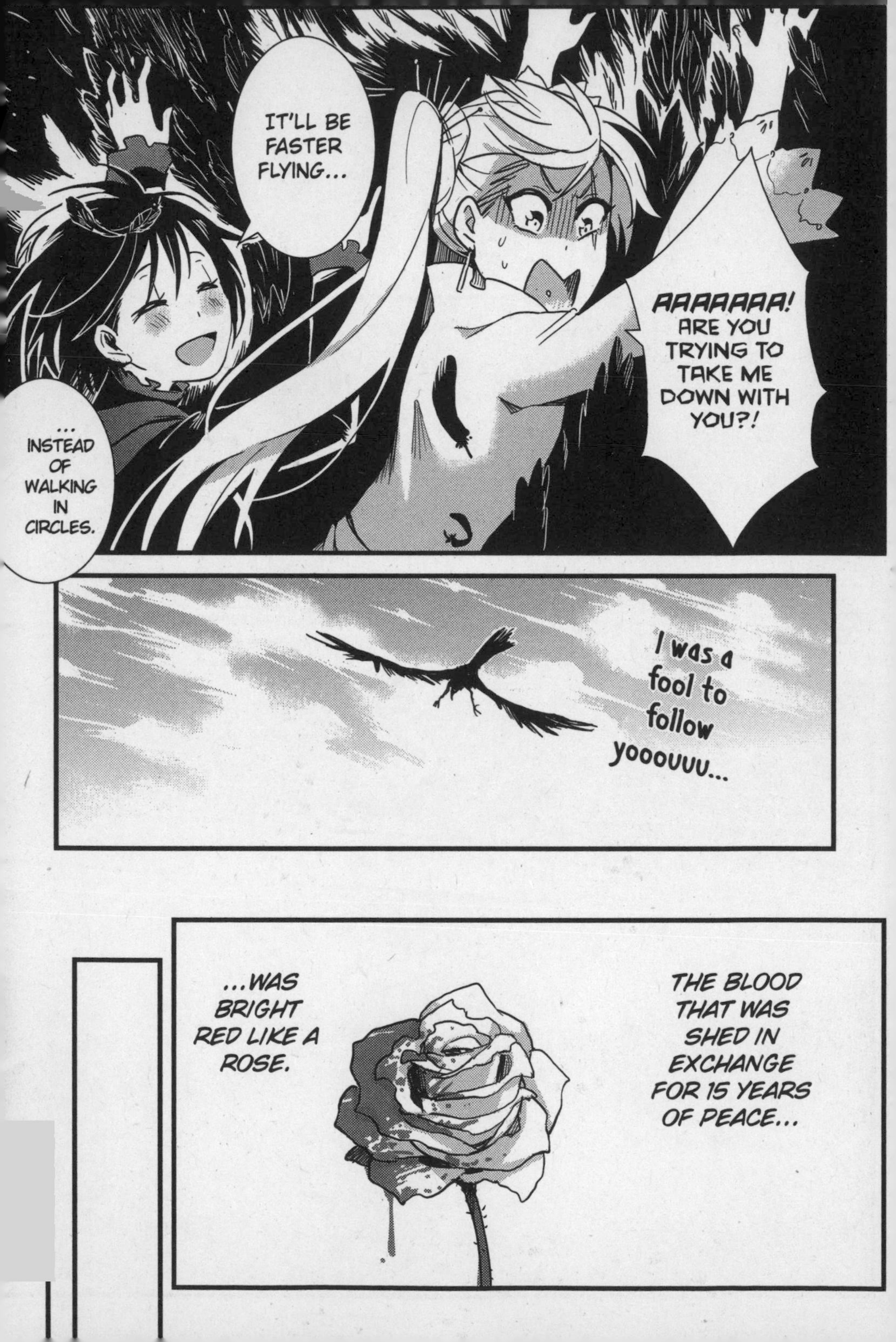
IT'LL BE FASTER FLYING...
...INSTEAD OF WALKING IN CIRCLES.
AAAAAAA! ARE YOU TRYING TO TAKE ME DOWN WITH YOU?!
I was a fool to follow yooouuu...
THE BLOOD THAT WAS SHED IN EXCHANGE FOR 15 YEARS OF PEACE...
...WAS BRIGHT RED LIKE A ROSE.

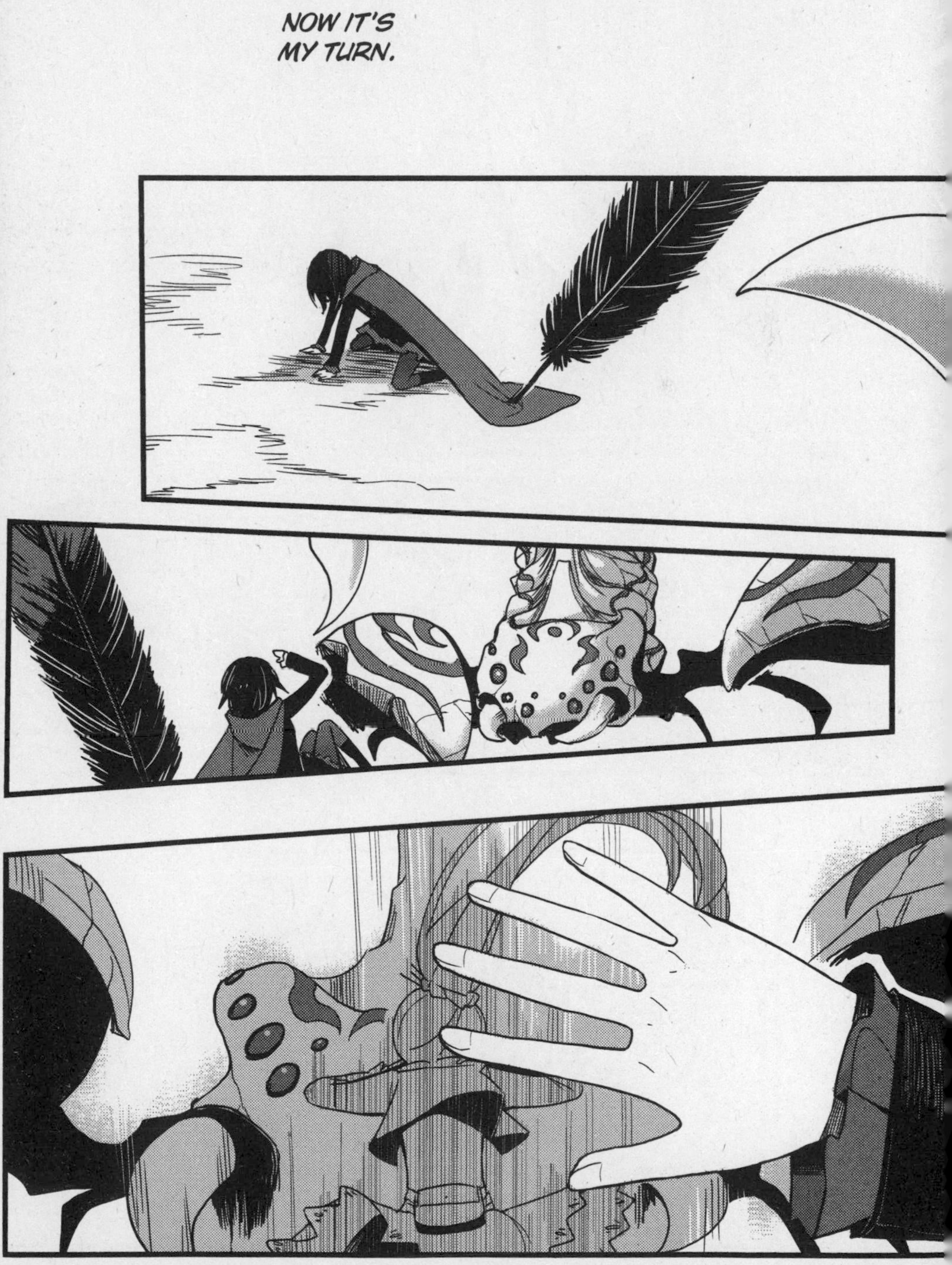
NOW IT'S MY TURN.

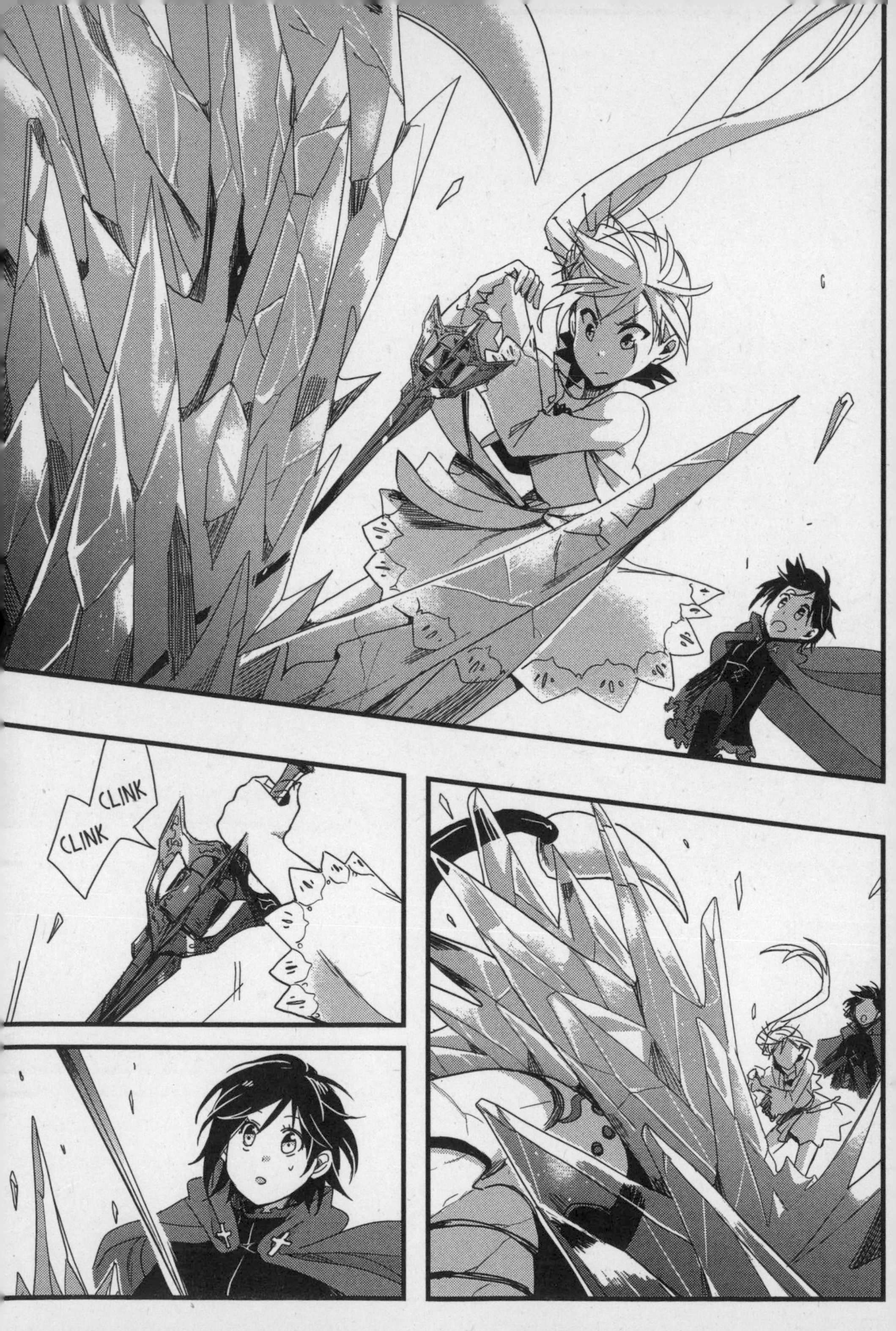
CLINK
CLINK

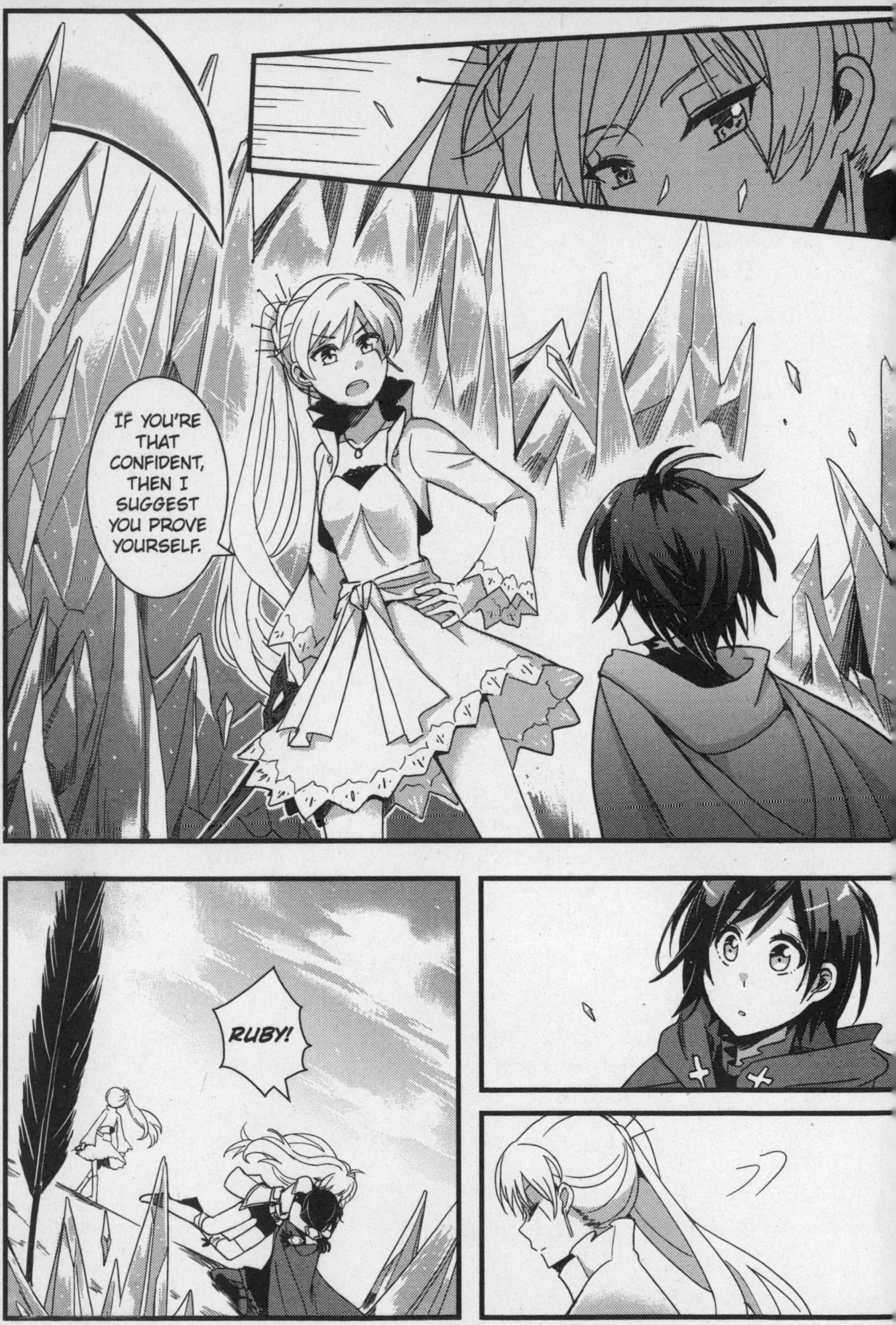
IF YOU'RE THAT CONFIDENT, THEN I SUGGEST YOU PROVE YOURSELF.
RUBY!

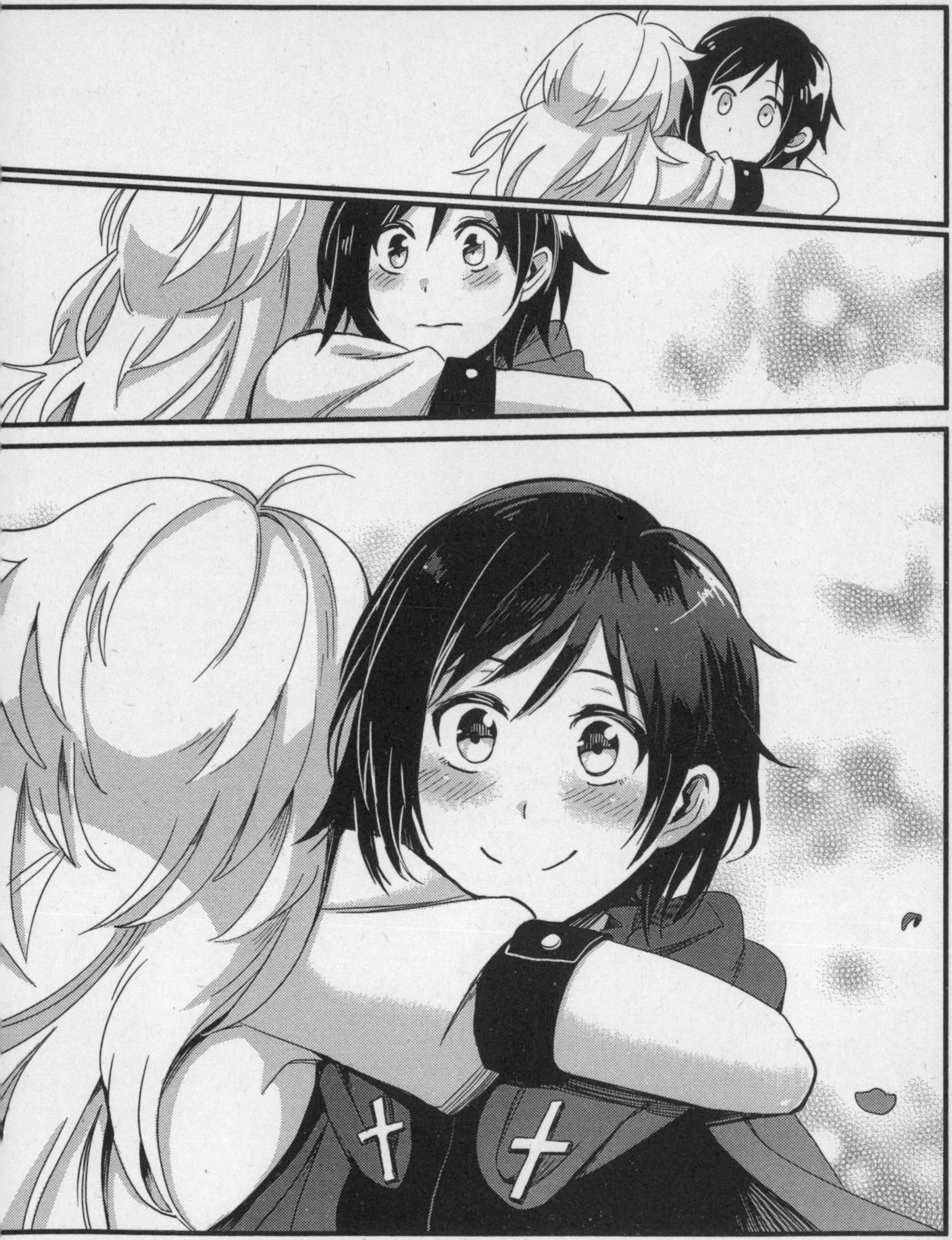

That Is Why I'm Here/END

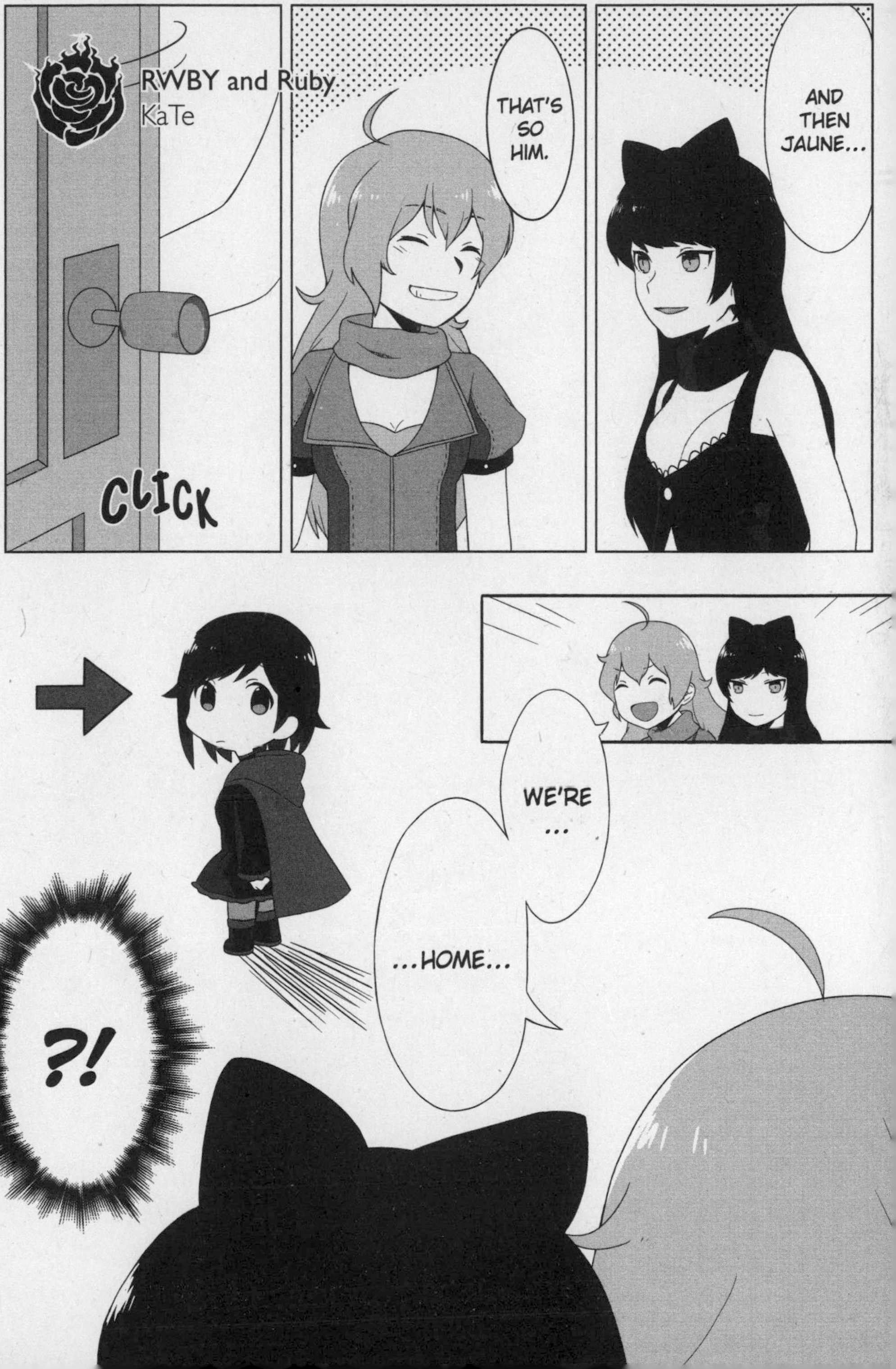
AND THEN JAUNE...
THAT'S SO HIM.
RWBY and Ruby
KaTe
CLICK
WE'RE ...
...HOME...
?!

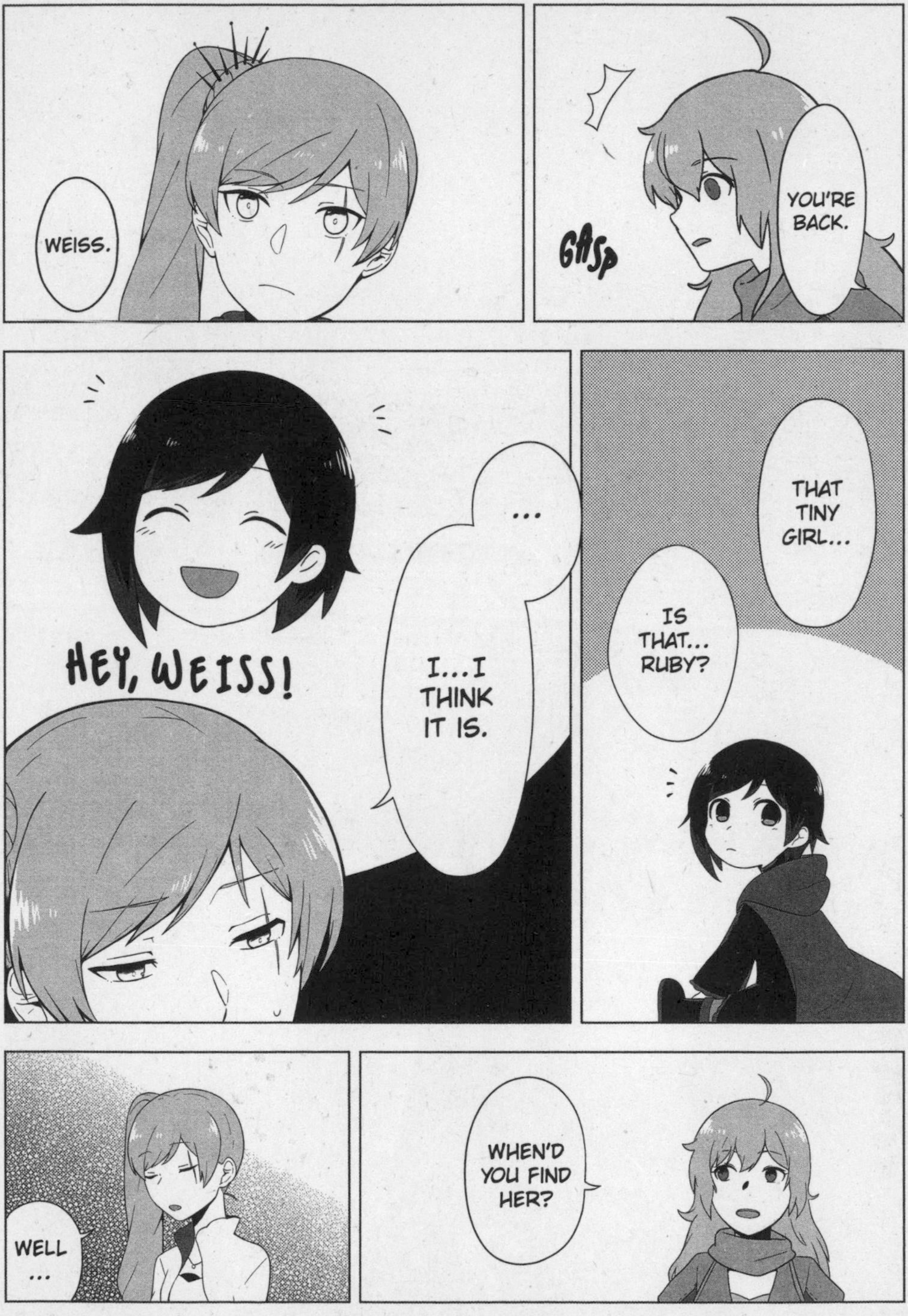
GASP
YOU'RE BACK.
WEISS.
THAT TINY GIRL...
IS THAT... RUBY?
...
I...I THINK IT IS.
HEY, WEISS!
WHEN'D YOU FIND HER?
WELL ...

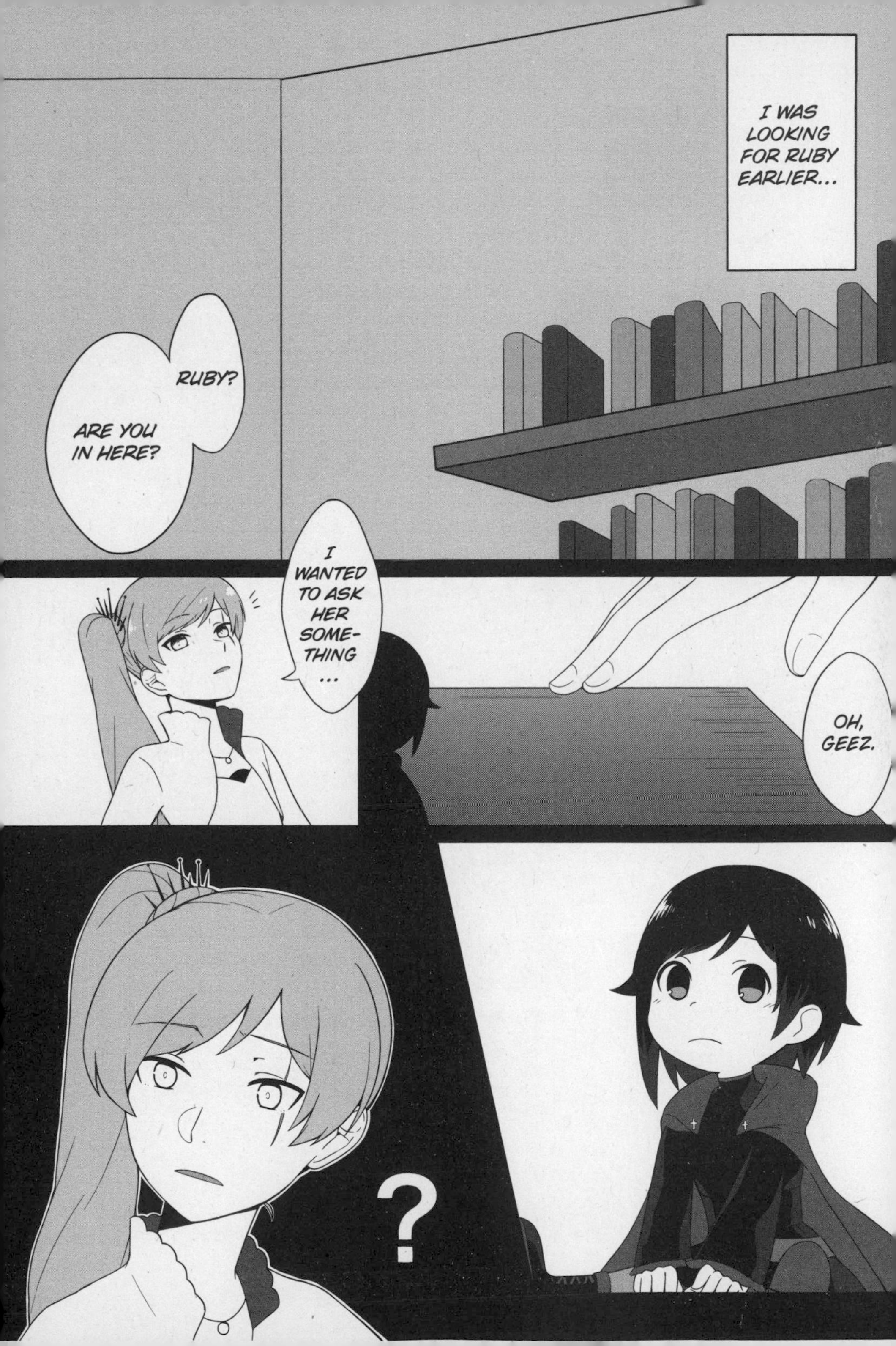
I WAS LOOKING FOR RUBY EARLIER...
RUBY? ARE YOU IN HERE?
I WANTED TO ASK HER SOME-THING...
OH, GEEZ.
?

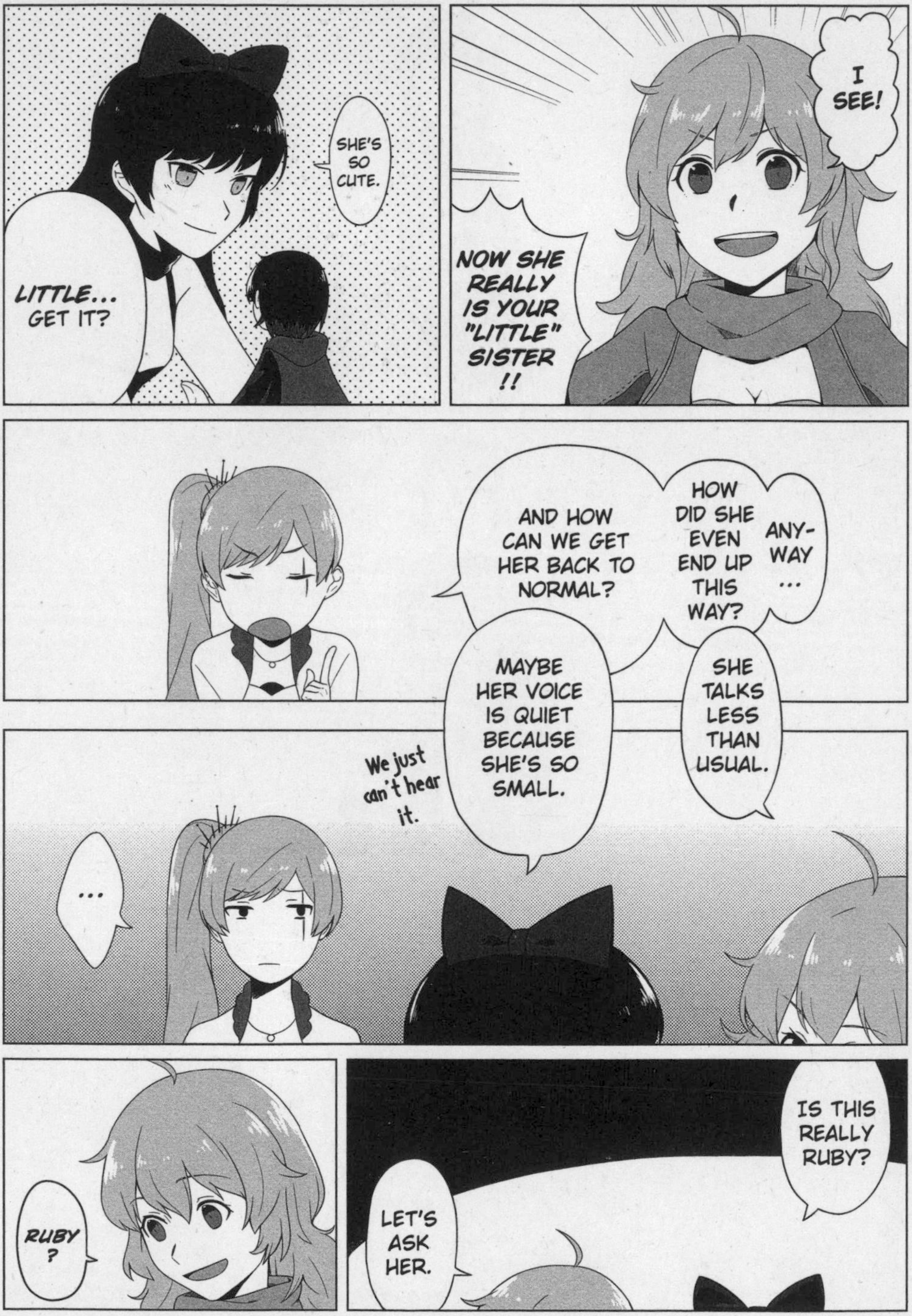
I SEE!
NOW SHE REALLY IS YOUR "LITTLE" SISTER !!
SHE'S SO CUTE.
LITTLE... GET IT?
ANY-WAY ...
HOW DID SHE EVEN END UP THIS WAY?
AND HOW CAN WE GET HER BACK TO NORMAL?
SHE TALKS LESS THAN USUAL.
MAYBE HER VOICE IS QUIET BECAUSE SHE'S SO SMALL.
We just can't hear it.
...
IS THIS REALLY RUBY?
LET'S ASK HER.
RUBY ?

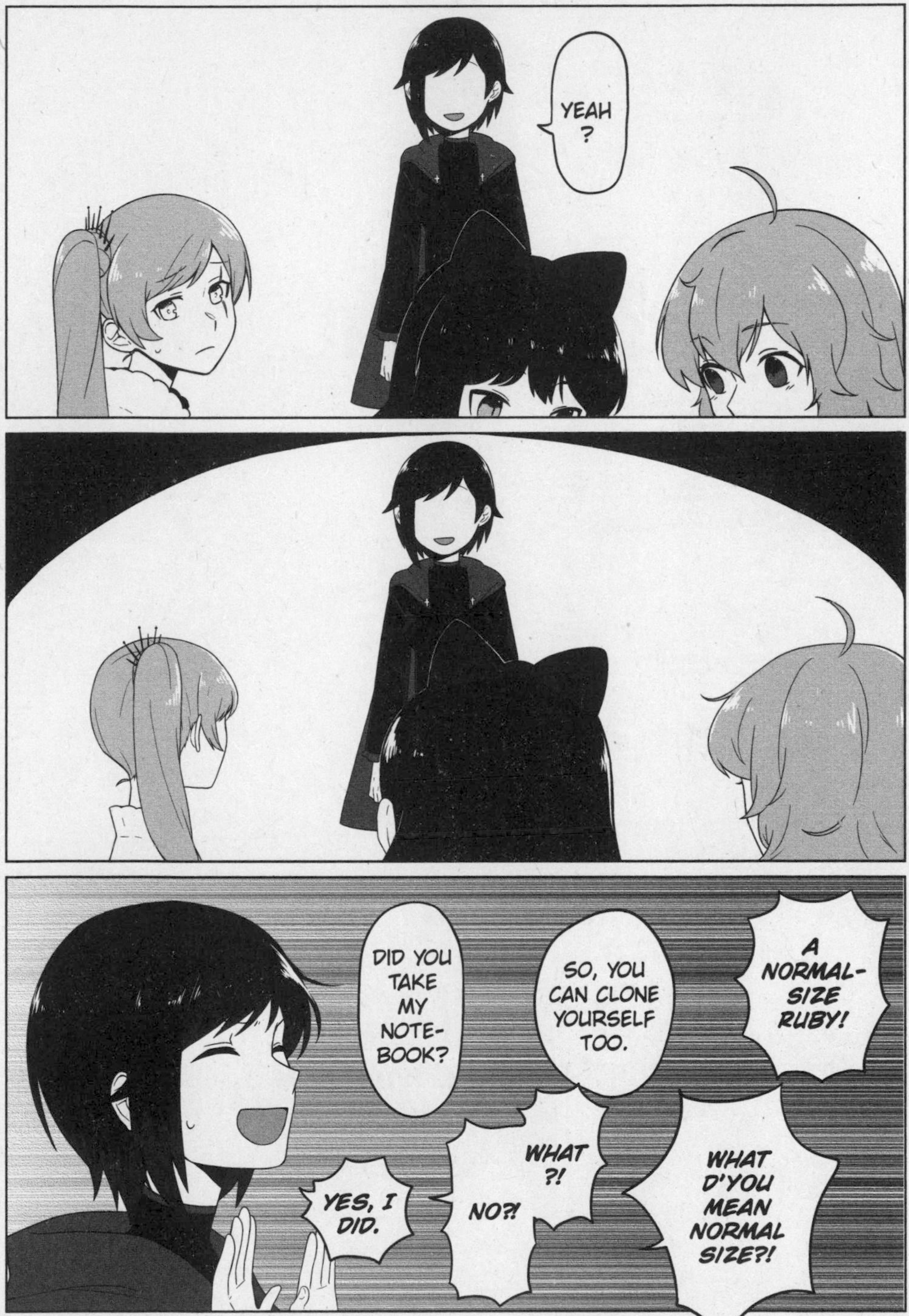
YEAH ?
A NORMAL-SIZE RUBY!
SO, YOU CAN CLONE YOURSELF TOO.
DID YOU TAKE MY NOTE-BOOK?
WHAT D'YOU MEAN NORMAL SIZE?!
WHAT ?!
NO?!
YES, I DID.

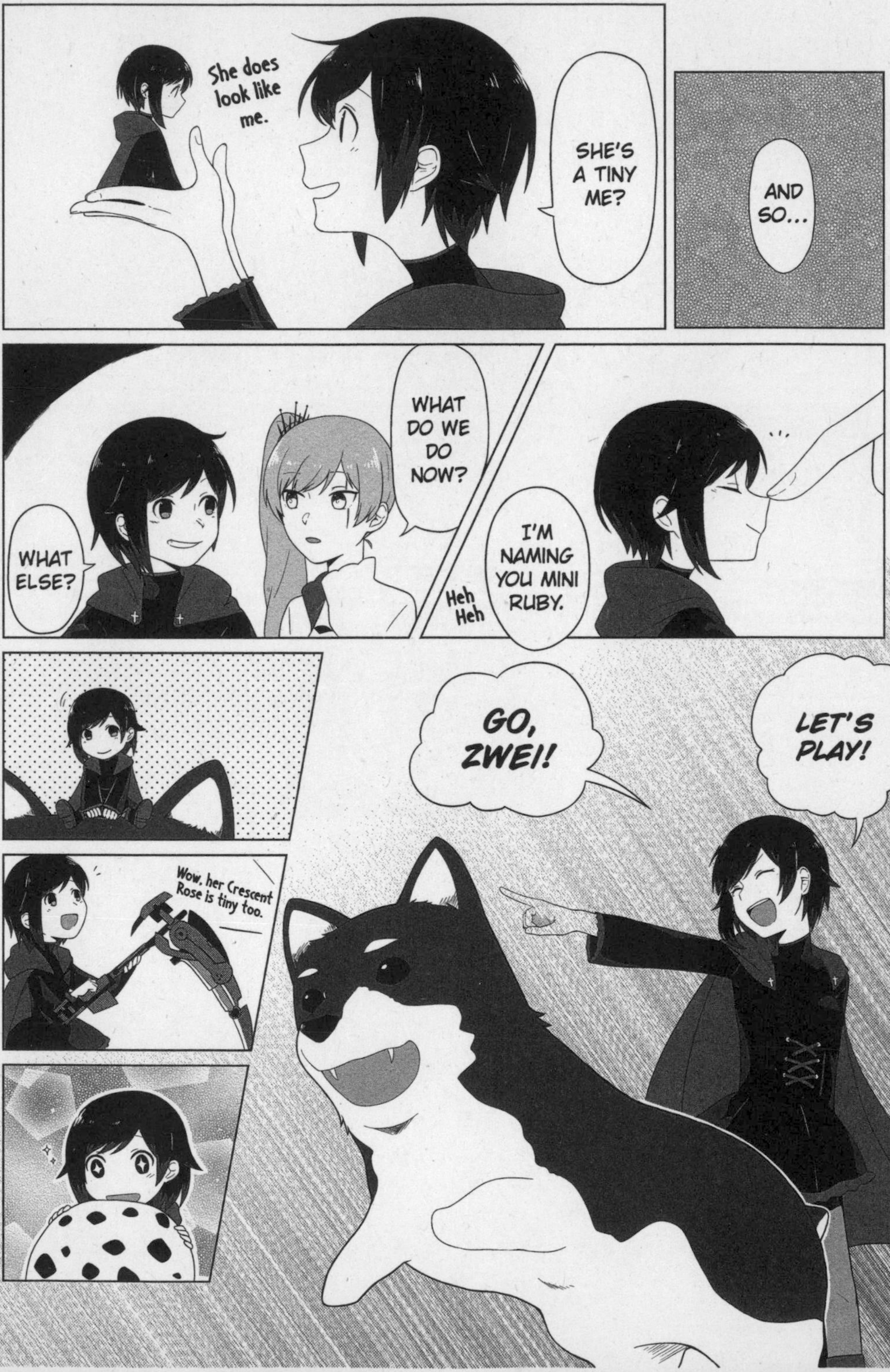
AND SO...
SHE'S A TINY ME?
She does look like me.
I'M NAMING YOU MINI RUBY.
Heh Heh
WHAT DO WE DO NOW?
WHAT ELSE?
LET'S PLAY!
GO, ZWEI!
Wow, her Crescent Rose is tiny too.

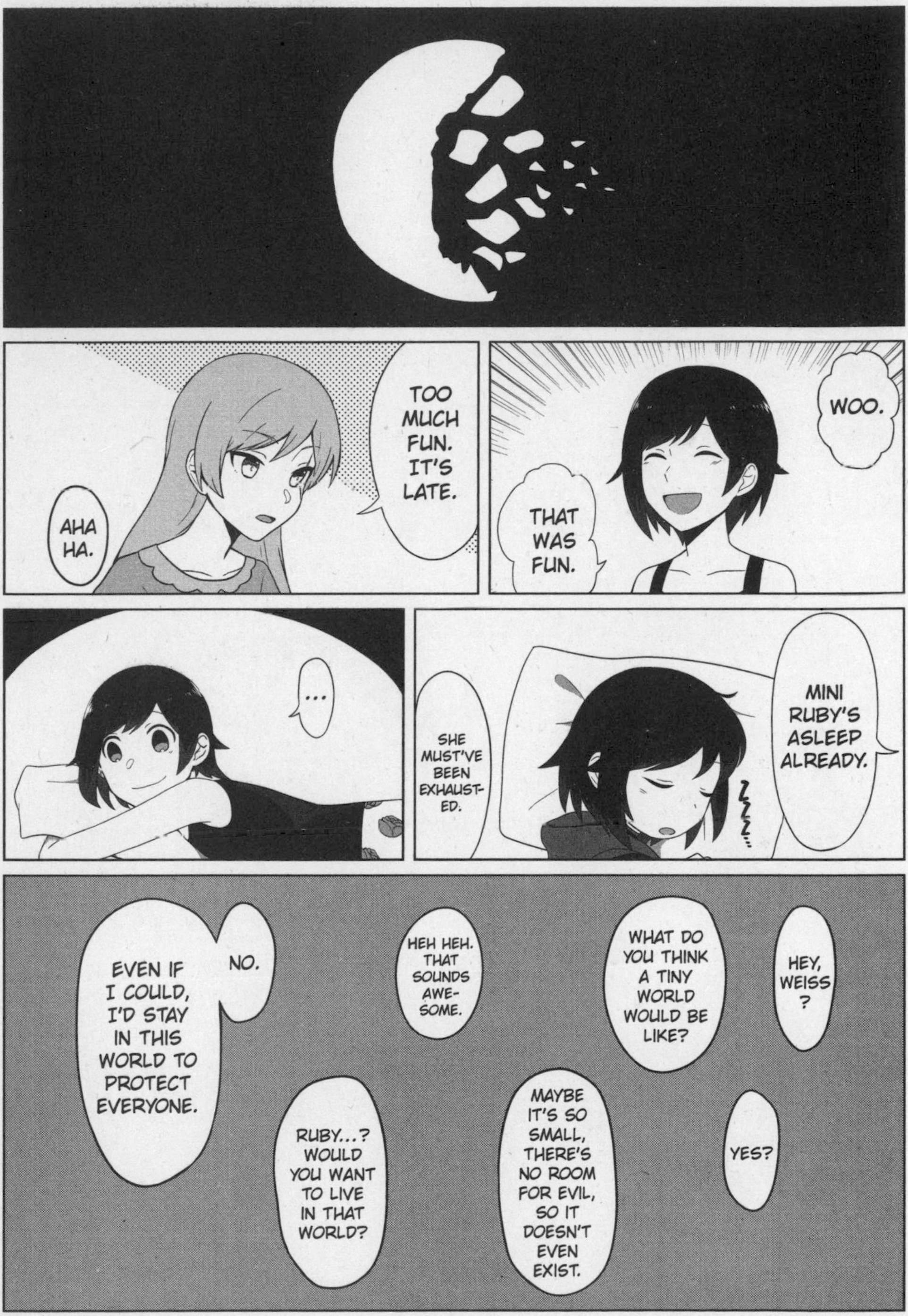
WOO.
THAT WAS FUN.
TOO MUCH FUN. IT'S LATE.
AHA HA.
MINI RUBY'S ASLEEP ALREADY.
SHE MUST'VE BEEN EXHAUSTED.
...
HEY, WEISS?
WHAT DO YOU THINK A TINY WORLD WOULD BE LIKE?
YES?
MAYBE IT'S SO SMALL, THERE'S NO ROOM FOR EVIL, SO IT DOESN'T EVEN EXIST.
HEH HEH. THAT SOUNDS AWESOME.
RUBY...? WOULD YOU WANT TO LIVE IN THAT WORLD?
NO.
EVEN IF I COULD, I'D STAY IN THIS WORLD TO PROTECT EVERYONE.

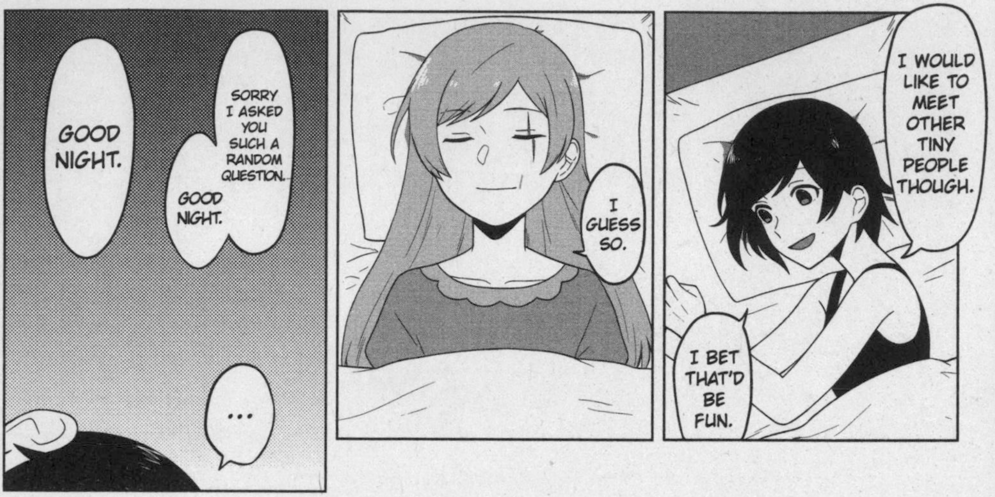
I WOULD LIKE TO MEET OTHER TINY PEOPLE THOUGH.
I BET THAT'D BE FUN.
I GUESS SO.
SORRY I ASKED YOU SUCH A RANDOM QUESTION.
GOOD NIGHT.
GOOD NIGHT.
...

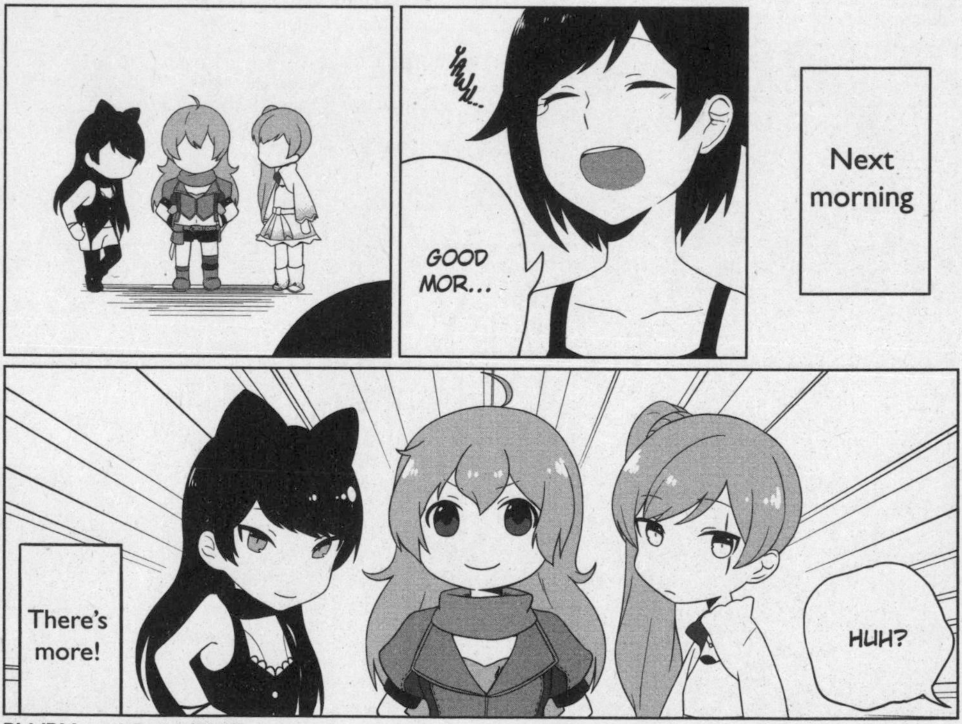
Next morning
YAWN...
GOOD MOR...
HUH?
There's more!

RWBY and Ruby/END

Who's Afraid of Little Red Riding Hood If We All Attack at Once!

Xily

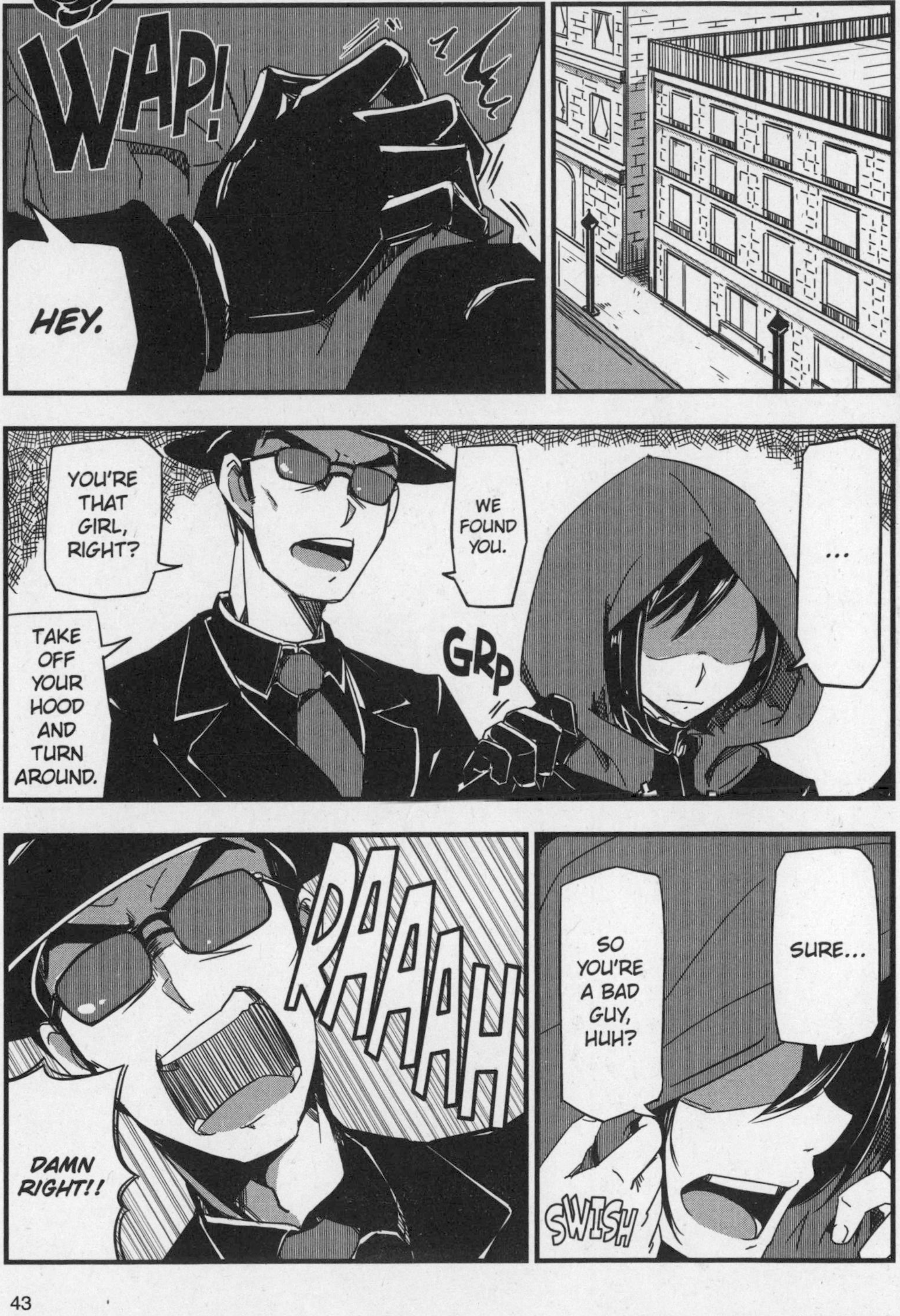
WAP!
HEY.
...
WE FOUND YOU.
YOU'RE THAT GIRL, RIGHT?
GRP
TAKE OFF YOUR HOOD AND TURN AROUND.
SURE...
SO YOU'RE A BAD GUY, HUH?
SWISH
RAAAH
DAMN RIGHT!!

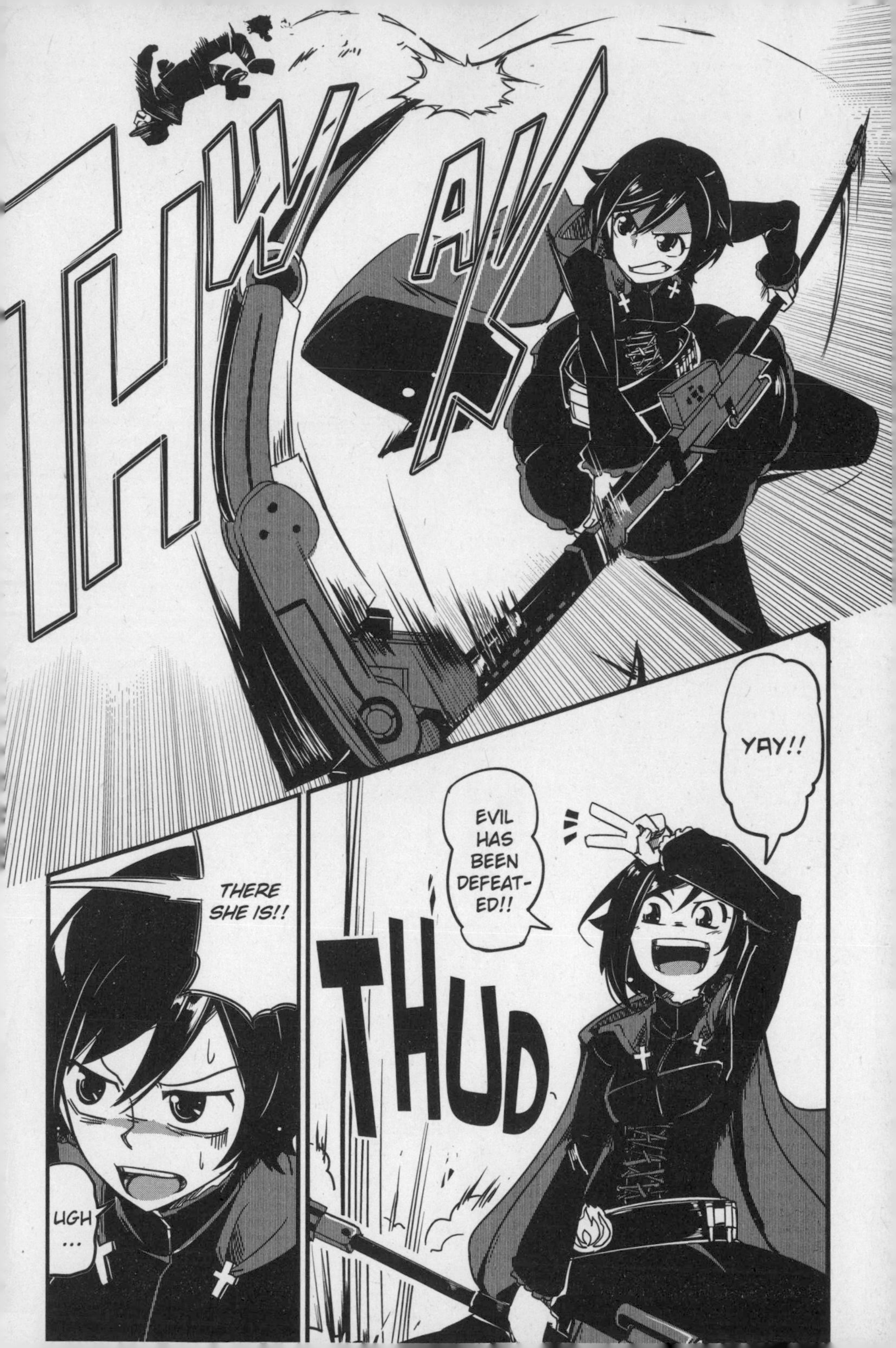
THWAK
YAY!!
EVIL HAS BEEN DEFEAT-ED!!
THUD
THERE SHE IS!!
UGH ...

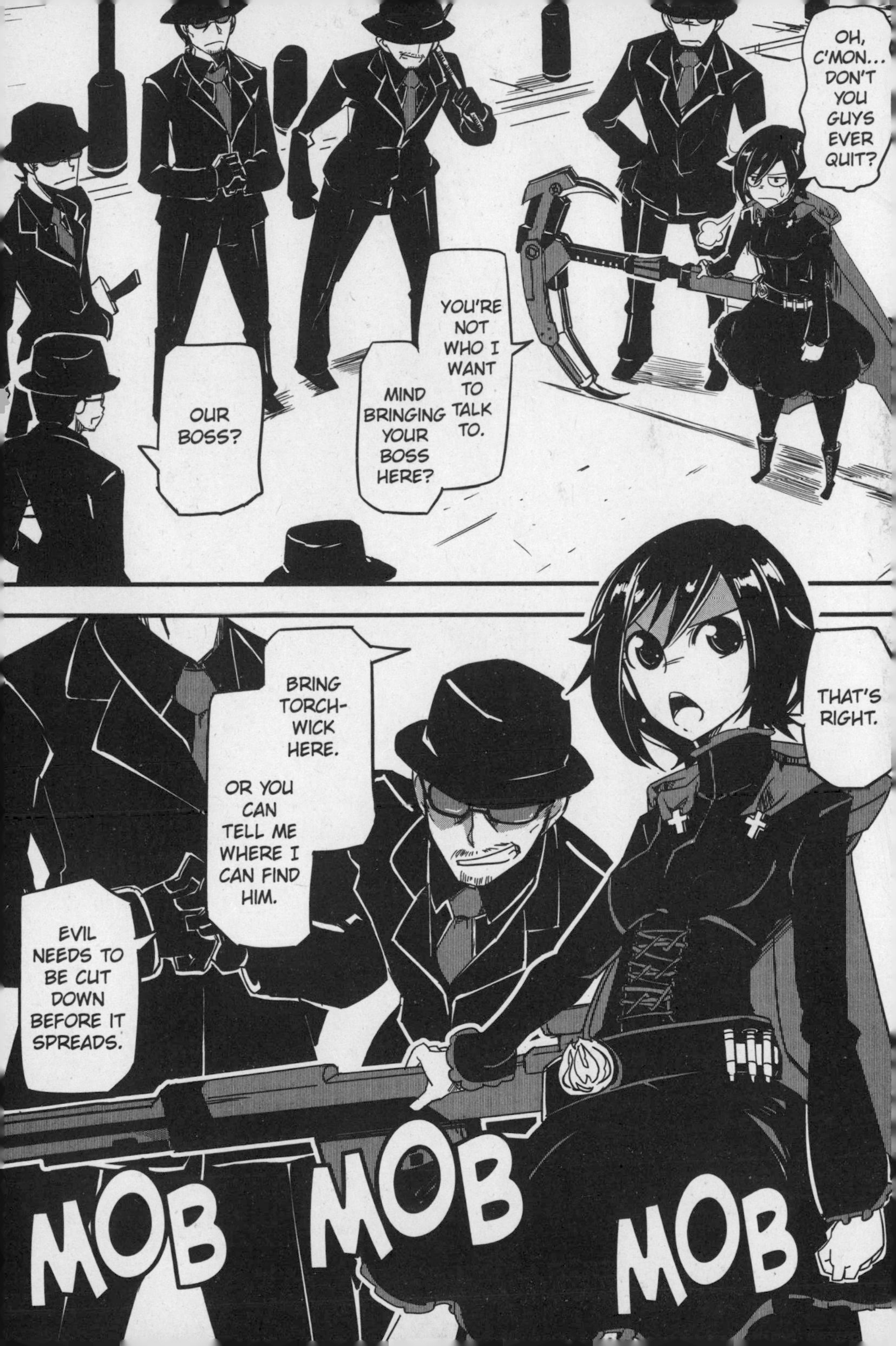
OH, C'MON... DON'T YOU GUYS EVER QUIT?
YOU'RE NOT WHO I WANT TO TALK TO.
MIND BRINGING YOUR BOSS HERE?
OUR BOSS?
THAT'S RIGHT.
BRING TORCH-WICK HERE.
OR YOU CAN TELL ME WHERE I CAN FIND HIM.
EVIL NEEDS TO BE CUT DOWN BEFORE IT SPREADS.
MOB
MOB
MOB

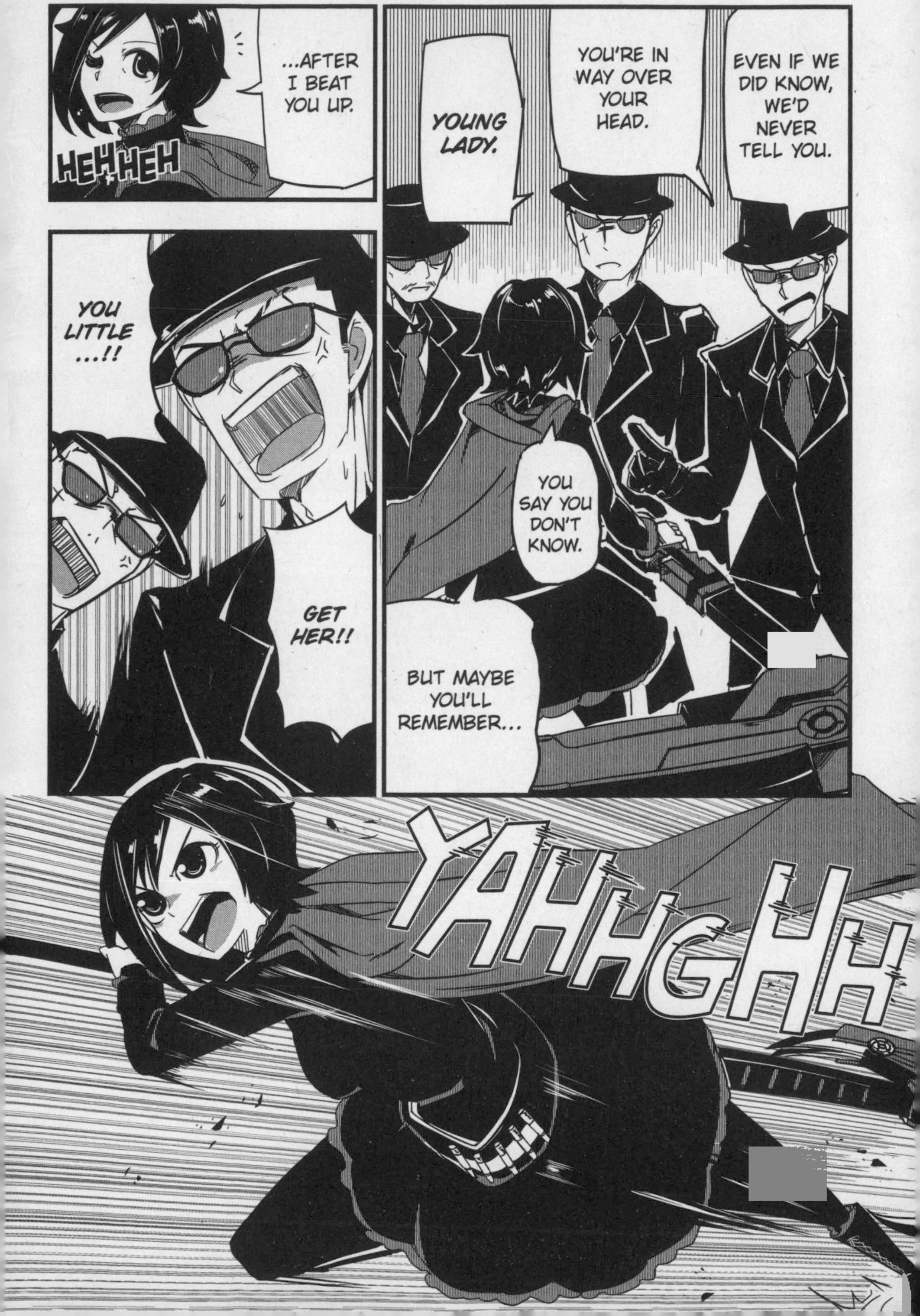
EVEN IF WE DID KNOW, WE'D NEVER TELL YOU.
YOU'RE IN WAY OVER YOUR HEAD.
YOUNG LADY.
YOU SAY YOU DON'T KNOW.
BUT MAYBE YOU'LL REMEMBER...
...AFTER I BEAT YOU UP.
HEHHEH
YOU LITTLE...!!
GET HER!!
YAHHGHH

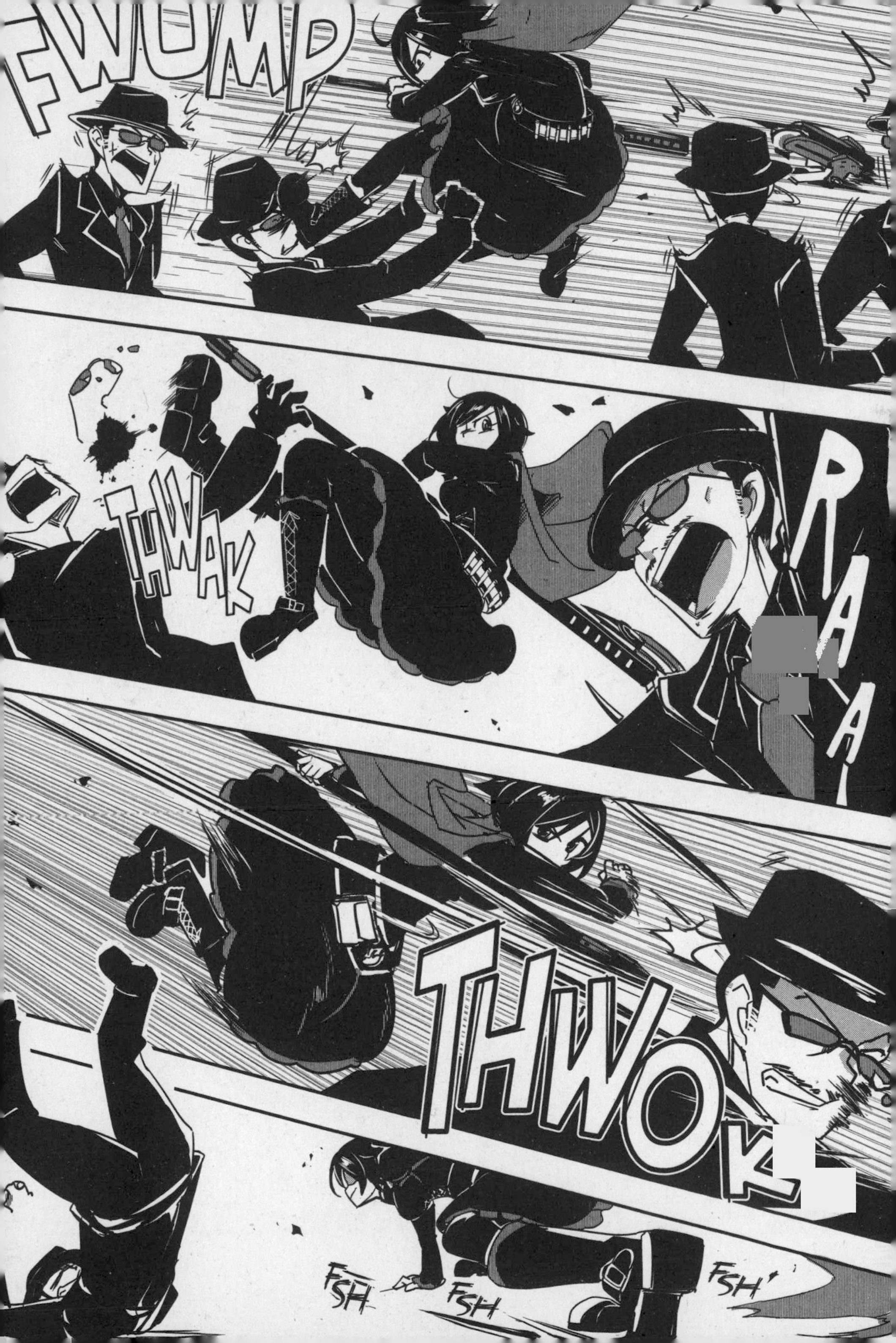
FWOMP
RAA
THWAK
THWOK
FSH
FSH
FSH

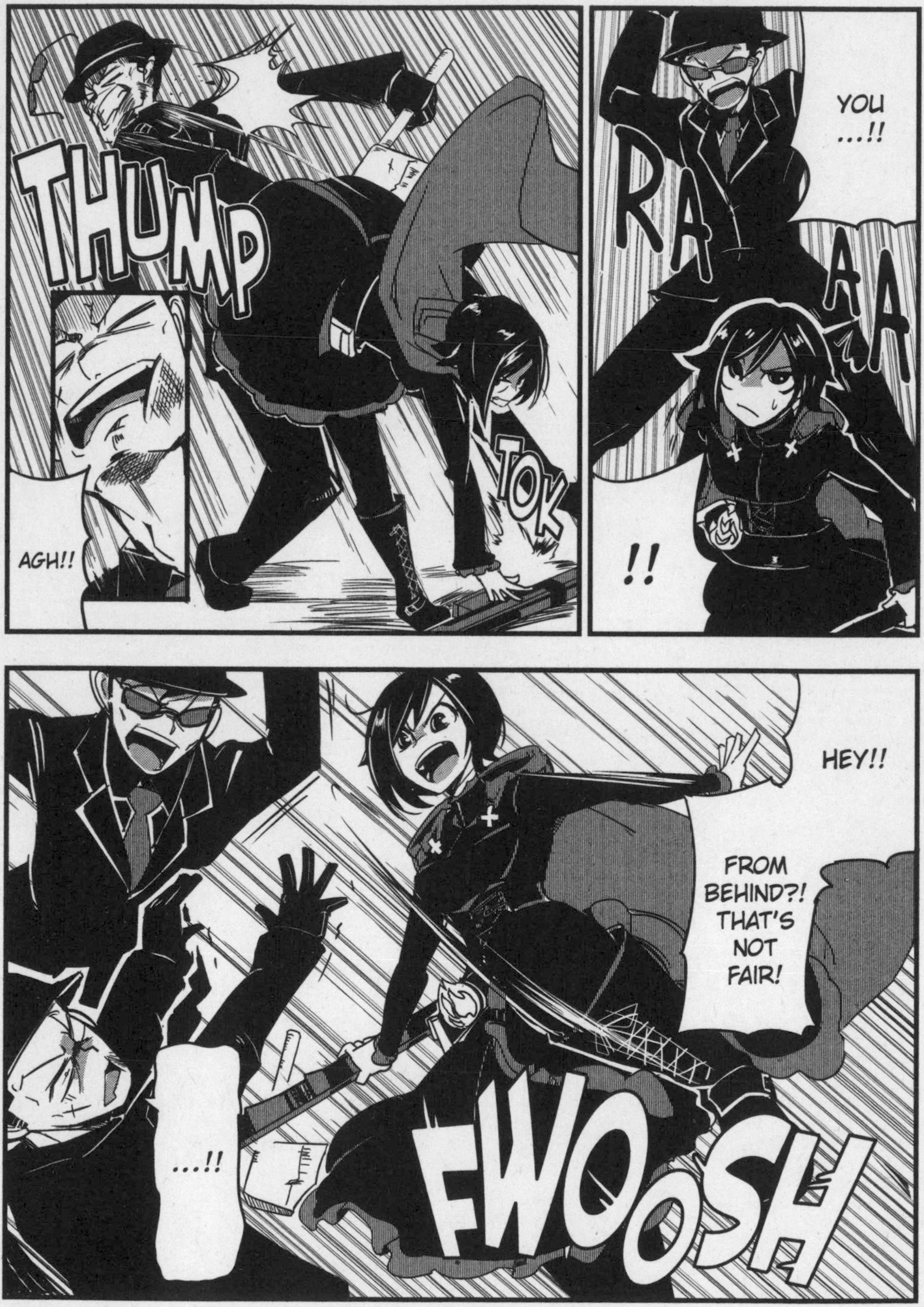

YOU ...!!
RAAA
!!
THUMP
TOK
AGH!!
HEY!!
FROM BEHIND?! THAT'S NOT FAIR!
...!!
FWOOOSH

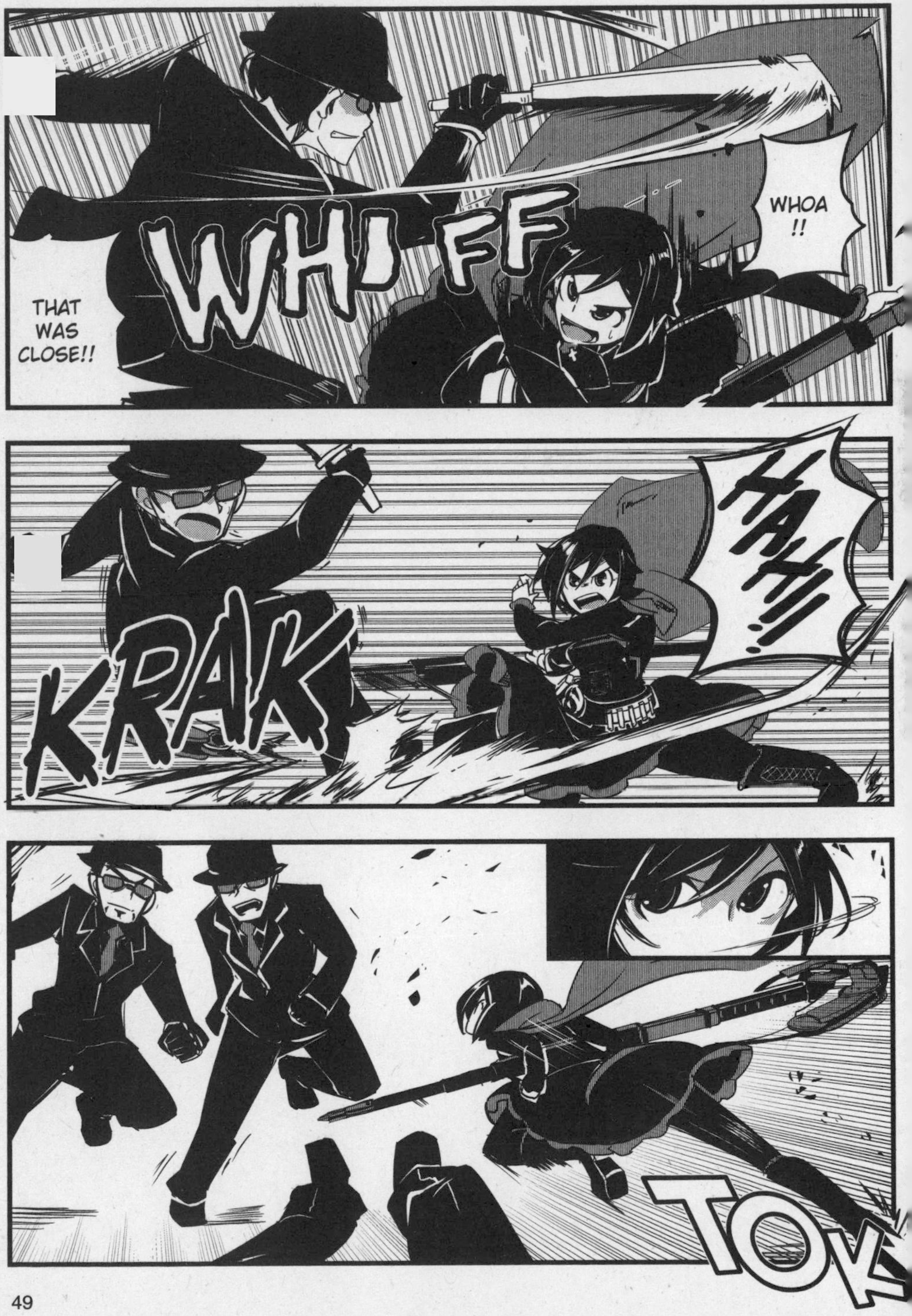
WHOA !!
WHIFF
THAT WAS CLOSE!!
HAH!!
KRAK
TOK

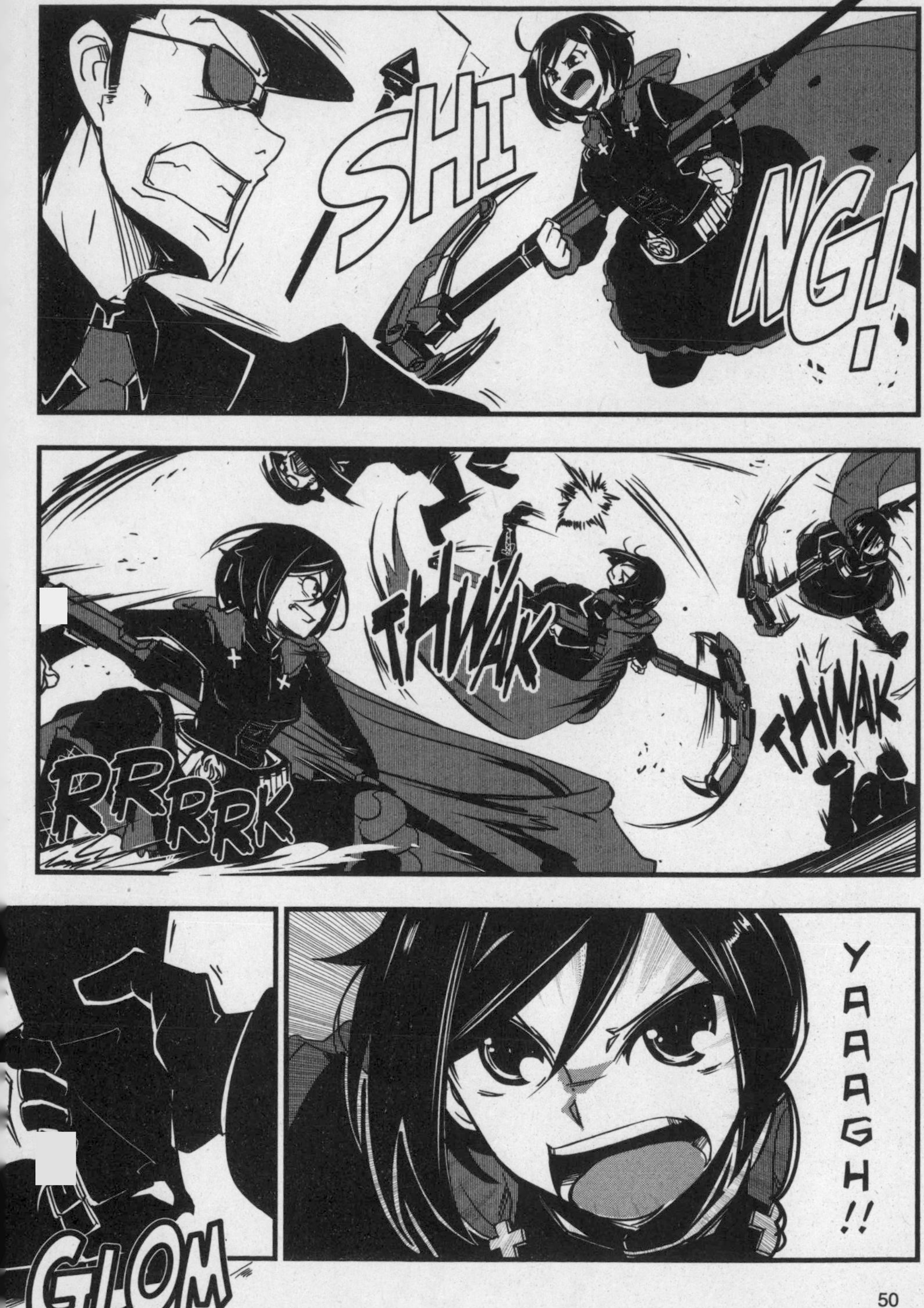

SHI
NG!
THWAK
THWAK
RRRRK
YAAAGH!!
GLOM

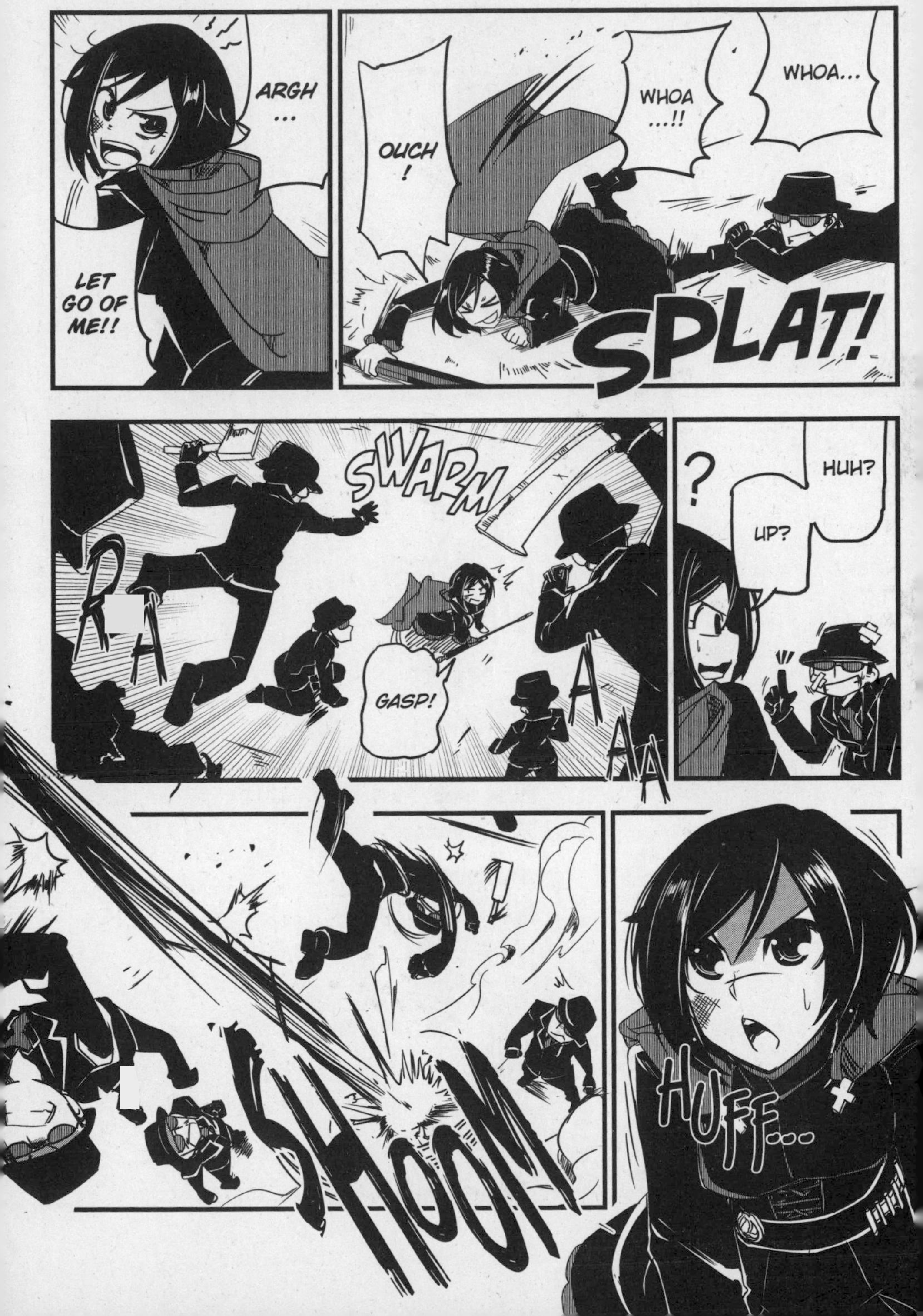
WHOA...
WHOA ...!!
OUCH !
SPLAT!
ARGH ...
LET GO OF ME!!
?
HUH?
UP?
SWARM
GASP!
HUFF...
SHOOM

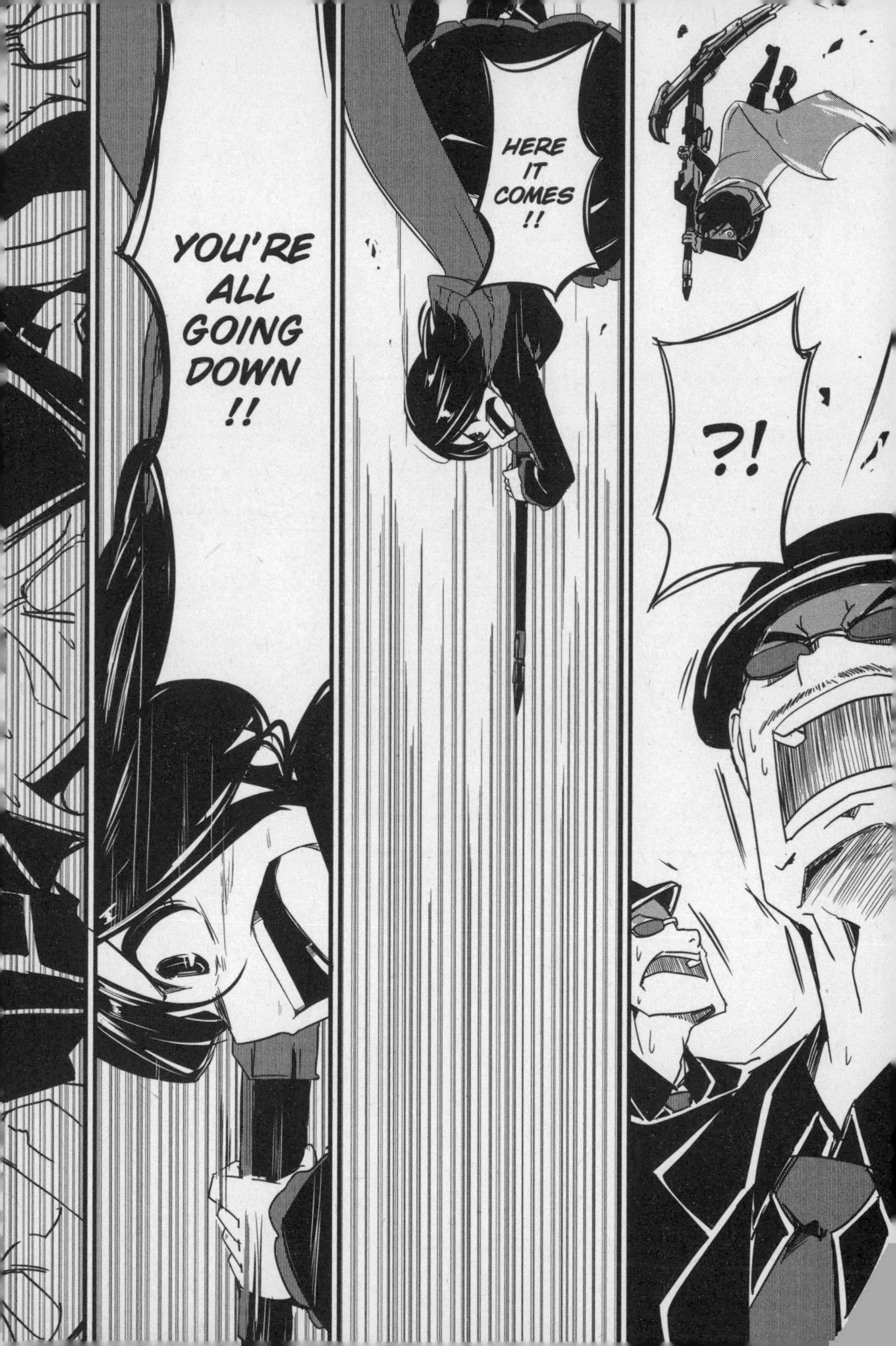
?!
HERE IT COMES !!
YOU'RE ALL GOING DOWN !!

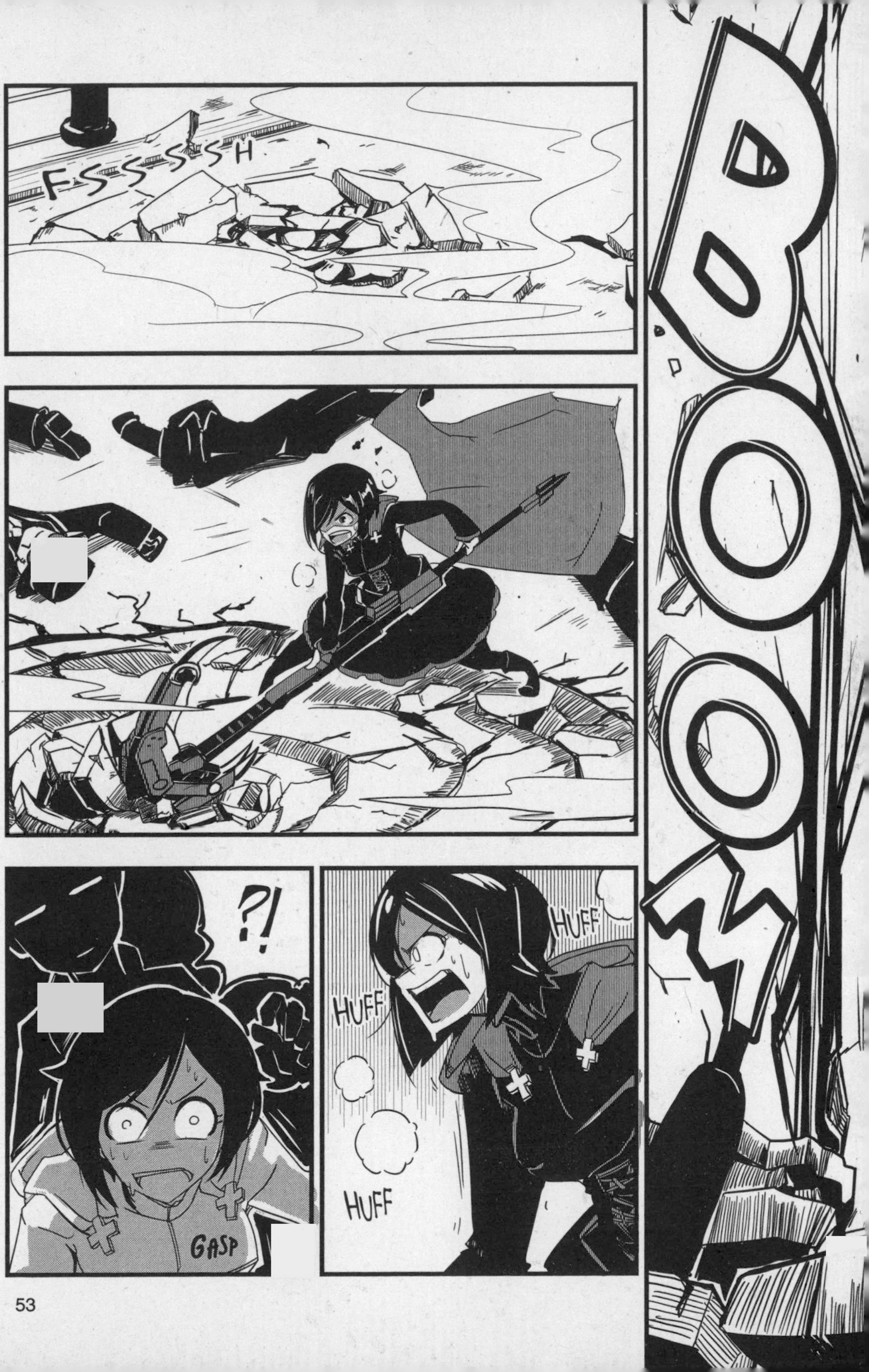
BOOM
FSSSSH
HUFF
HUFF
HUFF
?!
GASP

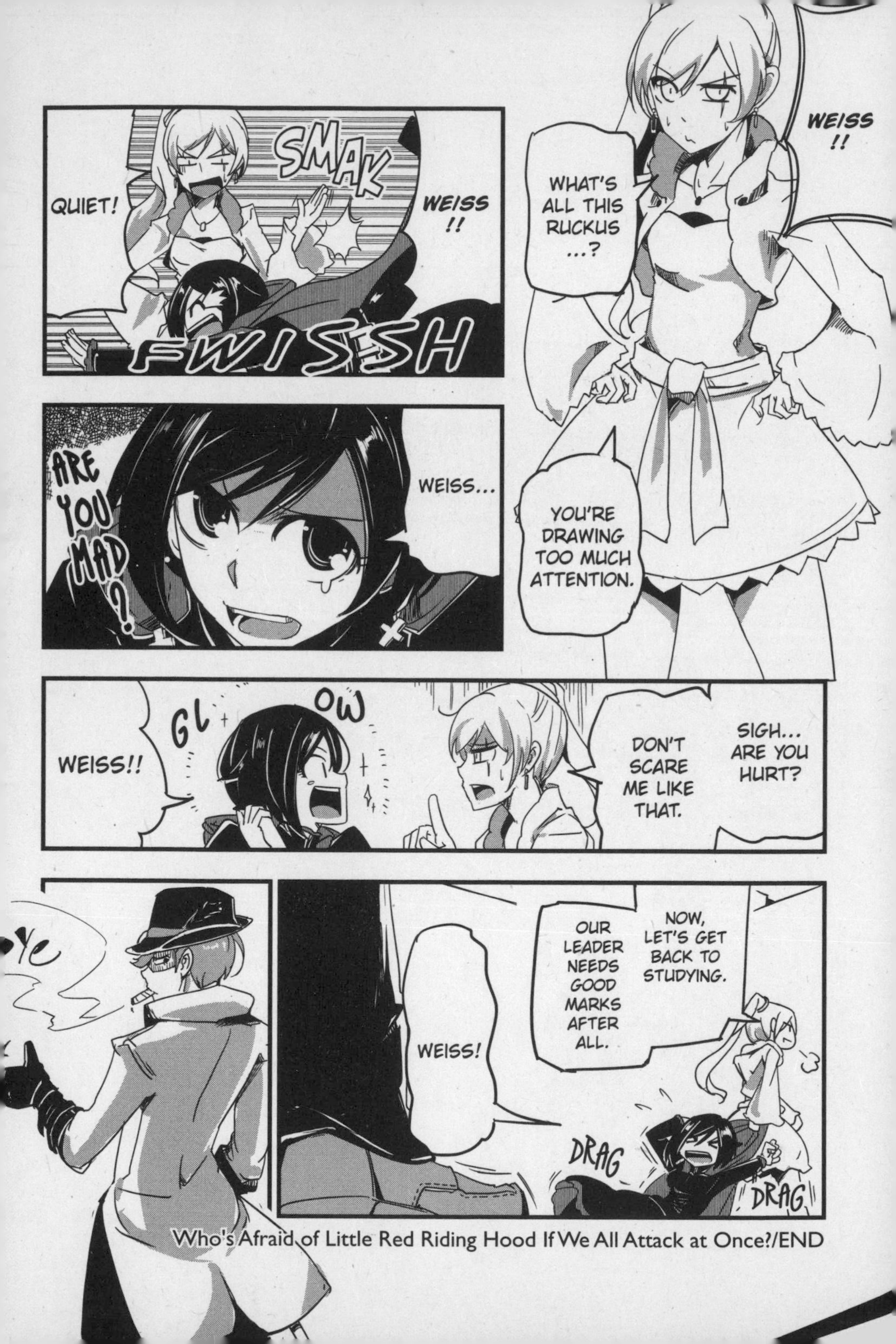
WEISS !!
WHAT'S ALL THIS RUCKUS ...?
YOU'RE DRAWING TOO MUCH ATTENTION.
WEISS !!
SMAK
QUIET!
FWISSH
WEISS...
ARE YOU MAD?
SIGH... ARE YOU HURT?
DON'T SCARE ME LIKE THAT.
GLOW
WEISS!!
NOW, LET'S GET BACK TO STUDYING.
OUR LEADER NEEDS GOOD MARKS AFTER ALL.
WEISS!
DRAG
DRAG
Who's Afraid of Little Red Riding Hood If We All Attack at Once?/END

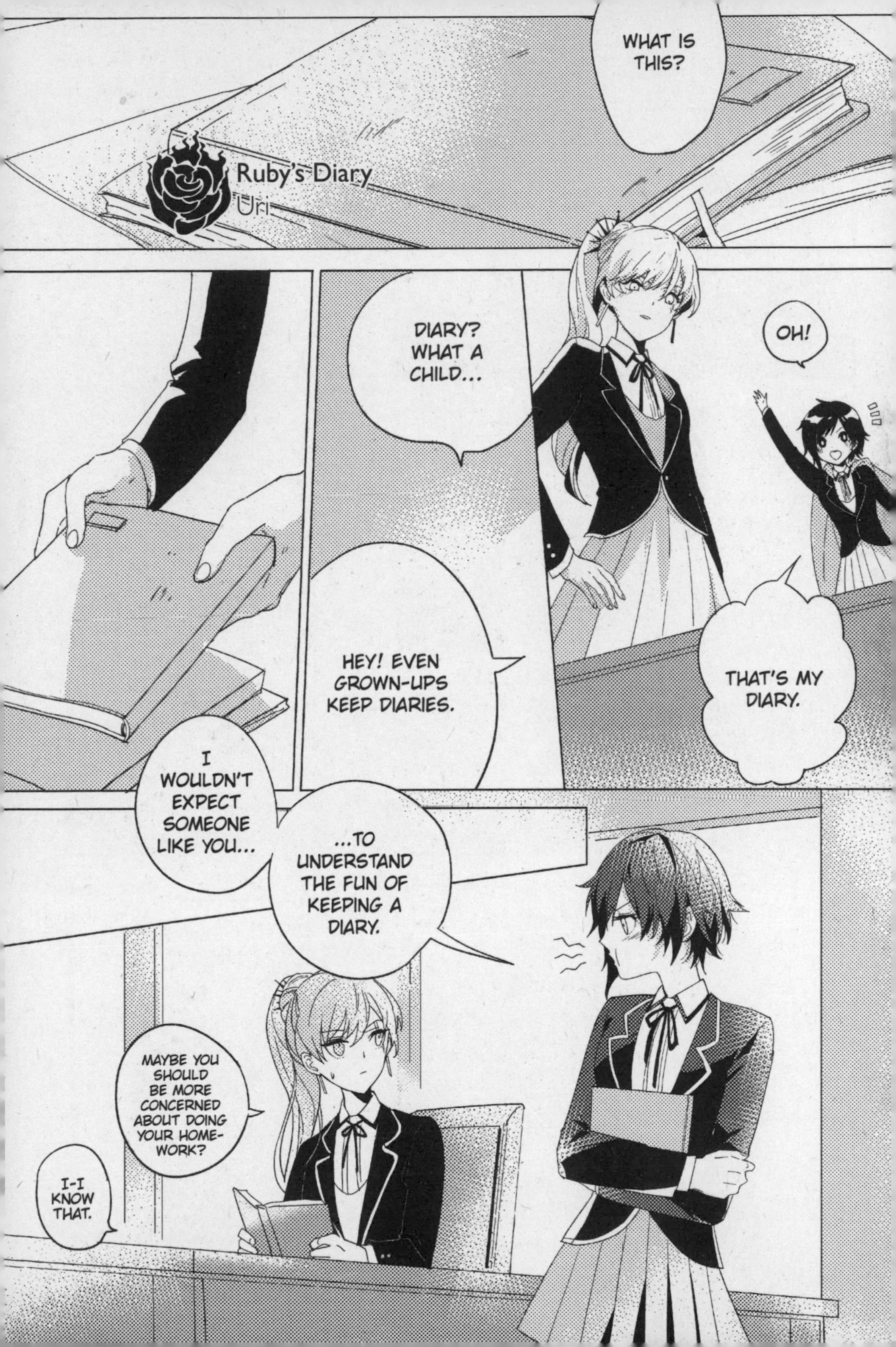
WHAT IS THIS?
Ruby's Diary
Uri
OH!
THAT'S MY DIARY.
DIARY? WHAT A CHILD...
HEY! EVEN GROWN-UPS KEEP DIARIES.
I WOULDN'T EXPECT SOMEONE LIKE YOU...
...TO UNDERSTAND THE FUN OF KEEPING A DIARY.
MAYBE YOU SHOULD BE MORE CONCERNED ABOUT DOING YOUR HOME-WORK?
I-I KNOW THAT.

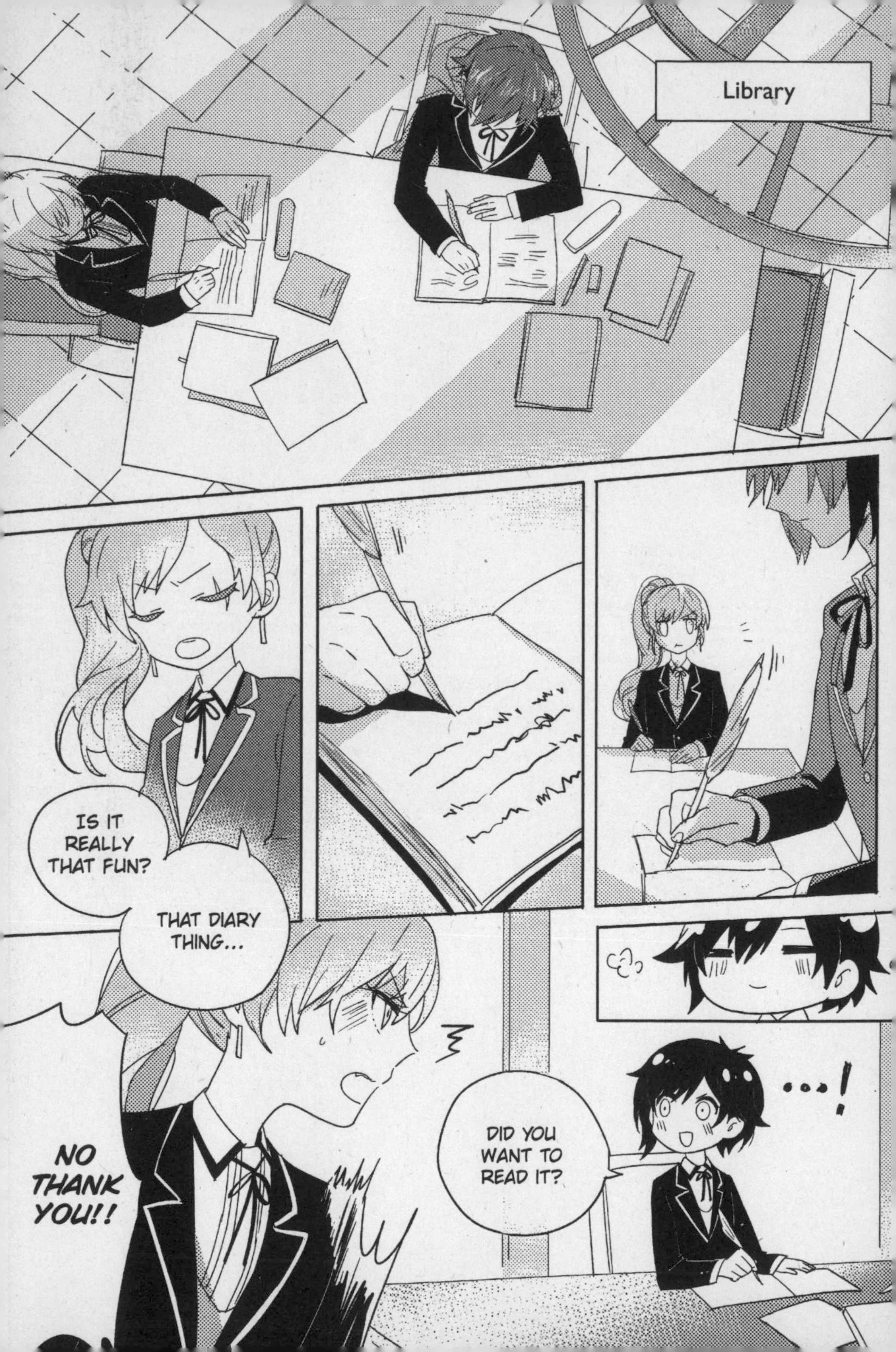

Library
IS IT REALLY THAT FUN?
THAT DIARY THING...
...!
DID YOU WANT TO READ IT?
NO THANK YOU!!

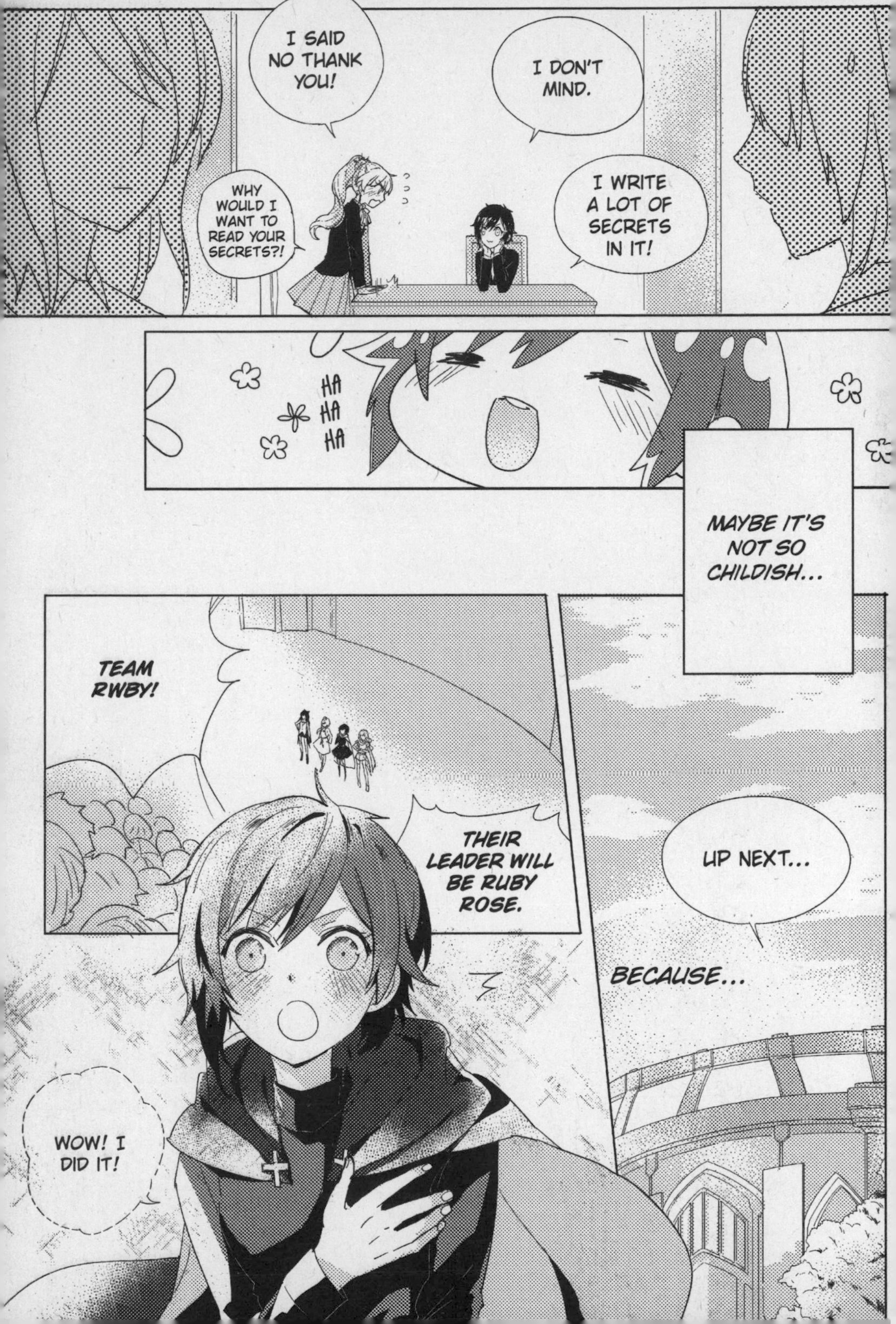
I DON'T MIND.
I SAID NO THANK YOU!
I WRITE A LOT OF SECRETS IN IT!
WHY WOULD I WANT TO READ YOUR SECRETS?!
HA HA HA
MAYBE IT'S NOT SO CHILDISH...
UP NEXT...
BECAUSE...
TEAM RWBY!
THEIR LEADER WILL BE RUBY ROSE.
WOW! I DID IT!

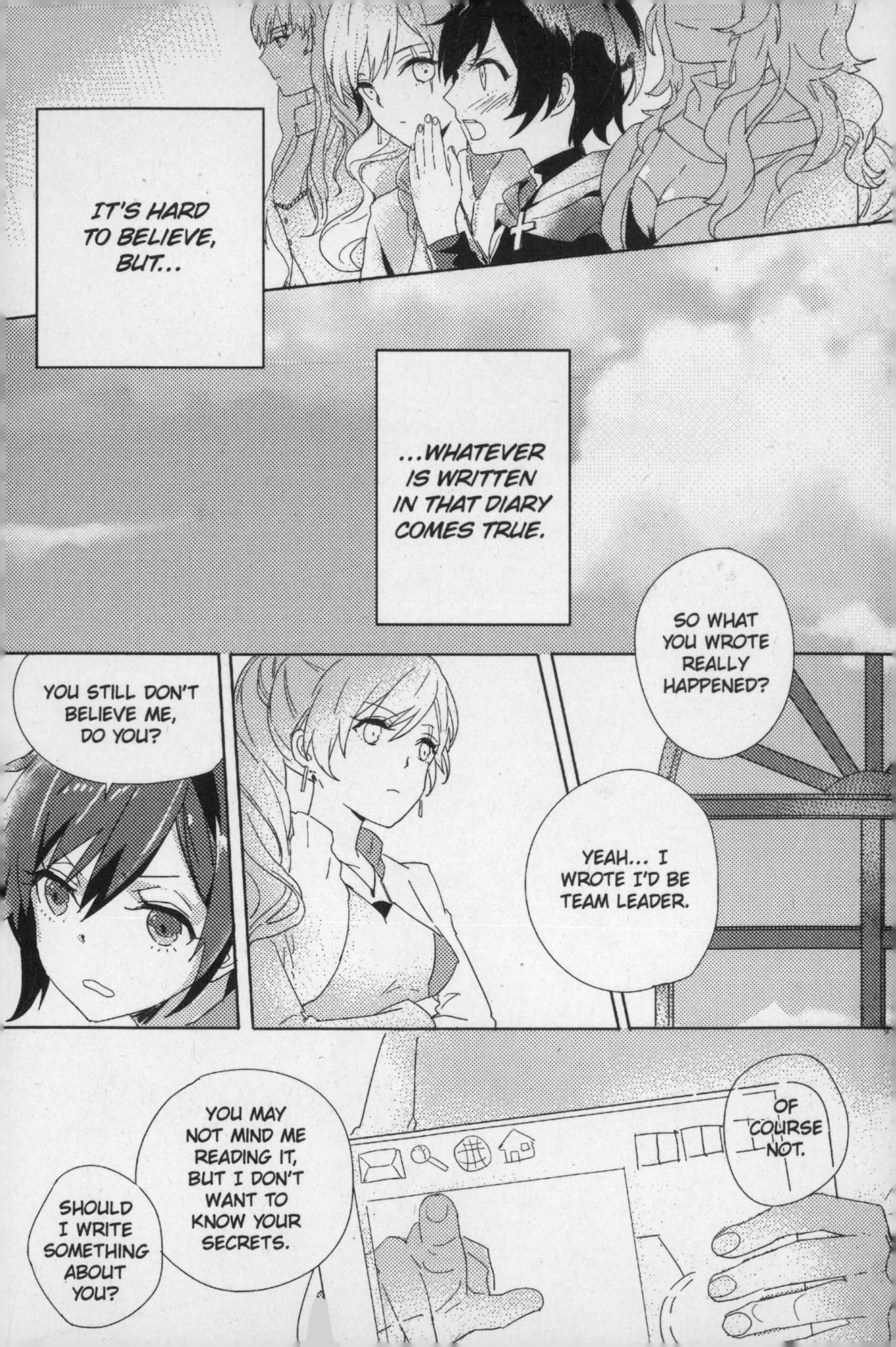
IT'S HARD TO BELIEVE, BUT...
...WHATEVER IS WRITTEN IN THAT DIARY COMES TRUE.
SO WHAT YOU WROTE REALLY HAPPENED?
YEAH... I WROTE I'D BE TEAM LEADER.
YOU STILL DON'T BELIEVE ME, DO YOU?
OF COURSE NOT.
YOU MAY NOT MIND ME READING IT, BUT I DON'T WANT TO KNOW YOUR SECRETS.
SHOULD I WRITE SOMETHING ABOUT YOU?

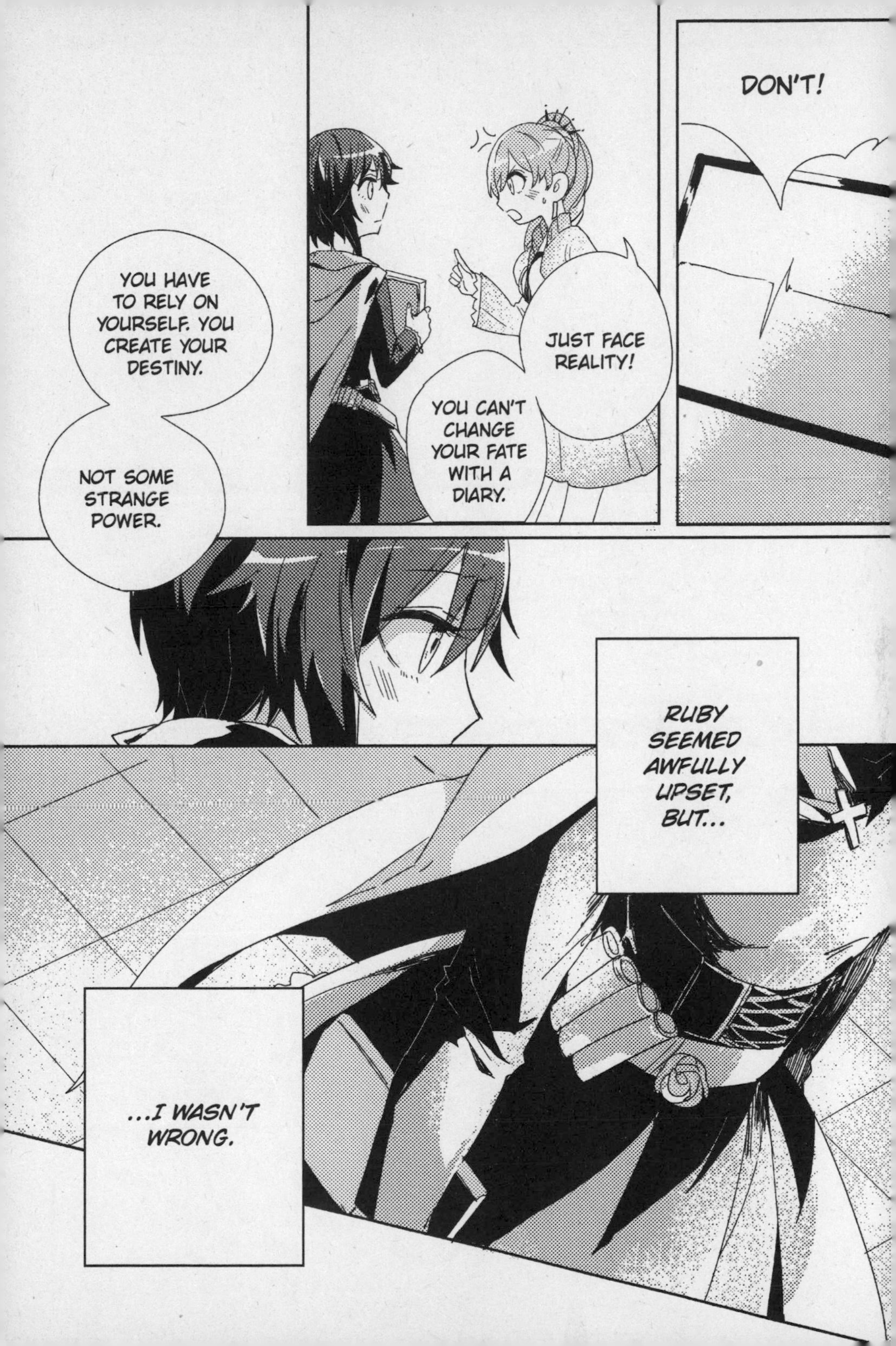
DON'T!
JUST FACE REALITY!
YOU CAN'T CHANGE YOUR FATE WITH A DIARY.
YOU HAVE TO RELY ON YOURSELF. YOU CREATE YOUR DESTINY.
NOT SOME STRANGE POWER.
RUBY SEEMED AWFULLY UPSET, BUT...
...I WASN'T WRONG.

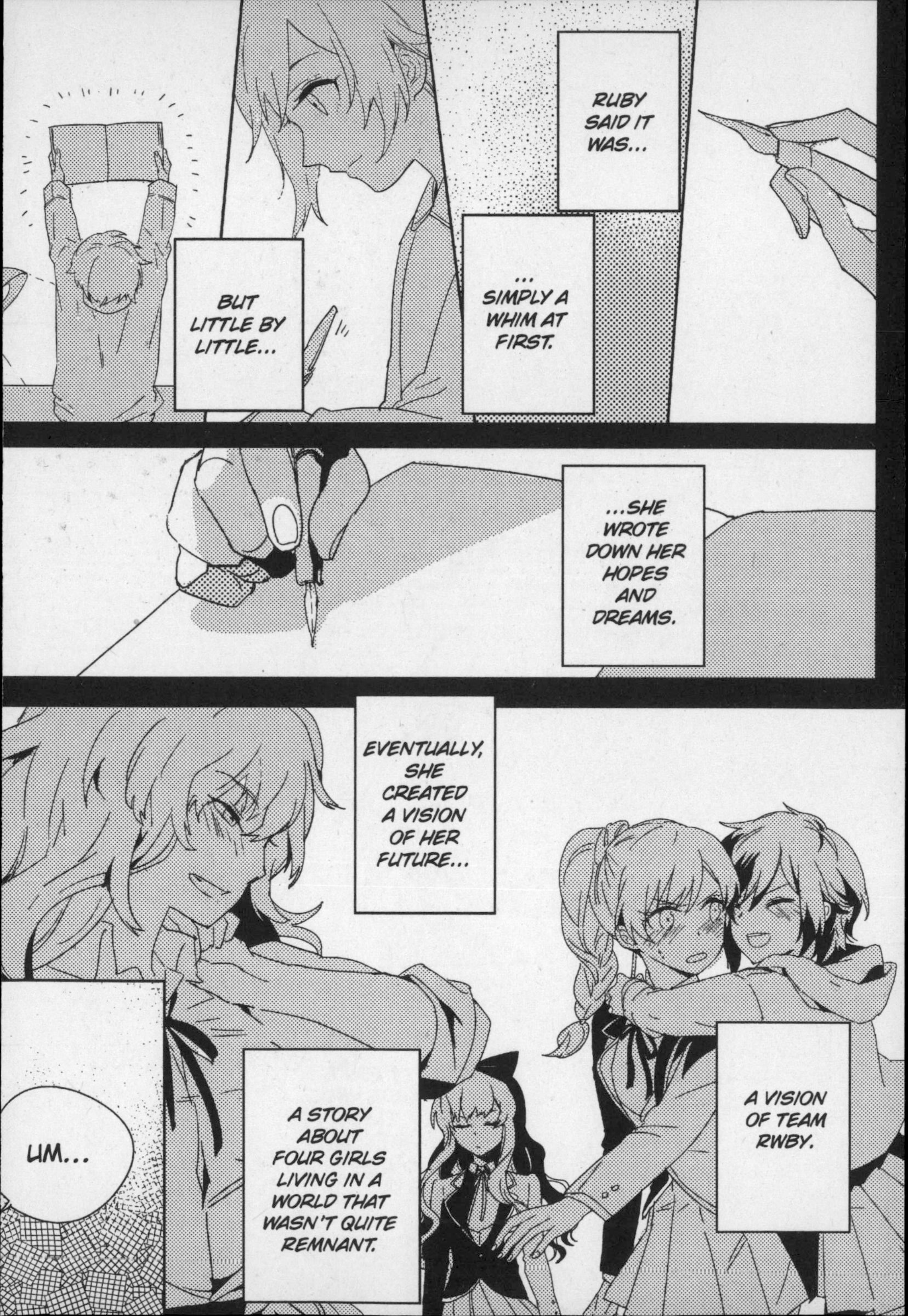
RUBY SAID IT WAS...
... SIMPLY A WHIM AT FIRST.
BUT LITTLE BY LITTLE...
...SHE WROTE DOWN HER HOPES AND DREAMS.
EVENTUALLY, SHE CREATED A VISION OF HER FUTURE...
A VISION OF TEAM RWBY.
A STORY ABOUT FOUR GIRLS LIVING IN A WORLD THAT WASN'T QUITE REMNANT.
UM...

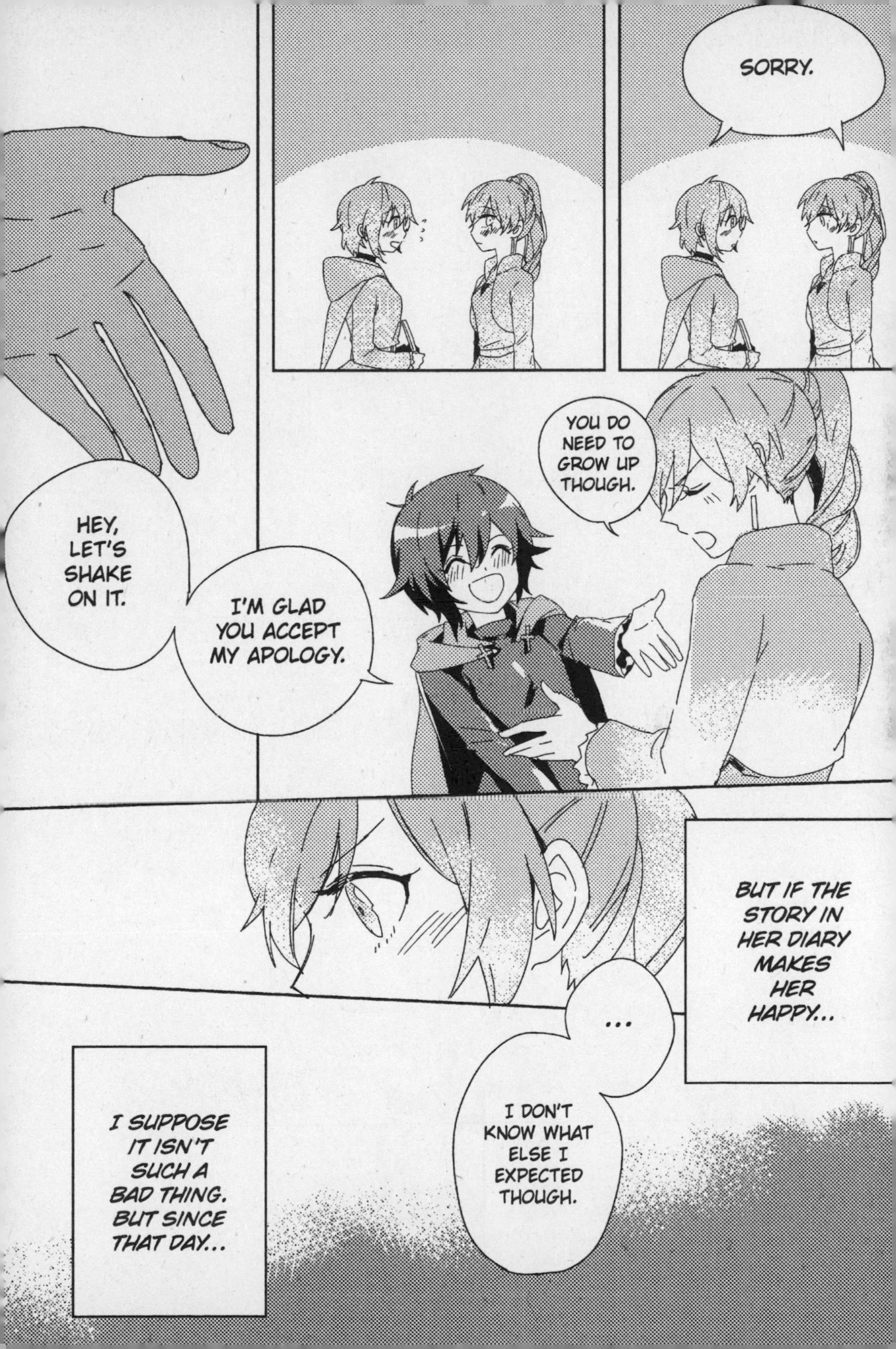

SORRY.
YOU DO NEED TO GROW UP THOUGH.
I'M GLAD YOU ACCEPT MY APOLOGY.
HEY, LET'S SHAKE ON IT.
BUT IF THE STORY IN HER DIARY MAKES HER HAPPY...
...
I DON'T KNOW WHAT ELSE I EXPECTED THOUGH.
I SUPPOSE IT ISN'T SUCH A BAD THING. BUT SINCE THAT DAY...

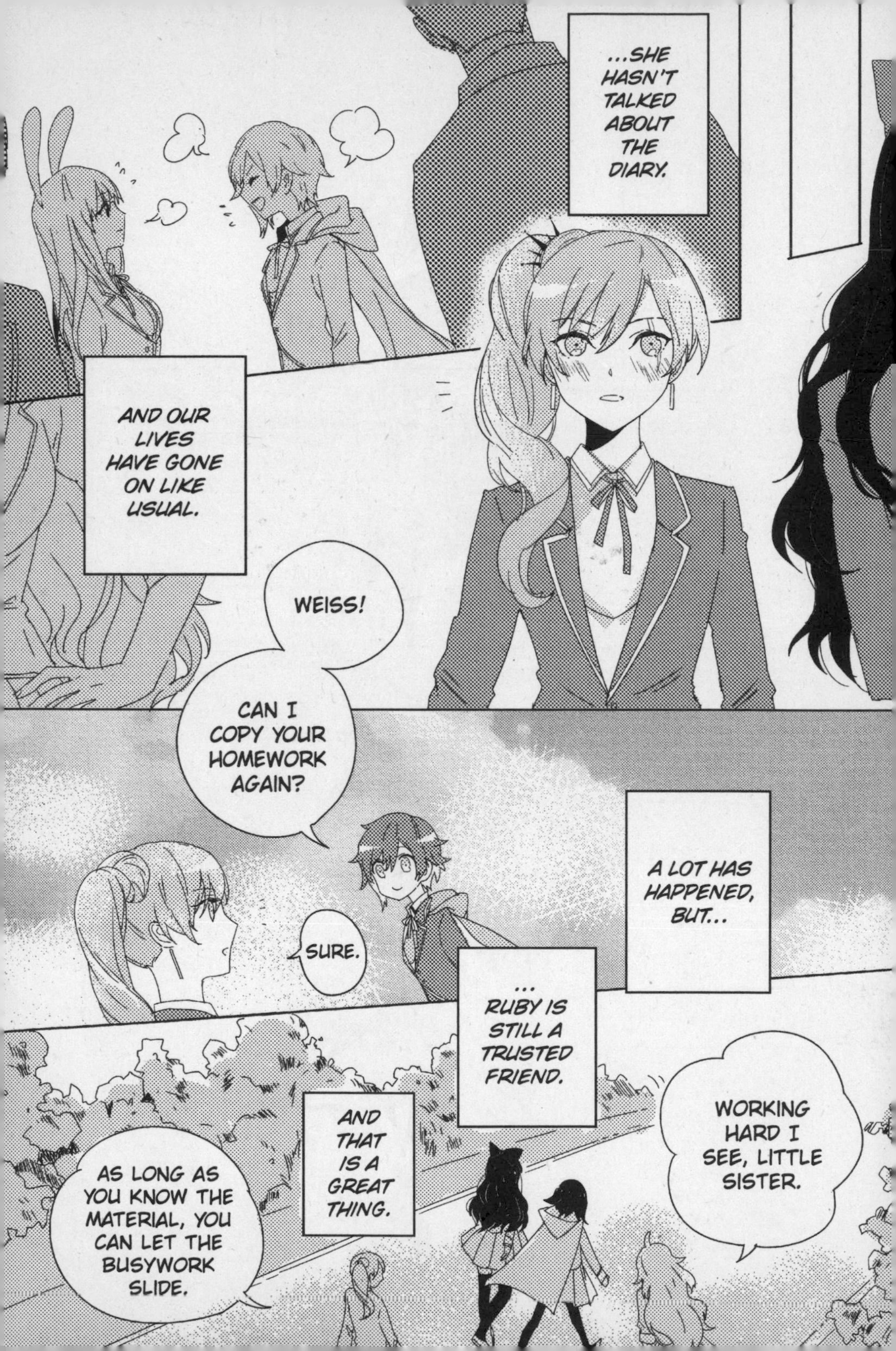
...SHE HASN'T TALKED ABOUT THE DIARY.
AND OUR LIVES HAVE GONE ON LIKE USUAL.
WEISS!
CAN I COPY YOUR HOMEWORK AGAIN?
A LOT HAS HAPPENED, BUT...
SURE.
... RUBY IS STILL A TRUSTED FRIEND.
WORKING HARD I SEE, LITTLE SISTER.
AND THAT IS A GREAT THING.
AS LONG AS YOU KNOW THE MATERIAL, YOU CAN LET THE BUSYWORK SLIDE.

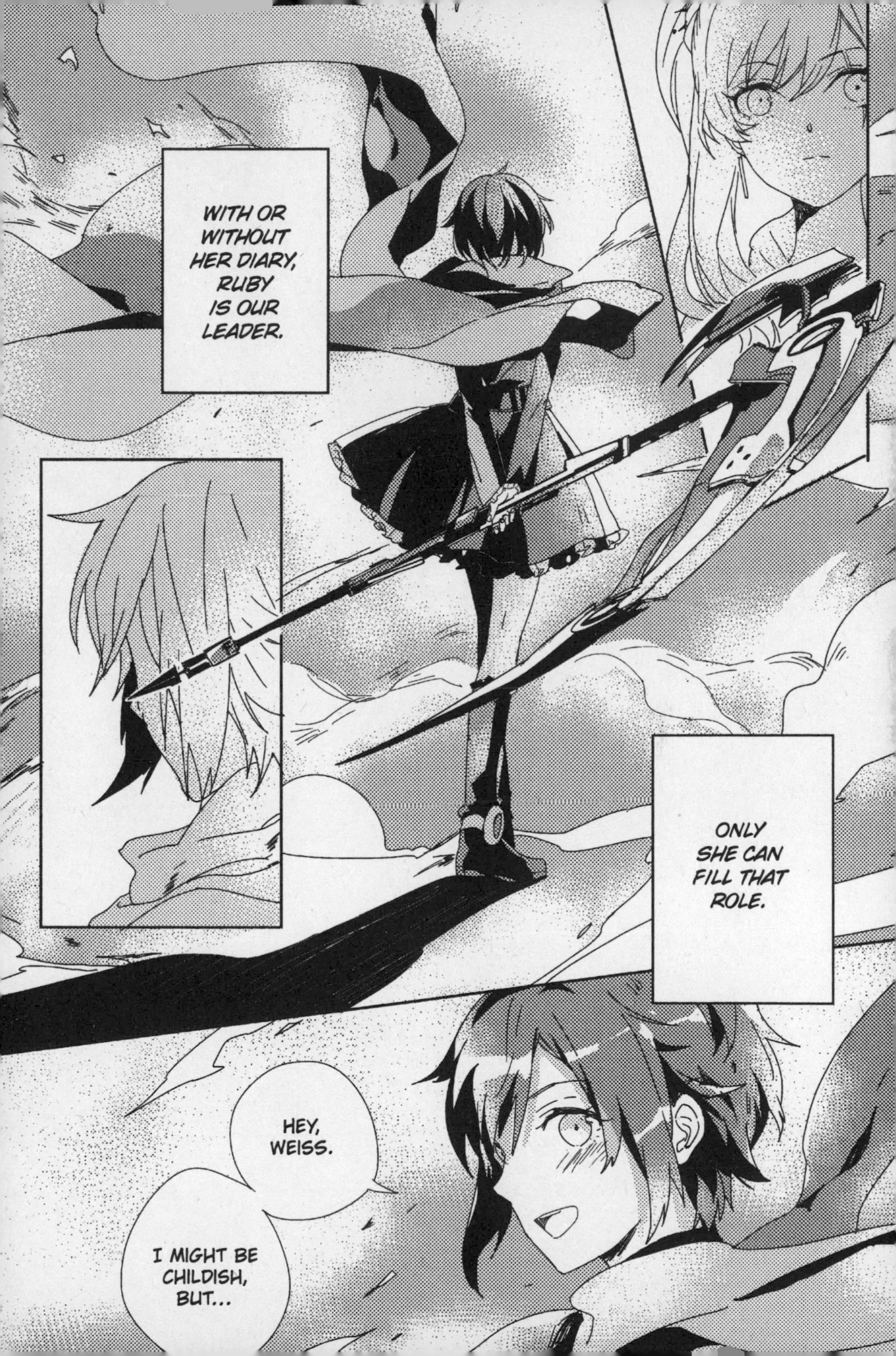
WITH OR WITHOUT HER DIARY, RUBY IS OUR LEADER.
ONLY SHE CAN FILL THAT ROLE.
HEY, WEISS.
I MIGHT BE CHILDISH, BUT...

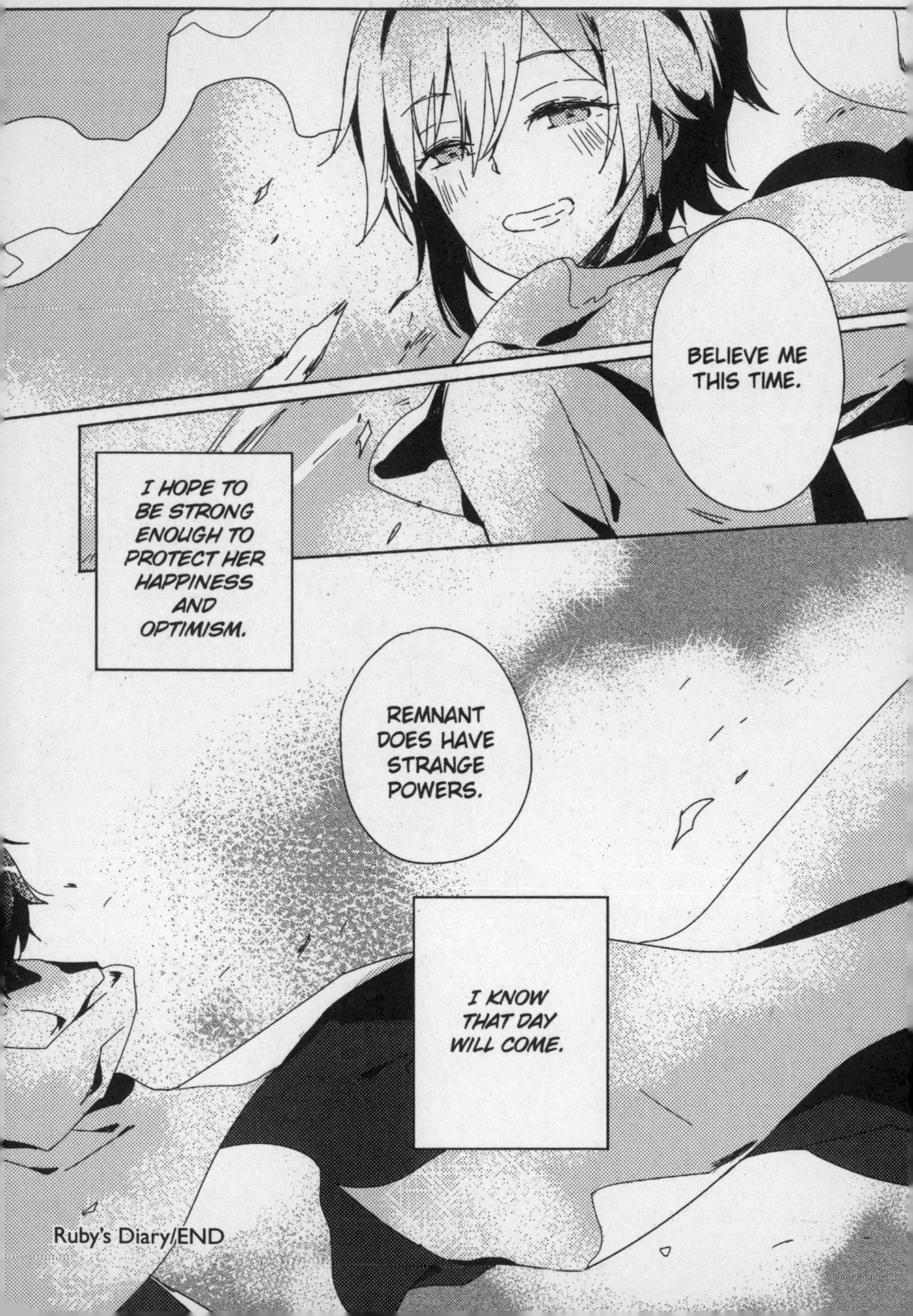
BELIEVE ME THIS TIME.
I HOPE TO BE STRONG ENOUGH TO PROTECT HER HAPPINESS AND OPTIMISM.
REMNANT DOES HAVE STRANGE POWERS.
I KNOW THAT DAY WILL COME.
Ruby's Diary/END

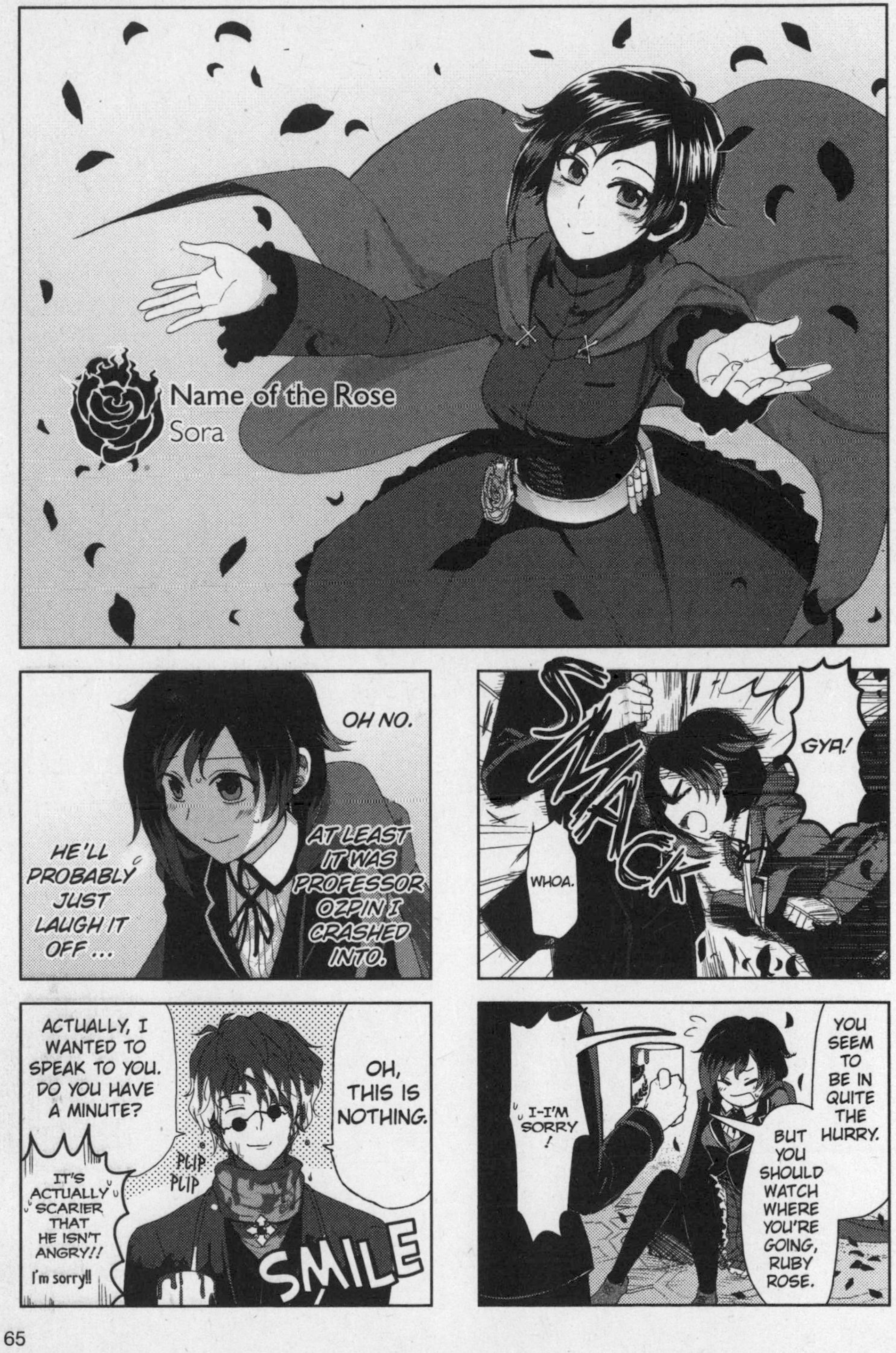

Name of the Rose
Sora
GYA!
SMACK
WHOA.
OH NO.
AT LEAST IT WAS PROFESSOR OZPIN I CRASHED INTO.
HE'LL PROBABLY JUST LAUGH IT OFF ...
YOU SEEM TO BE IN QUITE THE HURRY.
BUT YOU SHOULD WATCH WHERE YOU'RE GOING, RUBY ROSE.
I-I'M SORRY!
OH, THIS IS NOTHING.
ACTUALLY, I WANTED TO SPEAK TO YOU. DO YOU HAVE A MINUTE?
PLIP PLIP
SMILE
IT'S ACTUALLY SCARIER THAT HE ISN'T ANGRY!!
I'm sorry!!

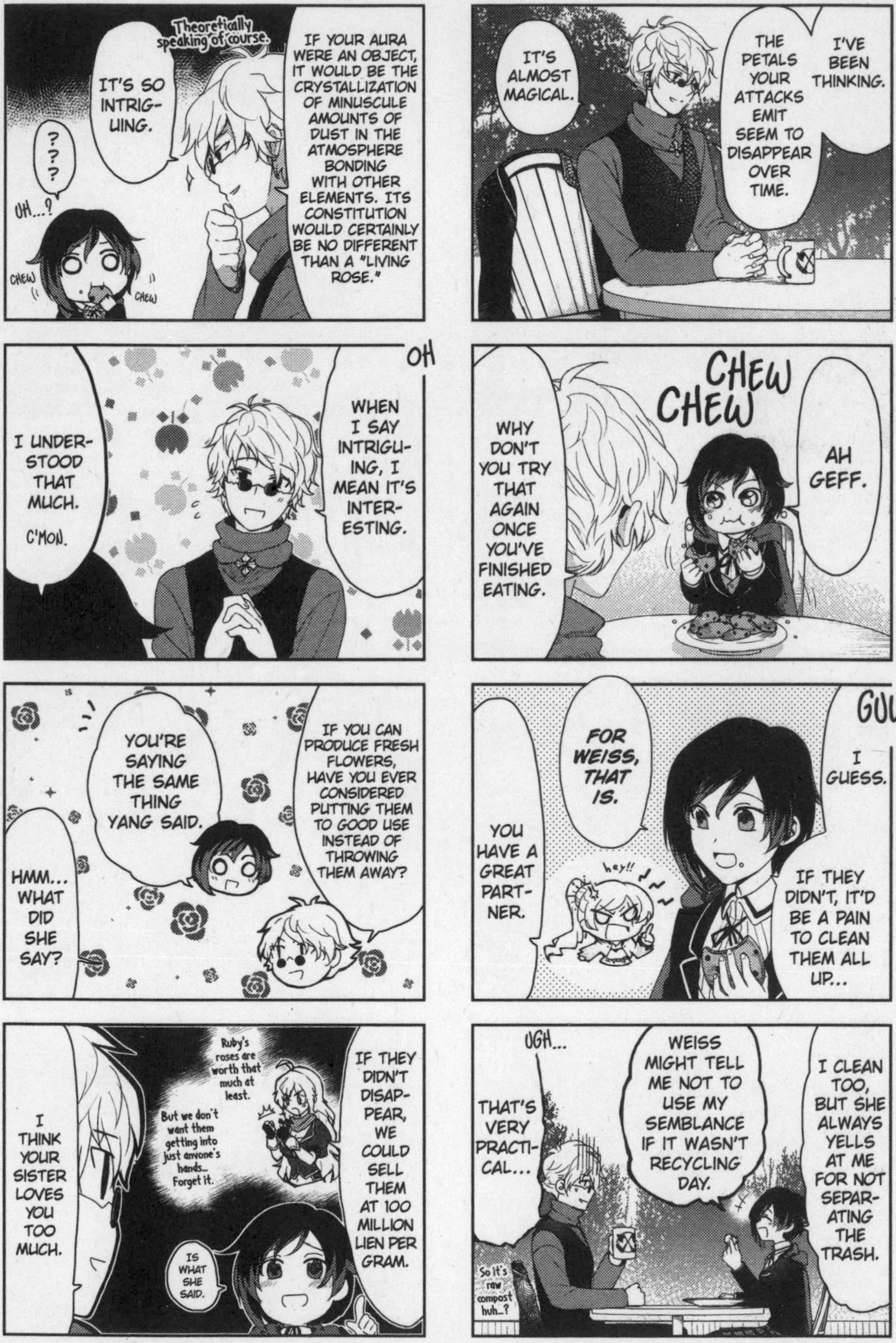
I'VE BEEN THINKING.
THE PETALS YOUR ATTACKS EMIT SEEM TO DISAPPEAR OVER TIME.
IT'S ALMOST MAGICAL.
IF YOUR AURA WERE AN OBJECT, IT WOULD BE THE CRYSTALLIZATION OF MINUSCULE AMOUNTS OF DUST IN THE ATMOSPHERE BONDING WITH OTHER ELEMENTS. ITS CONSTITUTION WOULD CERTAINLY BE NO DIFFERENT THAN A "LIVING ROSE."
Theoretically speaking of course.
IT'S SO INTRIGU-UING.
???
UH...?
CHEW
CHEW
CHEW CHEW
AH GEFF.
WHY DON'T YOU TRY THAT AGAIN ONCE YOU'VE FINISHED EATING.
OH
WHEN I SAY INTRIGU-ING, I MEAN IT'S INTER-ESTING.
I UNDER-STOOD THAT MUCH.
C'MON.
GULP
I GUESS.
FOR WEISS, THAT IS.
IF THEY DIDN'T, IT'D BE A PAIN TO CLEAN THEM ALL UP...
YOU HAVE A GREAT PART-NER.
hey!!
IF YOU CAN PRODUCE FRESH FLOWERS, HAVE YOU EVER CONSIDERED PUTTING THEM TO GOOD USE INSTEAD OF THROWING THEM AWAY?
YOU'RE SAYING THE SAME THING YANG SAID.
HMM... WHAT DID SHE SAY?
I CLEAN TOO, BUT SHE ALWAYS YELLS AT ME FOR NOT SEPARA-TING THE TRASH.
WEISS MIGHT TELL ME NOT TO USE MY SEMBLANCE IF IT WASN'T RECYCLING DAY.
UGH...
THAT'S VERY PRACTI-CAL...
So it's raw compost huh...?
IF THEY DIDN'T DISAP-PEAR, WE COULD SELL THEM AT 100 MILLION LIEN PER GRAM.
Ruby's roses are worth that much at least.
But we don't want them getting into just anyone's hands... Forget it.
IS WHAT SHE SAID.
I THINK YOUR SISTER LOVES YOU TOO MUCH.

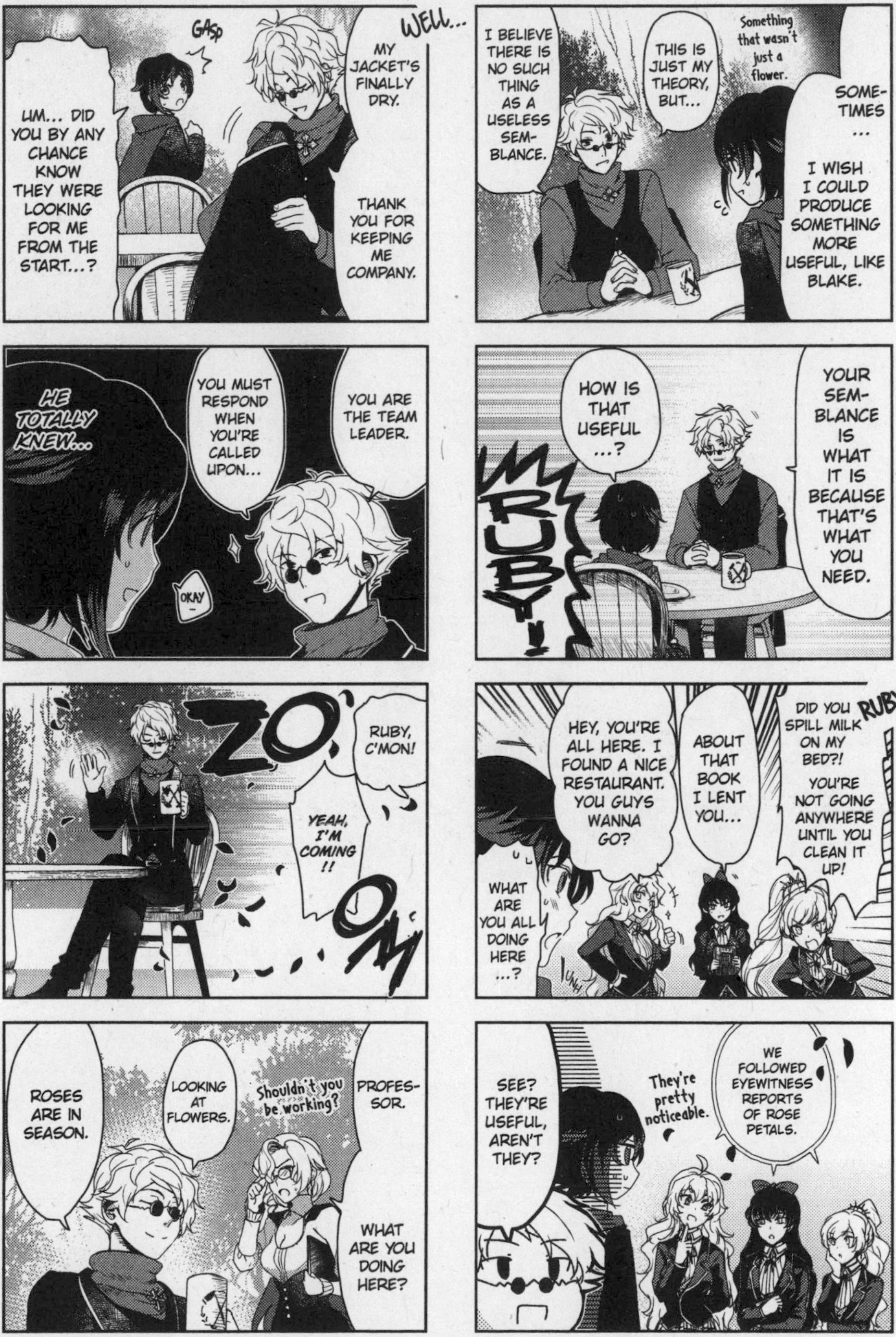
SOME-TIMES...
I WISH I COULD PRODUCE SOMETHING MORE USEFUL, LIKE BLAKE.
Something that wasn't just a flower.
THIS IS JUST MY THEORY, BUT...
I BELIEVE THERE IS NO SUCH THING AS A USELESS SEM-BLANCE.
WELL...
MY JACKET'S FINALLY DRY.
THANK YOU FOR KEEPING ME COMPANY.
GASP
UM... DID YOU BY ANY CHANCE KNOW THEY WERE LOOKING FOR ME FROM THE START...?
YOUR SEM-BLANCE IS WHAT IT IS BECAUSE THAT'S WHAT YOU NEED.
HOW IS THAT USEFUL...?
RUBY!!
YOU ARE THE TEAM LEADER.
YOU MUST RESPOND WHEN YOU'RE CALLED UPON...
HE TOTALLY KNEW...
OKAY
RUBY!
DID YOU SPILL MILK ON MY BED?!
YOU'RE NOT GOING ANYWHERE UNTIL YOU CLEAN IT UP!
ABOUT THAT BOOK I LENT YOU...
HEY, YOU'RE ALL HERE. I FOUND A NICE RESTAURANT. YOU GUYS WANNA GO?
WHAT ARE YOU ALL DOING HERE...?
UNH
RUBY, C'MON!
ZO
YEAH, I'M COMING!!
OM
WE FOLLOWED EYEWITNESS REPORTS OF ROSE PETALS.
They're pretty noticeable.
SEE? THEY'RE USEFUL, AREN'T THEY?
PROFES-SOR.
WHAT ARE YOU DOING HERE?
Shouldn't you be working?
LOOKING AT FLOWERS.
ROSES ARE IN SEASON.

Name of the Rose/END

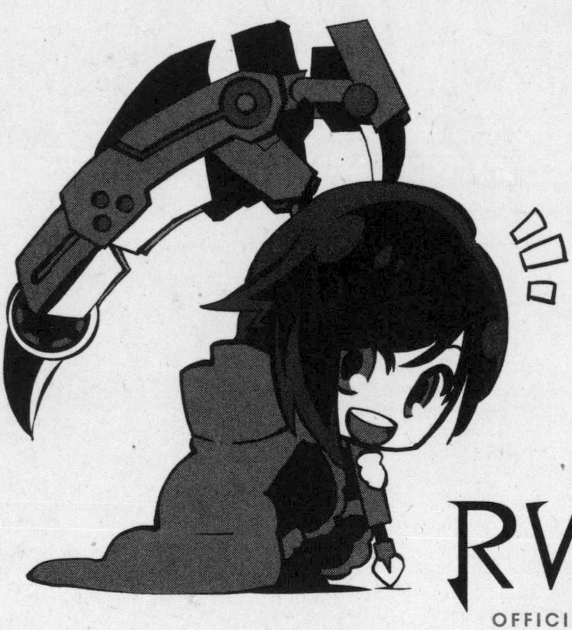

RWBY

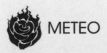

OFFICIAL MANGA ANTHOLOGY
VOLUME 1 RED LIKE ROSES

METEO

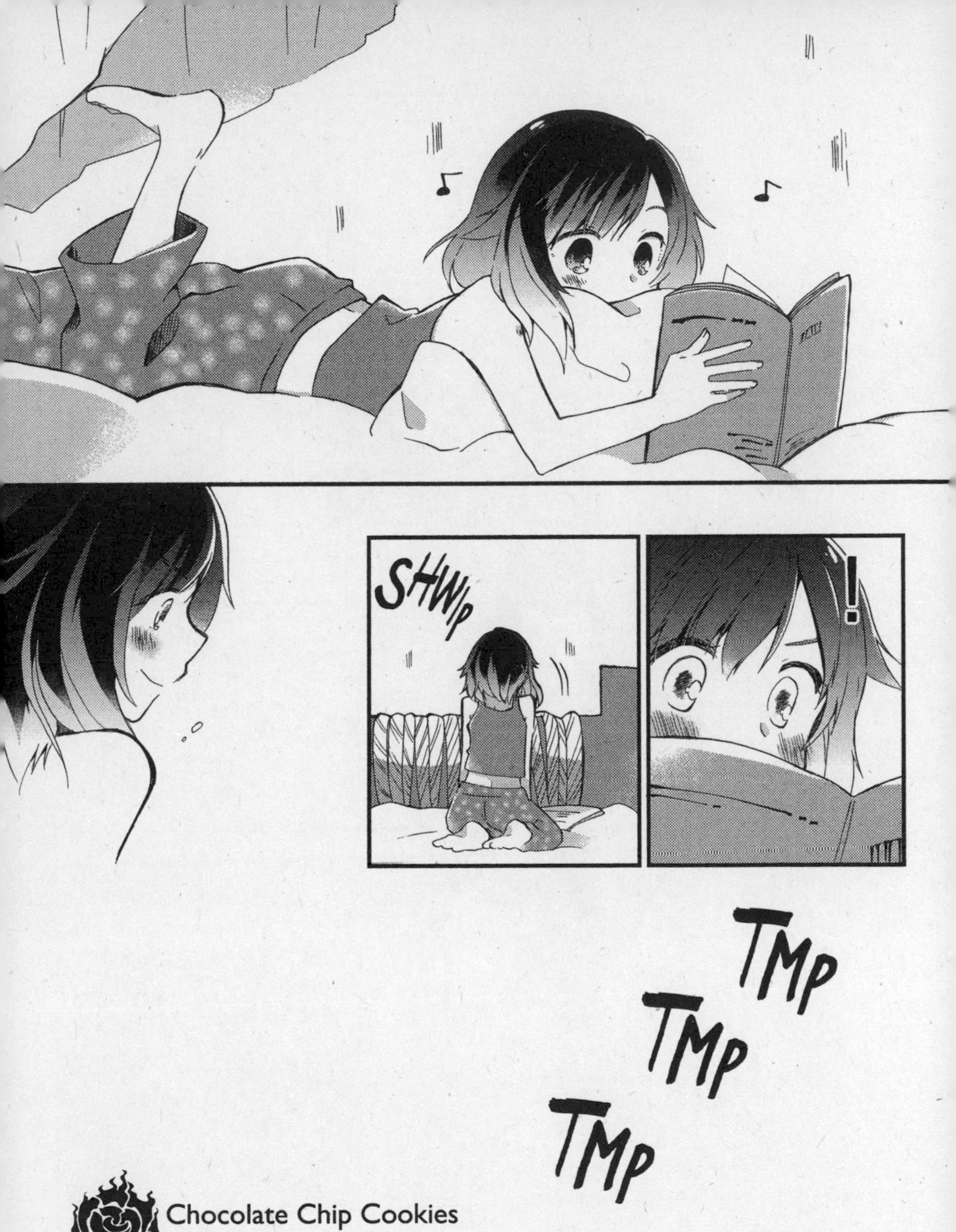
!
SHWIP
TMP
TMP
TMP

Chocolate Chip Cookies
Amaya

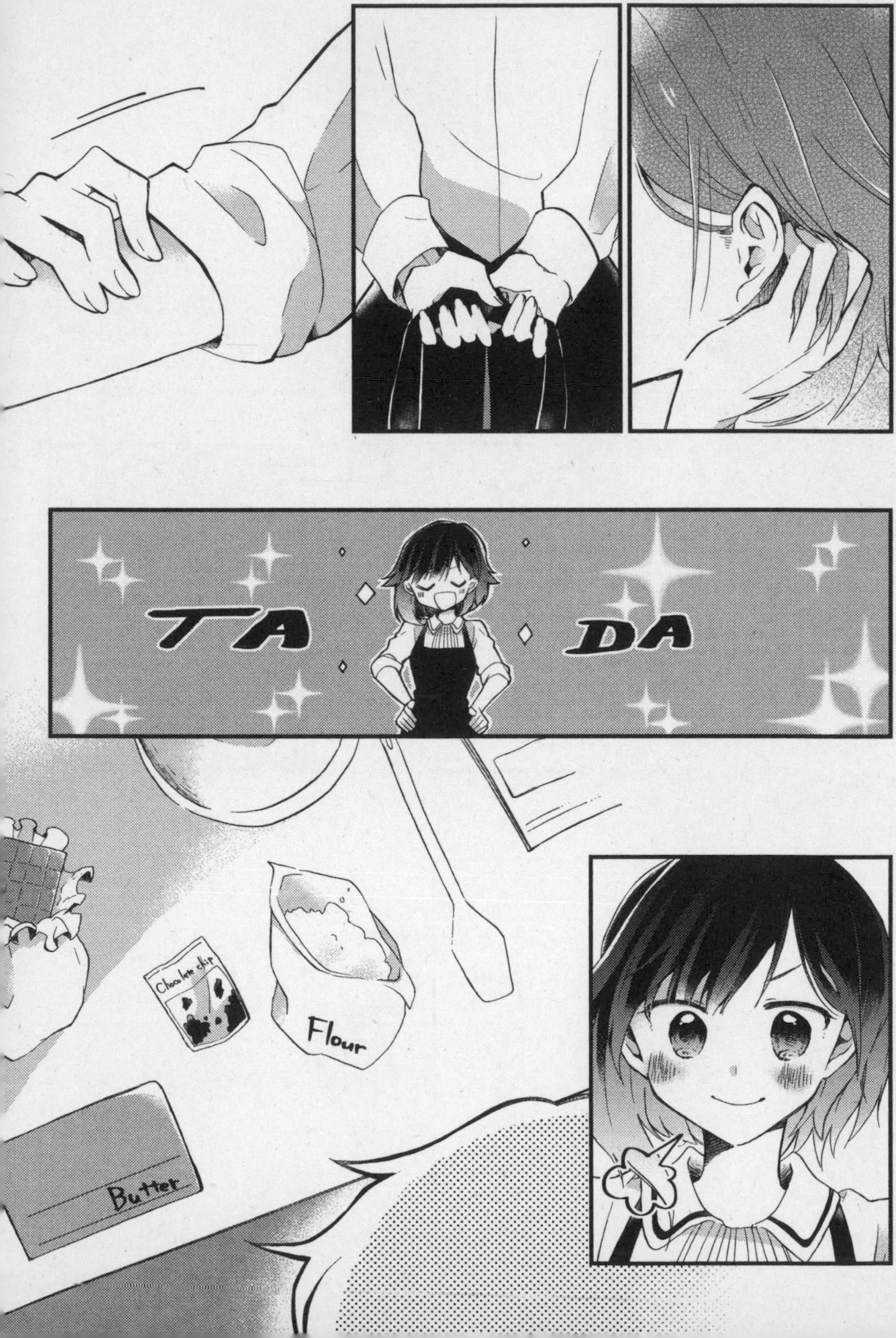
TA
DA
Flour
Chocolate chip
Butter

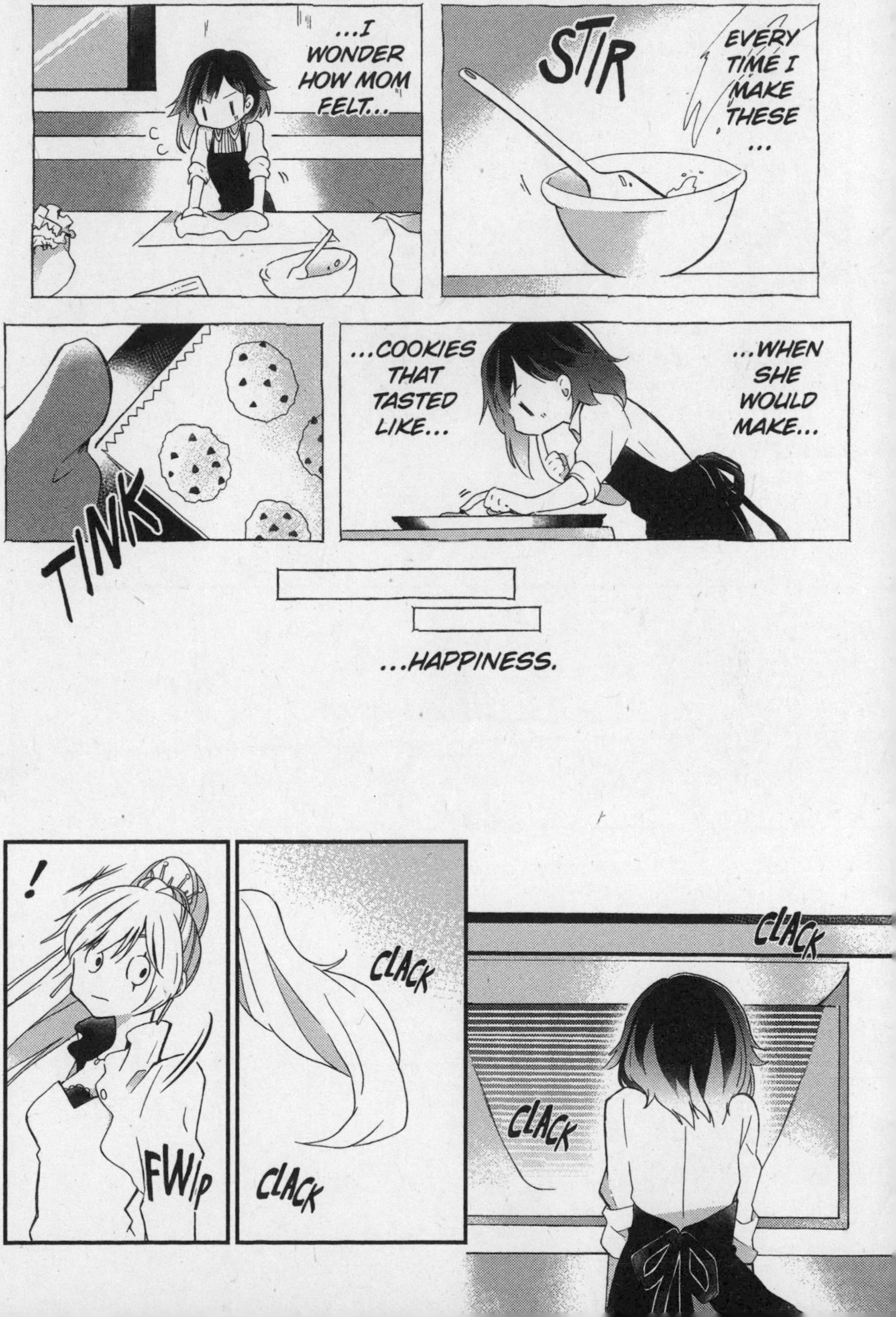
STIR
EVERY TIME I MAKE THESE...
...I WONDER HOW MOM FELT...
...WHEN SHE WOULD MAKE...
...COOKIES THAT TASTED LIKE...
TINK
...HAPPINESS.
CLACK
CLACK
CLACK
CLACK
!
FWIP

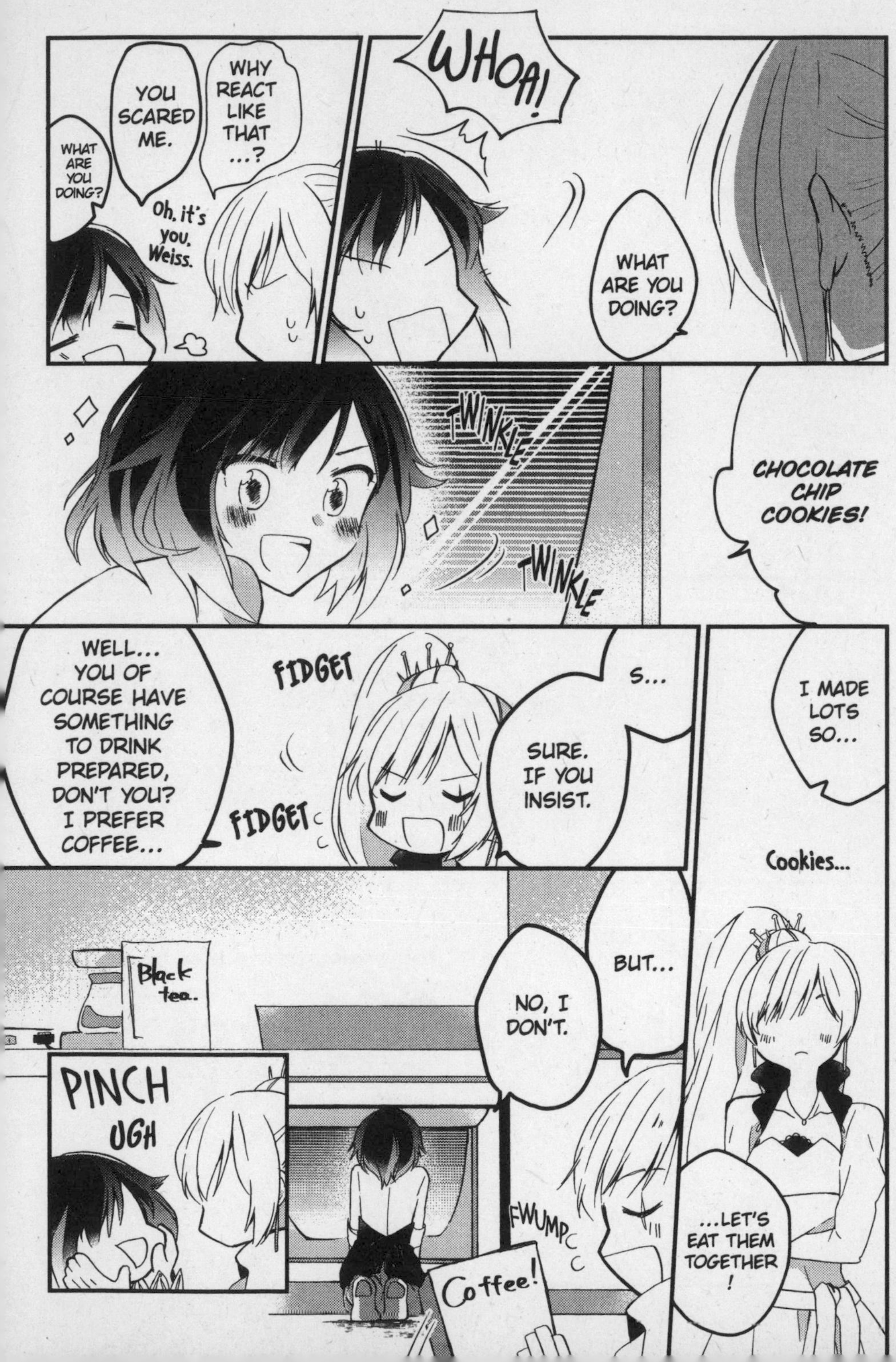
WHAT ARE YOU DOING?
WHOA!
WHY REACT LIKE THAT...?
YOU SCARED ME.
Oh, it's you, Weiss.
WHAT ARE YOU DOING?
CHOCOLATE CHIP COOKIES!
TWINKLE
TWINKLE
I MADE LOTS SO...
Cookies...
...LET'S EAT THEM TOGETHER!
S...
SURE. IF YOU INSIST.
FIDGET
WELL... YOU OF COURSE HAVE SOMETHING TO DRINK PREPARED, DON'T YOU? I PREFER COFFEE...
FIDGET
BUT...
NO, I DON'T.
Black tea..
FWUMP
Coffee!
PINCH
UGH

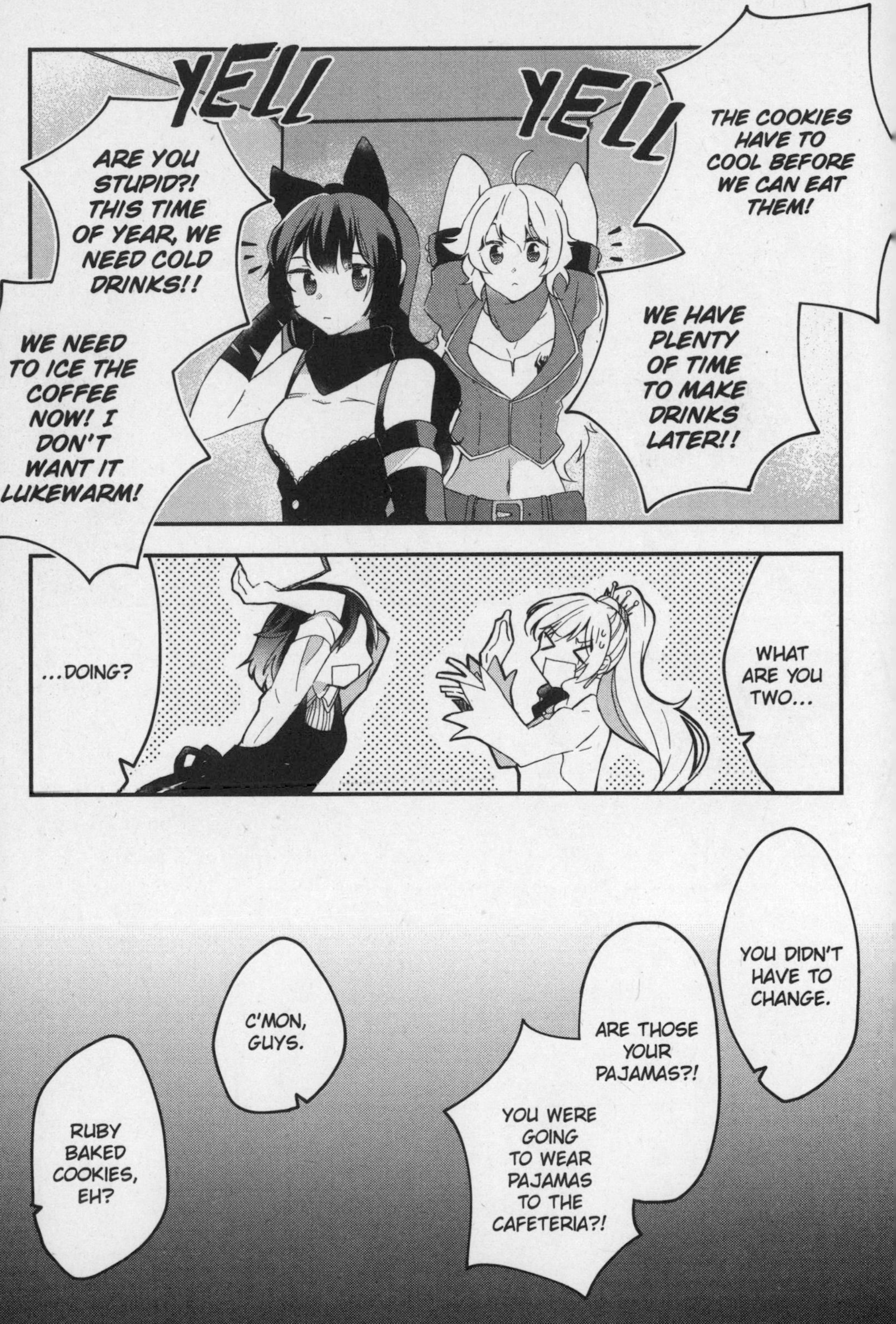
YELL
YELL
THE COOKIES HAVE TO COOL BEFORE WE CAN EAT THEM!
ARE YOU STUPID?! THIS TIME OF YEAR, WE NEED COLD DRINKS!!
WE HAVE PLENTY OF TIME TO MAKE DRINKS LATER!!
WE NEED TO ICE THE COFFEE NOW! I DON'T WANT IT LUKEWARM!
WHAT ARE YOU TWO...
...DOING?
YOU DIDN'T HAVE TO CHANGE.
ARE THOSE YOUR PAJAMAS?!
YOU WERE GOING TO WEAR PAJAMAS TO THE CAFETERIA?!
C'MON, GUYS.
RUBY BAKED COOKIES, EH?

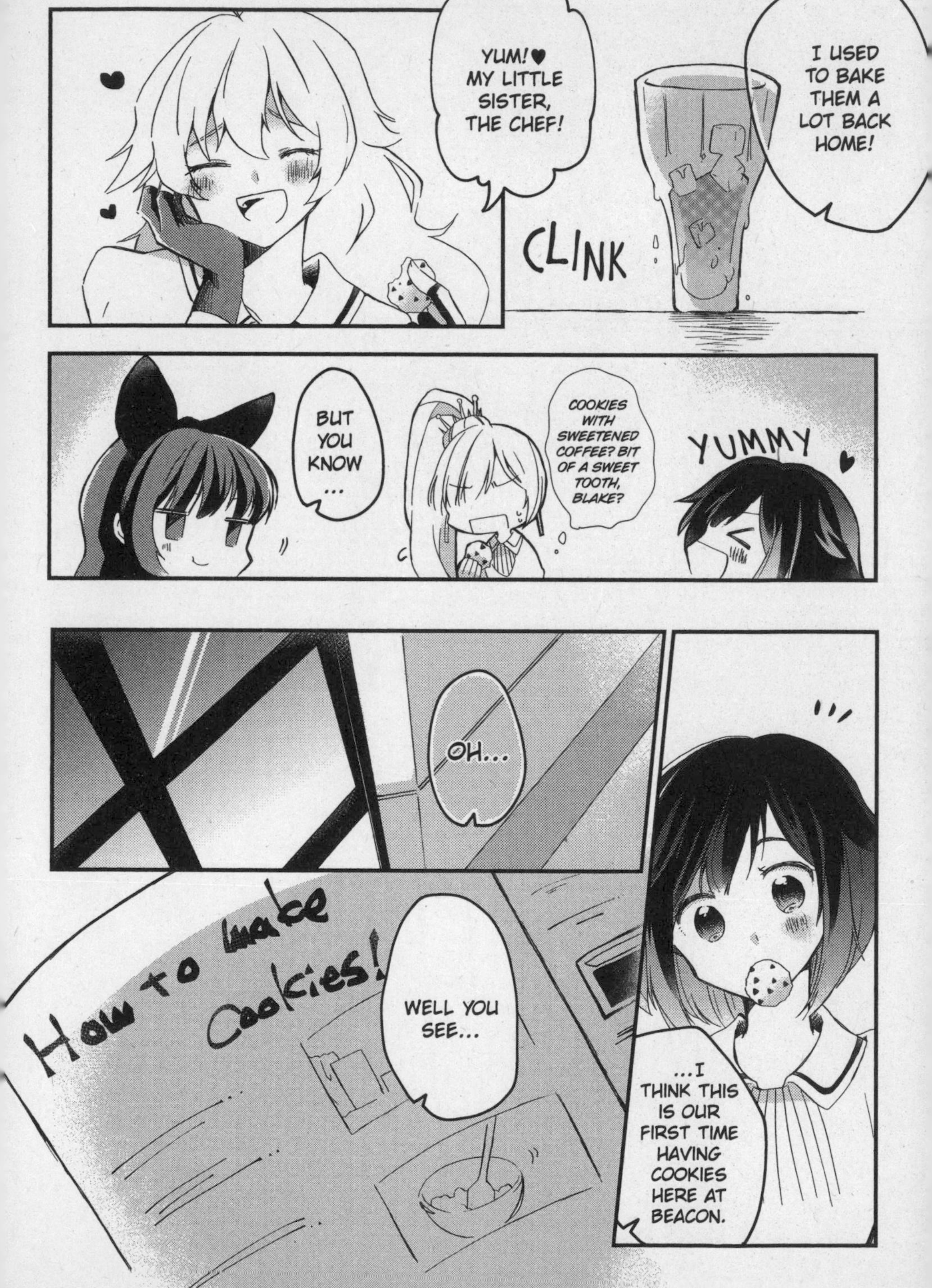
I USED TO BAKE THEM A LOT BACK HOME!
CLINK
YUM!♥ MY LITTLE SISTER, THE CHEF!
YUMMY
COOKIES WITH SWEETENED COFFEE? BIT OF A SWEET TOOTH, BLAKE?
BUT YOU KNOW ...
...I THINK THIS IS OUR FIRST TIME HAVING COOKIES HERE AT BEACON.
OH...
WELL YOU SEE...
How to make Cookies!

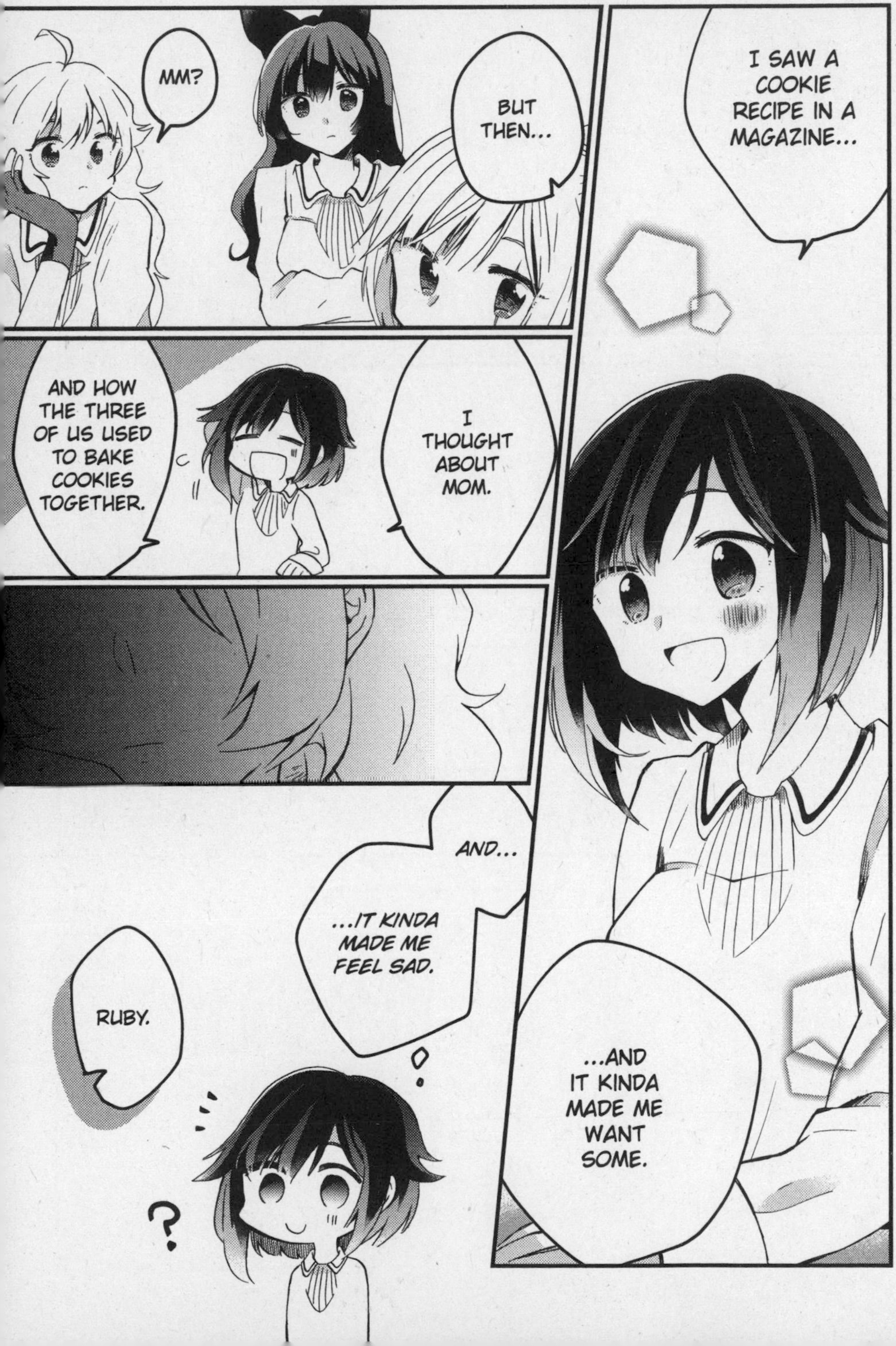
I SAW A COOKIE RECIPE IN A MAGAZINE...
...AND IT KINDA MADE ME WANT SOME.
BUT THEN...
MM?
I THOUGHT ABOUT MOM.
AND HOW THE THREE OF US USED TO BAKE COOKIES TOGETHER.
AND...
...IT KINDA MADE ME FEEL SAD.
RUBY.

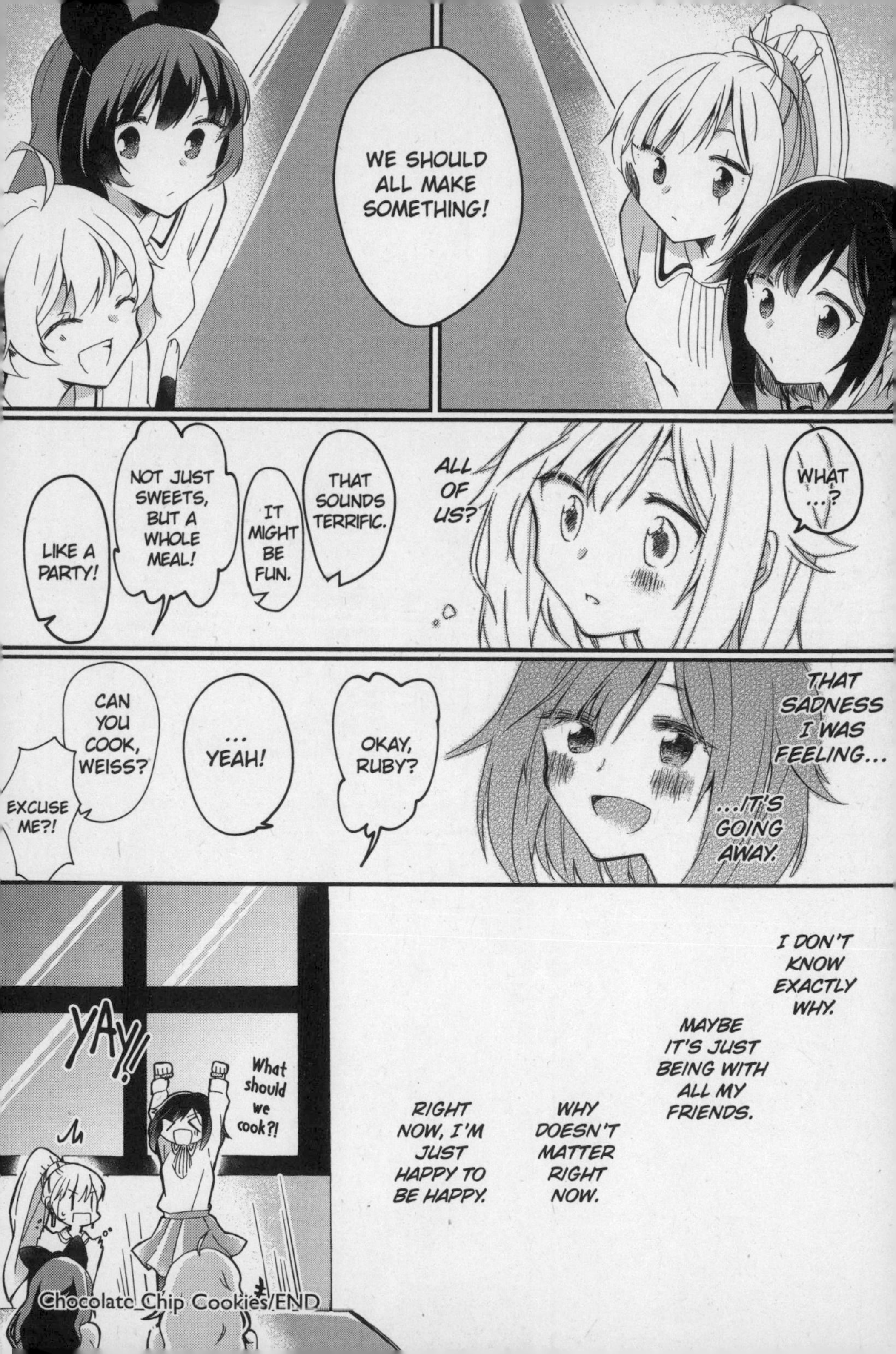
WE SHOULD ALL MAKE SOMETHING!
WHAT ...?
ALL OF US?
THAT SOUNDS TERRIFIC.
IT MIGHT BE FUN.
NOT JUST SWEETS, BUT A WHOLE MEAL!
LIKE A PARTY!
THAT SADNESS I WAS FEELING...
...IT'S GOING AWAY.
OKAY, RUBY?
...YEAH!
CAN YOU COOK, WEISS?
EXCUSE ME?!
I DON'T KNOW EXACTLY WHY.
MAYBE IT'S JUST BEING WITH ALL MY FRIENDS.
WHY DOESN'T MATTER RIGHT NOW.
RIGHT NOW, I'M JUST HAPPY TO BE HAPPY.
YAY!!
What should we cook?!
Chocolate Chip Cookies/END

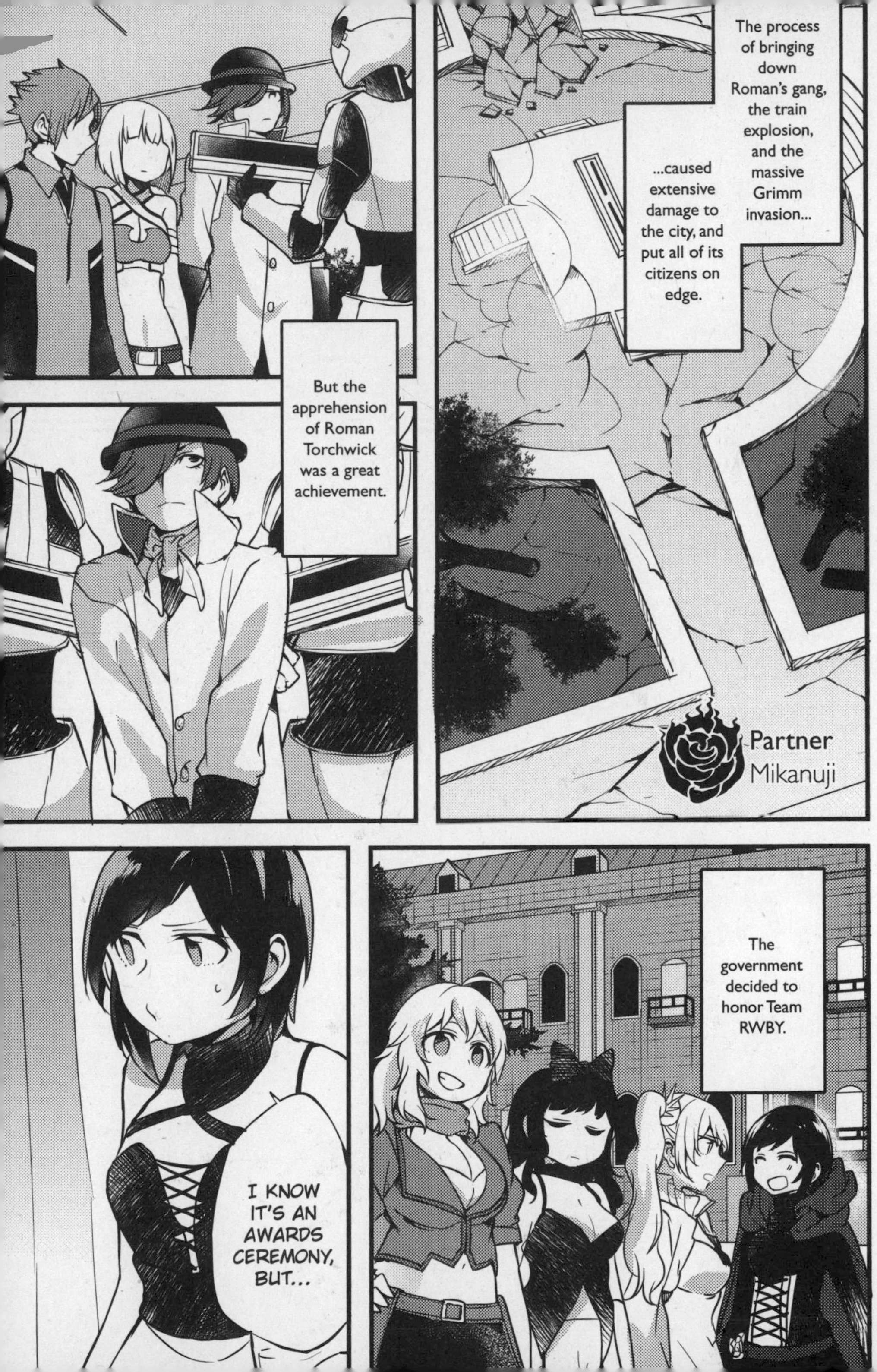
The process of bringing down Roman's gang, the train explosion, and the massive Grimm invasion...
...caused extensive damage to the city, and put all of its citizens on edge.
Partner
Mikanuji
But the apprehension of Roman Torchwick was a great achievement.
The government decided to honor Team RWBY.
I KNOW IT'S AN AWARDS CEREMONY, BUT...

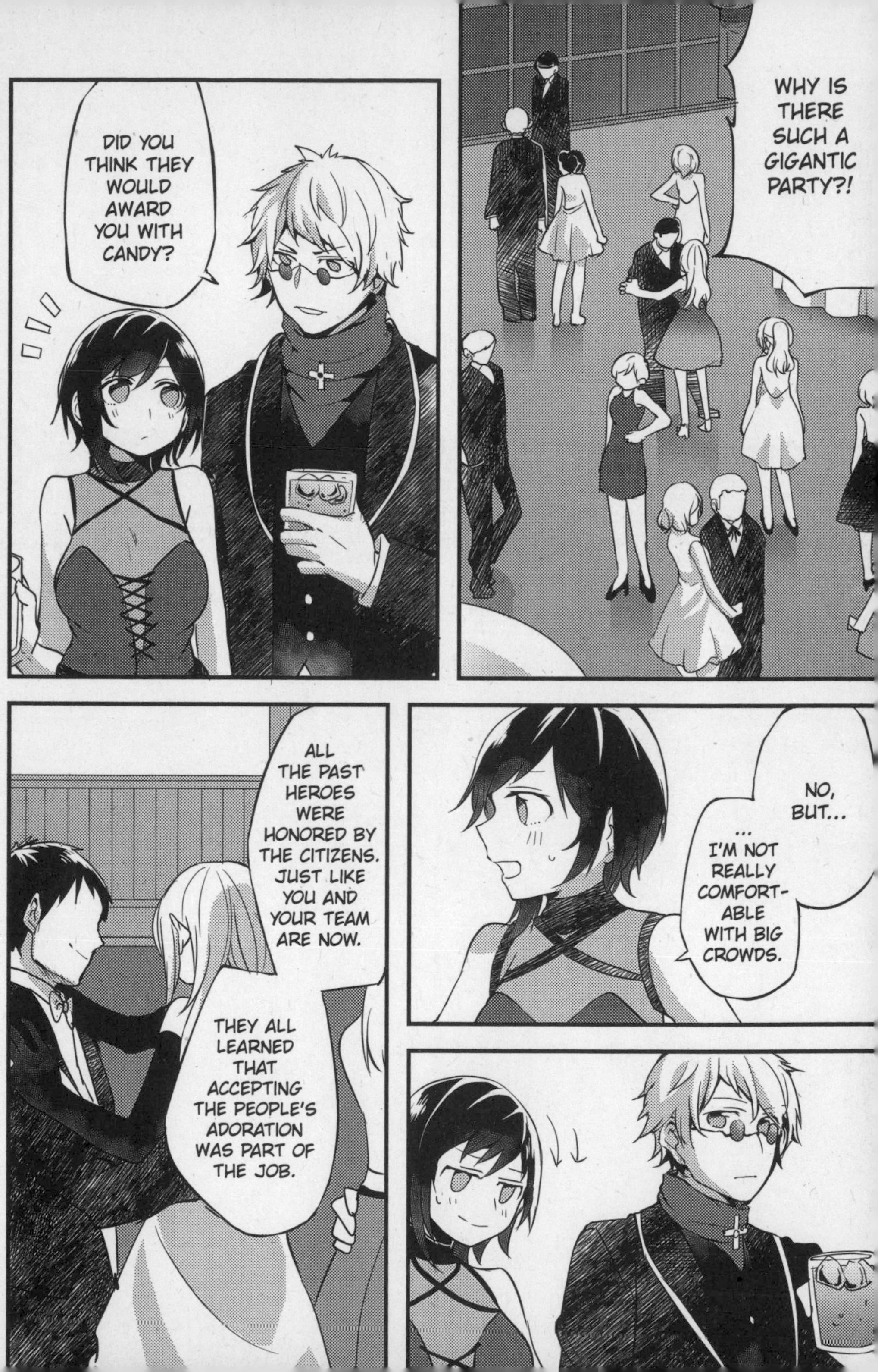
WHY IS THERE SUCH A GIGANTIC PARTY?!
DID YOU THINK THEY WOULD AWARD YOU WITH CANDY?
NO, BUT...
... I'M NOT REALLY COMFORT-ABLE WITH BIG CROWDS.
ALL THE PAST HEROES WERE HONORED BY THE CITIZENS. JUST LIKE YOU AND YOUR TEAM ARE NOW.
THEY ALL LEARNED THAT ACCEPTING THE PEOPLE'S ADORATION WAS PART OF THE JOB.

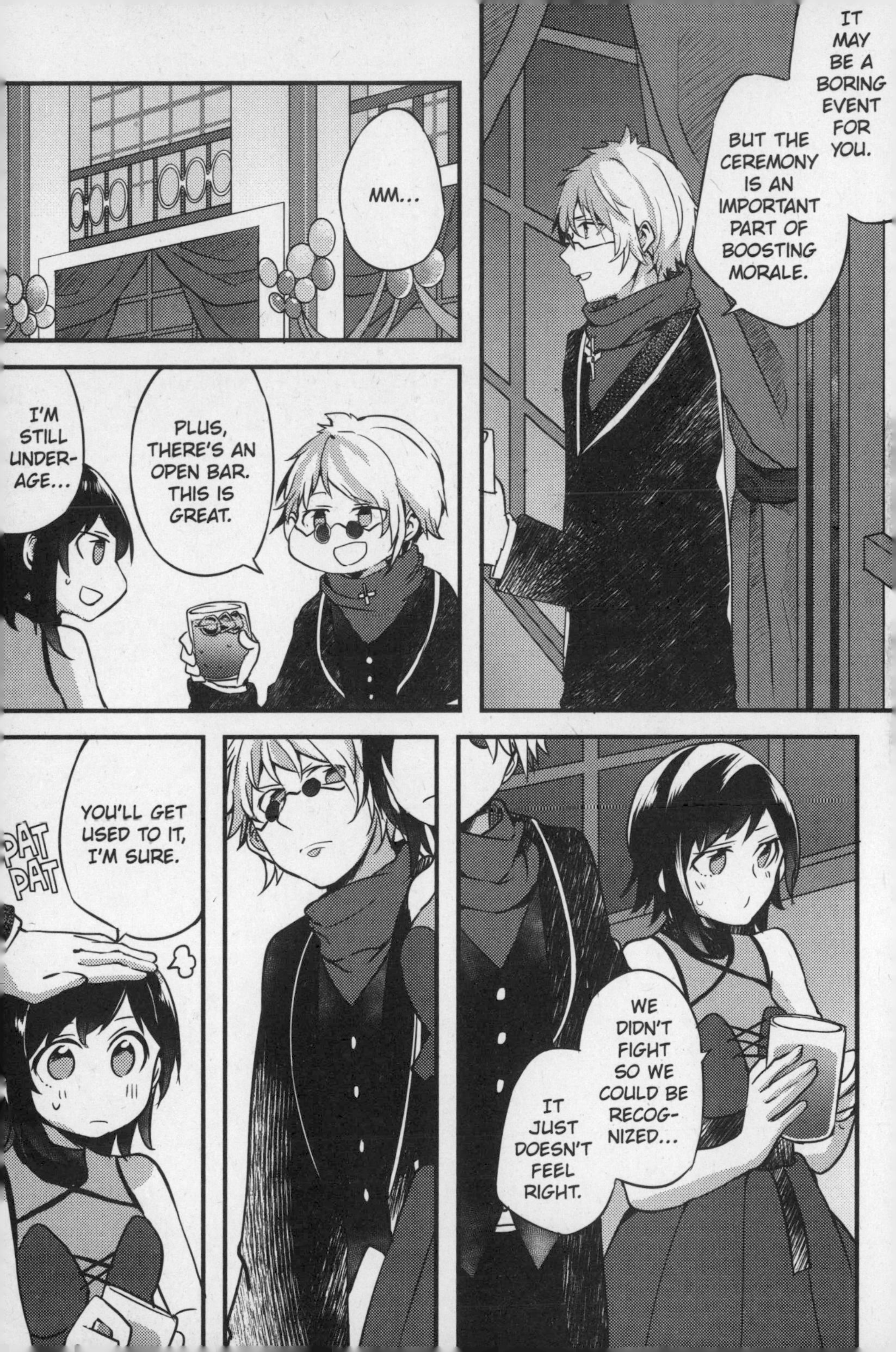
IT MAY BE A BORING EVENT FOR YOU.
BUT THE CEREMONY IS AN IMPORTANT PART OF BOOSTING MORALE.
MM...
PLUS, THERE'S AN OPEN BAR. THIS IS GREAT.
I'M STILL UNDER-AGE...
WE DIDN'T FIGHT SO WE COULD BE RECOG-NIZED...
IT JUST DOESN'T FEEL RIGHT.
YOU'LL GET USED TO IT, I'M SURE.
PAT PAT

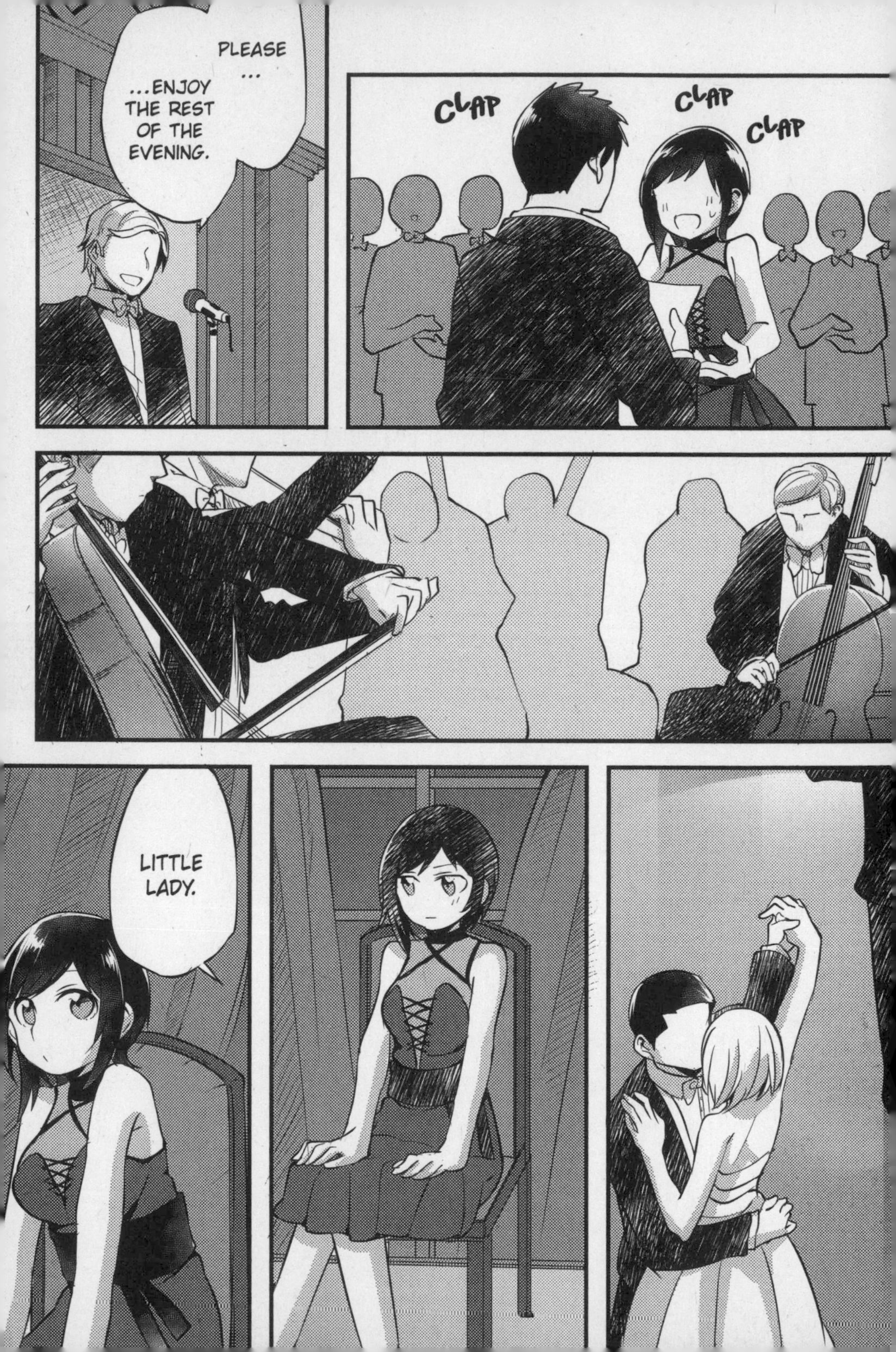
CLAP
CLAP
CLAP
PLEASE ...
...ENJOY THE REST OF THE EVENING.
LITTLE LADY.

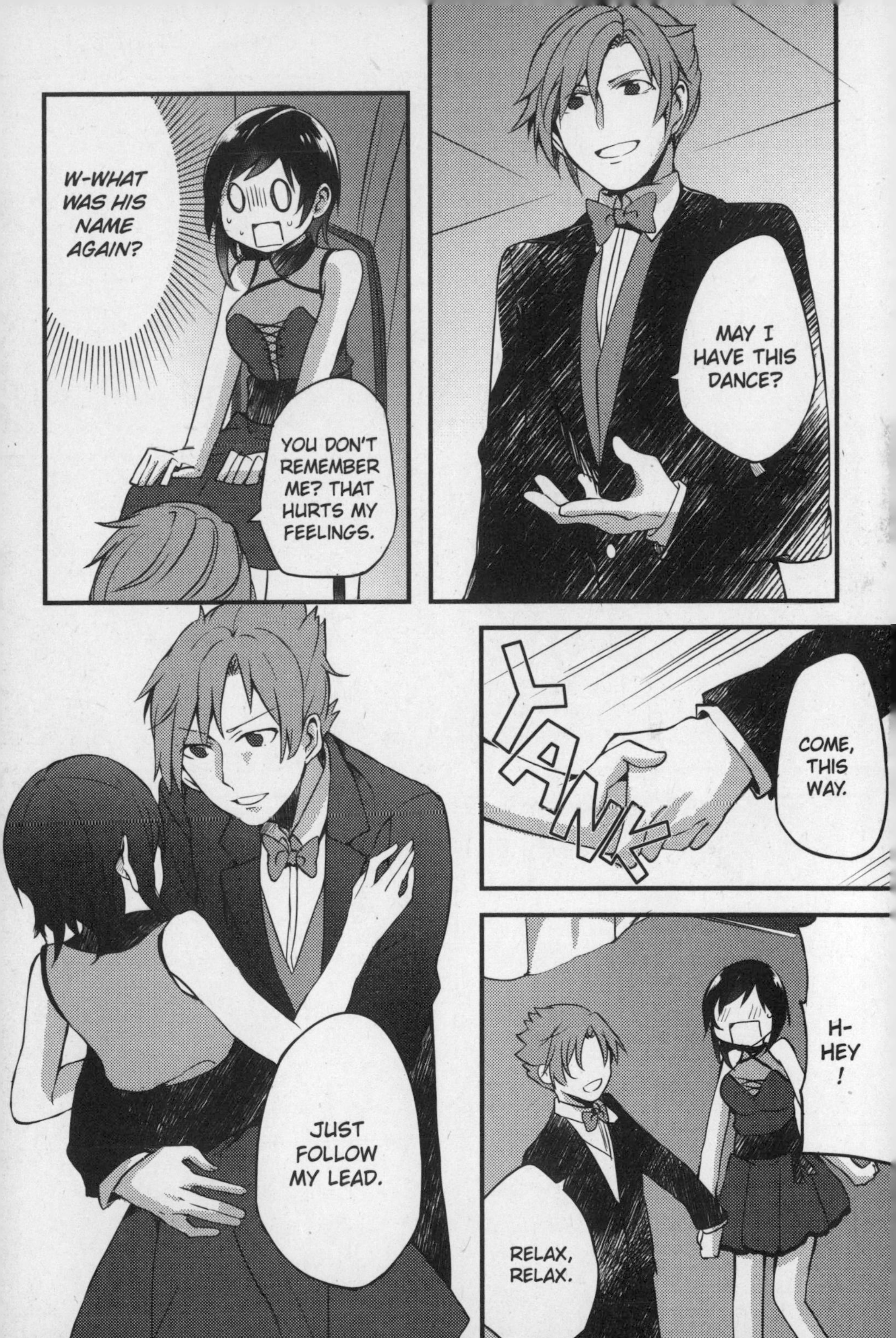
MAY I HAVE THIS DANCE?
W-WHAT WAS HIS NAME AGAIN?
YOU DON'T REMEMBER ME? THAT HURTS MY FEELINGS.
YANK
COME, THIS WAY.
H-HEY!
RELAX, RELAX.
JUST FOLLOW MY LEAD.

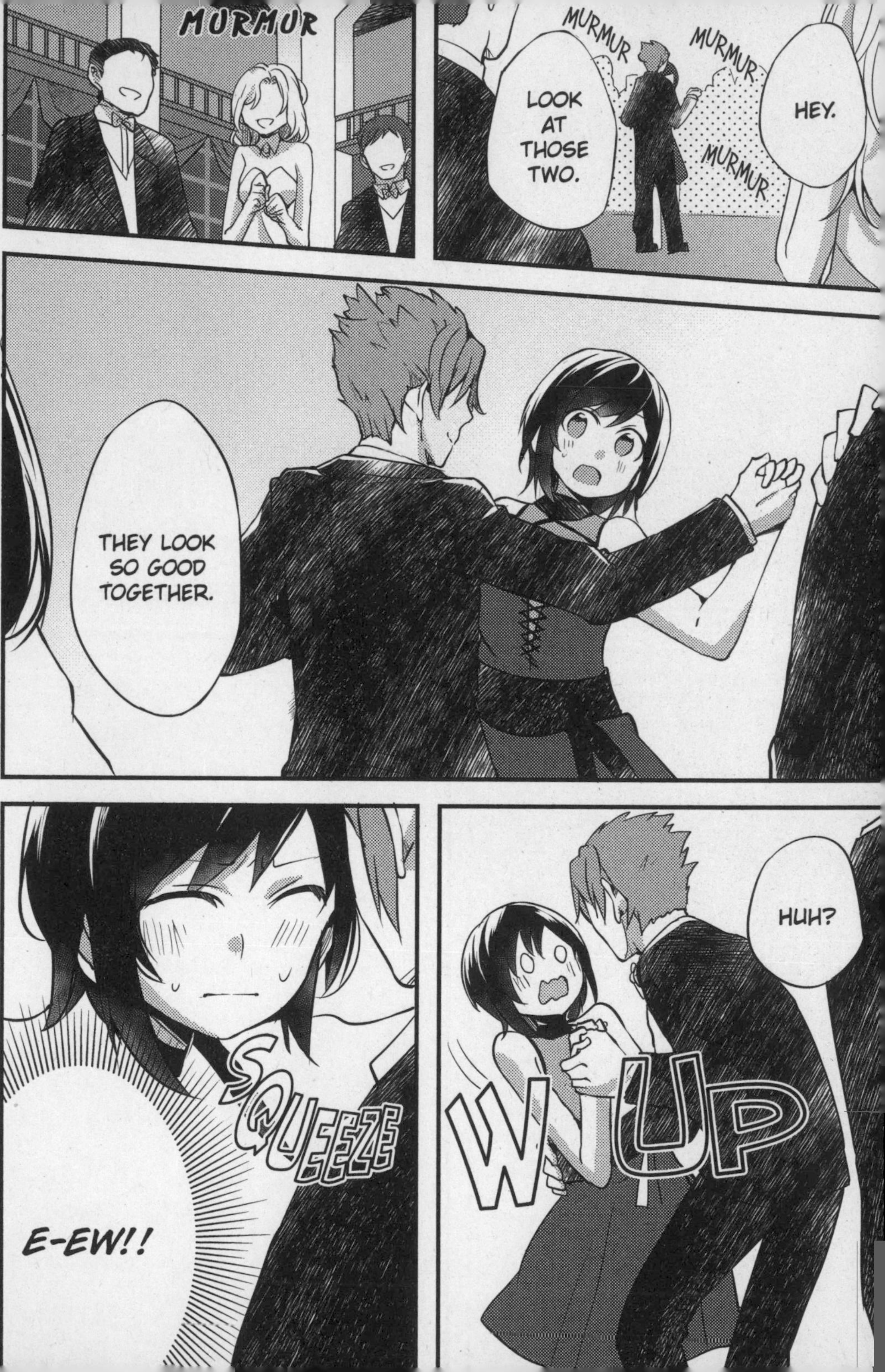
HEY.
MURMUR
MURMUR
MURMUR
LOOK AT THOSE TWO.
MURMUR
MURMUR
THEY LOOK SO GOOD TOGETHER.
HUH?
WUP
SQUEEZE
E-EW!!

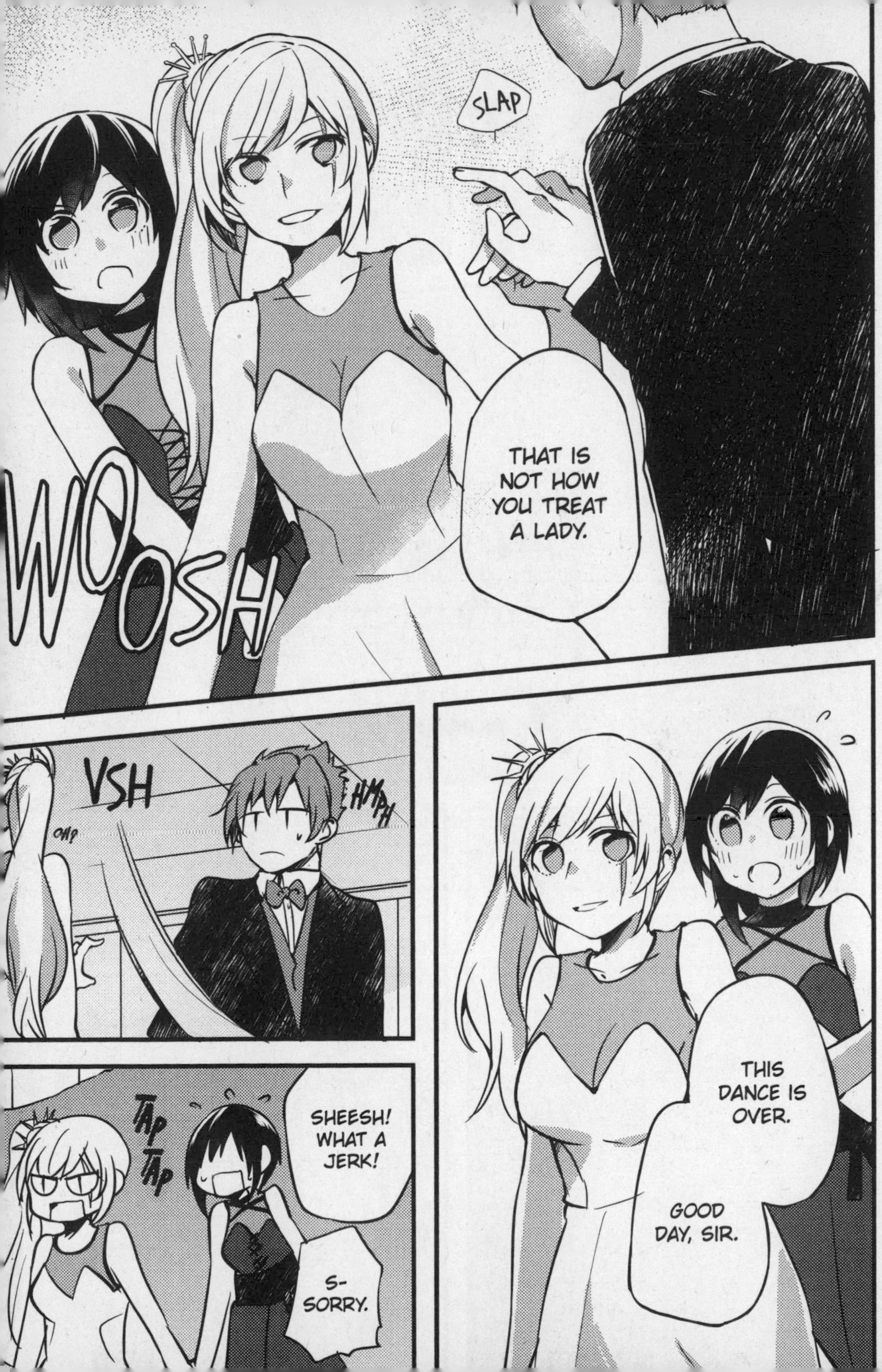
SLAP
THAT IS NOT HOW YOU TREAT A LADY.
WOOSH
THIS DANCE IS OVER.
GOOD DAY, SIR.
HMPH
VSH
SHEESH! WHAT A JERK!
S- SORRY.
TAP TAP

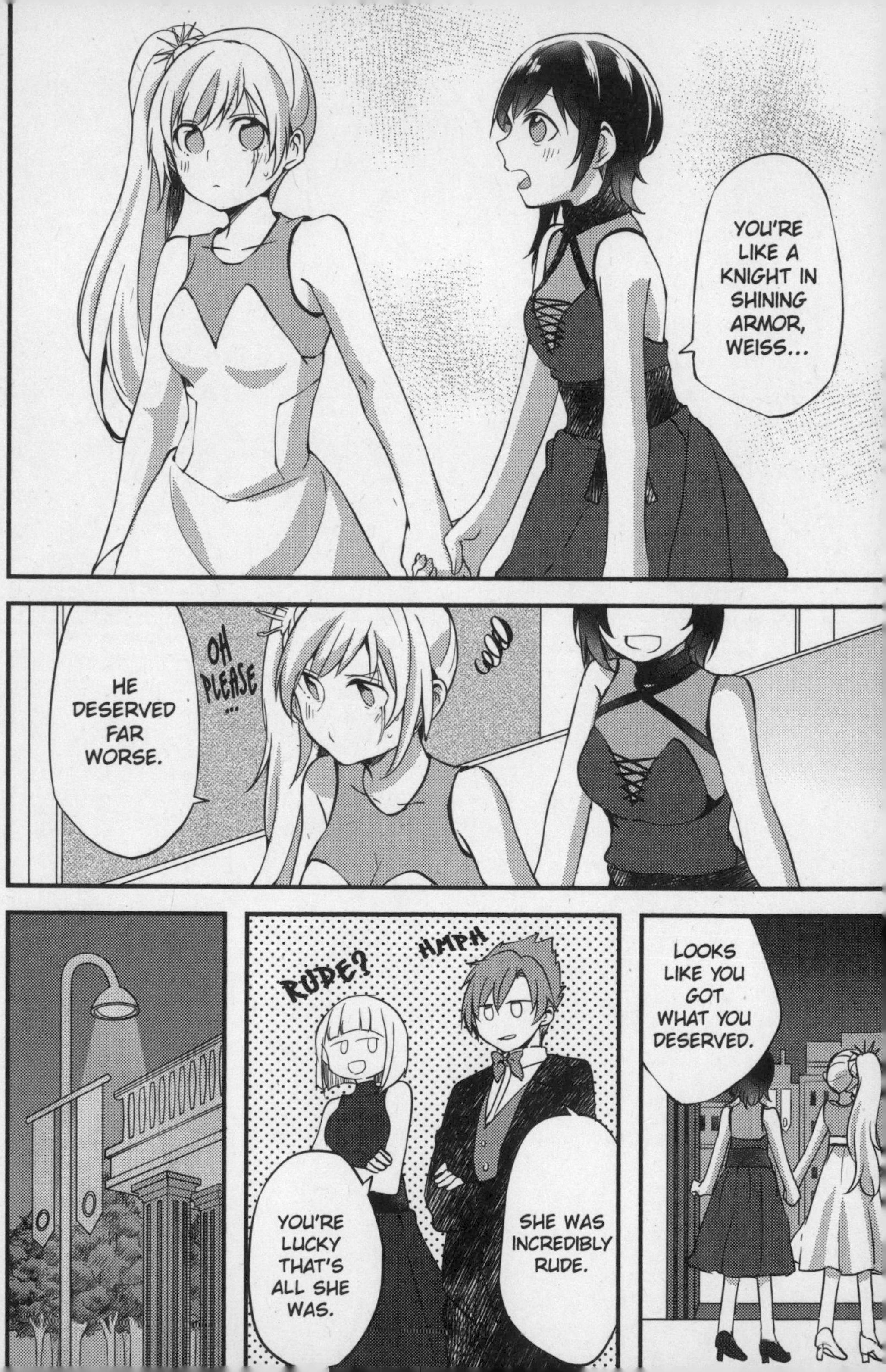

YOU'RE LIKE A KNIGHT IN SHINING ARMOR, WEISS...
OH PLEASE...
HE DESERVED FAR WORSE.
LOOKS LIKE YOU GOT WHAT YOU DESERVED.
HMPH
RUDE?
SHE WAS INCREDIBLY RUDE.
YOU'RE LUCKY THAT'S ALL SHE WAS.

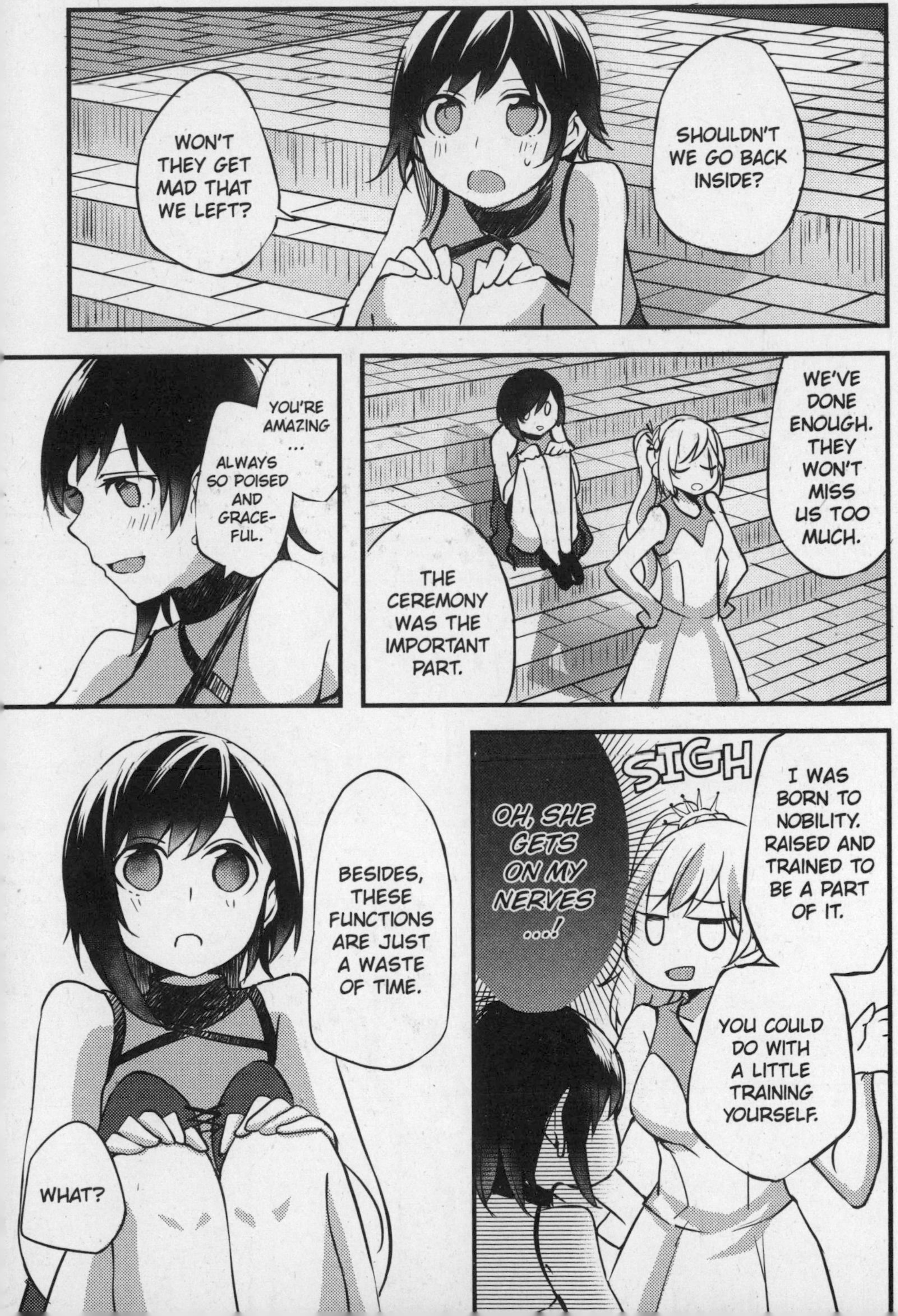
SHOULDN'T WE GO BACK INSIDE?
WON'T THEY GET MAD THAT WE LEFT?
WE'VE DONE ENOUGH. THEY WON'T MISS US TOO MUCH.
THE CEREMONY WAS THE IMPORTANT PART.
YOU'RE AMAZING... ALWAYS SO POISED AND GRACE-FUL.
I WAS BORN TO NOBILITY. RAISED AND TRAINED TO BE A PART OF IT.
SIGH
OH, SHE GETS ON MY NERVES...!
YOU COULD DO WITH A LITTLE TRAINING YOURSELF.
BESIDES, THESE FUNCTIONS ARE JUST A WASTE OF TIME.
WHAT?

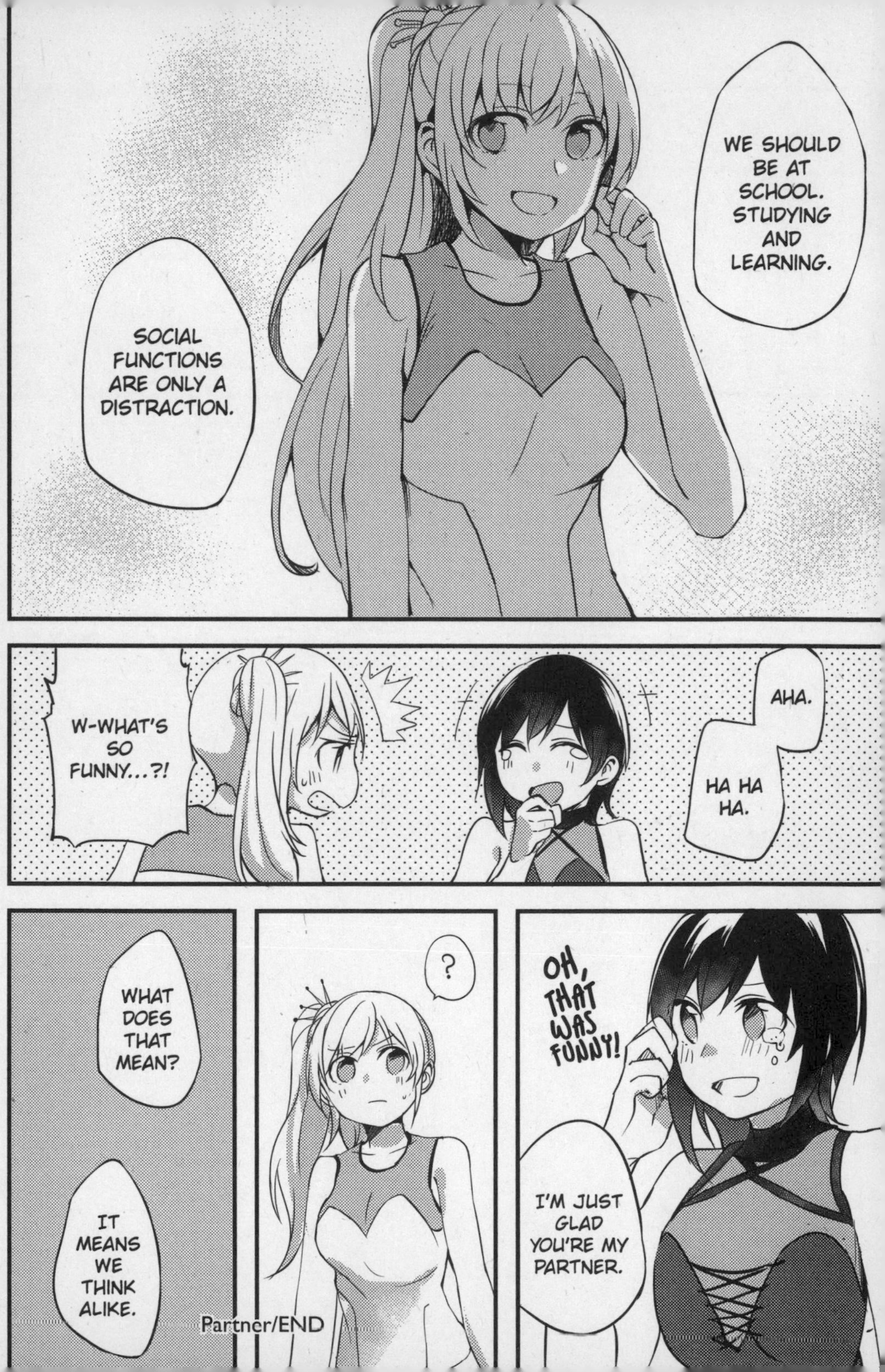
WE SHOULD BE AT SCHOOL. STUDYING AND LEARNING.
SOCIAL FUNCTIONS ARE ONLY A DISTRACTION.
AHA.
HA HA HA.
W-WHAT'S SO FUNNY...?!
OH, THAT WAS FUNNY!
I'M JUST GLAD YOU'RE MY PARTNER.
?
WHAT DOES THAT MEAN?
IT MEANS WE THINK ALIKE.
Partner/END

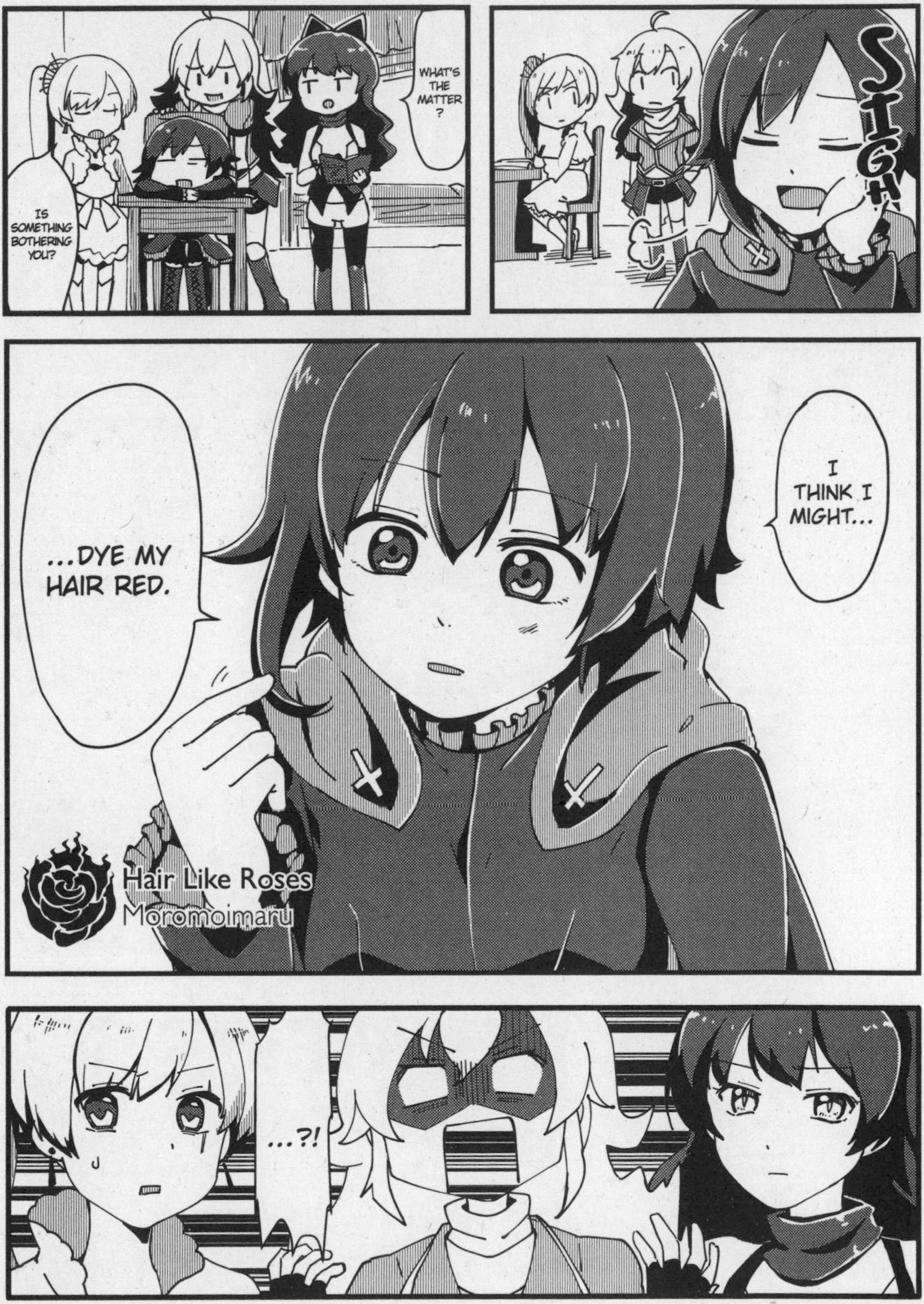
SIGH
WHAT'S THE MATTER?
IS SOMETHING BOTHERING YOU?
I THINK I MIGHT...
...DYE MY HAIR RED.
Hair Like Roses
Moromoimaru
...?!

Whimsical

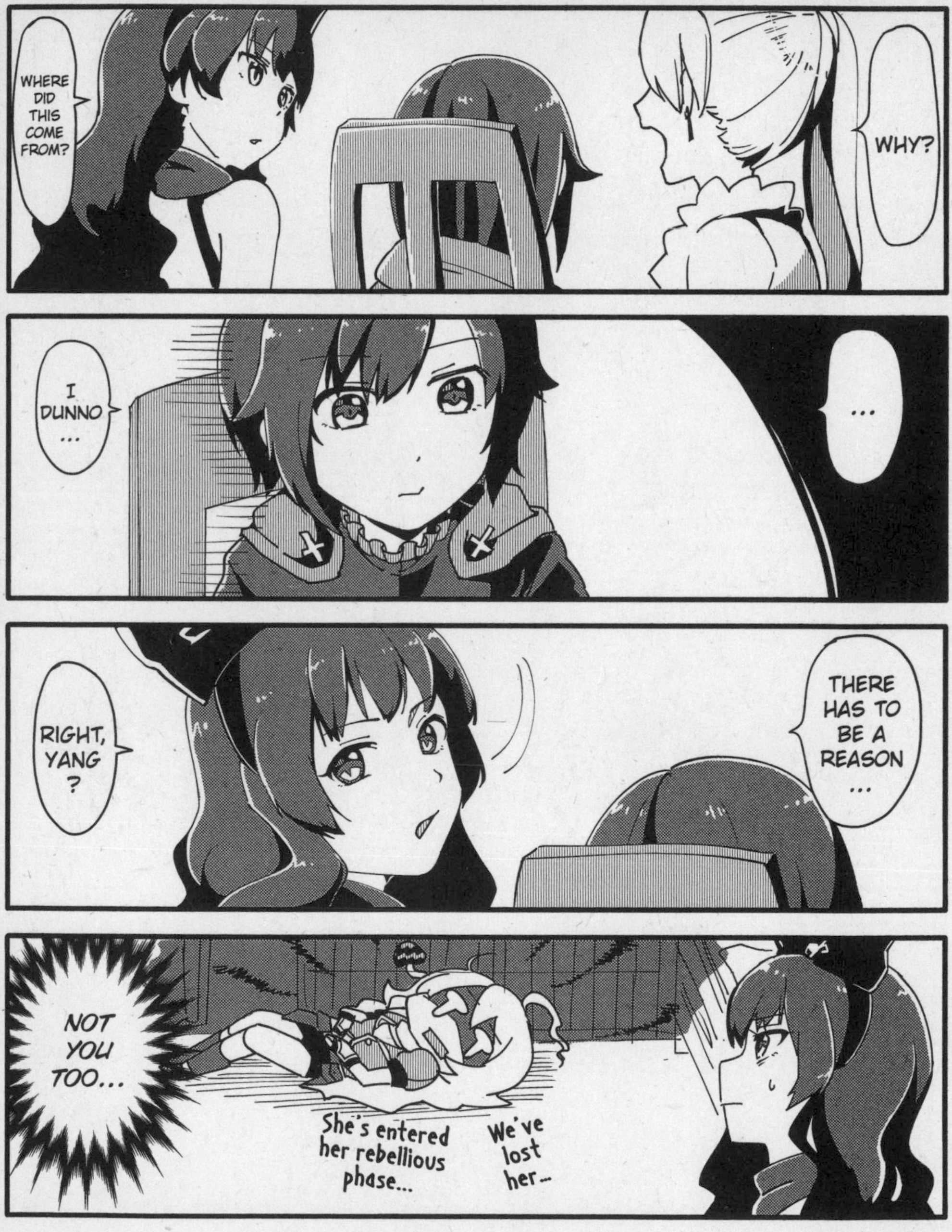

WHY?
WHERE DID THIS COME FROM?
...
I DUNNO...
THERE HAS TO BE A REASON...
RIGHT, YANG?
NOT YOU TOO...
We've lost her...
She's entered her rebellious phase...

Rebellious Phase

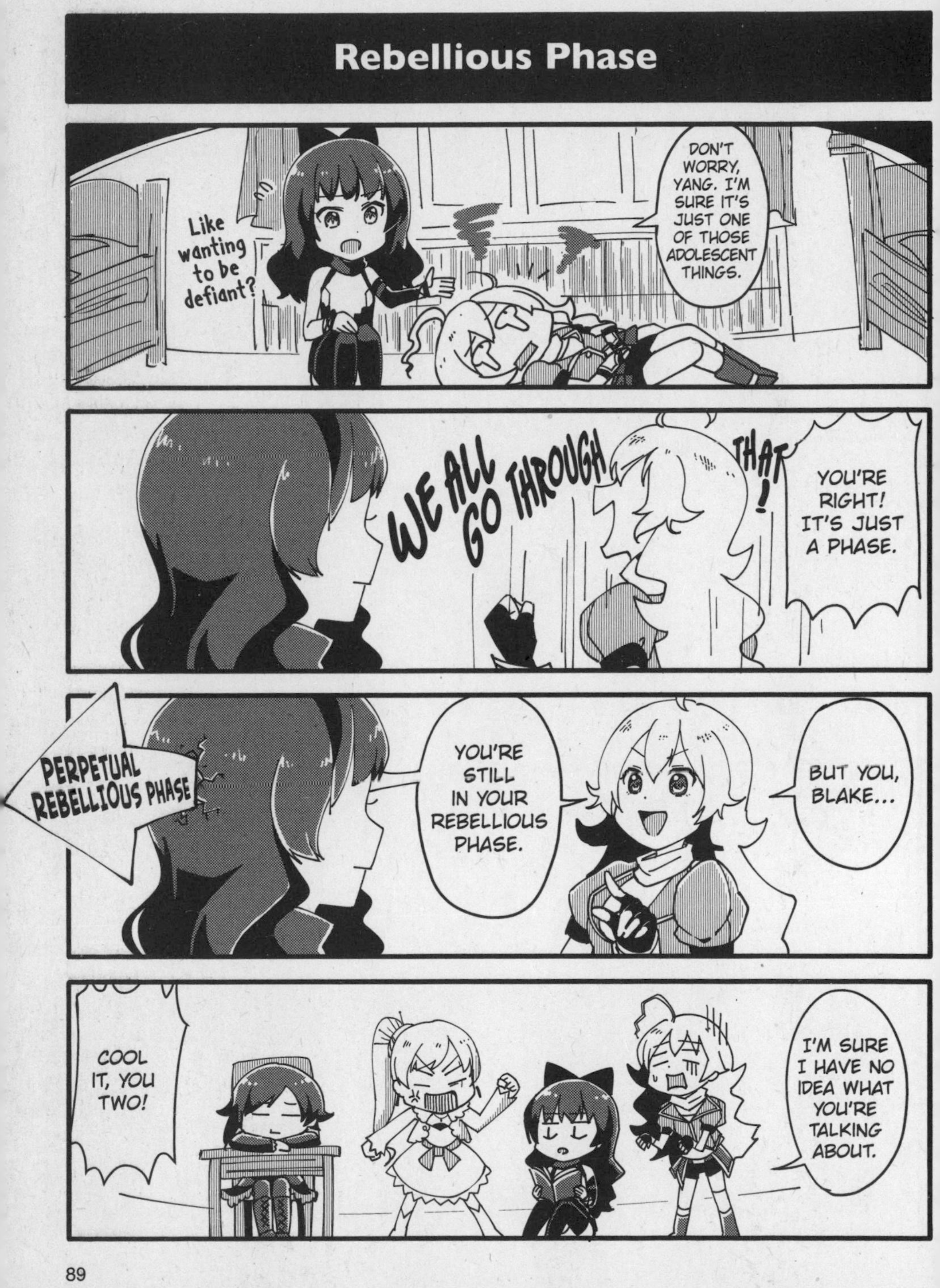
DON'T WORRY, YANG. I'M SURE IT'S JUST ONE OF THOSE ADOLESCENT THINGS.
Like wanting to be defiant?
YOU'RE RIGHT! IT'S JUST A PHASE.
WE ALL GO THROUGH THAT!
BUT YOU, BLAKE...
YOU'RE STILL IN YOUR REBELLIOUS PHASE.
PERPETUAL REBELLIOUS PHASE
I'M SURE I HAVE NO IDEA WHAT YOU'RE TALKING ABOUT.
COOL IT, YOU TWO!

Confession

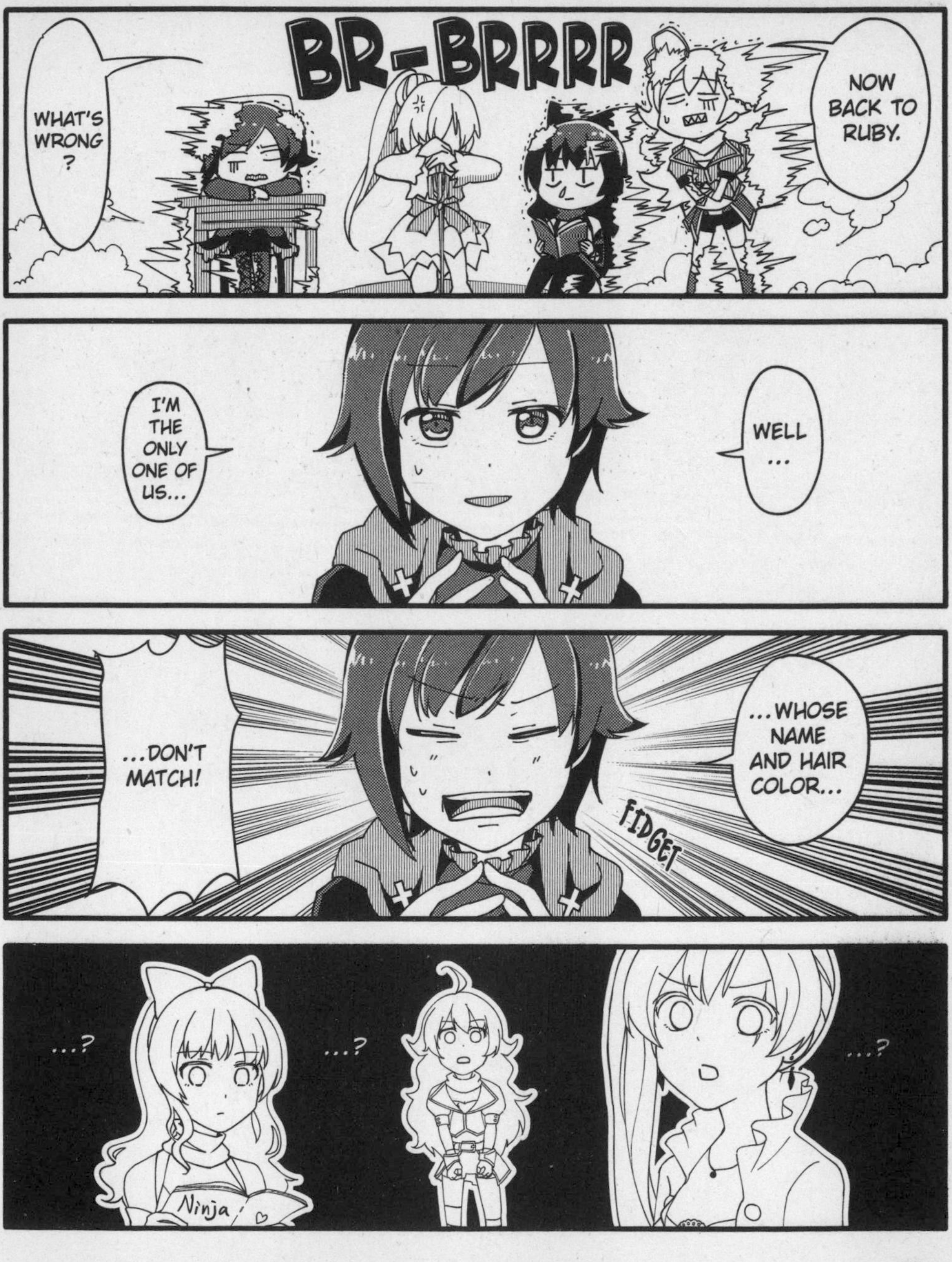
NOW BACK TO RUBY.
BR-BRRRR
WHAT'S WRONG?
WELL...
I'M THE ONLY ONE OF US...
...WHOSE NAME AND HAIR COLOR...
FIDGET
...DON'T MATCH!
...?
...?
...?
Ninja

Team RWBY

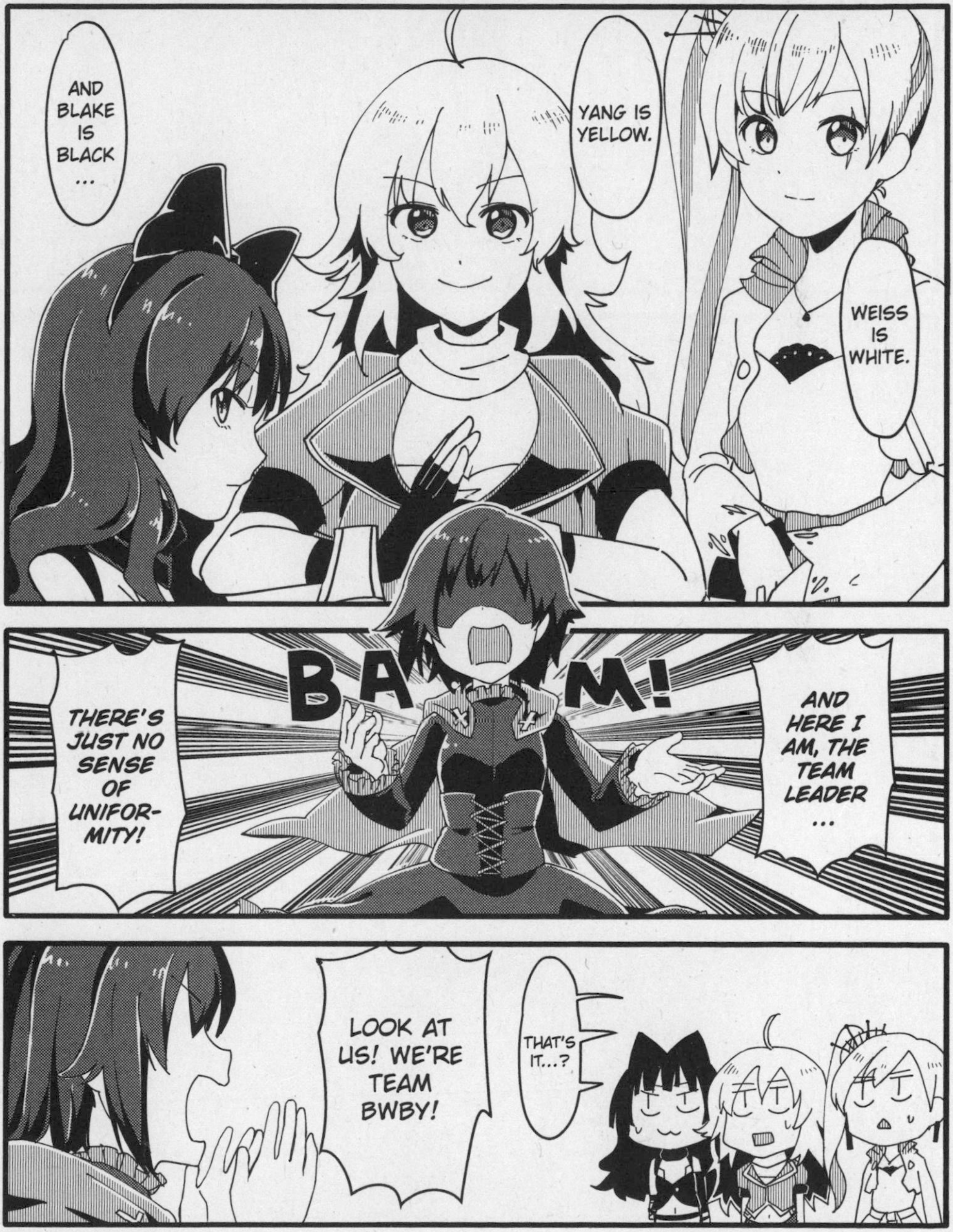

WEISS IS WHITE.
YANG IS YELLOW.
AND BLAKE IS BLACK ...
AND HERE I AM, THE TEAM LEADER ...
BAM!
THERE'S JUST NO SENSE OF UNIFORMITY!
THAT'S IT...?
LOOK AT US! WE'RE TEAM BWBY!

Stating a Case

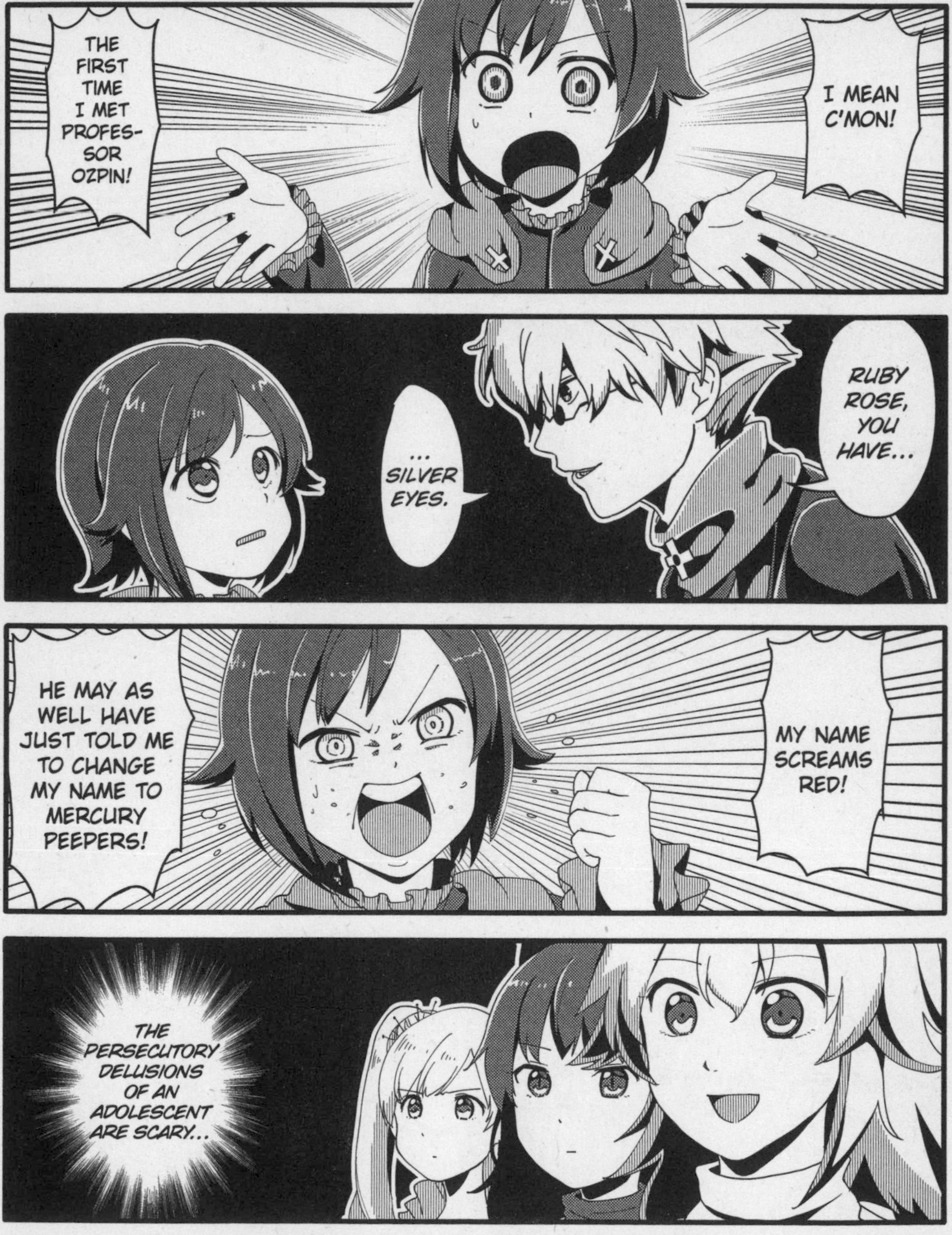

I MEAN C'MON!
THE FIRST TIME I MET PROFES-SOR OZPIN!
RUBY ROSE, YOU HAVE...
... SILVER EYES.
MY NAME SCREAMS RED!
HE MAY AS WELL HAVE JUST TOLD ME TO CHANGE MY NAME TO MERCURY PEEPERS!
THE PERSECUTORY DELUSIONS OF AN ADOLESCENT ARE SCARY...

Advice

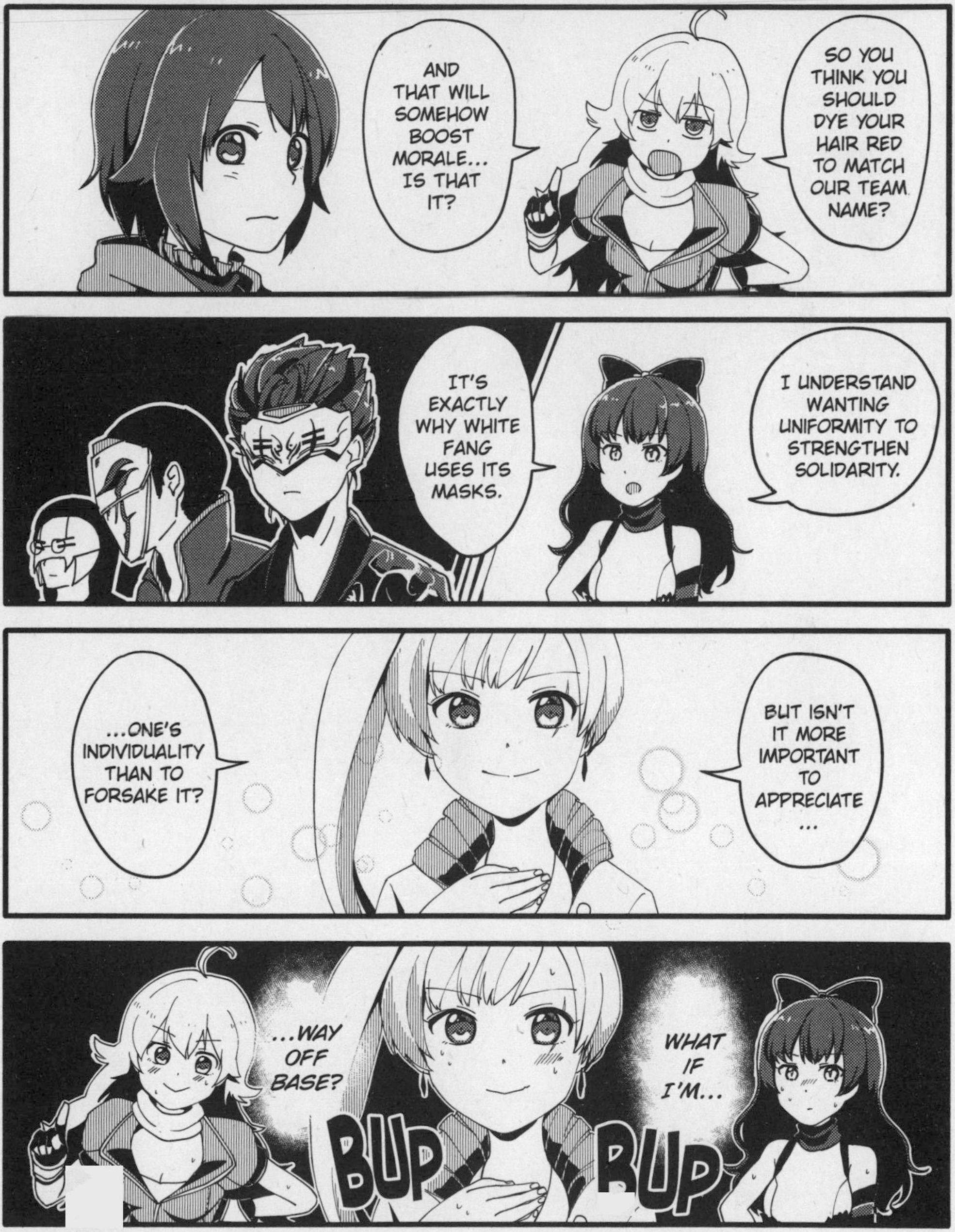
SO YOU THINK YOU SHOULD DYE YOUR HAIR RED TO MATCH OUR TEAM NAME?
AND THAT WILL SOMEHOW BOOST MORALE... IS THAT IT?
I UNDERSTAND WANTING UNIFORMITY TO STRENGTHEN SOLIDARITY.
IT'S EXACTLY WHY WHITE FANG USES ITS MASKS.
BUT ISN'T IT MORE IMPORTANT TO APPRECIATE ...
...ONE'S INDIVIDUALITY THAN TO FORSAKE IT?
WHAT IF I'M...
...WAY OFF BASE?
BUP
BUP

Scamper

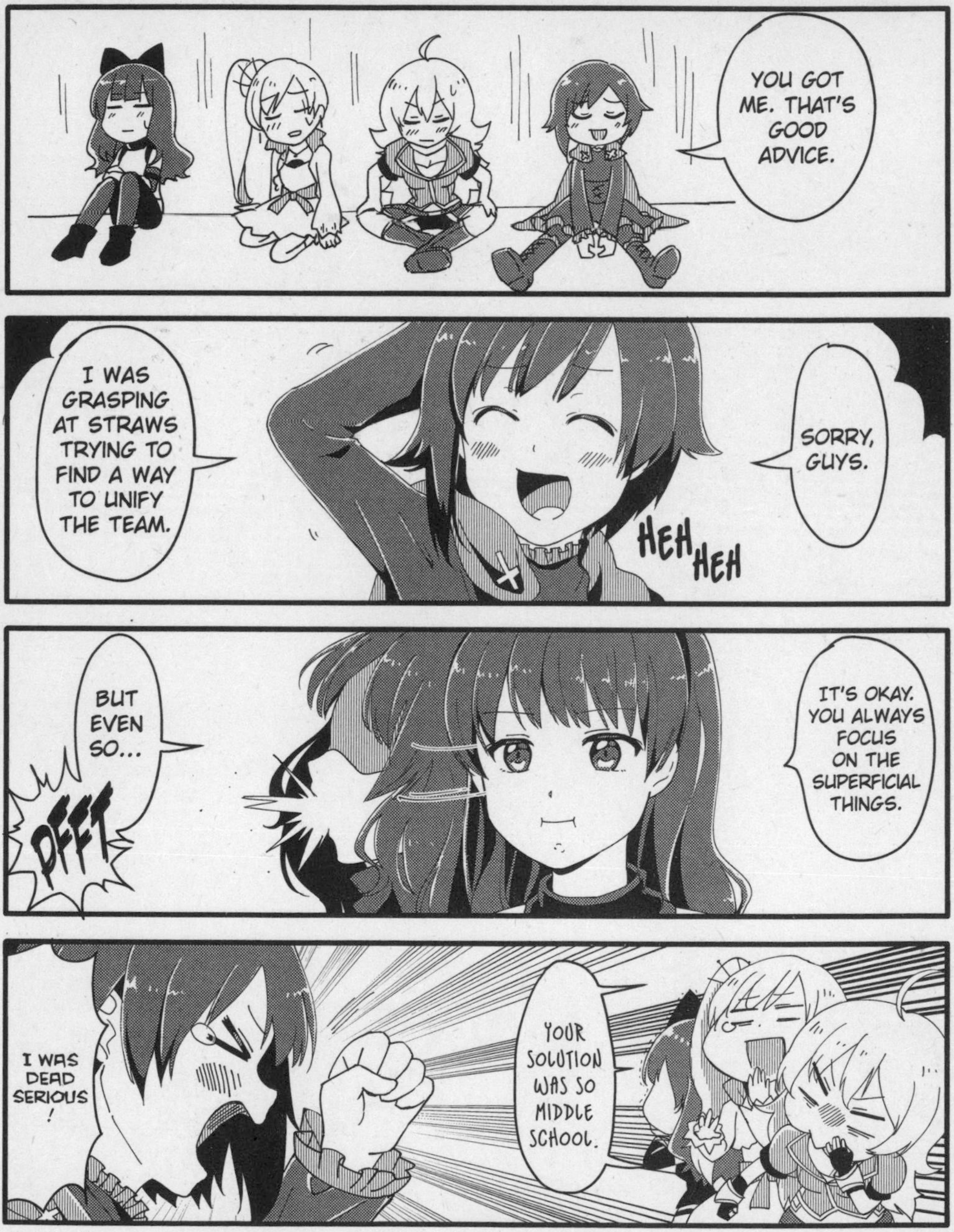
YOU GOT ME. THAT'S GOOD ADVICE.
SORRY, GUYS.
I WAS GRASPING AT STRAWS TRYING TO FIND A WAY TO UNIFY THE TEAM.
HEH HEH
IT'S OKAY. YOU ALWAYS FOCUS ON THE SUPERFICIAL THINGS.
BUT EVEN SO...
PFFT
YOUR SOLUTION WAS SO MIDDLE SCHOOL.
I WAS DEAD SERIOUS!

Solution

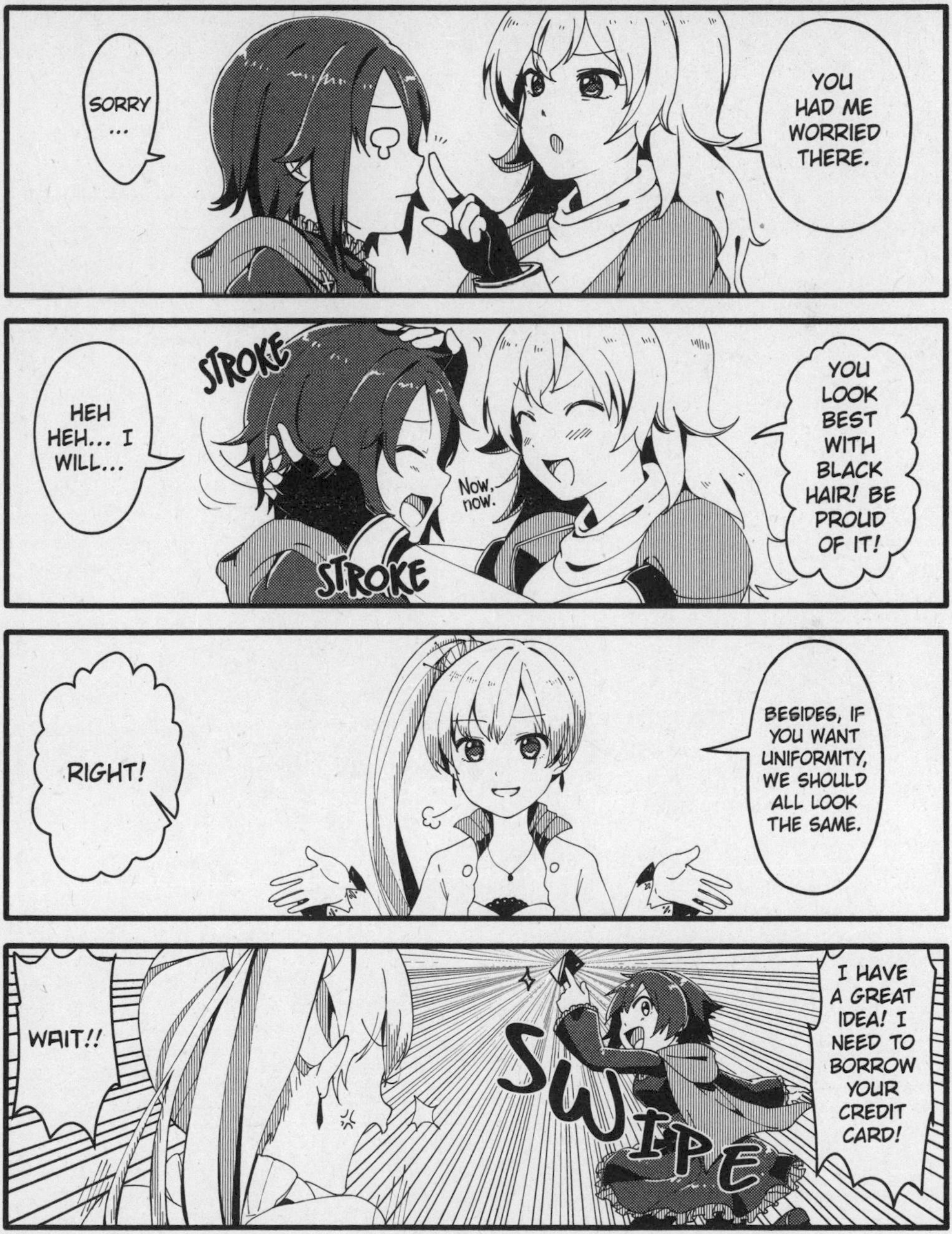

YOU HAD ME WORRIED THERE.
SORRY...
YOU LOOK BEST WITH BLACK HAIR! BE PROUD OF IT!
Now, now.
STROKE
HEH HEH... I WILL...
STROKE
BESIDES, IF YOU WANT UNIFORMITY, WE SHOULD ALL LOOK THE SAME.
RIGHT!
I HAVE A GREAT IDEA! I NEED TO BORROW YOUR CREDIT CARD!
SWIPE
WAIT!!

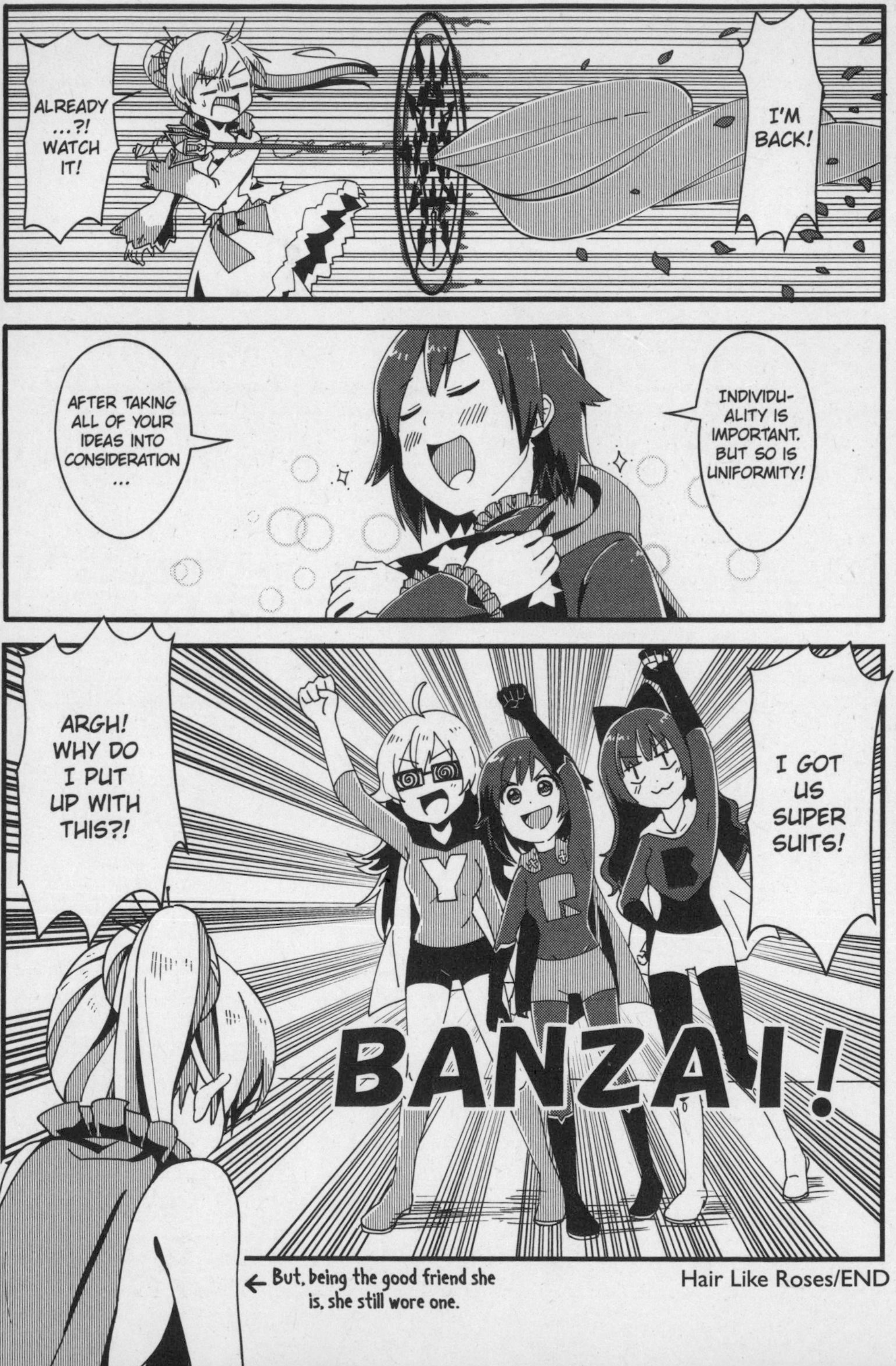
I'M BACK!
ALREADY ...?! WATCH IT!
INDIVIDU-ALITY IS IMPORTANT. BUT SO IS UNIFORMITY!
AFTER TAKING ALL OF YOUR IDEAS INTO CONSIDERATION ...
I GOT US SUPER SUITS!
ARGH! WHY DO I PUT UP WITH THIS?!
BANZAI!

Hair Like Roses/END

← But, being the good friend she is, she still wore one.

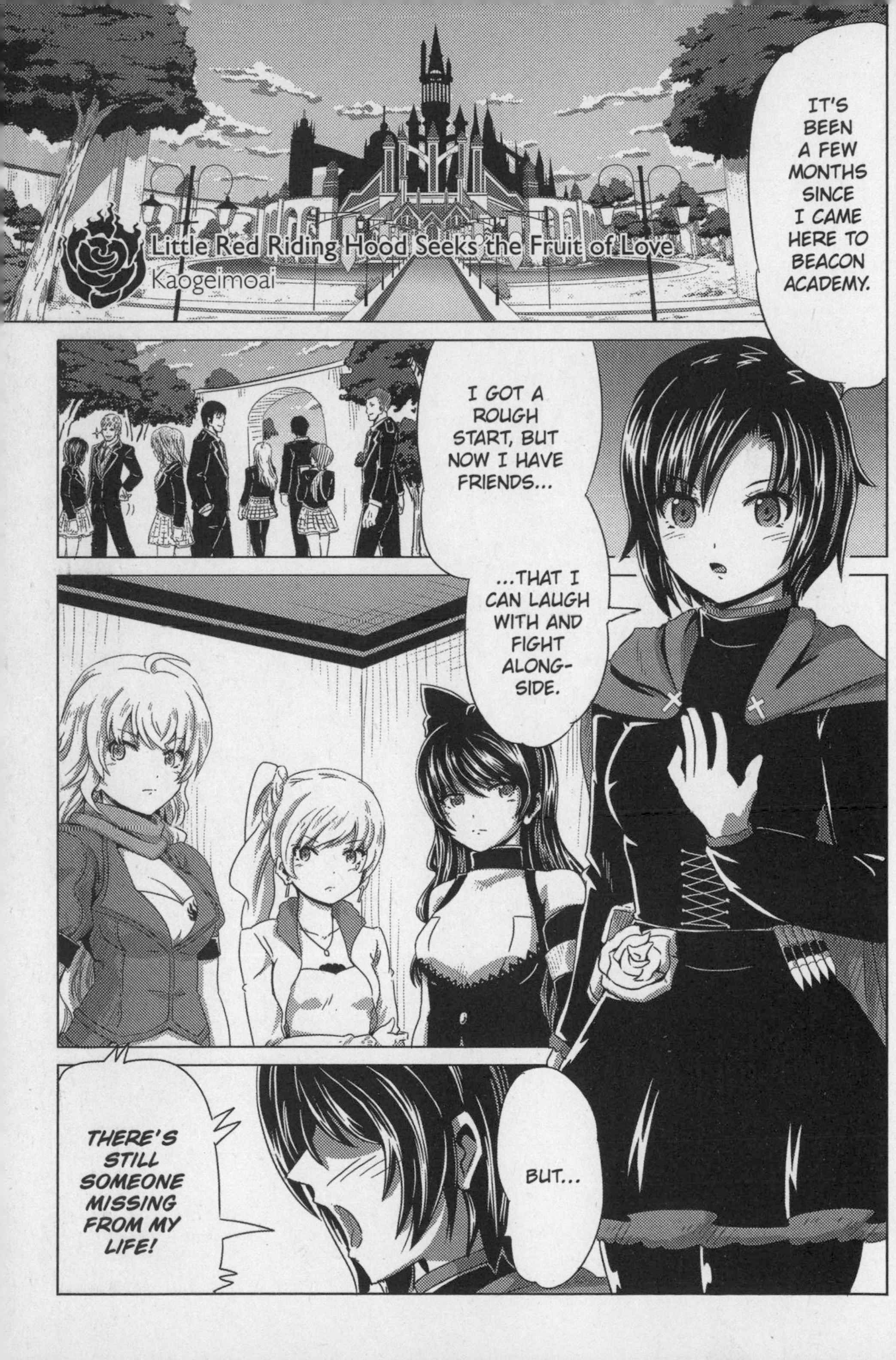
Little Red Riding Hood Seeks the Fruit of Love
Kaogeimoai
IT'S BEEN A FEW MONTHS SINCE I CAME HERE TO BEACON ACADEMY.
I GOT A ROUGH START, BUT NOW I HAVE FRIENDS...
...THAT I CAN LAUGH WITH AND FIGHT ALONG-SIDE.
BUT...
THERE'S STILL SOMEONE MISSING FROM MY LIFE!

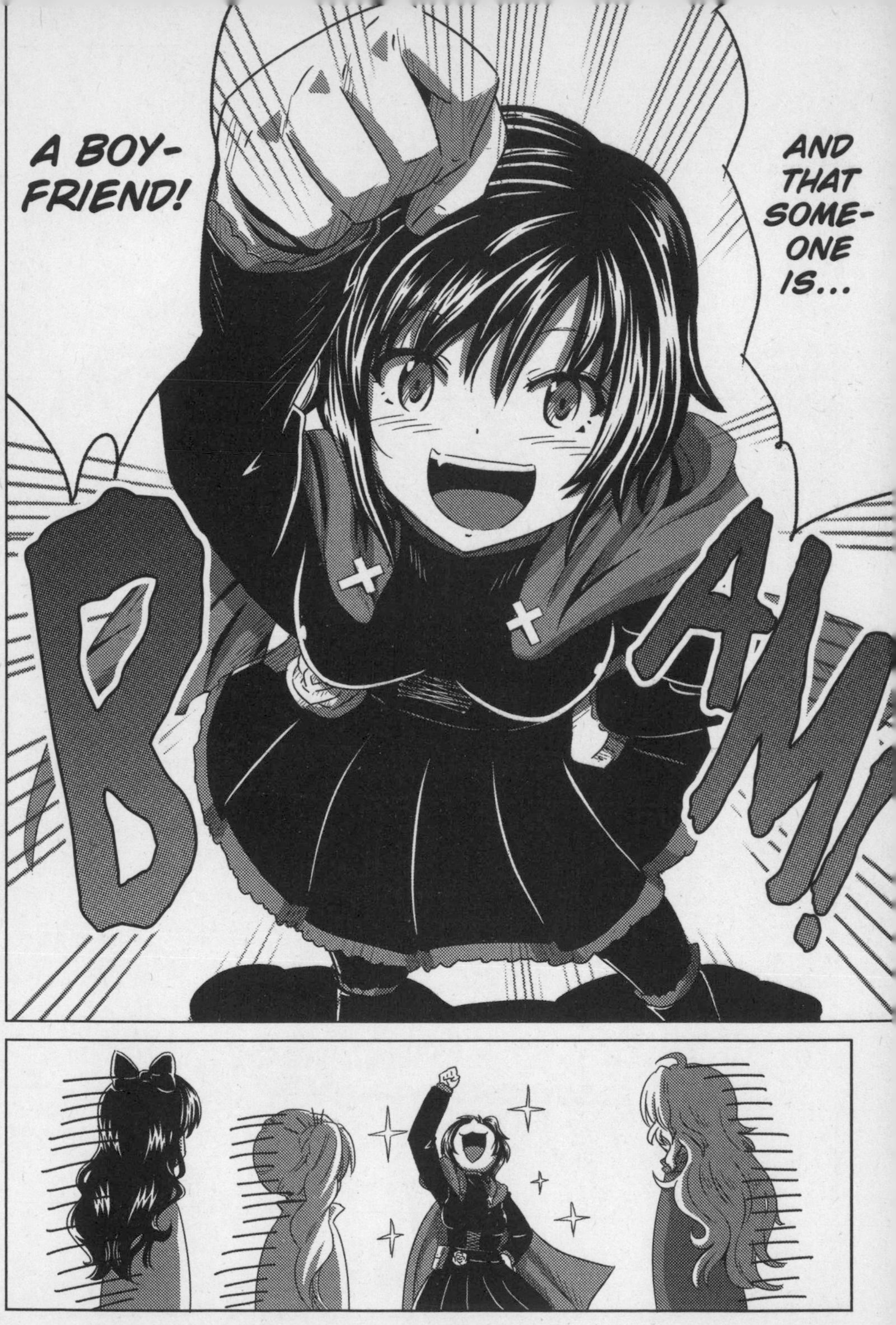
AND THAT SOMEONE IS...
A BOYFRIEND!
BAM!

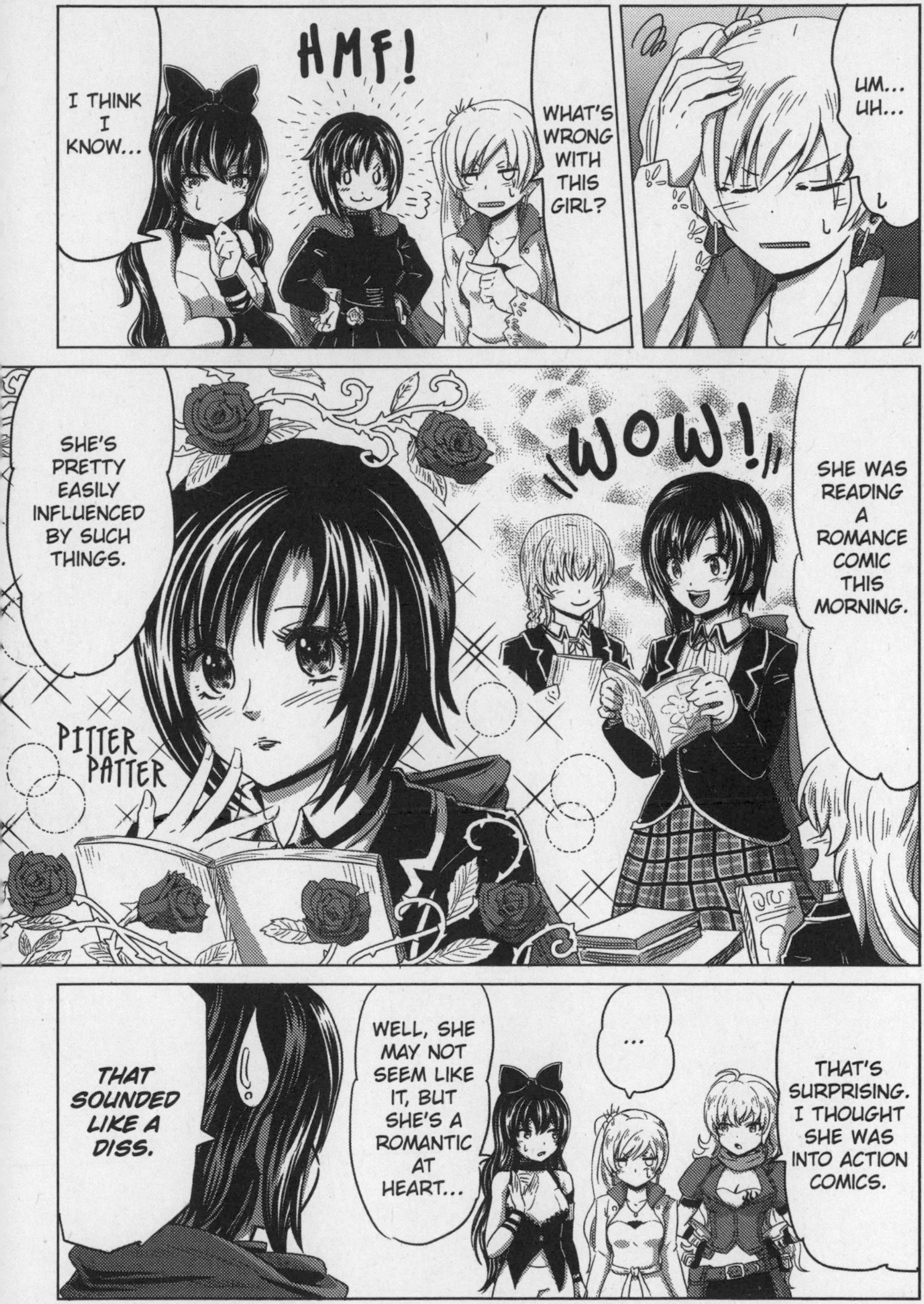
UM... UH...
WHAT'S WRONG WITH THIS GIRL?
HMF!
I THINK I KNOW...
SHE WAS READING A ROMANCE COMIC THIS MORNING.
WOW!
SHE'S PRETTY EASILY INFLUENCED BY SUCH THINGS.
PITTER PATTER
THAT'S SURPRISING. I THOUGHT SHE WAS INTO ACTION COMICS.
...
WELL, SHE MAY NOT SEEM LIKE IT, BUT SHE'S A ROMANTIC AT HEART...
THAT SOUNDED LIKE A DISS.

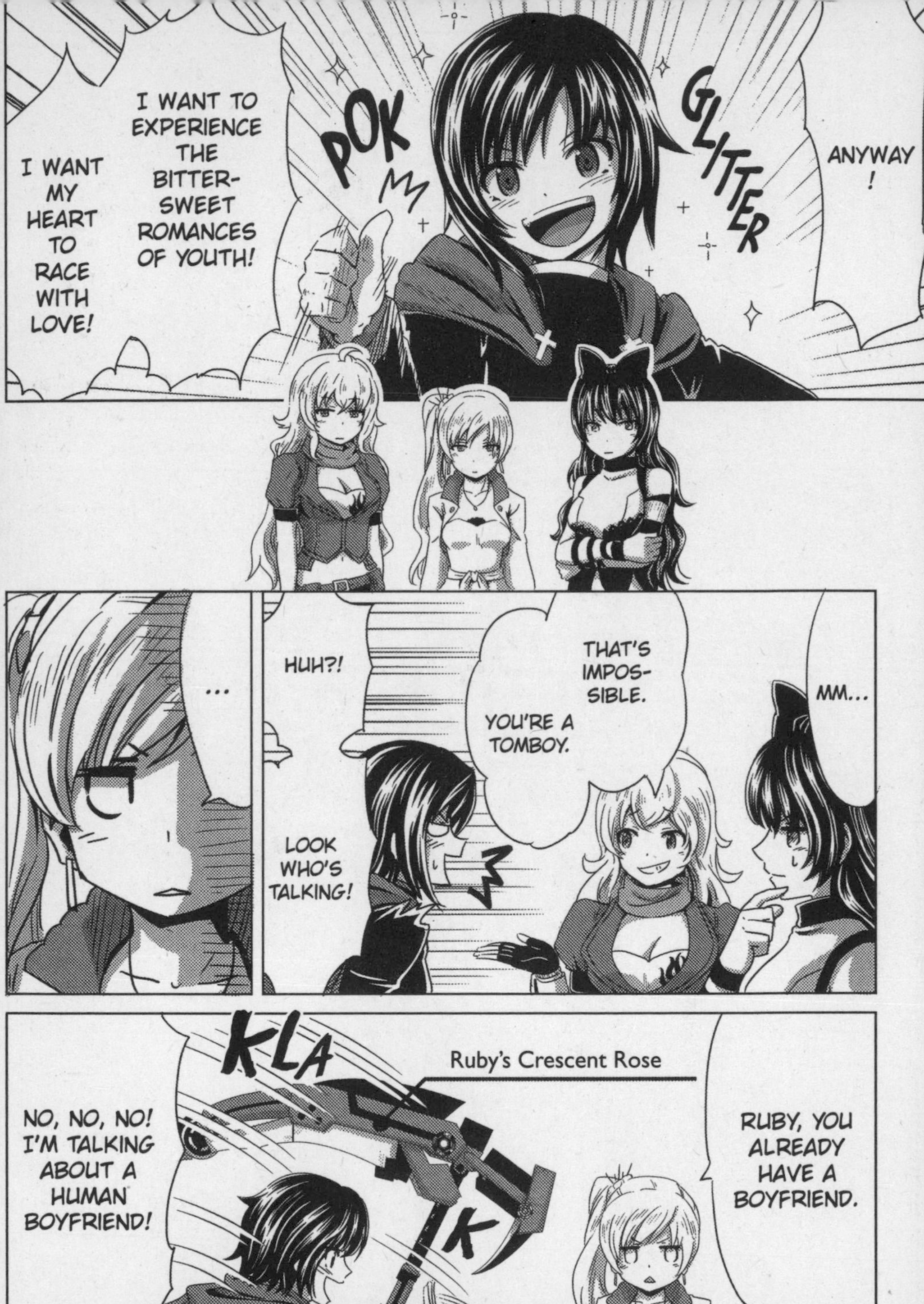
ANYWAY!
GLITTER
POK
I WANT TO EXPERIENCE THE BITTER-SWEET ROMANCES OF YOUTH!
I WANT MY HEART TO RACE WITH LOVE!
MM...
THAT'S IMPOSSIBLE. YOU'RE A TOMBOY.
HUH?!
LOOK WHO'S TALKING!
...
RUBY, YOU ALREADY HAVE A BOYFRIEND.
Ruby's Crescent Rose
KLA
K
NO, NO, NO! I'M TALKING ABOUT A HUMAN BOYFRIEND!

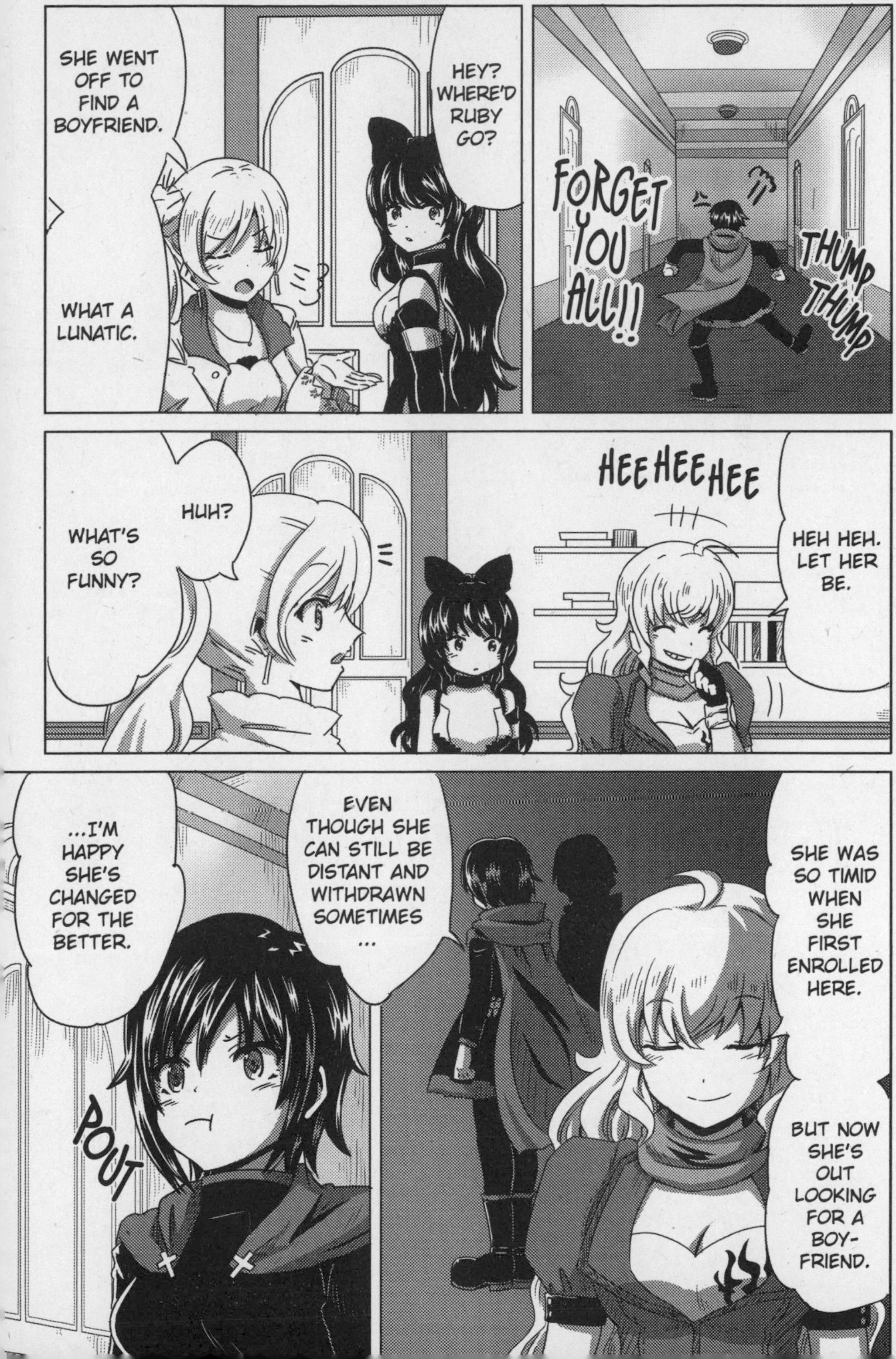
FORGET YOU ALL!!
THUMP THUMP
HEY? WHERE'D RUBY GO?
SHE WENT OFF TO FIND A BOYFRIEND.
WHAT A LUNATIC.
HEE HEE HEE
HEH HEH. LET HER BE.
HUH?
WHAT'S SO FUNNY?
SHE WAS SO TIMID WHEN SHE FIRST ENROLLED HERE.
EVEN THOUGH SHE CAN STILL BE DISTANT AND WITHDRAWN SOMETIMES ...
BUT NOW SHE'S OUT LOOKING FOR A BOY-FRIEND.
...I'M HAPPY SHE'S CHANGED FOR THE BETTER.
POUT

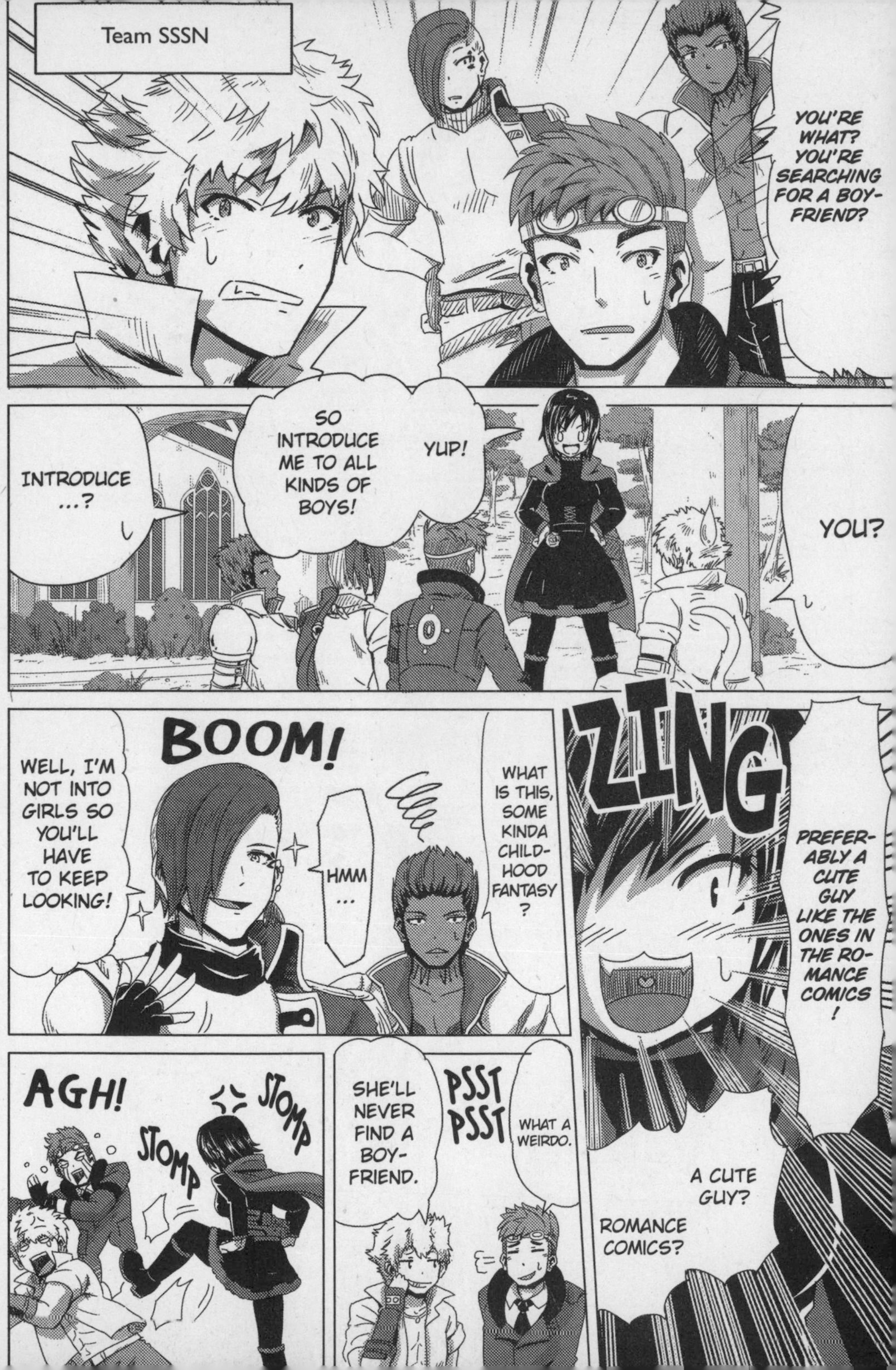
Team SSSN
YOU'RE WHAT? YOU'RE SEARCHING FOR A BOY-FRIEND?
YOU?
YUP!
SO INTRODUCE ME TO ALL KINDS OF BOYS!
INTRODUCE ...?
ZING
PREFER-ABLY A CUTE GUY LIKE THE ONES IN THE RO-MANCE COMICS!
A CUTE GUY?
ROMANCE COMICS?
WHAT IS THIS, SOME KINDA CHILD-HOOD FANTASY?
HMM ...
BOOM!
WELL, I'M NOT INTO GIRLS SO YOU'LL HAVE TO KEEP LOOKING!
WHAT A WEIRDO.
PSST PSST
SHE'LL NEVER FIND A BOY-FRIEND.
STOMP
STOMP
AGH!

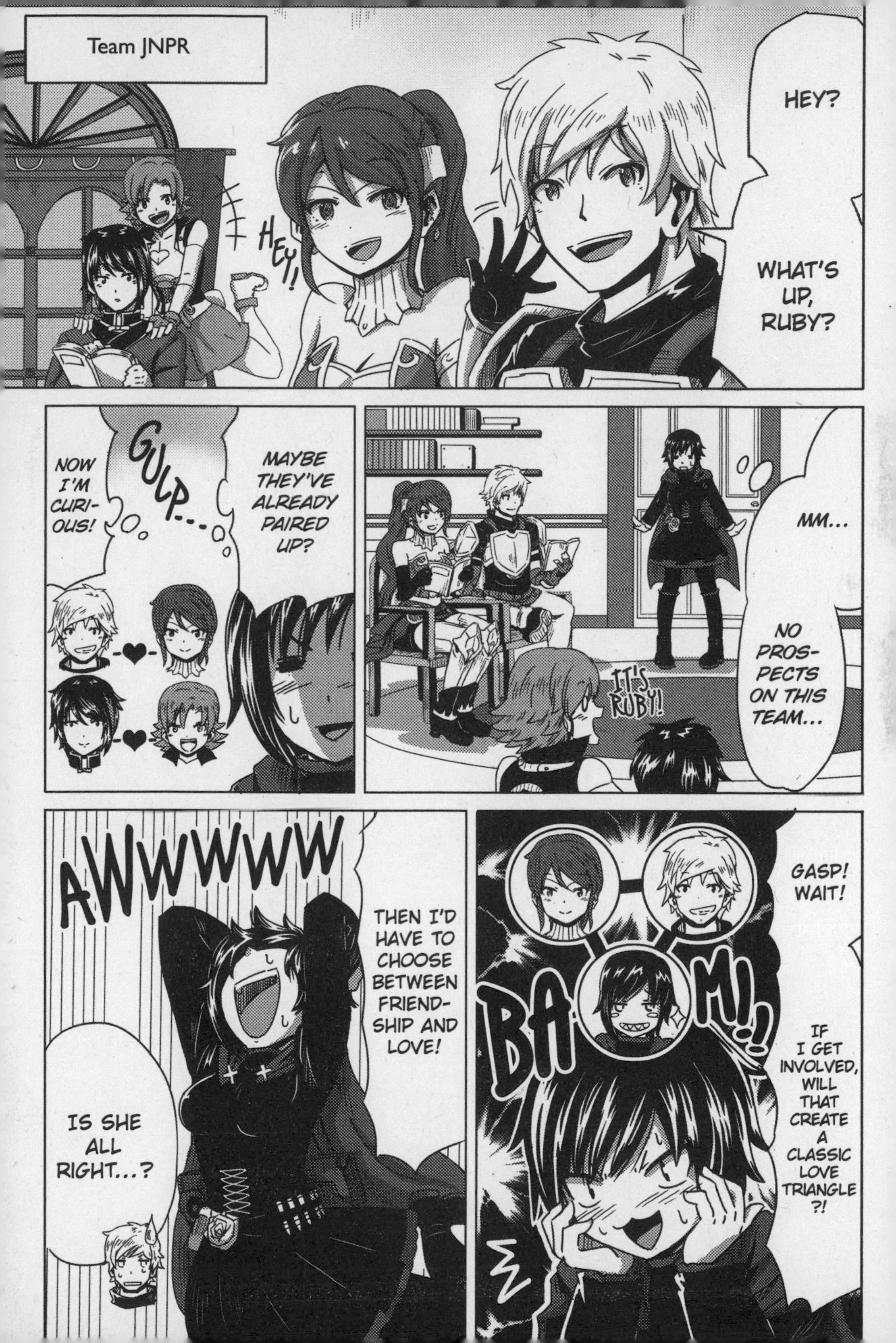

Team JNPR
HEY?
WHAT'S UP, RUBY?
HEY!
MM...
NO PROSPECTS ON THIS TEAM...
IT'S RUBY!
MAYBE THEY'VE ALREADY PAIRED UP?
GULP...
NOW I'M CURIOUS!
GASP! WAIT!
BAM!!
IF I GET INVOLVED, WILL THAT CREATE A CLASSIC LOVE TRIANGLE?!
THEN I'D HAVE TO CHOOSE BETWEEN FRIENDSHIP AND LOVE!
AWWWWWW
IS SHE ALL RIGHT...?

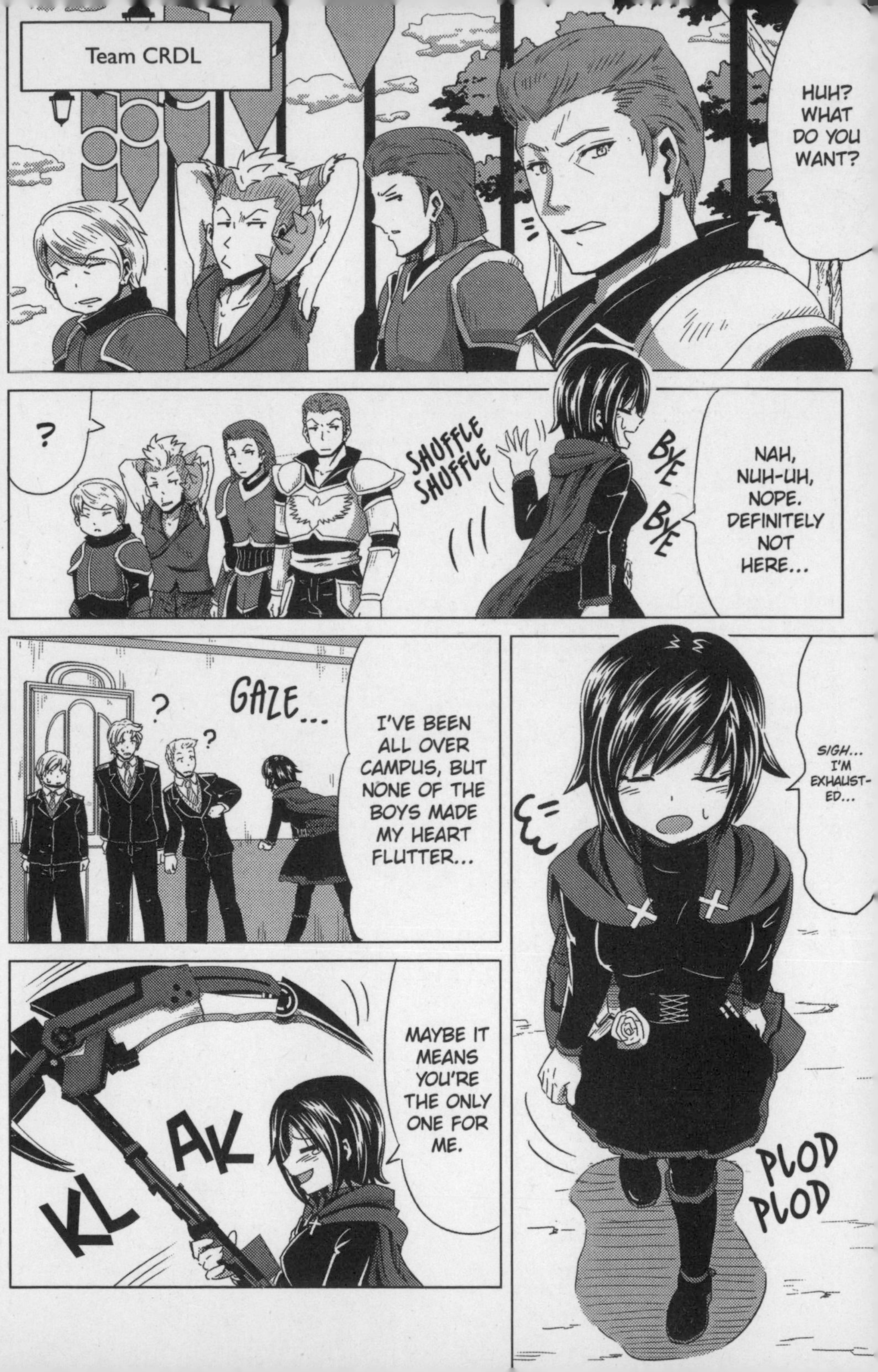
Team CRDL
HUH? WHAT DO YOU WANT?
NAH, NUH-UH, NOPE. DEFINITELY NOT HERE...
BYE BYE
SHUFFLE SHUFFLE
?
SIGH... I'M EXHAUST-ED...
PLOD PLOD
I'VE BEEN ALL OVER CAMPUS, BUT NONE OF THE BOYS MADE MY HEART FLUTTER...
GAZE...
?
?
MAYBE IT MEANS YOU'RE THE ONLY ONE FOR ME.
KLAK

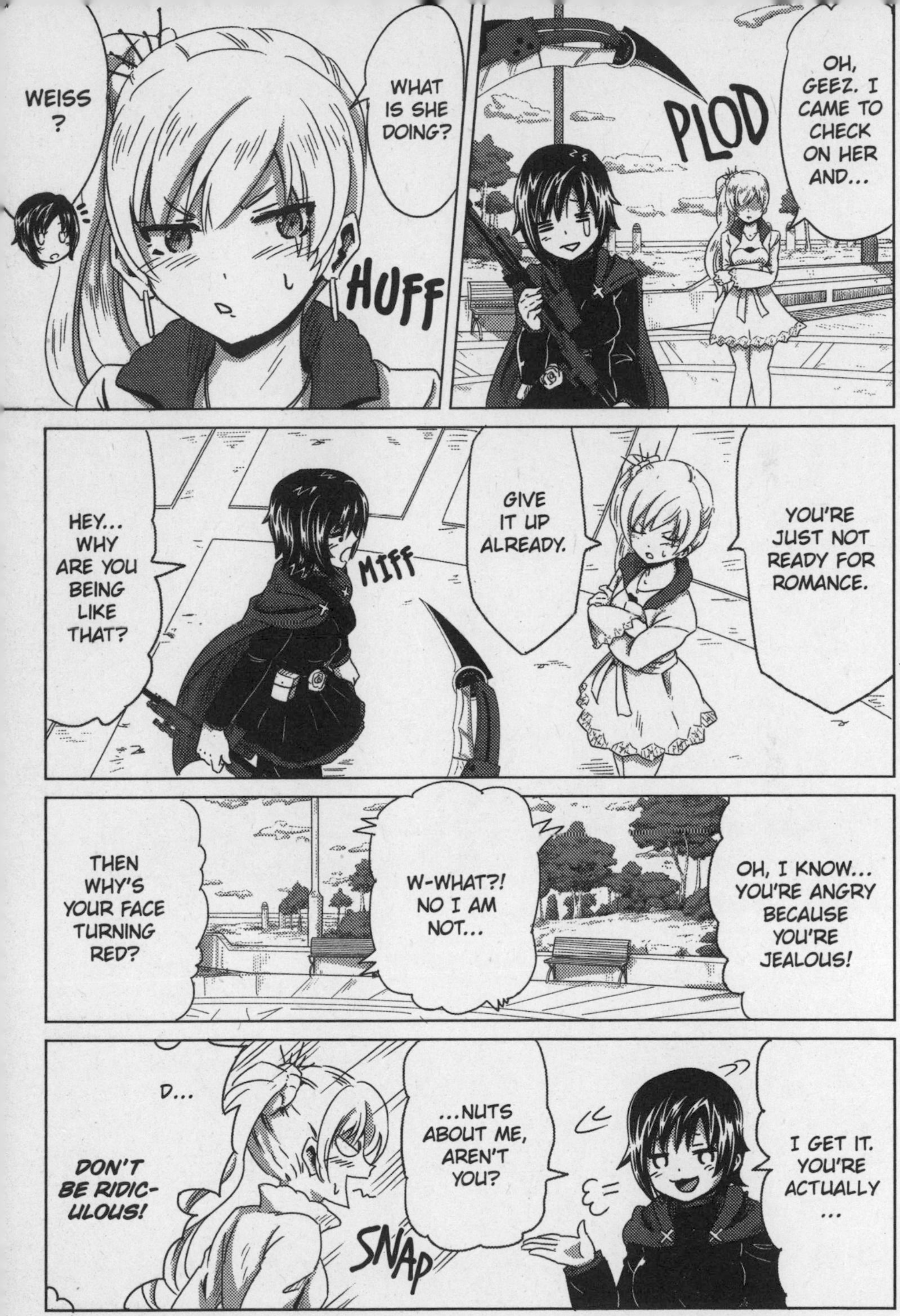
OH, GEEZ. I CAME TO CHECK ON HER AND...
PLOD
WHAT IS SHE DOING?
HUFF
WEISS ?
YOU'RE JUST NOT READY FOR ROMANCE.
GIVE IT UP ALREADY.
MIFF
HEY... WHY ARE YOU BEING LIKE THAT?
OH, I KNOW... YOU'RE ANGRY BECAUSE YOU'RE JEALOUS!
W-WHAT?! NO I AM NOT...
THEN WHY'S YOUR FACE TURNING RED?
I GET IT. YOU'RE ACTUALLY ...
...NUTS ABOUT ME, AREN'T YOU?
SNAP
D...
DON'T BE RIDIC-ULOUS!

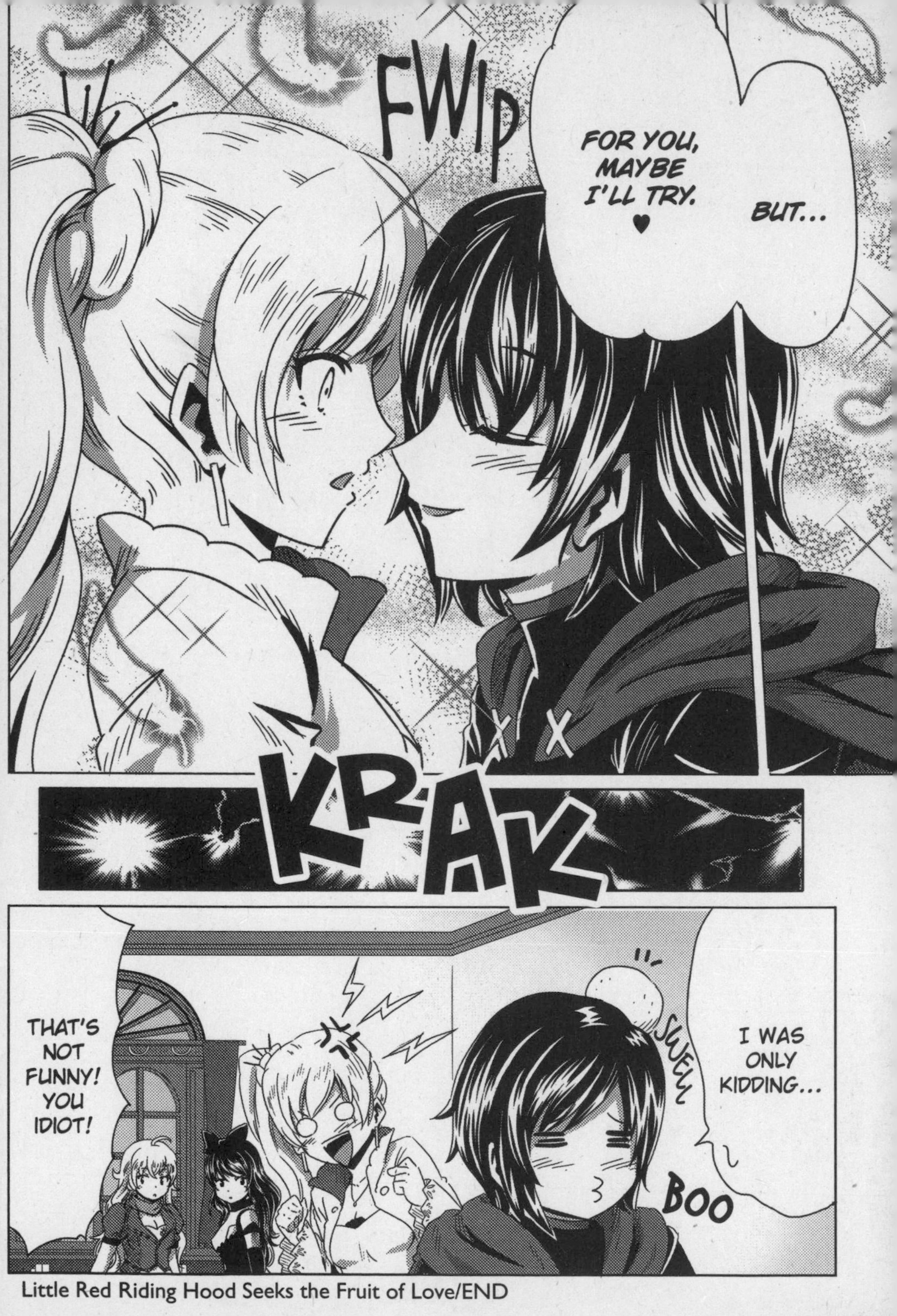
FOR YOU, MAYBE I'LL TRY. ♥
BUT...
FWIP
KRAK
I WAS ONLY KIDDING...
SWEW
BOO
THAT'S NOT FUNNY! YOU IDIOT!

Little Red Riding Hood Seeks the Fruit of Love/END

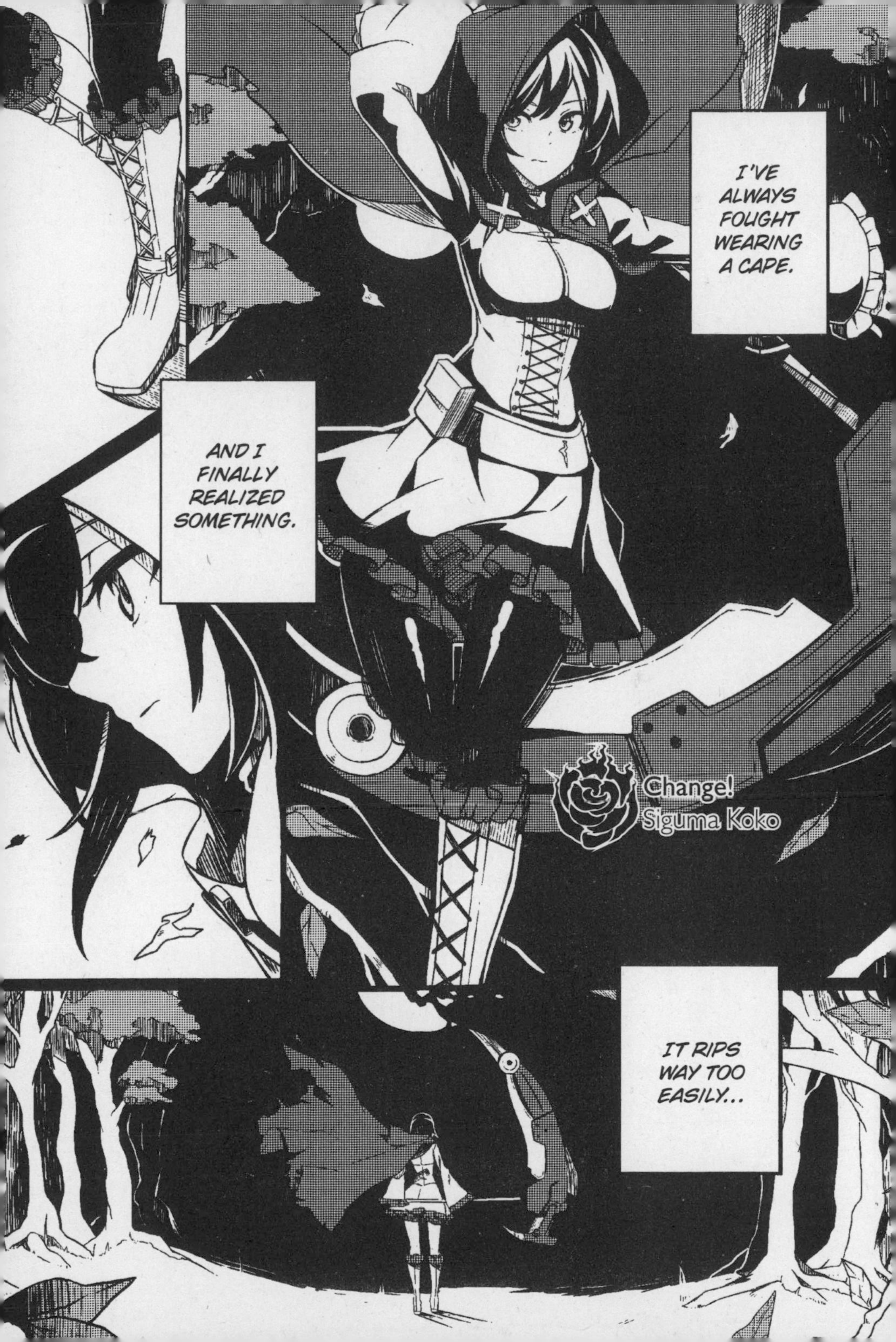
I'VE ALWAYS FOUGHT WEARING A CAPE.
AND I FINALLY REALIZED SOMETHING.
Change!
Siguma Koko
IT RIPS WAY TOO EASILY...

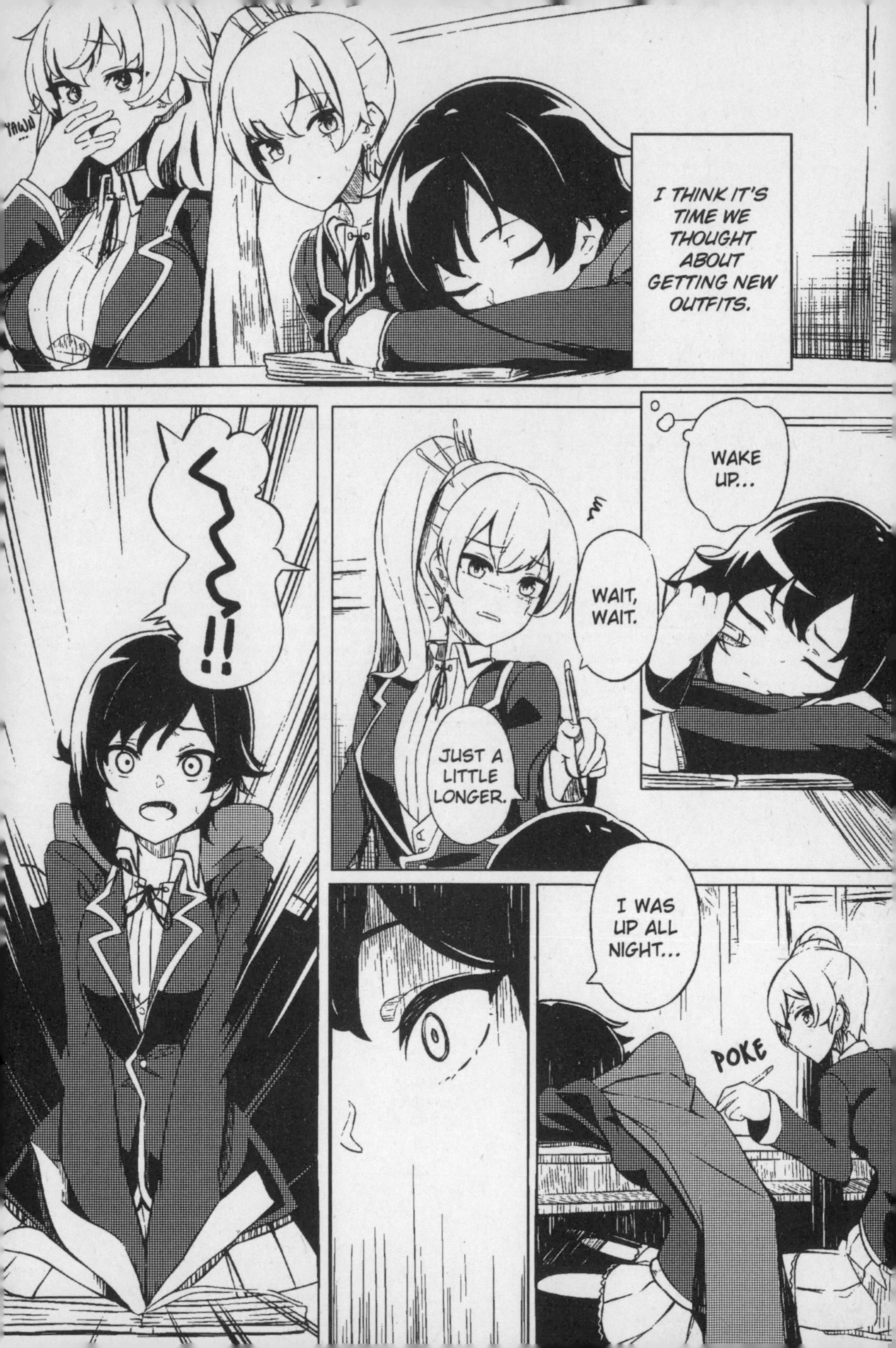

I THINK IT'S TIME WE THOUGHT ABOUT GETTING NEW OUTFITS.
YAWN...
WAKE UP...
WAIT, WAIT.
JUST A LITTLE LONGER.
I WAS UP ALL NIGHT...
POKE
!!

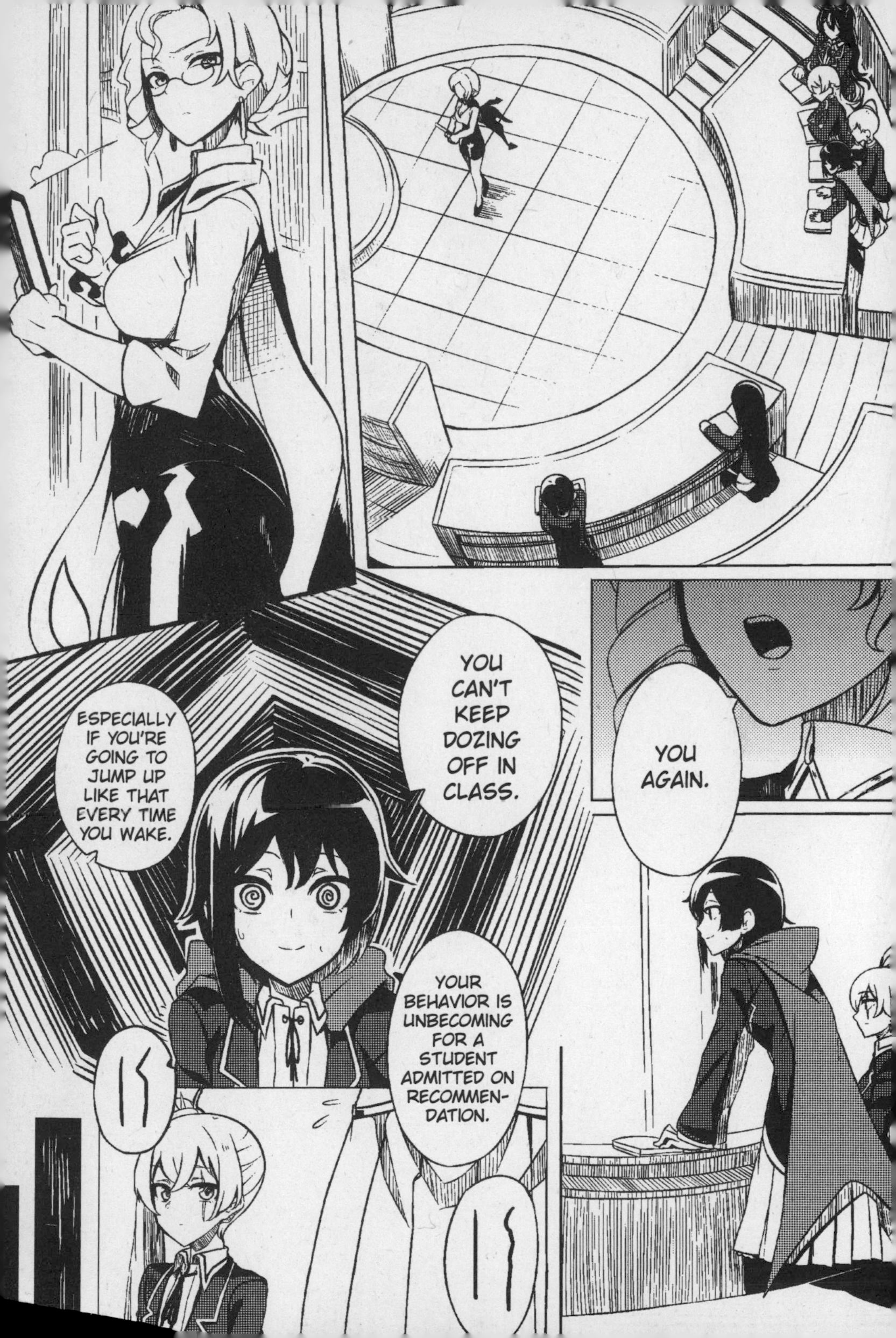
YOU AGAIN.
YOU CAN'T KEEP DOZING OFF IN CLASS.
ESPECIALLY IF YOU'RE GOING TO JUMP UP LIKE THAT EVERY TIME YOU WAKE.
YOUR BEHAVIOR IS UNBECOMING FOR A STUDENT ADMITTED ON RECOMMEN-DATION.

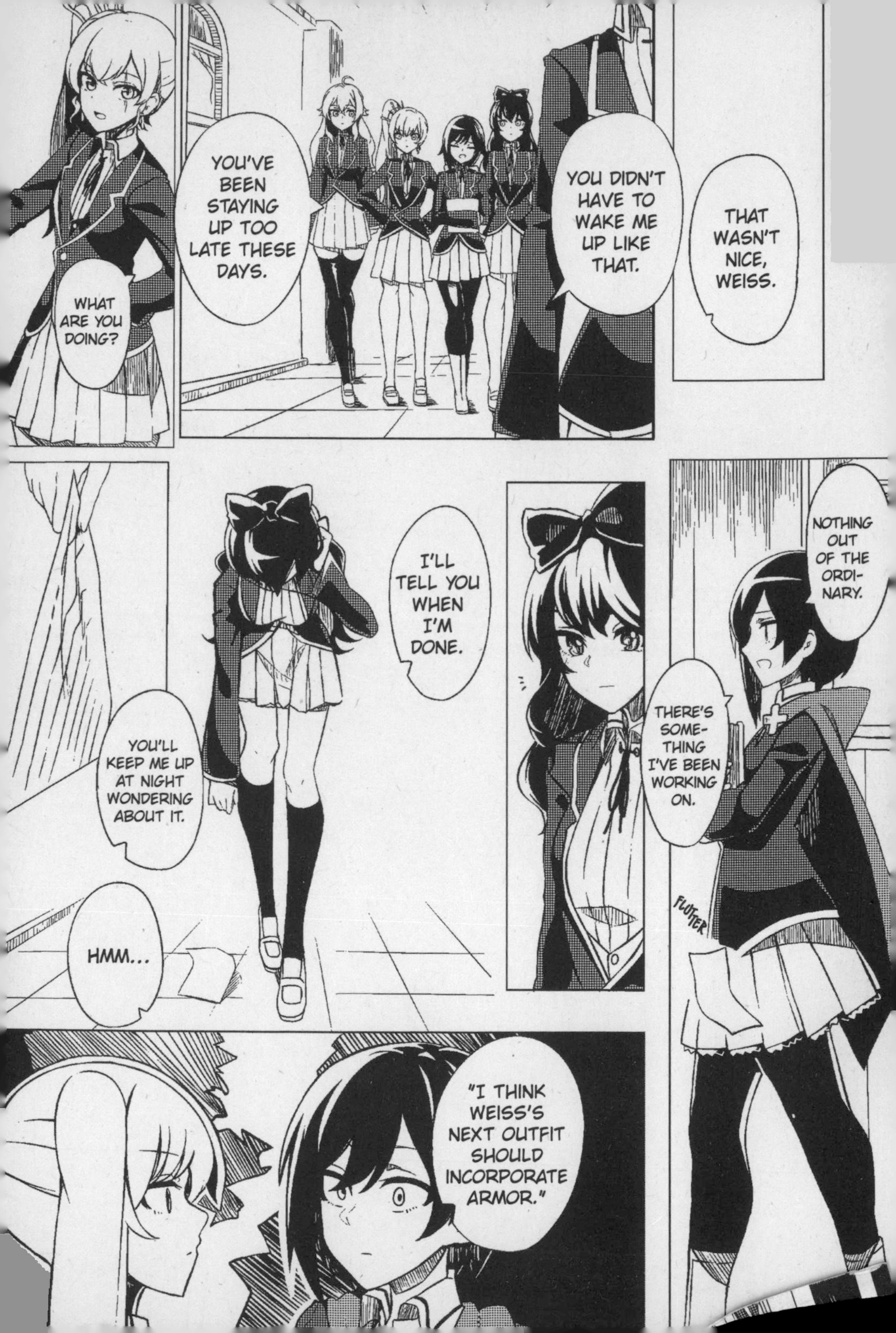
THAT WASN'T NICE, WEISS.
YOU DIDN'T HAVE TO WAKE ME UP LIKE THAT.
YOU'VE BEEN STAYING UP TOO LATE THESE DAYS.
WHAT ARE YOU DOING?
NOTHING OUT OF THE ORDINARY.
THERE'S SOMETHING I'VE BEEN WORKING ON.
FLUTTER
I'LL TELL YOU WHEN I'M DONE.
YOU'LL KEEP ME UP AT NIGHT WONDERING ABOUT IT.
HMM...
"I THINK WEISS'S NEXT OUTFIT SHOULD INCORPORATE ARMOR."

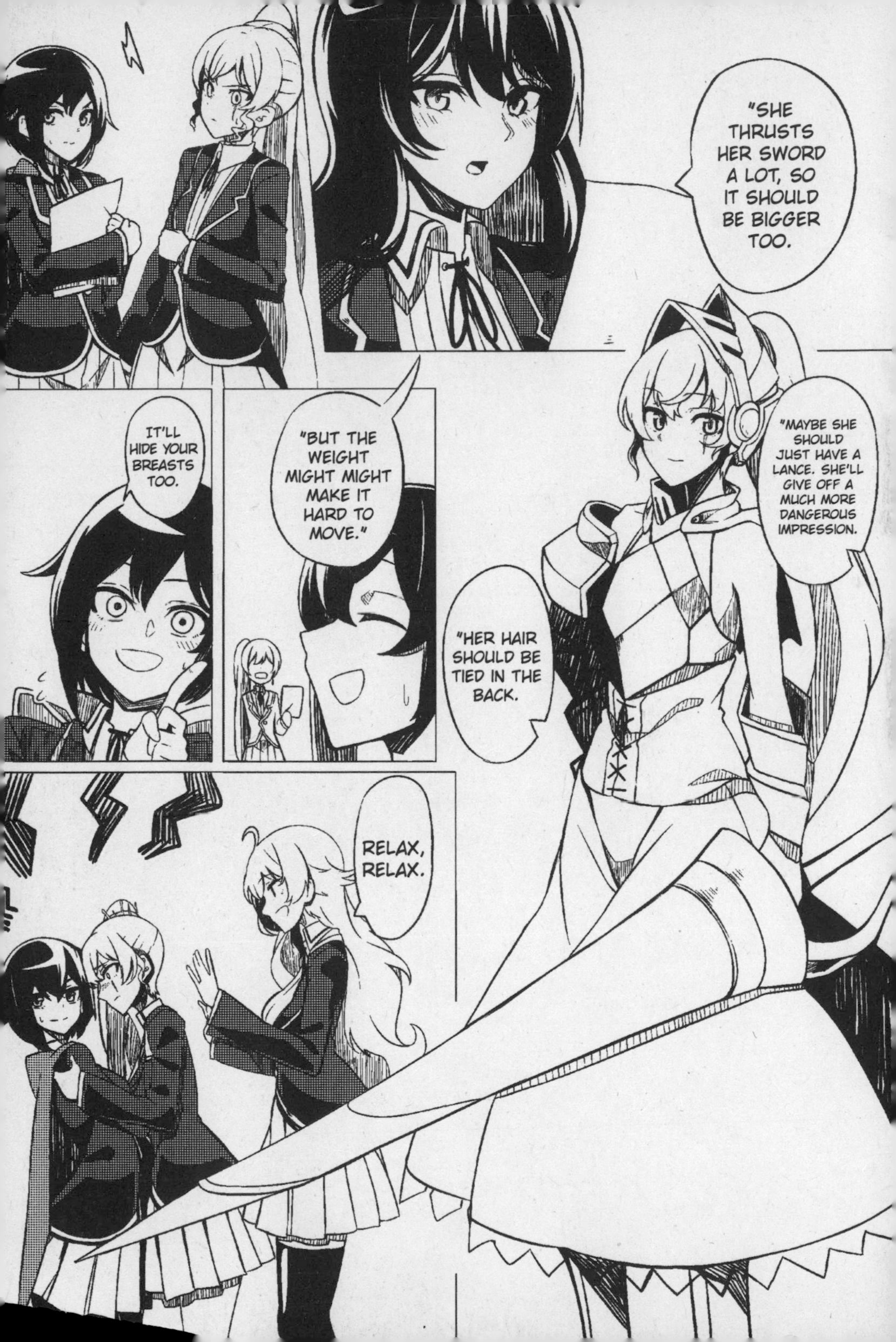
"SHE THRUSTS HER SWORD A LOT, SO IT SHOULD BE BIGGER TOO.
"MAYBE SHE SHOULD JUST HAVE A LANCE. SHE'LL GIVE OFF A MUCH MORE DANGEROUS IMPRESSION.
"HER HAIR SHOULD BE TIED IN THE BACK.
"BUT THE WEIGHT MIGHT MIGHT MAKE IT HARD TO MOVE."
IT'LL HIDE YOUR BREASTS TOO.
RELAX, RELAX.

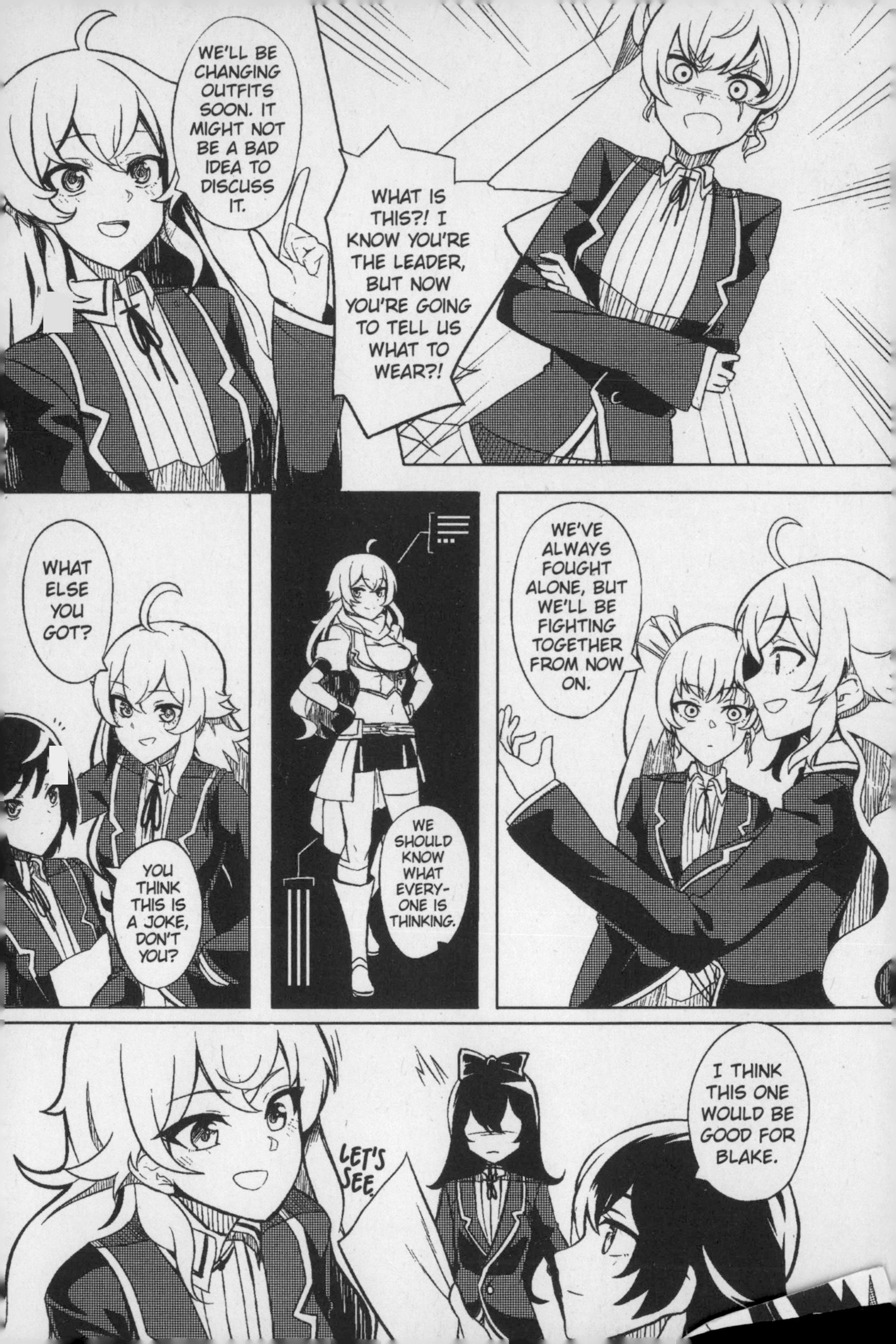
WHAT IS THIS?! I KNOW YOU'RE THE LEADER, BUT NOW YOU'RE GOING TO TELL US WHAT TO WEAR?!
WE'LL BE CHANGING OUTFITS SOON. IT MIGHT NOT BE A BAD IDEA TO DISCUSS IT.
WE'VE ALWAYS FOUGHT ALONE, BUT WE'LL BE FIGHTING TOGETHER FROM NOW ON.
WE SHOULD KNOW WHAT EVERY-ONE IS THINKING.
WHAT ELSE YOU GOT?
YOU THINK THIS IS A JOKE, DON'T YOU?
I THINK THIS ONE WOULD BE GOOD FOR BLAKE.
LET'S SEE.

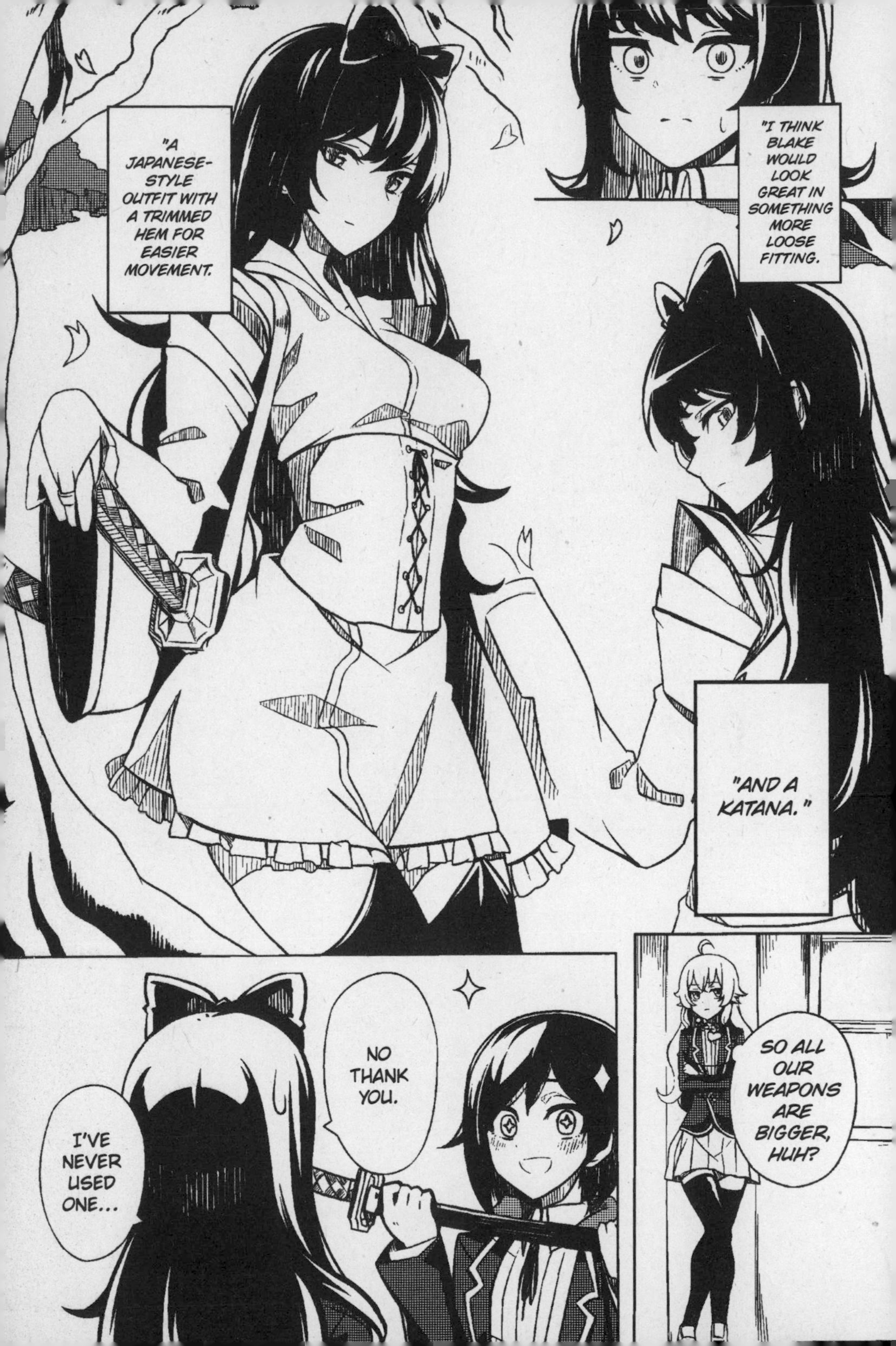

"I THINK BLAKE WOULD LOOK GREAT IN SOMETHING MORE LOOSE FITTING.
"A JAPANESE-STYLE OUTFIT WITH A TRIMMED HEM FOR EASIER MOVEMENT.
"AND A KATANA."
SO ALL OUR WEAPONS ARE BIGGER, HUH?
NO THANK YOU.
I'VE NEVER USED ONE...

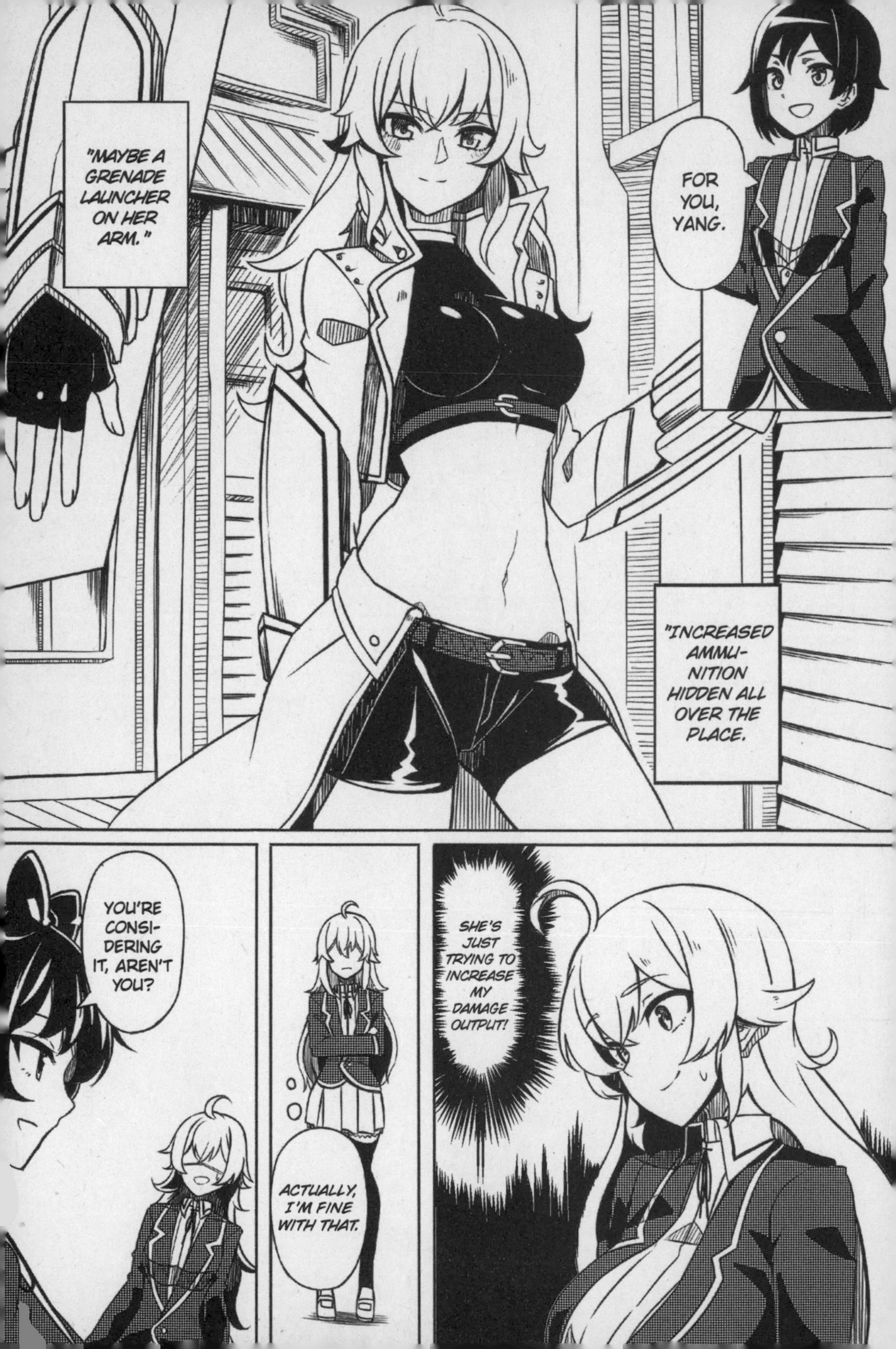

FOR YOU, YANG.
"MAYBE A GRENADE LAUNCHER ON HER ARM."
"INCREASED AMMU-NITION HIDDEN ALL OVER THE PLACE.
SHE'S JUST TRYING TO INCREASE MY DAMAGE OUTPUT!
ACTUALLY, I'M FINE WITH THAT.
YOU'RE CONSI-DERING IT, AREN'T YOU?

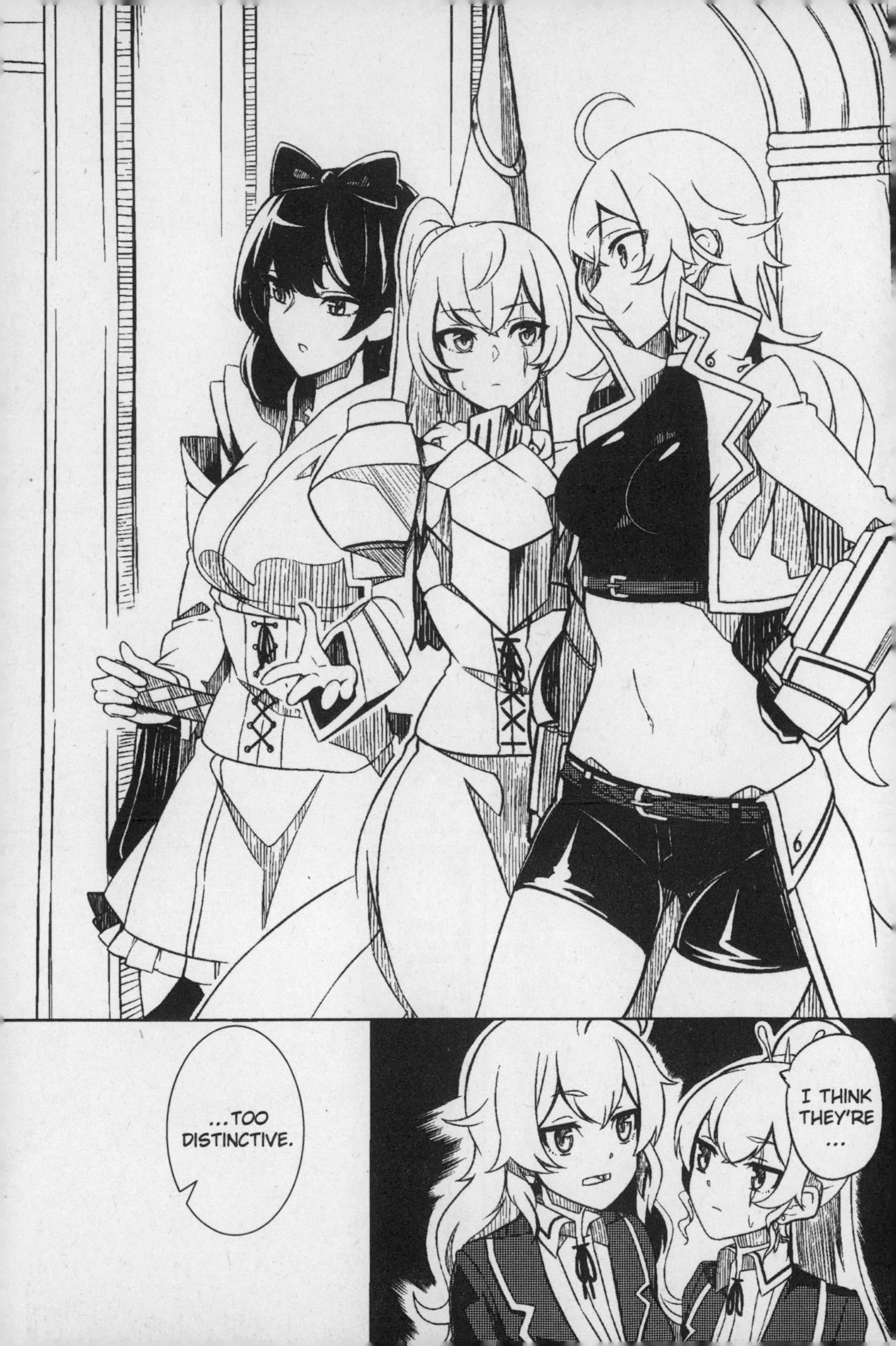
I THINK THEY'RE ...
...TOO DISTINCTIVE.

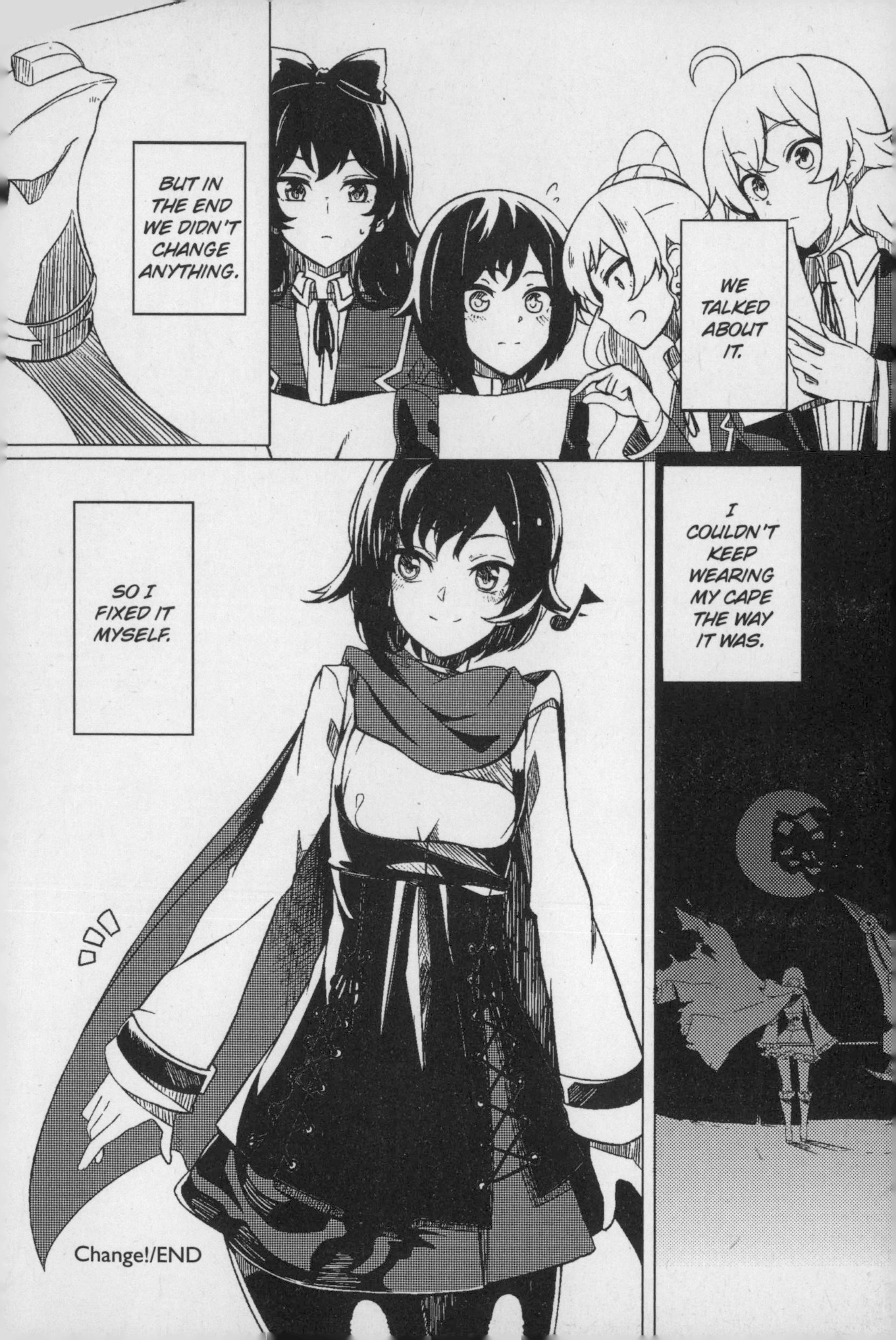
WE TALKED ABOUT IT.
BUT IN THE END WE DIDN'T CHANGE ANYTHING.
I COULDN'T KEEP WEARING MY CAPE THE WAY IT WAS.
SO I FIXED IT MYSELF.
Change!/END

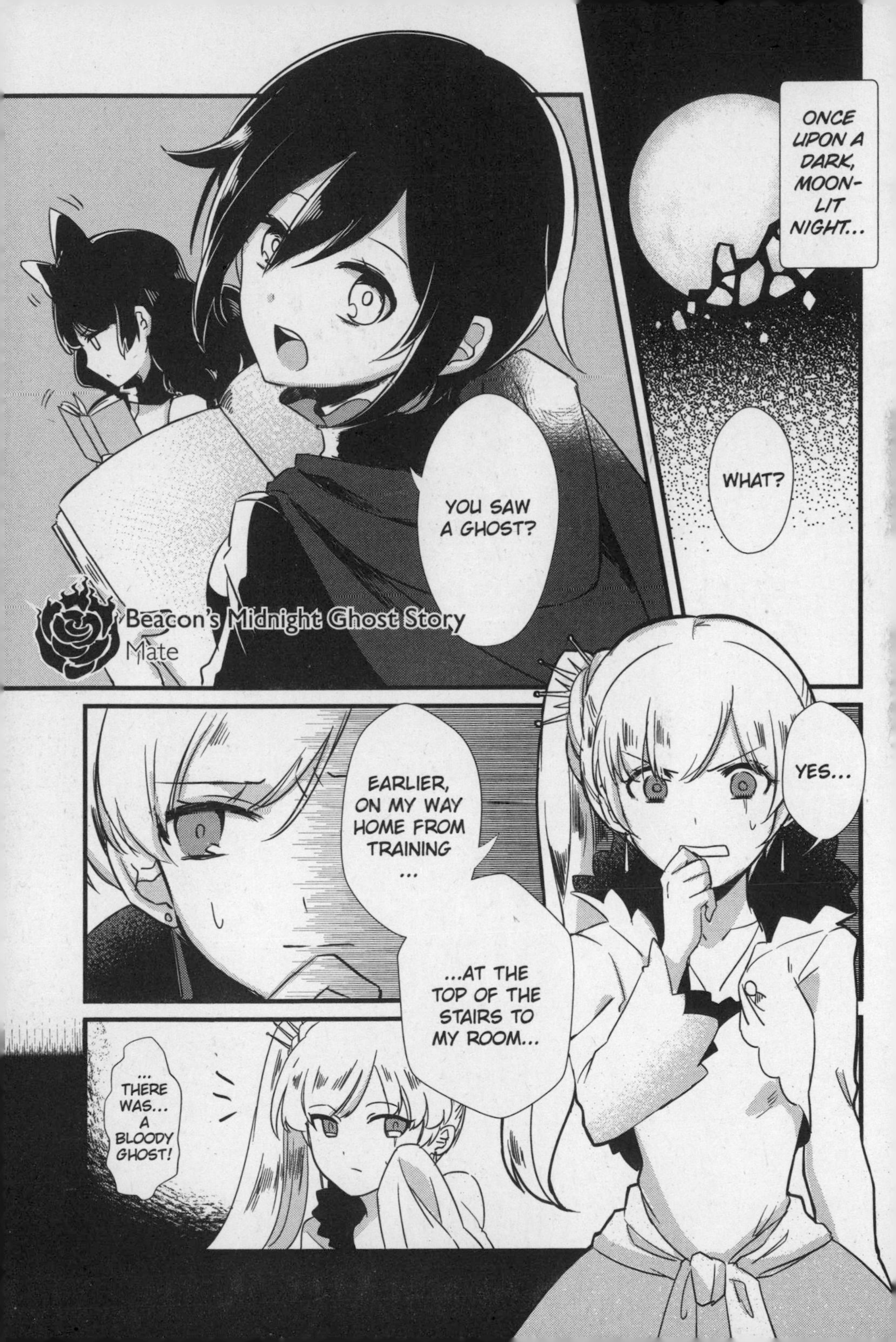
ONCE UPON A DARK, MOON-LIT NIGHT...
WHAT?
YOU SAW A GHOST?
Beacon's Midnight Ghost Story
Mate
YES...
EARLIER, ON MY WAY HOME FROM TRAINING ...
...AT THE TOP OF THE STAIRS TO MY ROOM...
... THERE WAS... A BLOODY GHOST!

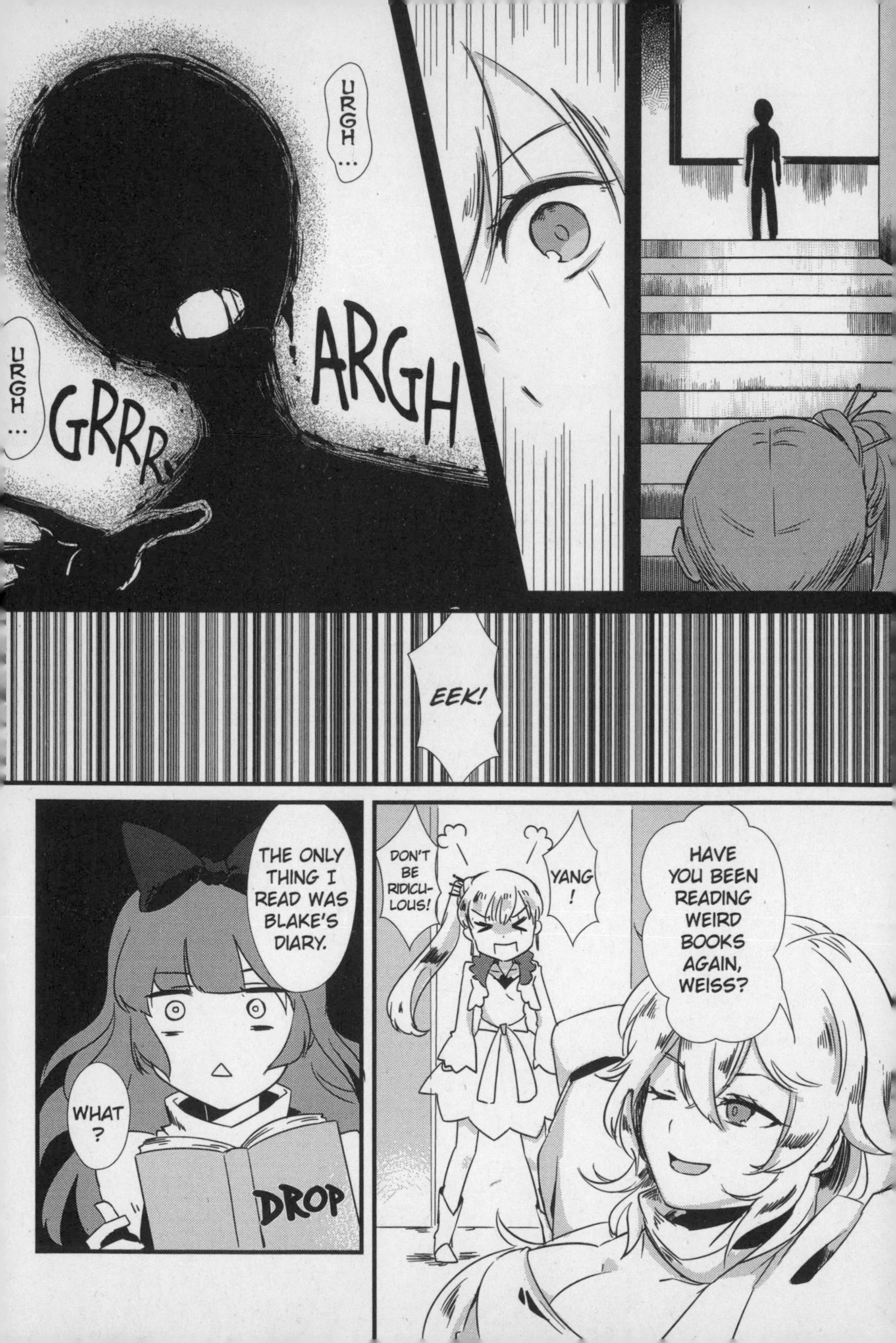
URGH...
ARGH
URGH...
GRRR
EEK!
HAVE YOU BEEN READING WEIRD BOOKS AGAIN, WEISS?
YANG!
DON'T BE RIDICU-LOUS!
THE ONLY THING I READ WAS BLAKE'S DIARY.
WHAT?
DROP

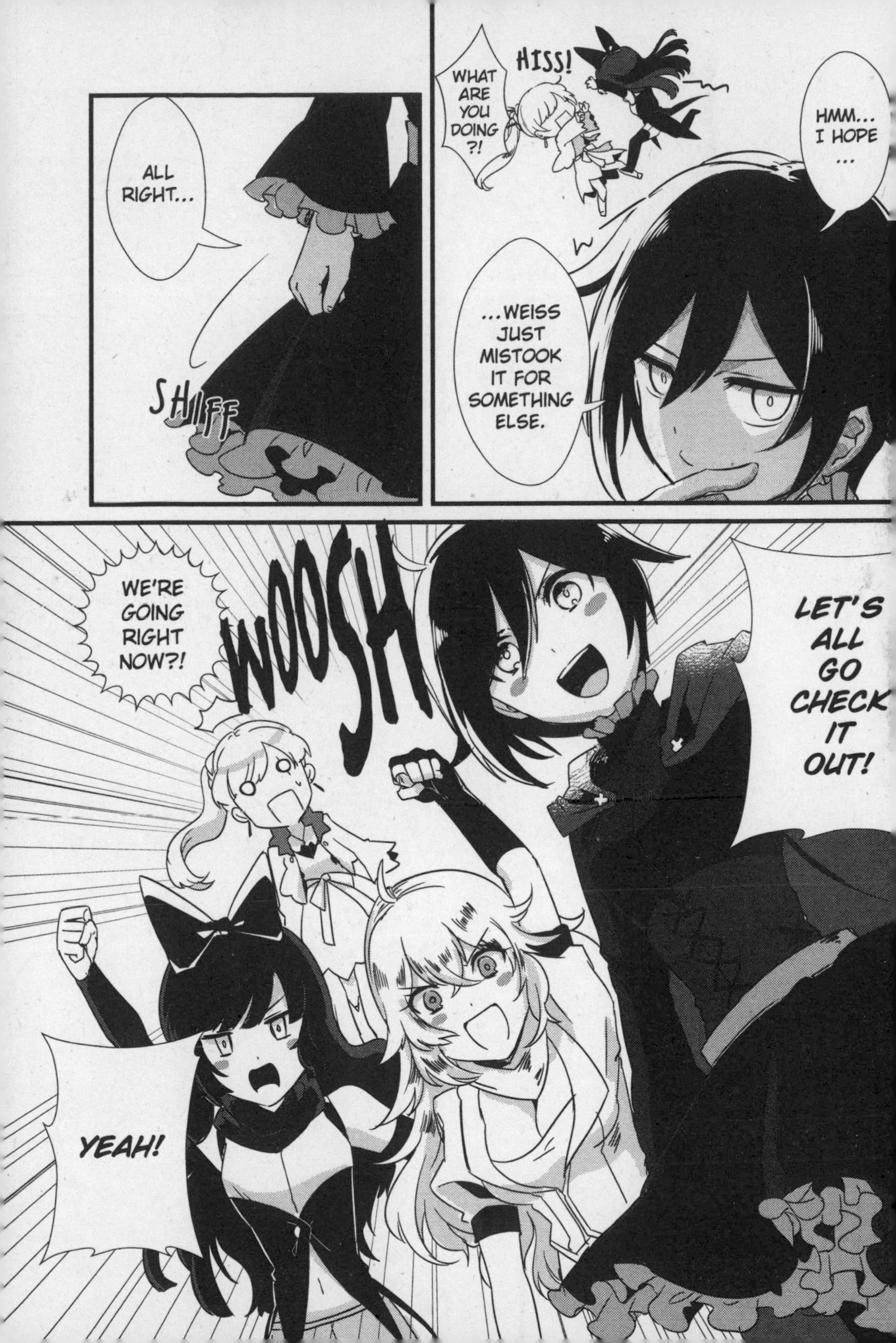
HMM... I HOPE ...
HISS!
WHAT ARE YOU DOING ?!
...WEISS JUST MISTOOK IT FOR SOMETHING ELSE.
ALL RIGHT...
SHIFF
LET'S ALL GO CHECK IT OUT!
WOOSH
WE'RE GOING RIGHT NOW?!
YEAH!

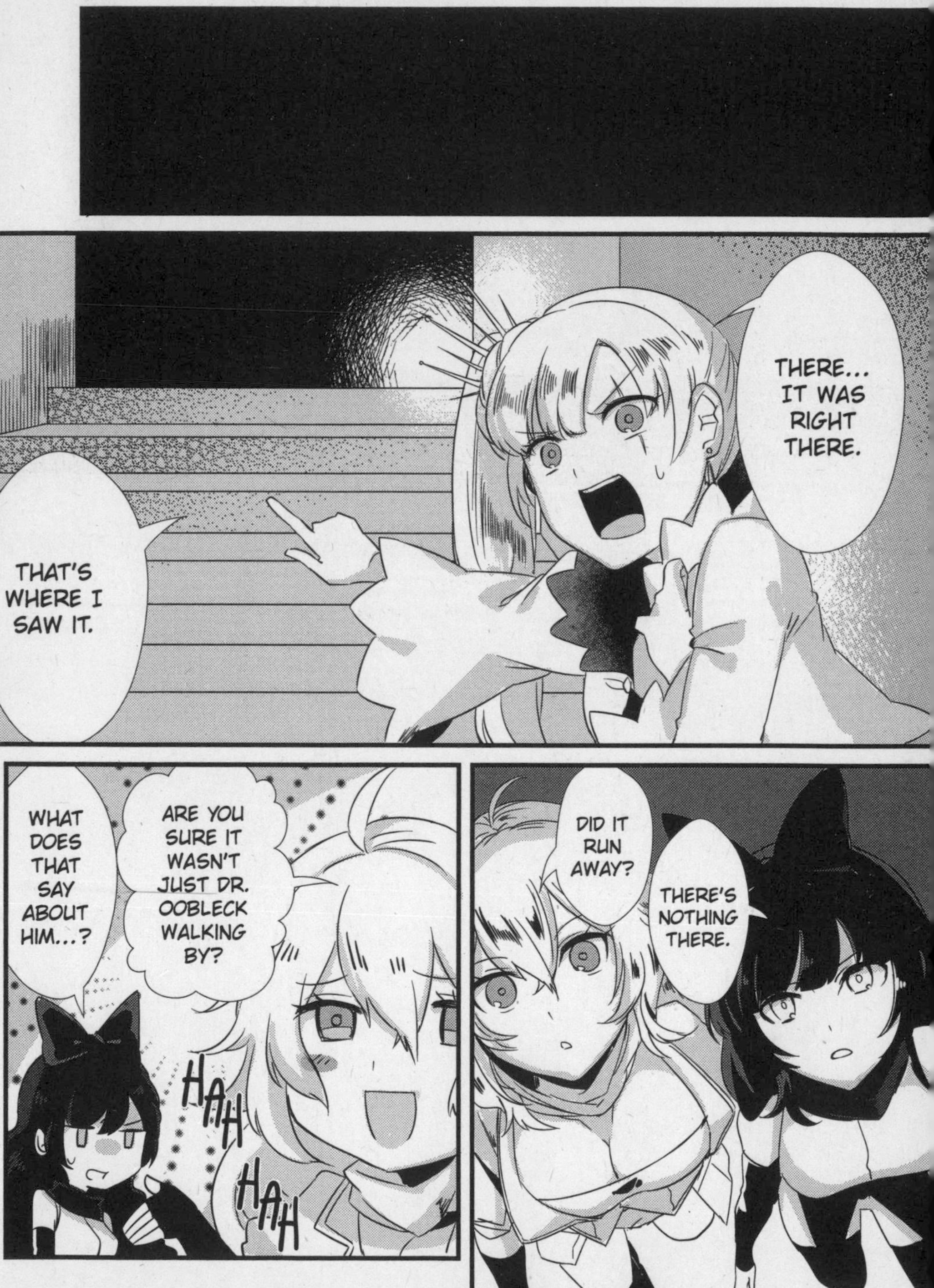
THERE... IT WAS RIGHT THERE.
THAT'S WHERE I SAW IT.
DID IT RUN AWAY?
THERE'S NOTHING THERE.
ARE YOU SURE IT WASN'T JUST DR. OOBLECK WALKING BY?
WHAT DOES THAT SAY ABOUT HIM...?
HAH
HAH

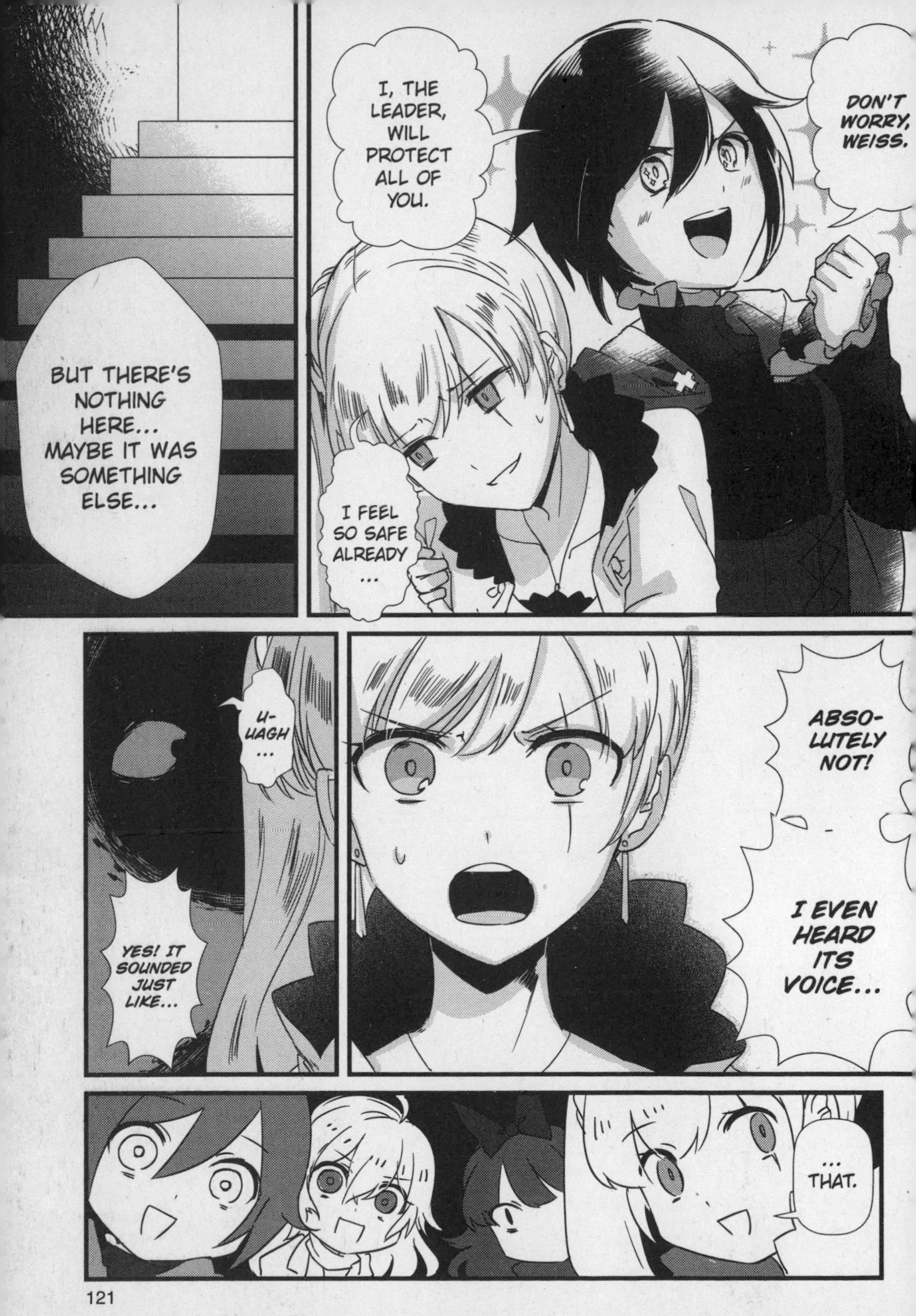
DON'T WORRY, WEISS.
I, THE LEADER, WILL PROTECT ALL OF YOU.
I FEEL SO SAFE ALREADY...
BUT THERE'S NOTHING HERE... MAYBE IT WAS SOMETHING ELSE...
ABSO-LUTELY NOT!
I EVEN HEARD ITS VOICE...
U-UAGH...
YES! IT SOUNDED JUST LIKE...
...THAT.

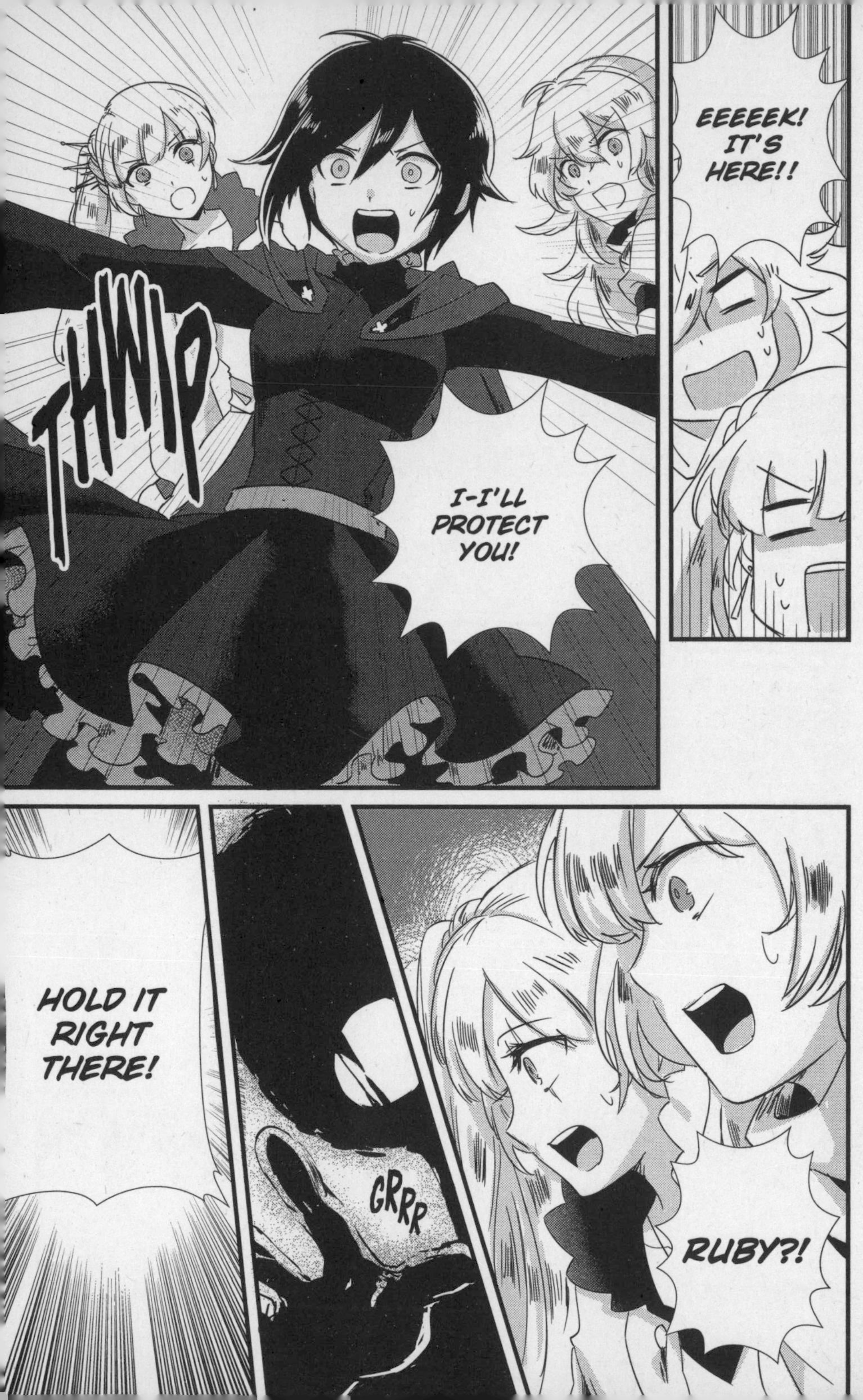
EEEEEK! IT'S HERE!!
THWIP
I-I'LL PROTECT YOU!
RUBY?!
GRRR
HOLD IT RIGHT THERE!

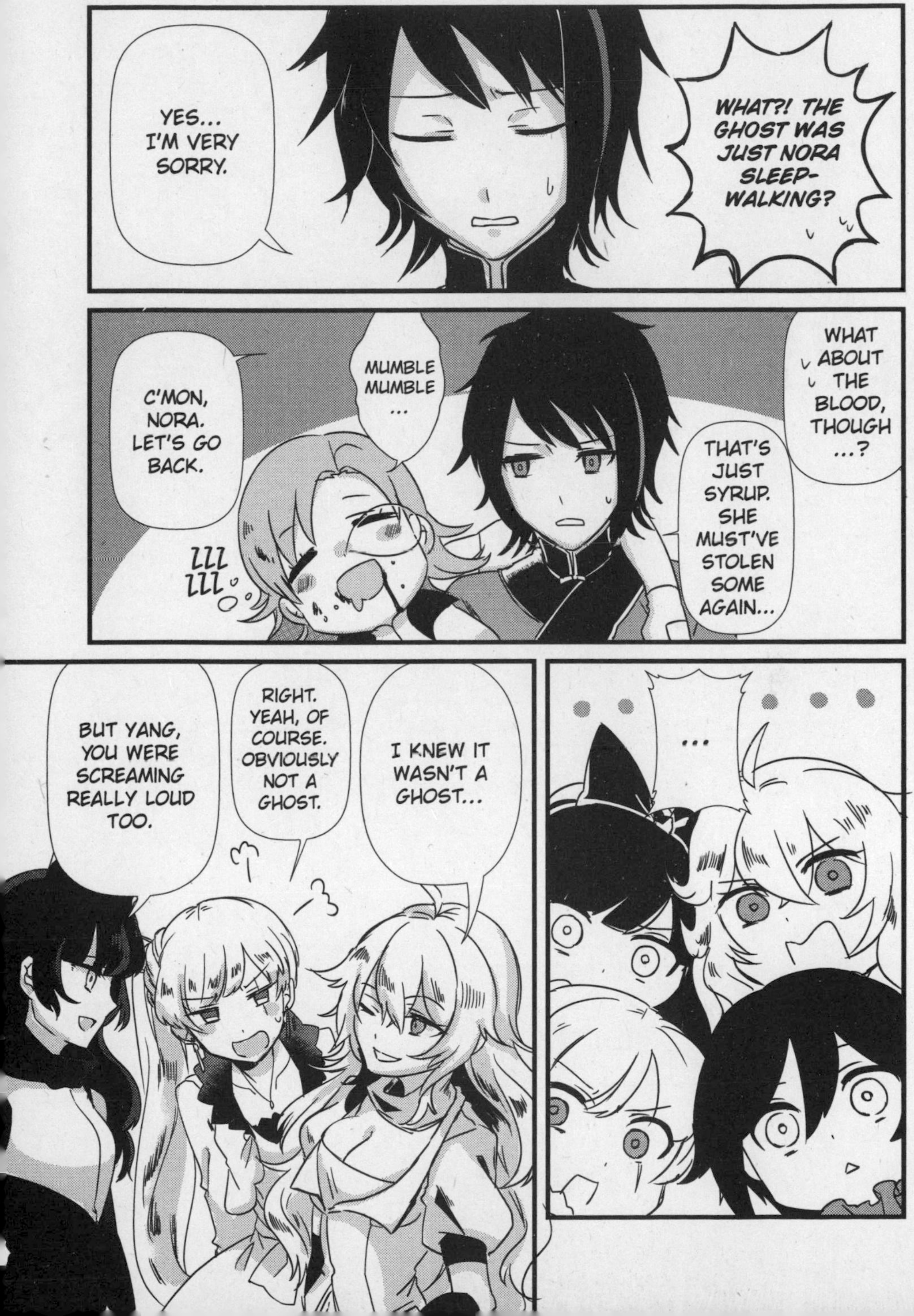
WHAT?! THE GHOST WAS JUST NORA SLEEP-WALKING?
YES... I'M VERY SORRY.
WHAT ABOUT THE BLOOD, THOUGH...?
THAT'S JUST SYRUP. SHE MUST'VE STOLEN SOME AGAIN...
MUMBLE MUMBLE ...
ZZZ ZZZ
C'MON, NORA. LET'S GO BACK.
...
I KNEW IT WASN'T A GHOST...
RIGHT. YEAH, OF COURSE. OBVIOUSLY NOT A GHOST.
BUT YANG, YOU WERE SCREAMING REALLY LOUD TOO.

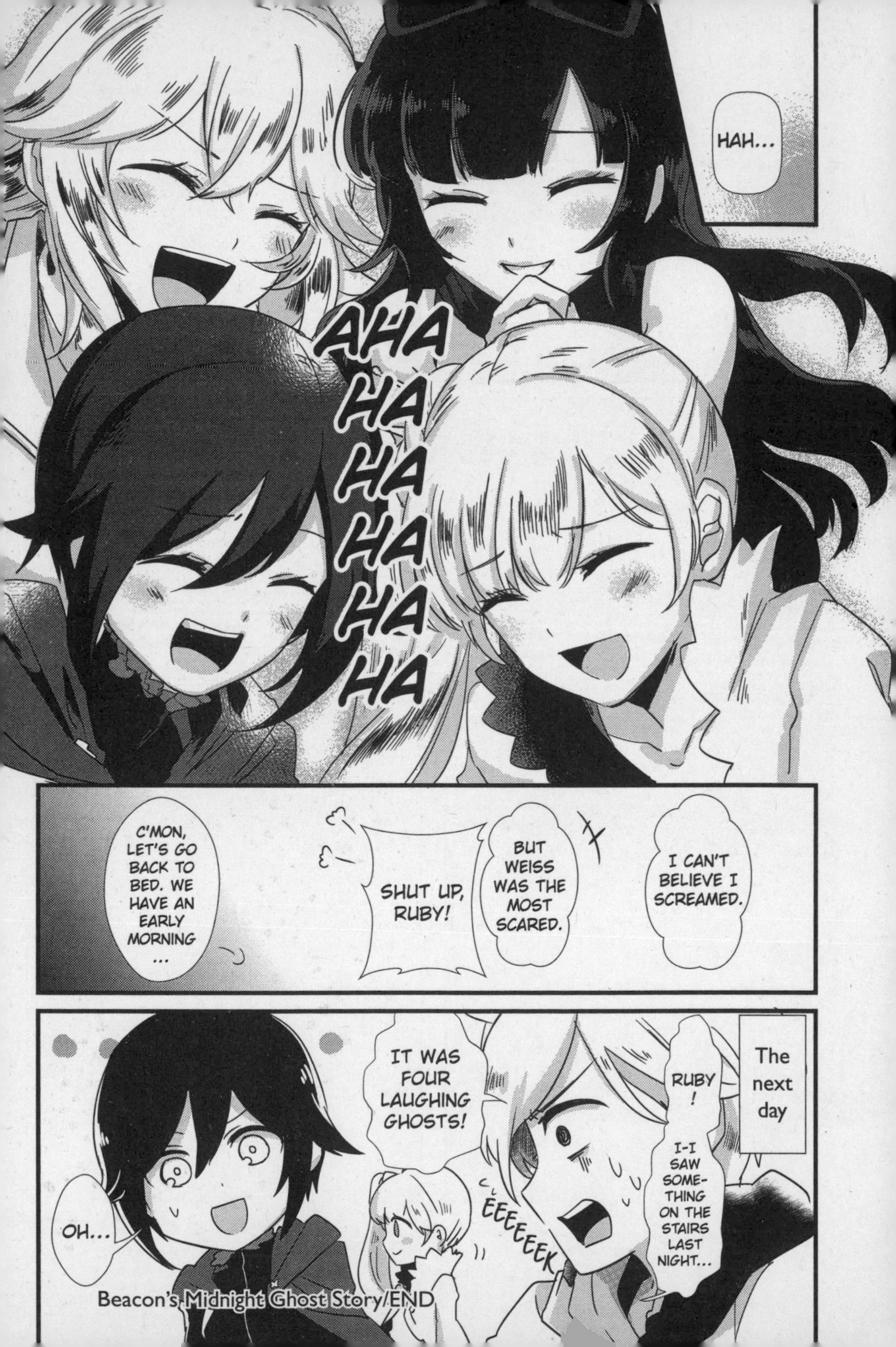
HAH...
AHA HA HA HA HA HA
I CAN'T BELIEVE I SCREAMED.
BUT WEISS WAS THE MOST SCARED.
SHUT UP, RUBY!
C'MON, LET'S GO BACK TO BED. WE HAVE AN EARLY MORNING ...
The next day
RUBY!
I-I SAW SOME-THING ON THE STAIRS LAST NIGHT...
EEEEEEK
IT WAS FOUR LAUGHING GHOSTS!
OH...
Beacon's Midnight Ghost Story/END

Beacon Days (Ruby)

Mojojoj

His Name Was Sid

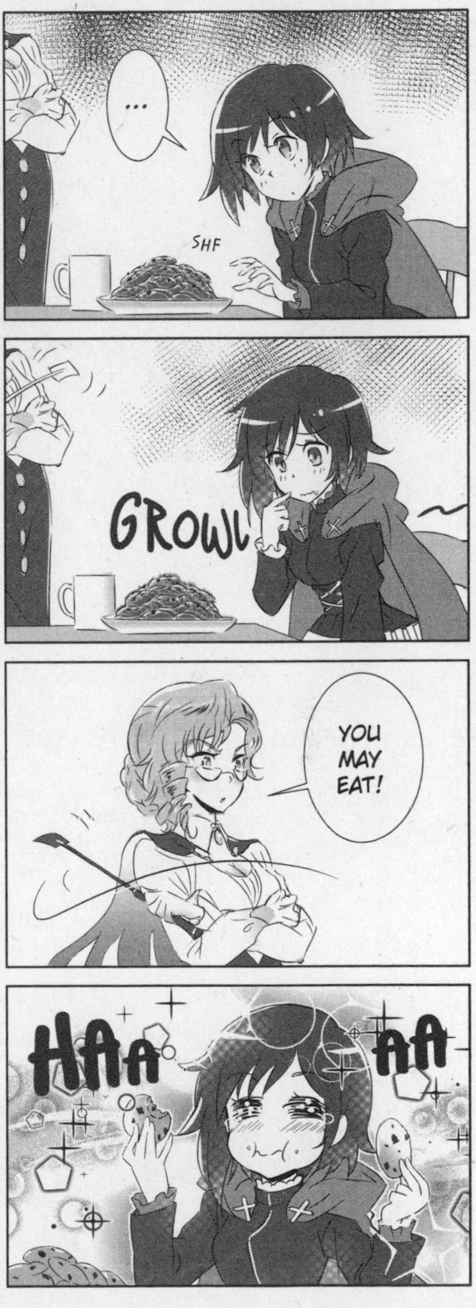
...
SHF
GROWL
YOU MAY EAT!
HAA
AA

Moonlight

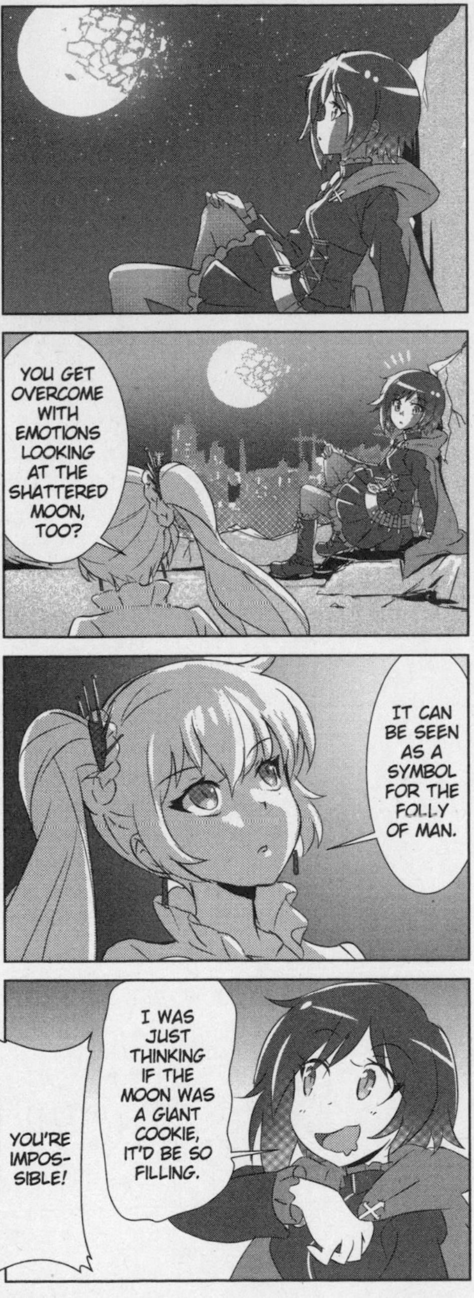
YOU GET OVERCOME WITH EMOTIONS LOOKING AT THE SHATTERED MOON, TOO?
IT CAN BE SEEN AS A SYMBOL FOR THE FOLLY OF MAN.
I WAS JUST THINKING IF THE MOON WAS A GIANT COOKIE, IT'D BE SO FILLING.
YOU'RE IMPOSSIBLE!

Team Leader

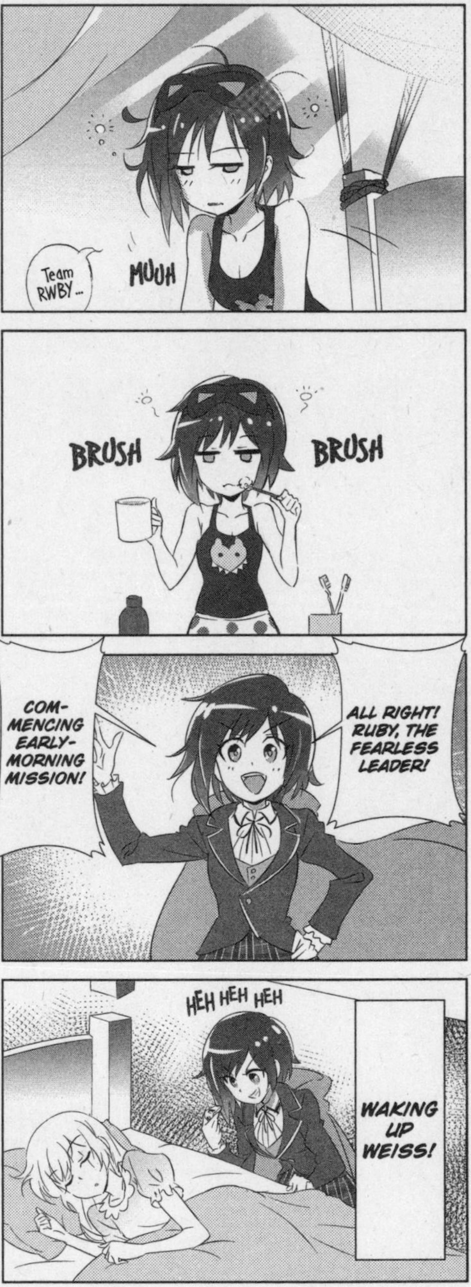
MUUH
Team RWBY...
BRUSH
BRUSH
ALL RIGHT! RUBY, THE FEARLESS LEADER!
COMMENCING EARLY-MORNING MISSION!
HEH HEH HEH
WAKING UP WEISS!

Speech

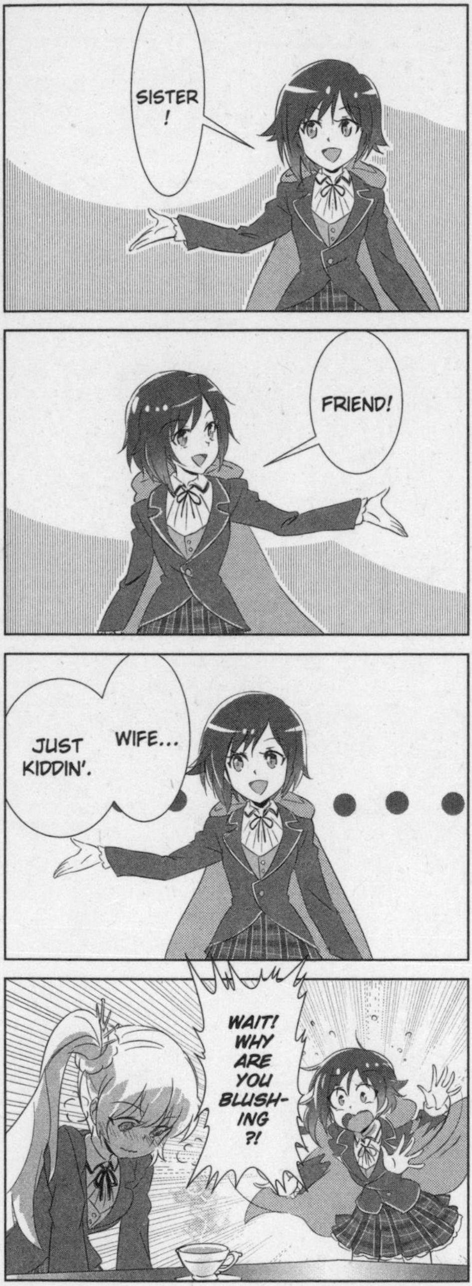
SISTER!
FRIEND!
WIFE...
JUST KIDDIN'.
WAIT! WHY ARE YOU BLUSHING?!

Different Version

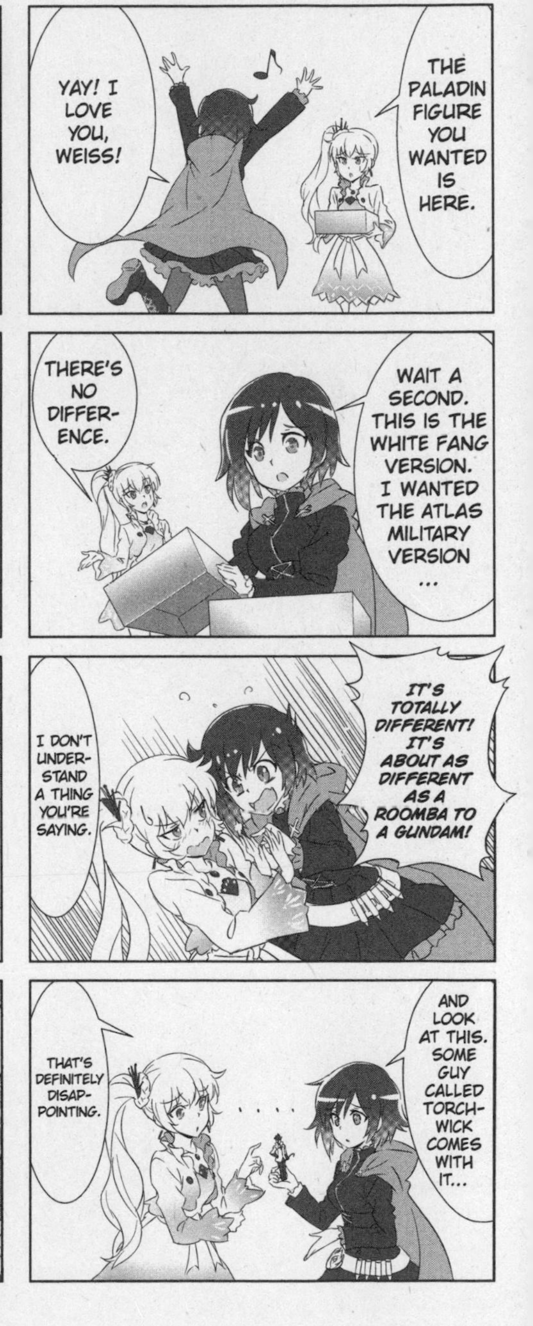
THE PALADIN FIGURE YOU WANTED IS HERE.
YAY! I LOVE YOU, WEISS!
WAIT A SECOND. THIS IS THE WHITE FANG VERSION. I WANTED THE ATLAS MILITARY VERSION ...
THERE'S NO DIFFERENCE.
IT'S TOTALLY DIFFERENT! IT'S ABOUT AS DIFFERENT AS A ROOMBA TO A GUNDAM!
I DON'T UNDERSTAND A THING YOU'RE SAYING.
AND LOOK AT THIS. SOME GUY CALLED TORCHWICK COMES WITH IT...
....
THAT'S DEFINITELY DISAPPOINTING.

Torchwick Guy

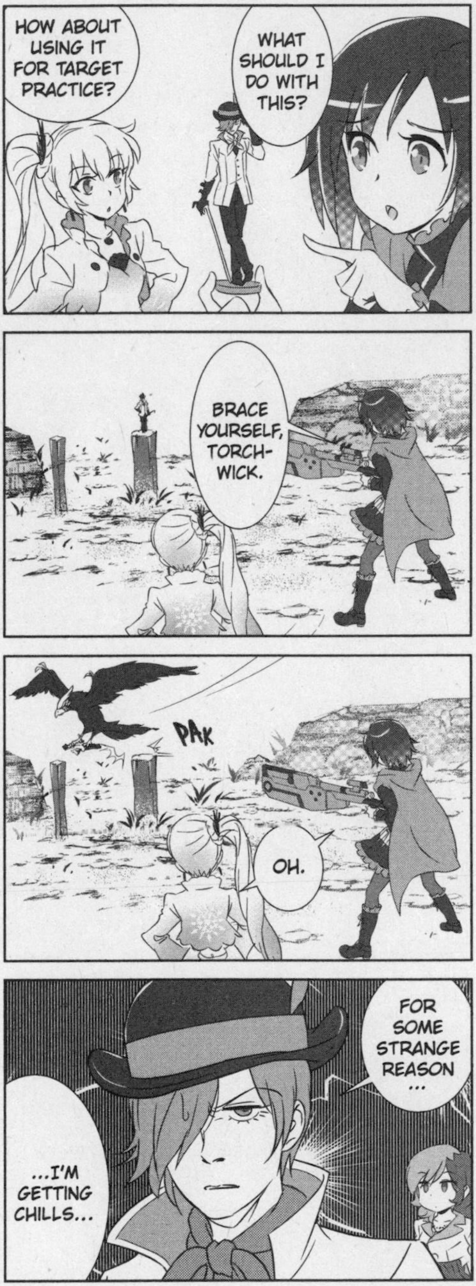
WHAT SHOULD I DO WITH THIS?
HOW ABOUT USING IT FOR TARGET PRACTICE?
BRACE YOURSELF, TORCHWICK.
PAK
OH.
FOR SOME STRANGE REASON ...
...I'M GETTING CHILLS...

Girl Talk

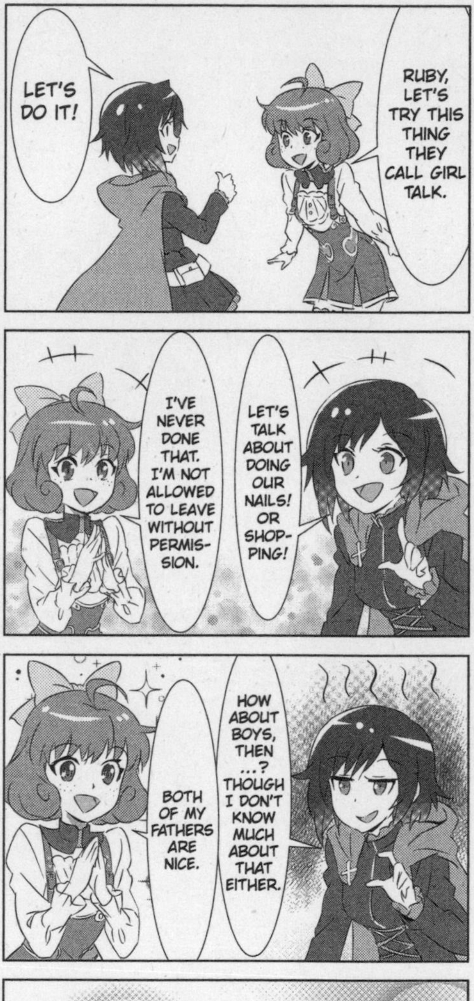
RUBY, LET'S TRY THIS THING THEY CALL GIRL TALK.
LET'S DO IT!
LET'S TALK ABOUT DOING OUR NAILS! OR SHOP-PING!
I'VE NEVER DONE THAT. I'M NOT ALLOWED TO LEAVE WITHOUT PERMIS-SION.
HOW ABOUT BOYS, THEN ...? THOUGH I DON'T KNOW MUCH ABOUT THAT EITHER.
BOTH OF MY FATHERS ARE NICE.
IN THE END...
...THEY TALKED ABOUT WEAPONS.

17-Year-Old High School Girl

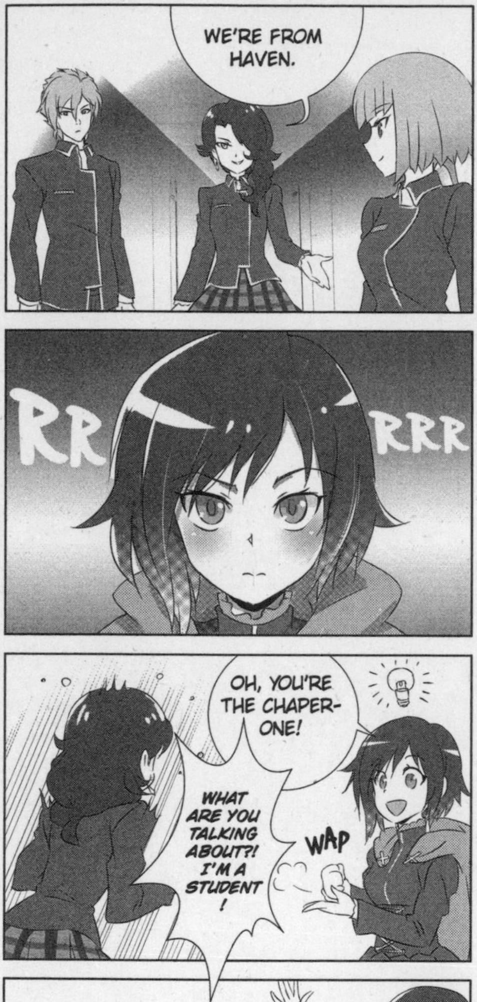
WE'RE FROM HAVEN.
RRR
RR
OH, YOU'RE THE CHAPER-ONE!
WAP
WHAT ARE YOU TALKING ABOUT?! I'M A STUDENT!
SHE MUST'VE REPEATED A YEAR ...

Beacon Days (Ruby)/END

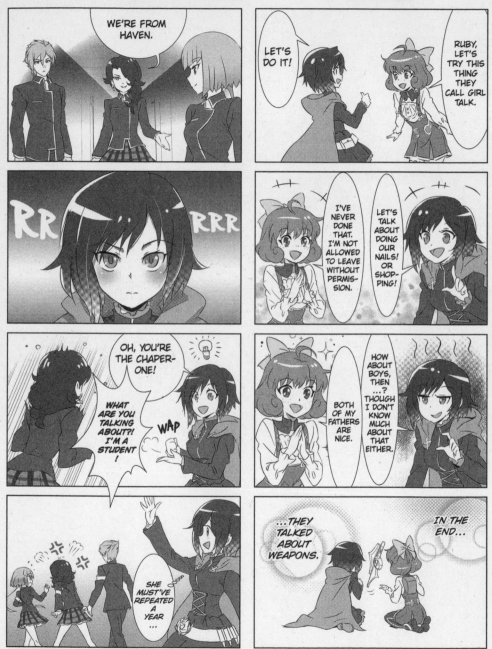

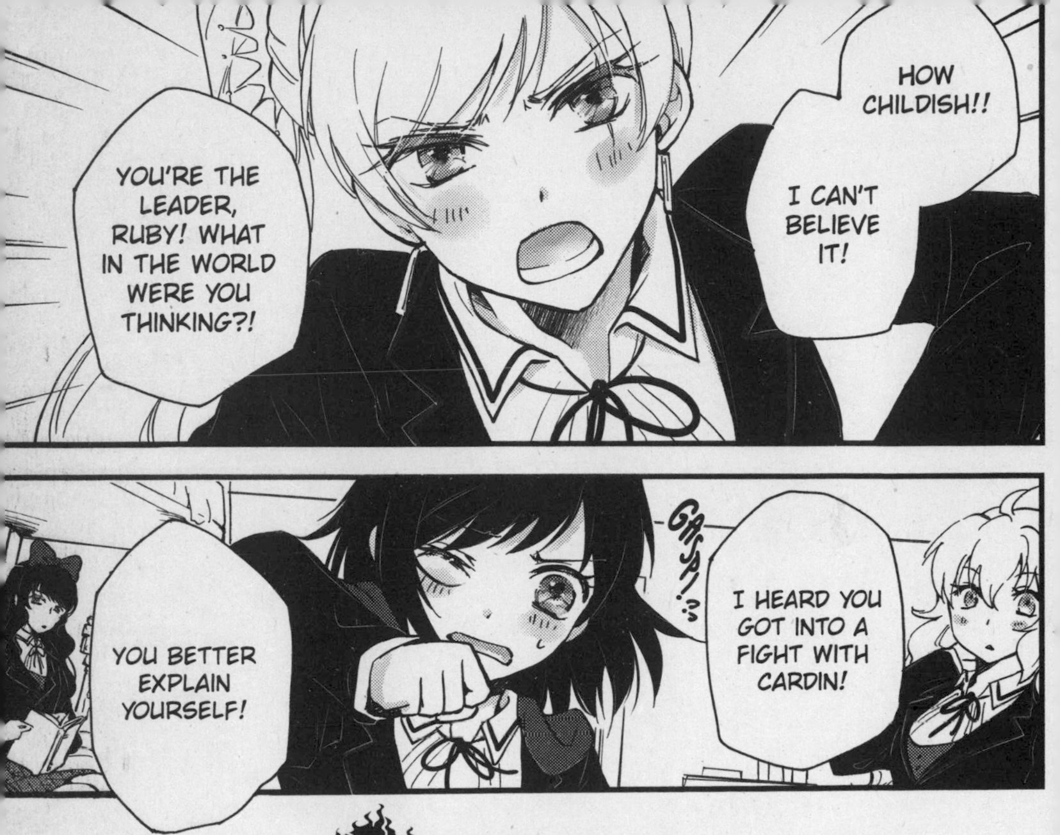
HOW CHILDISH!!
I CAN'T BELIEVE IT!
YOU'RE THE LEADER, RUBY! WHAT IN THE WORLD WERE YOU THINKING?!
GASP!?
I HEARD YOU GOT INTO A FIGHT WITH CARDIN!
YOU BETTER EXPLAIN YOURSELF!

Just Trying to Help

Amechan

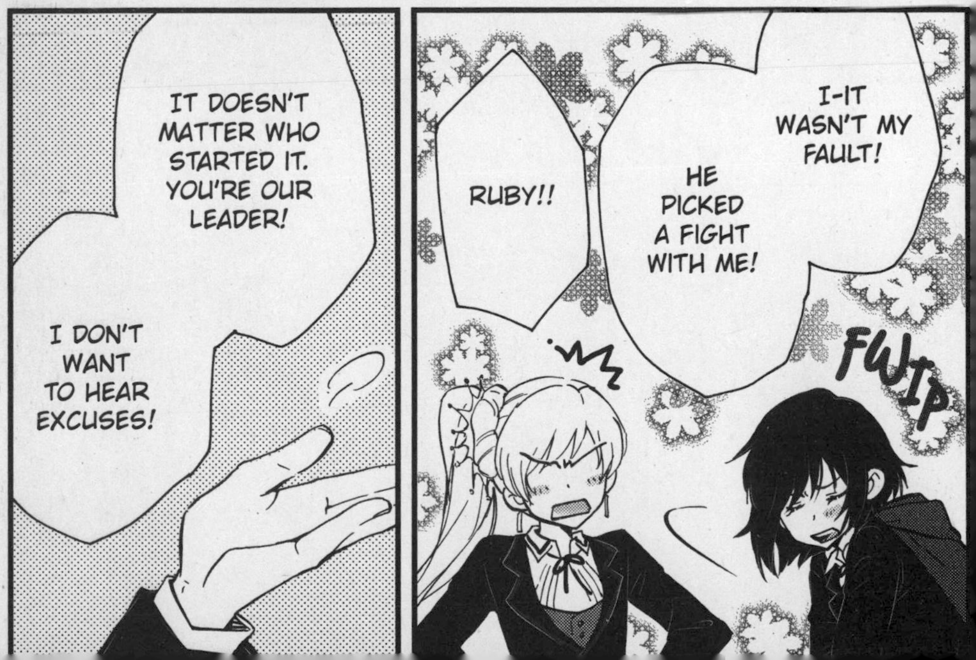
I-IT WASN'T MY FAULT!
HE PICKED A FIGHT WITH ME!
RUBY!!
FWIP
IT DOESN'T MATTER WHO STARTED IT. YOU'RE OUR LEADER!
I DON'T WANT TO HEAR EXCUSES!

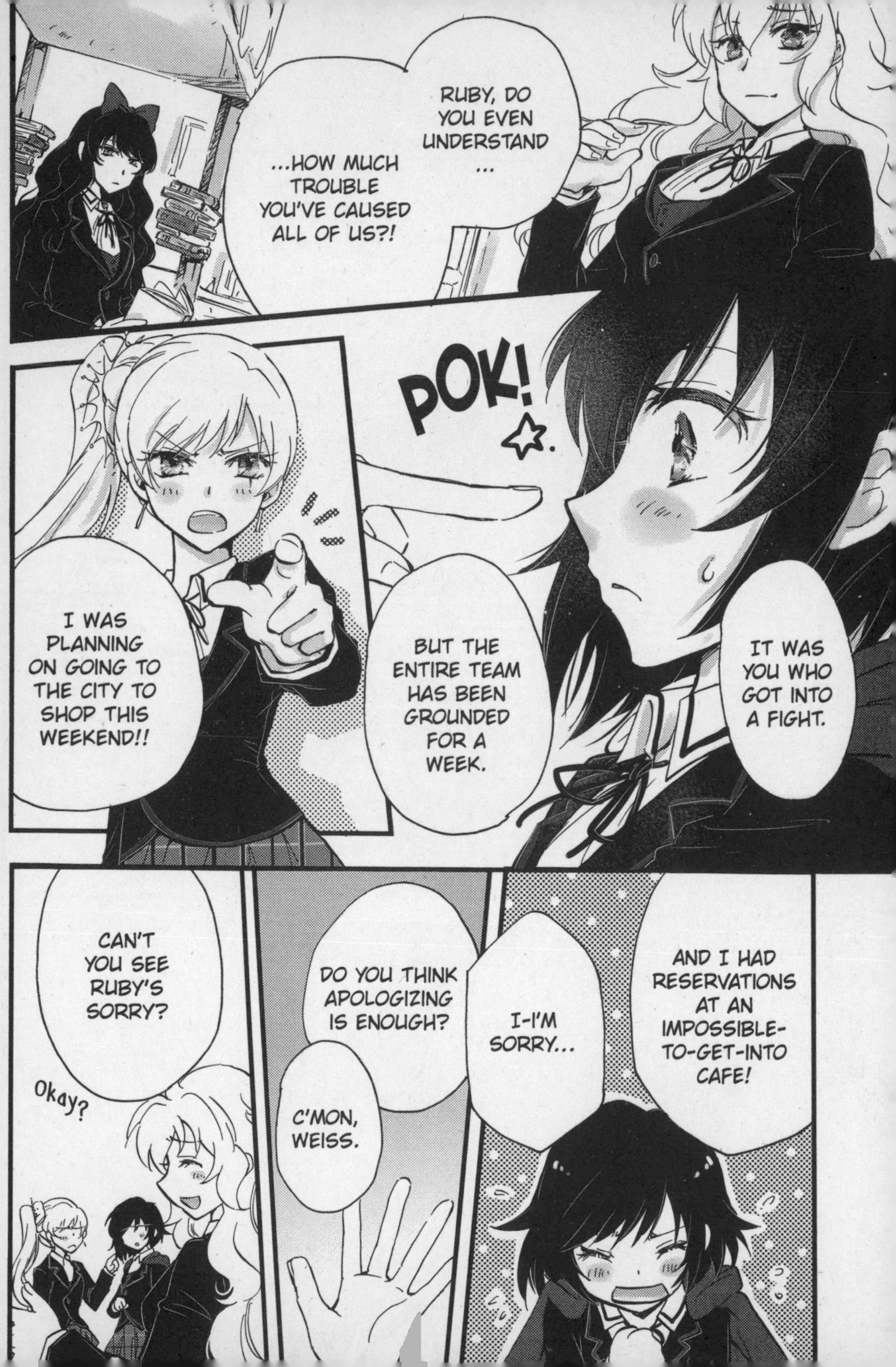
RUBY, DO YOU EVEN UNDERSTAND ...
...HOW MUCH TROUBLE YOU'VE CAUSED ALL OF US?!
POK!
IT WAS YOU WHO GOT INTO A FIGHT.
BUT THE ENTIRE TEAM HAS BEEN GROUNDED FOR A WEEK.
I WAS PLANNING ON GOING TO THE CITY TO SHOP THIS WEEKEND!!
AND I HAD RESERVATIONS AT AN IMPOSSIBLE-TO-GET-INTO CAFE!
I-I'M SORRY...
DO YOU THINK APOLOGIZING IS ENOUGH?
C'MON, WEISS.
CAN'T YOU SEE RUBY'S SORRY?
Okay?

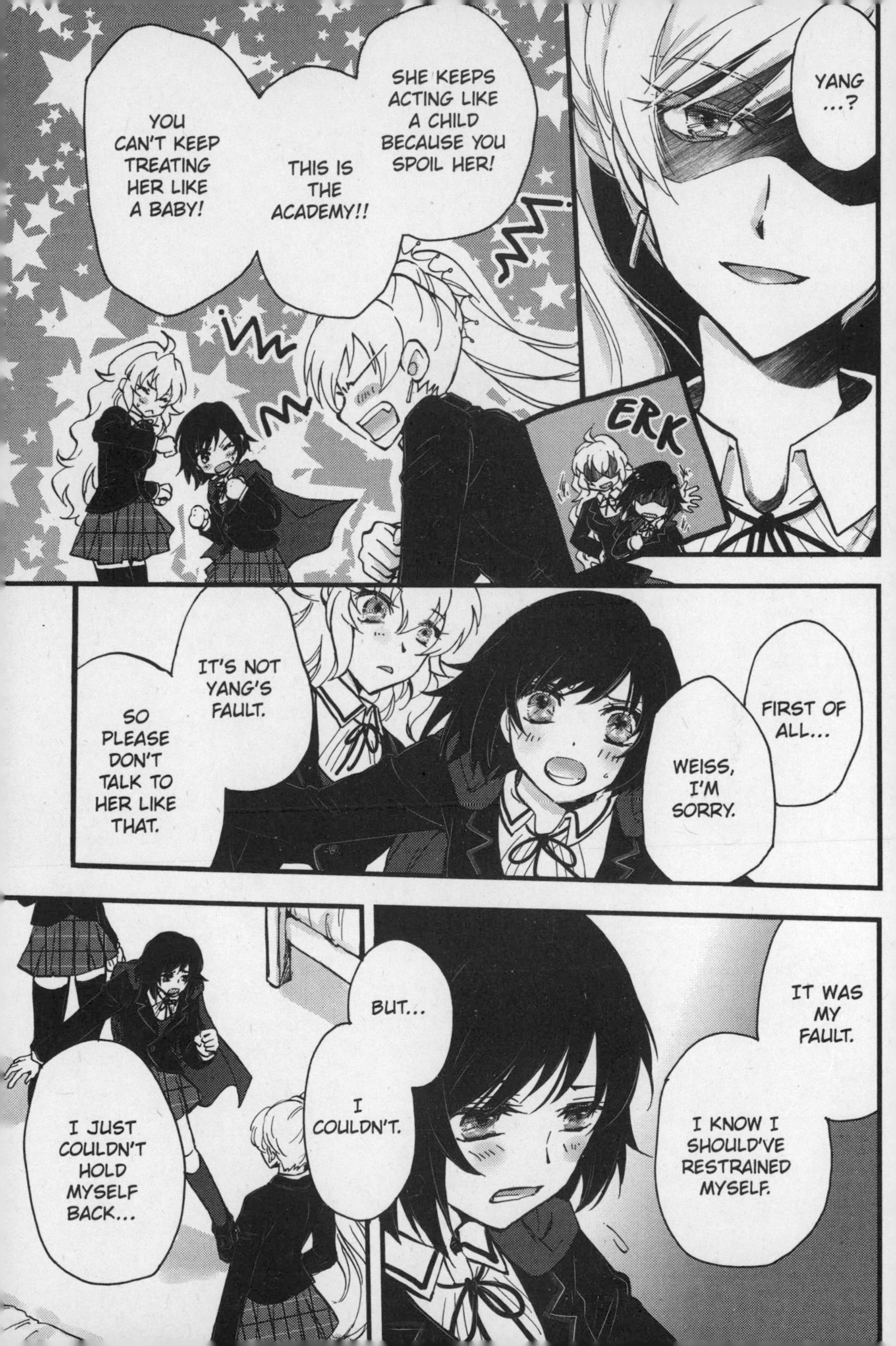
YANG ...?
ERK
SHE KEEPS ACTING LIKE A CHILD BECAUSE YOU SPOIL HER!
THIS IS THE ACADEMY!!
YOU CAN'T KEEP TREATING HER LIKE A BABY!
FIRST OF ALL...
WEISS, I'M SORRY.
IT'S NOT YANG'S FAULT.
SO PLEASE DON'T TALK TO HER LIKE THAT.
IT WAS MY FAULT.
I KNOW I SHOULD'VE RESTRAINED MYSELF.
BUT...
I COULDN'T.
I JUST COULDN'T HOLD MYSELF BACK...

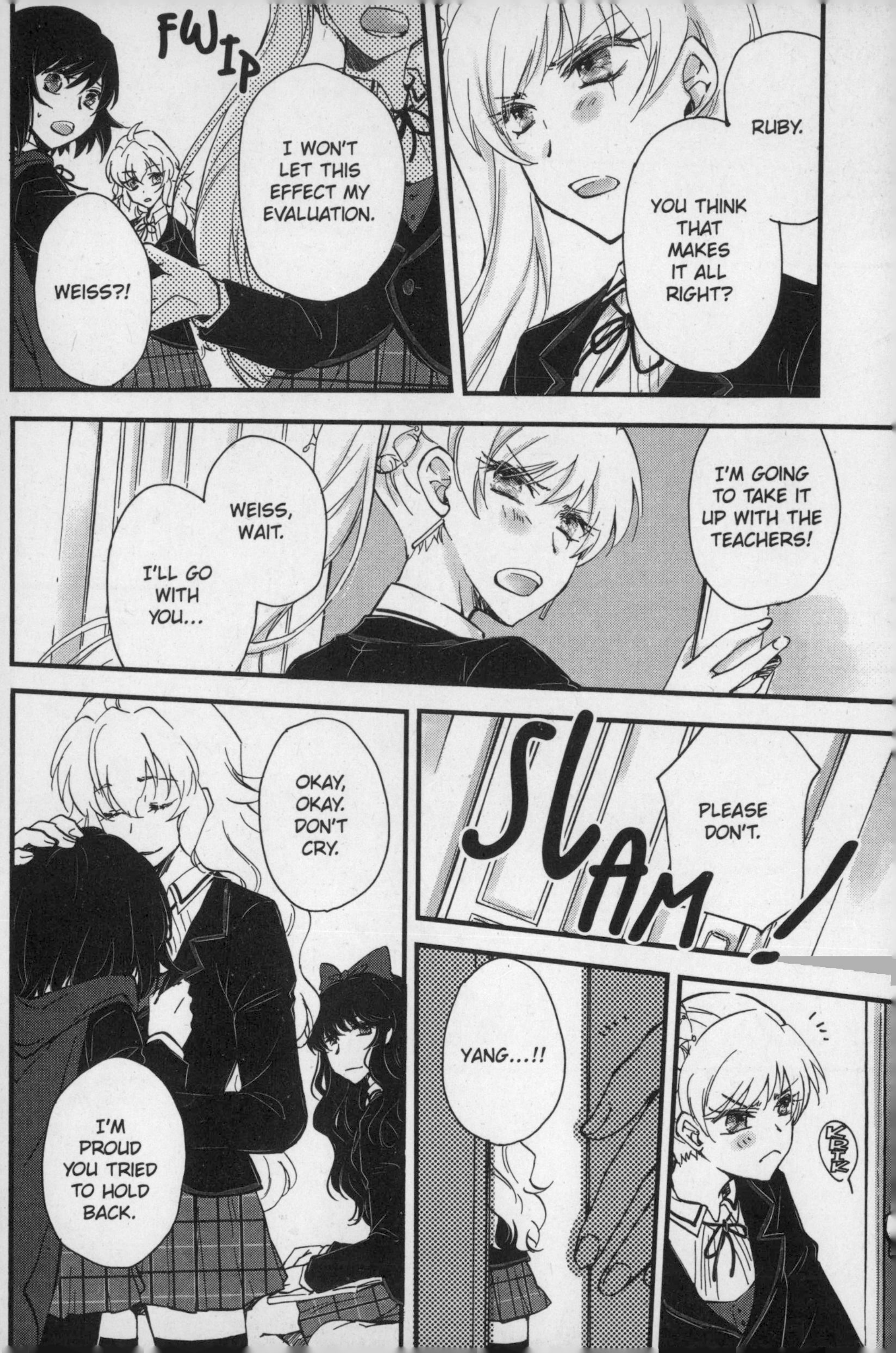
RUBY.
YOU THINK THAT MAKES IT ALL RIGHT?
FWIP
I WON'T LET THIS EFFECT MY EVALUATION.
WEISS?!
I'M GOING TO TAKE IT UP WITH THE TEACHERS!
WEISS, WAIT.
I'LL GO WITH YOU...
PLEASE DON'T.
SLAM!
KRIK
YANG...!!
OKAY, OKAY. DON'T CRY.
I'M PROUD YOU TRIED TO HOLD BACK.

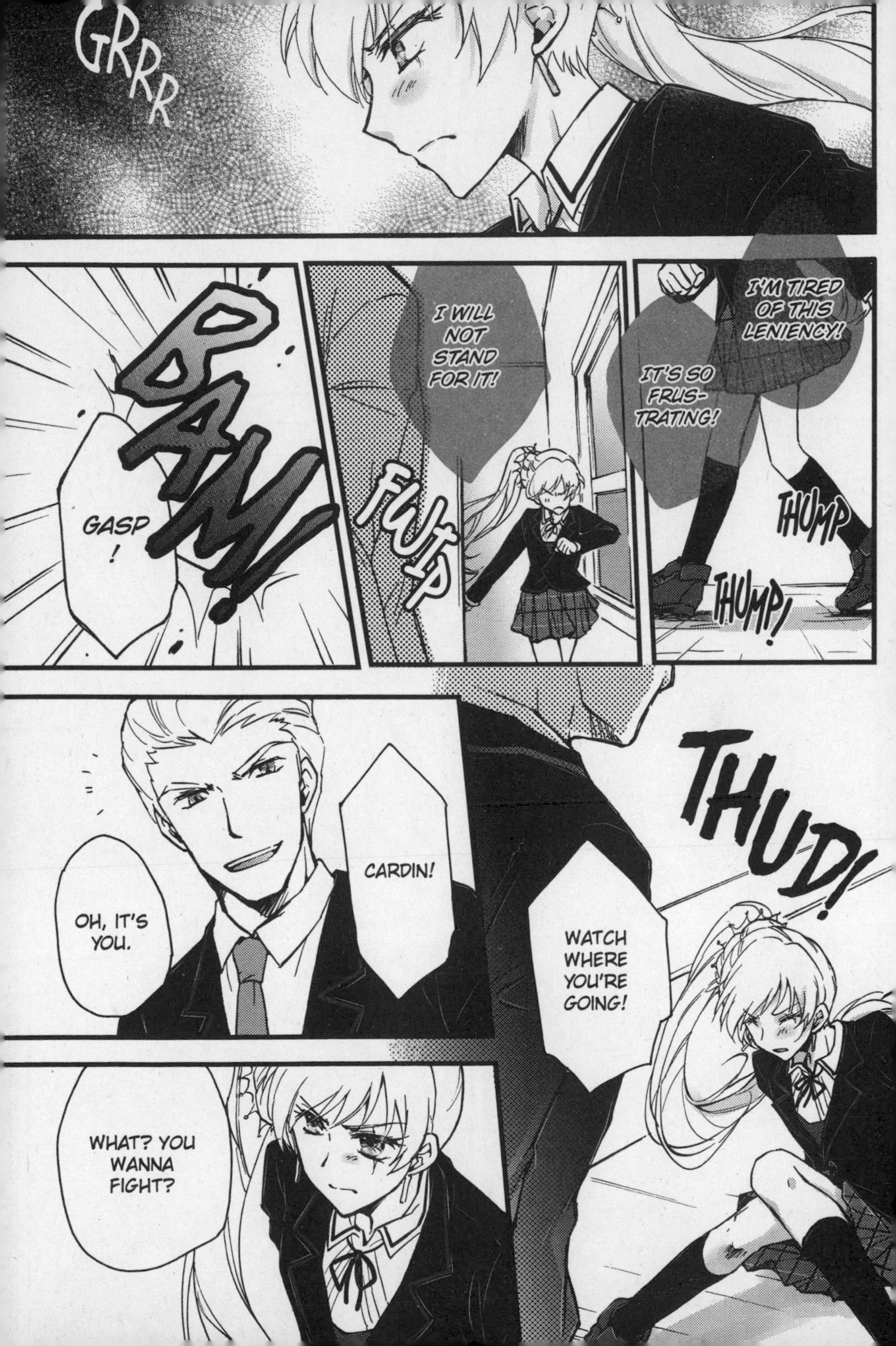
GRRRR
I'M TIRED OF THIS LENIENCY!
IT'S SO FRUS-TRATING!
THUMP
THUMP!
I WILL NOT STAND FOR IT!
FWIP
BAM!
GASP!
THUD!
WATCH WHERE YOU'RE GOING!
CARDIN!
OH, IT'S YOU.
WHAT? YOU WANNA FIGHT?

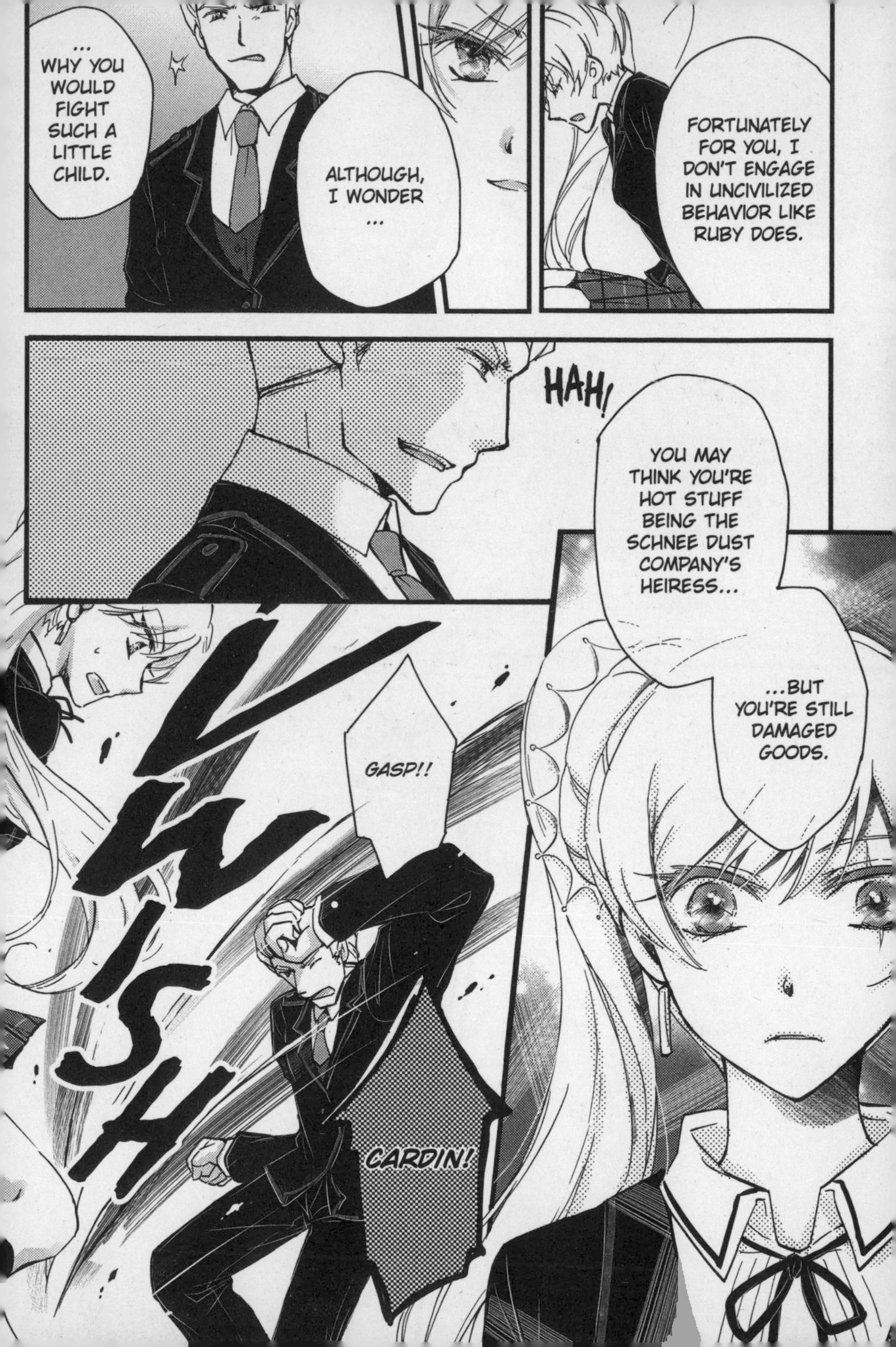
FORTUNATELY FOR YOU, I DON'T ENGAGE IN UNCIVILIZED BEHAVIOR LIKE RUBY DOES.
ALTHOUGH, I WONDER ...
... WHY YOU WOULD FIGHT SUCH A LITTLE CHILD.
HAH!
YOU MAY THINK YOU'RE HOT STUFF BEING THE SCHNEE DUST COMPANY'S HEIRESS...
...BUT YOU'RE STILL DAMAGED GOODS.
GASP!!
CARDIN!

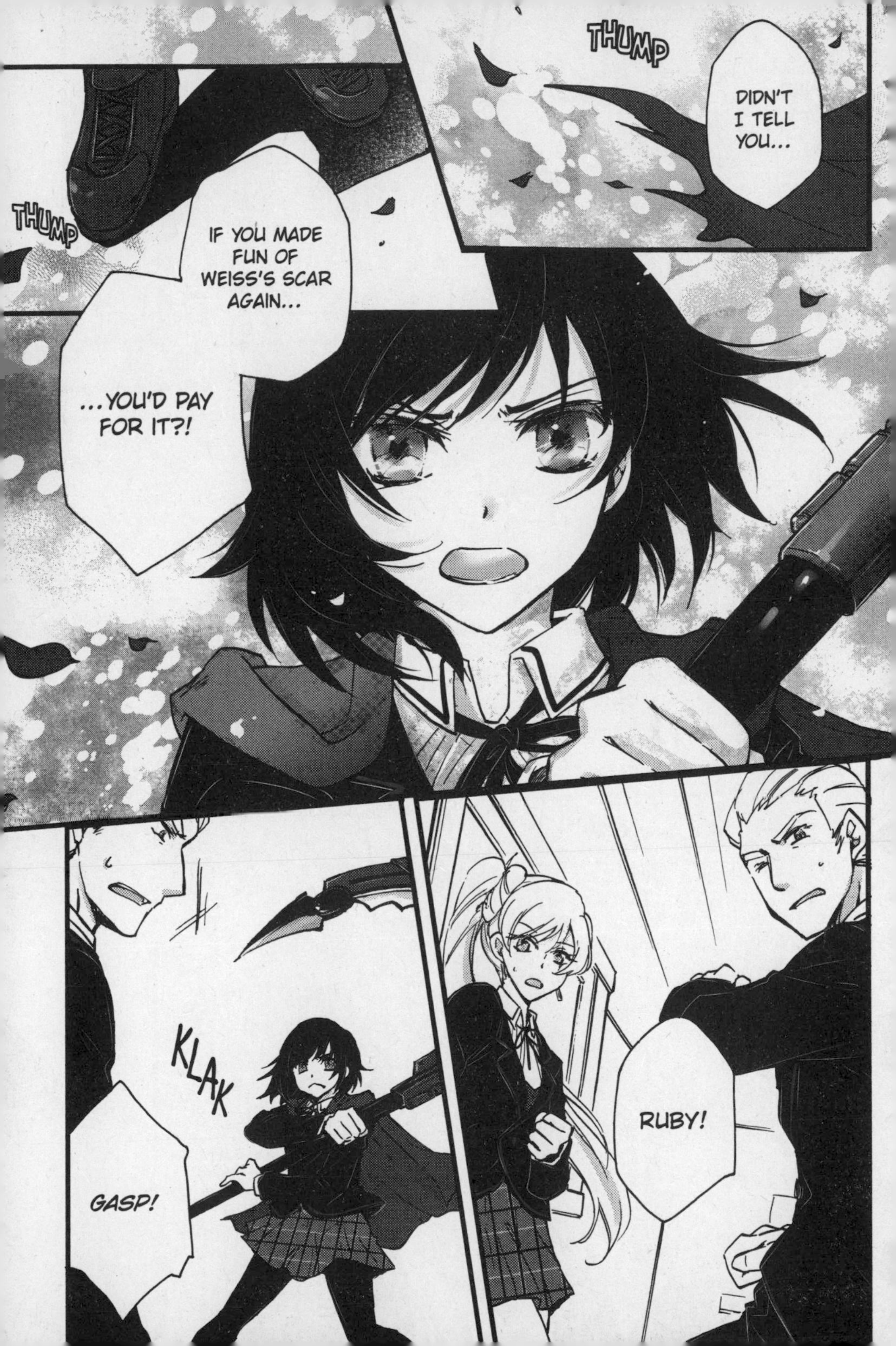
THUMP
DIDN'T I TELL YOU...
THUMP
IF YOU MADE FUN OF WEISS'S SCAR AGAIN...
...YOU'D PAY FOR IT?!
RUBY!
KLAK
GASP!

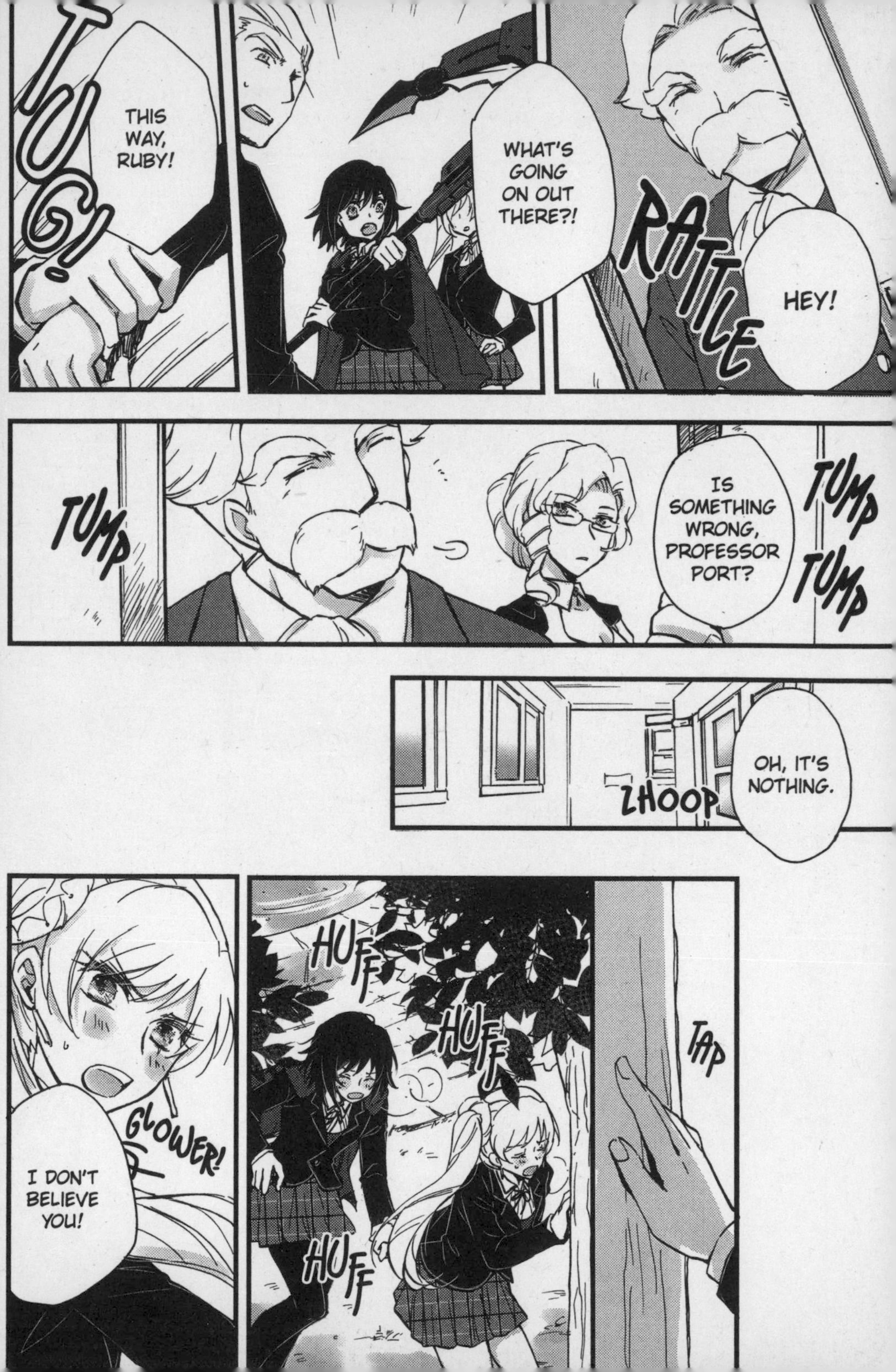
RATTLE
HEY!
WHAT'S GOING ON OUT THERE?!
THIS WAY, RUBY!
TUG!
TUMP
TUMP
IS SOMETHING WRONG, PROFESSOR PORT?
TUMP
ZHOOP
OH, IT'S NOTHING.
TAP
HUFF
HUFF
HUFF
GLOWER!
I DON'T BELIEVE YOU!

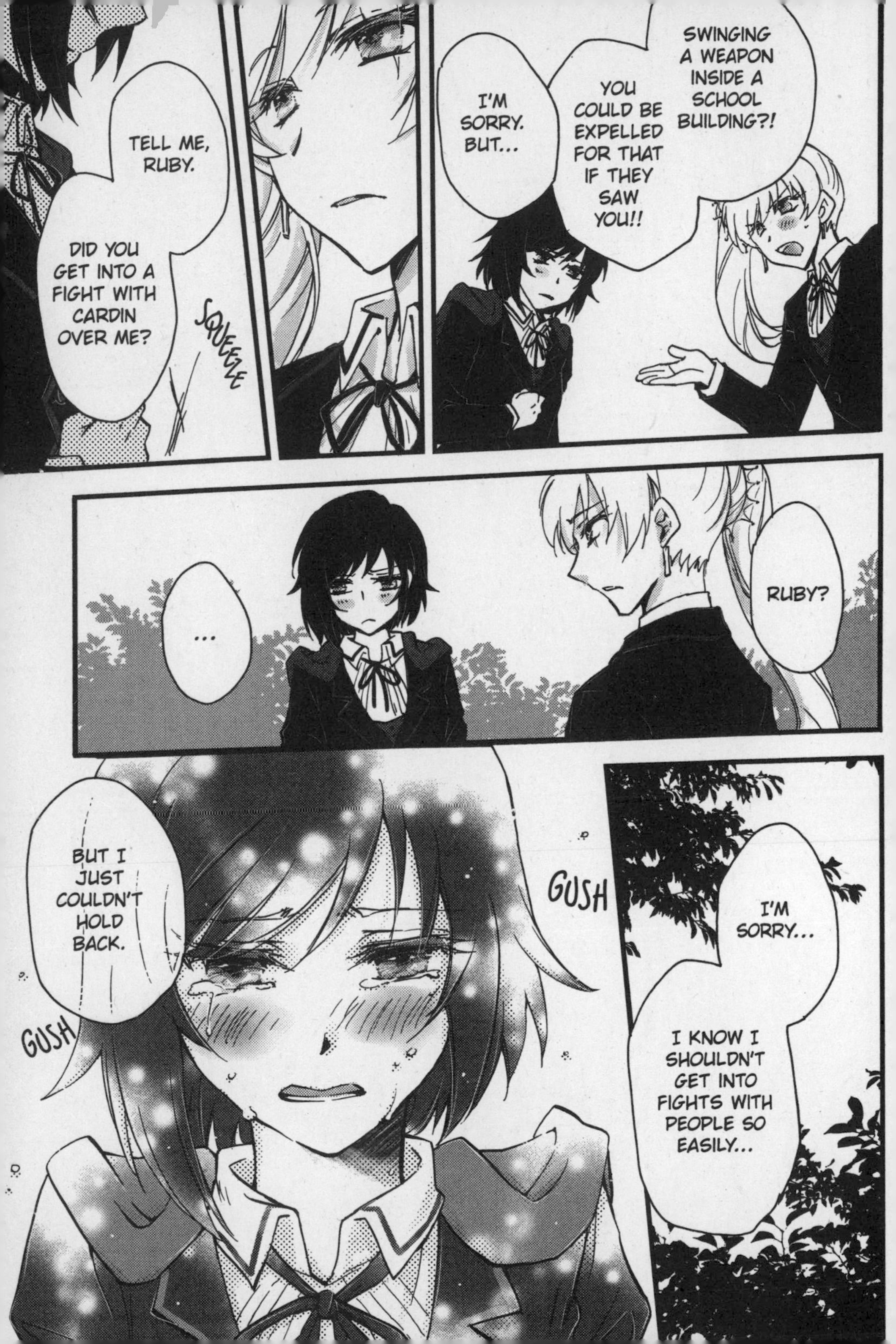
SWINGING A WEAPON INSIDE A SCHOOL BUILDING?!
YOU COULD BE EXPELLED FOR THAT IF THEY SAW YOU!!
I'M SORRY. BUT...
SQUEEZE
TELL ME, RUBY.
DID YOU GET INTO A FIGHT WITH CARDIN OVER ME?
RUBY?
...
I'M SORRY...
I KNOW I SHOULDN'T GET INTO FIGHTS WITH PEOPLE SO EASILY...
GUSH
BUT I JUST COULDN'T HOLD BACK.
GUSH

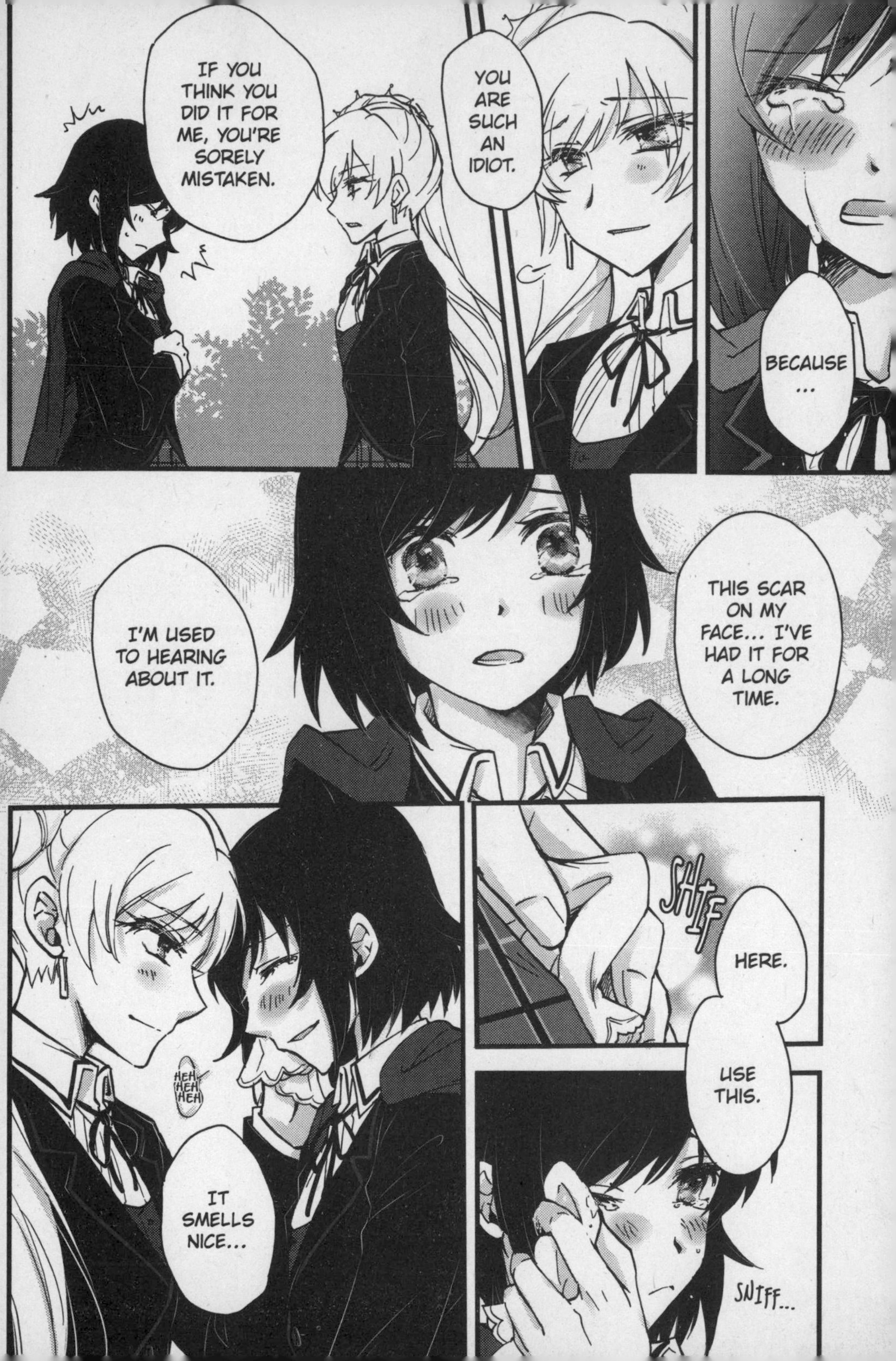
BECAUSE ...
YOU ARE SUCH AN IDIOT.
IF YOU THINK YOU DID IT FOR ME, YOU'RE SORELY MISTAKEN.
THIS SCAR ON MY FACE... I'VE HAD IT FOR A LONG TIME.
I'M USED TO HEARING ABOUT IT.
SHIFF
HERE.
USE THIS.
SNIFF...
HEH HEH HEH
IT SMELLS NICE...

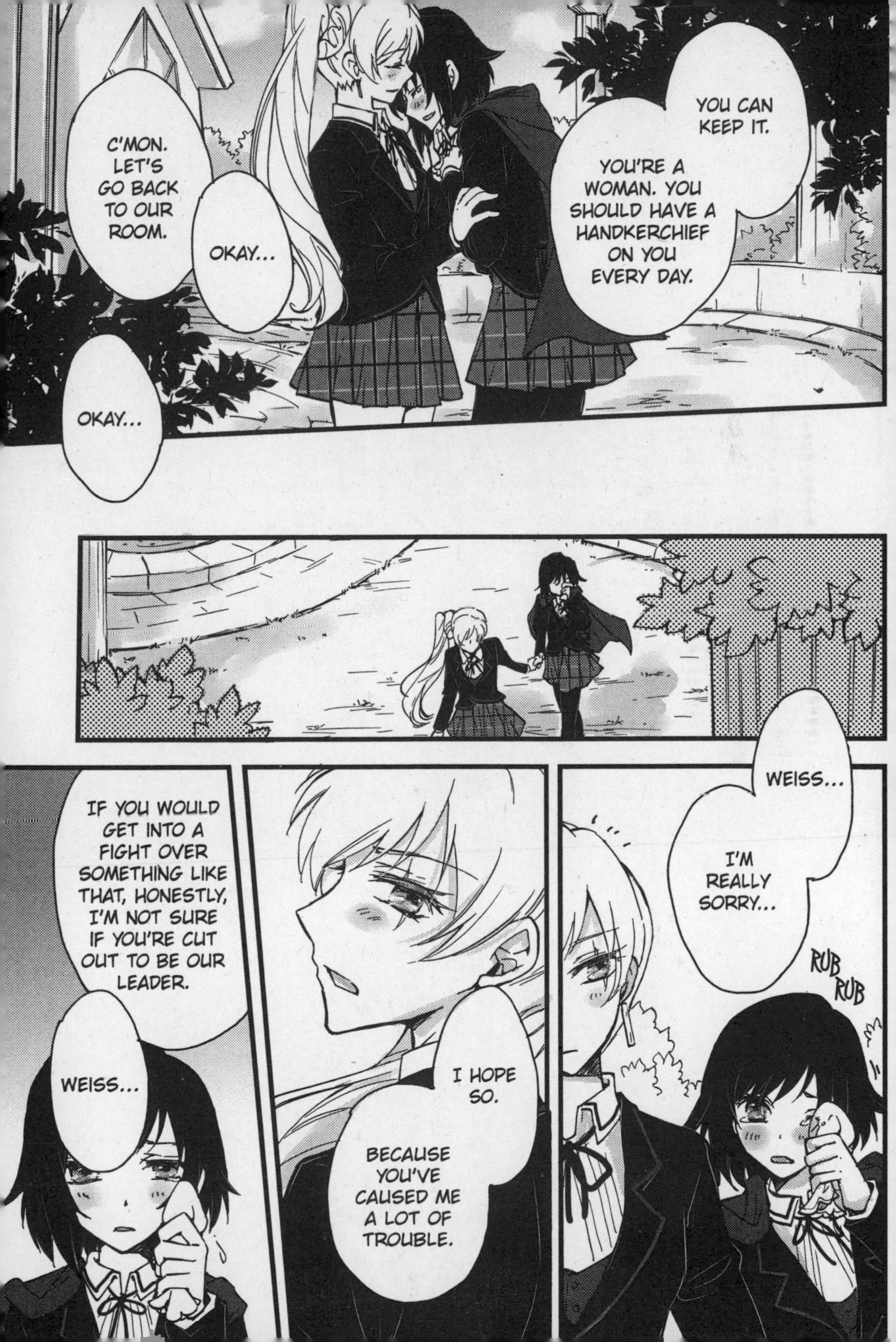
YOU CAN KEEP IT.
YOU'RE A WOMAN. YOU SHOULD HAVE A HANDKERCHIEF ON YOU EVERY DAY.
OKAY...
C'MON. LET'S GO BACK TO OUR ROOM.
OKAY...
WEISS...
I'M REALLY SORRY...
RUB RUB
...
I HOPE SO.
BECAUSE YOU'VE CAUSED ME A LOT OF TROUBLE.
IF YOU WOULD GET INTO A FIGHT OVER SOMETHING LIKE THAT, HONESTLY, I'M NOT SURE IF YOU'RE CUT OUT TO BE OUR LEADER.
WEISS...

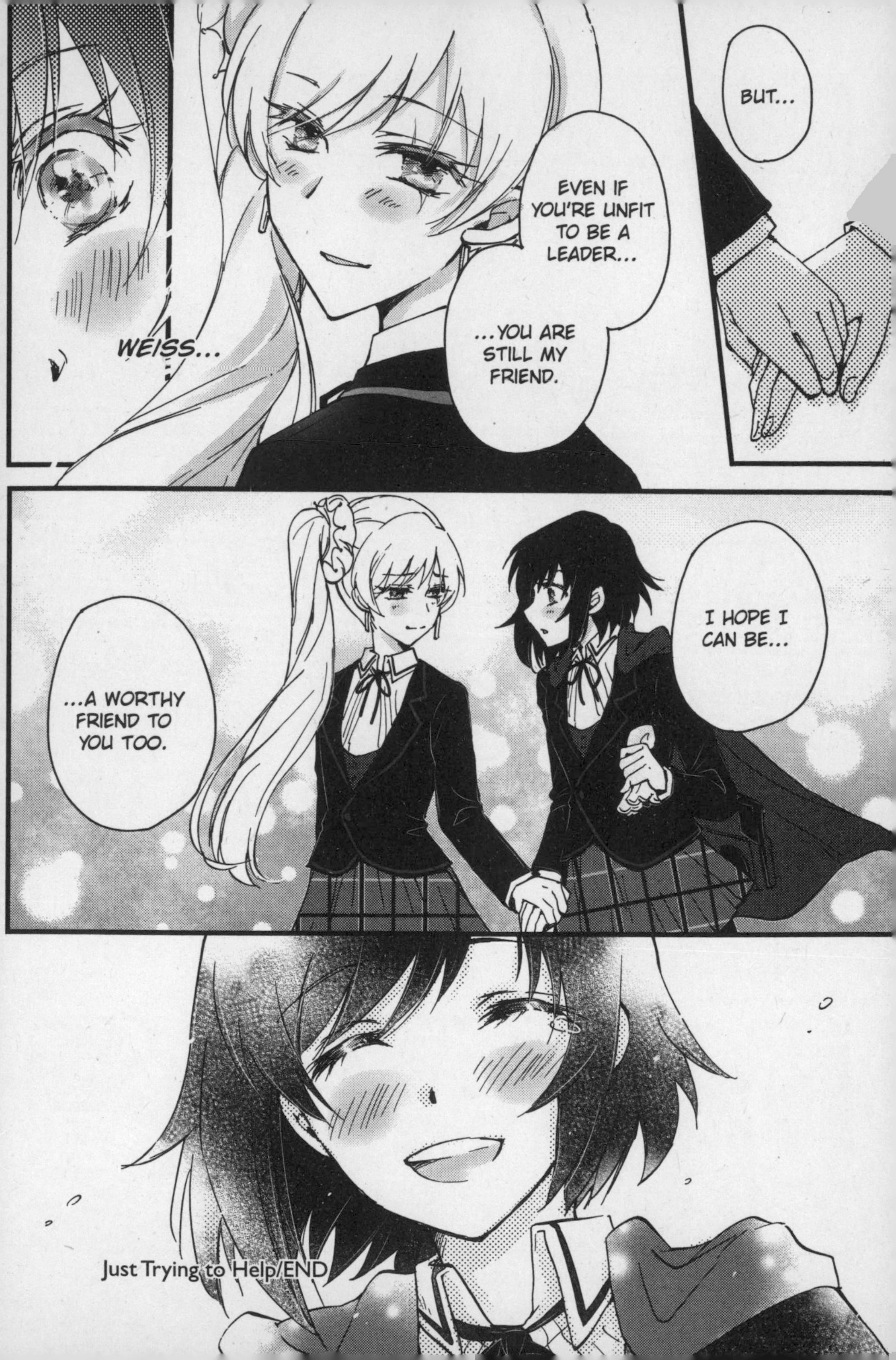
BUT...
EVEN IF YOU'RE UNFIT TO BE A LEADER...
...YOU ARE STILL MY FRIEND.
WEISS...
I HOPE I CAN BE...
...A WORTHY FRIEND TO YOU TOO.
Just Trying to Help/END

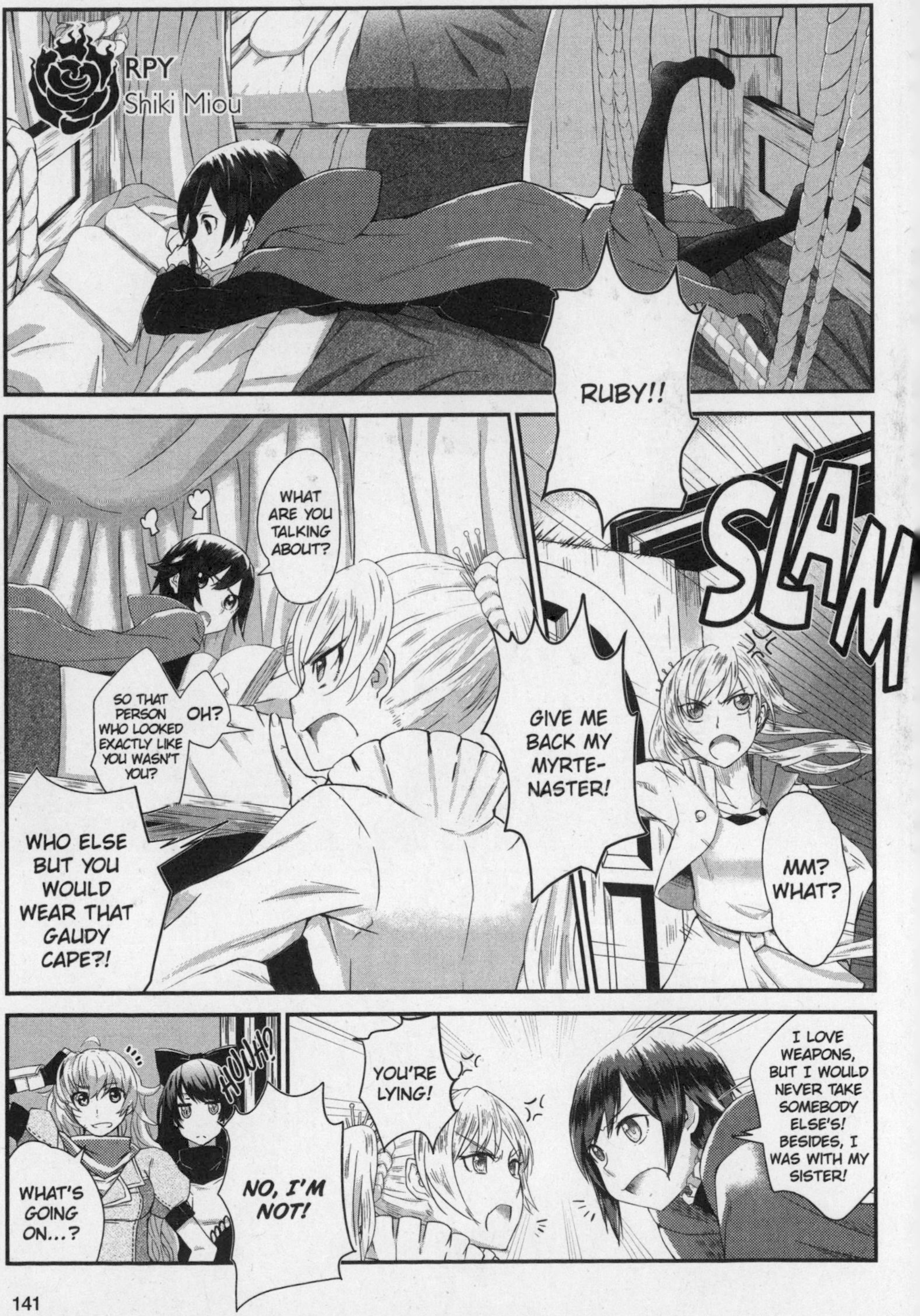
RPY
Shiki Miou
RUBY!!
SLAM
GIVE ME BACK MY MYRTE-NASTER!
MM? WHAT?
WHAT ARE YOU TALKING ABOUT?
OH?
SO THAT PERSON WHO LOOKED EXACTLY LIKE YOU WASN'T YOU?
WHO ELSE BUT YOU WOULD WEAR THAT GAUDY CAPE?!
I LOVE WEAPONS, BUT I WOULD NEVER TAKE SOMEBODY ELSE'S! BESIDES, I WAS WITH MY SISTER!
YOU'RE LYING!
NO, I'M NOT!
HUHH?
WHAT'S GOING ON...?

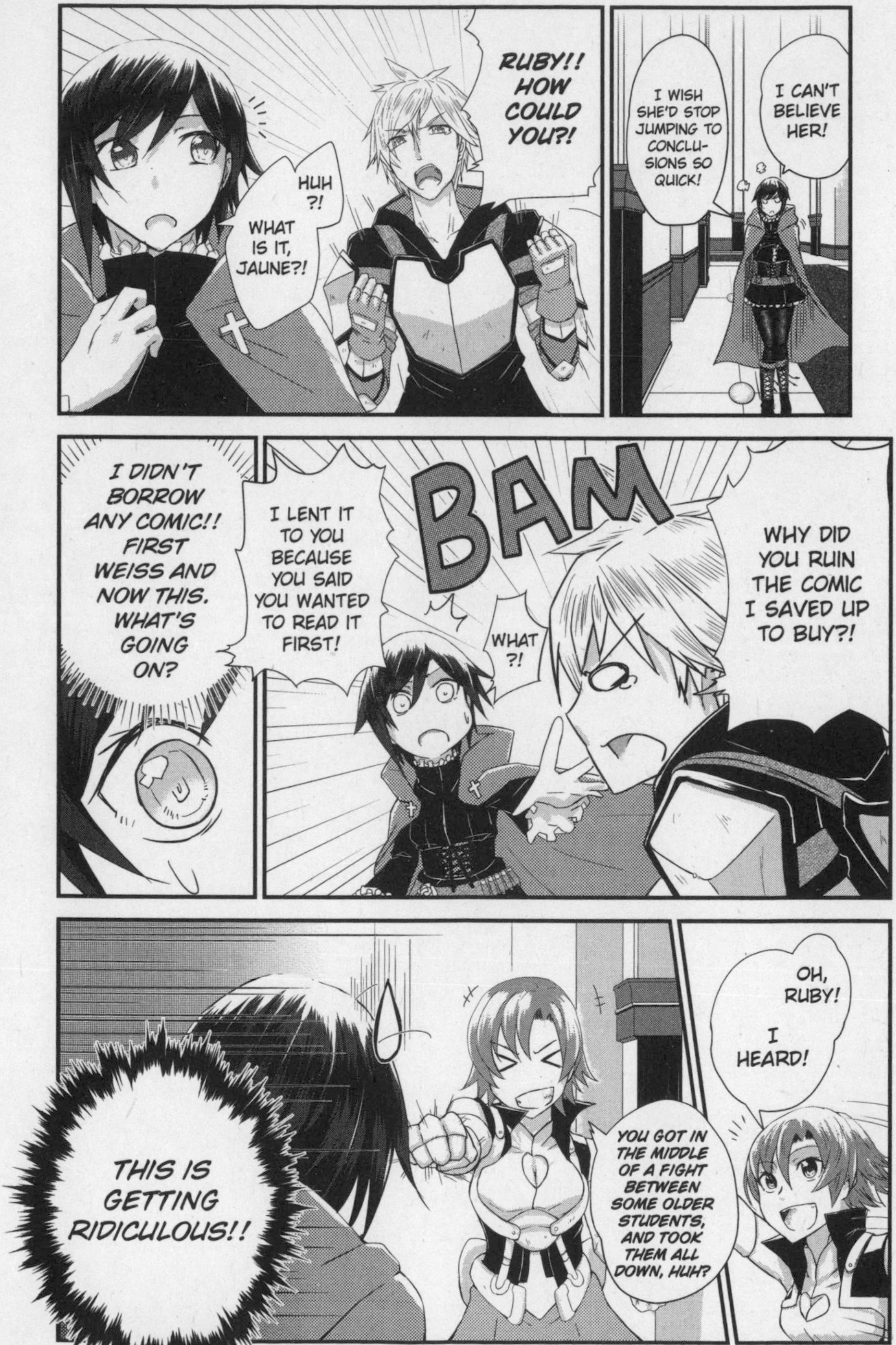
I CAN'T BELIEVE HER!
I WISH SHE'D STOP JUMPING TO CONCLUSIONS SO QUICK!
RUBY!! HOW COULD YOU?!
HUH ?!
WHAT IS IT, JAUNE?!
WHY DID YOU RUIN THE COMIC I SAVED UP TO BUY?!
BAM
WHAT ?!
I LENT IT TO YOU BECAUSE YOU SAID YOU WANTED TO READ IT FIRST!
I DIDN'T BORROW ANY COMIC!! FIRST WEISS AND NOW THIS. WHAT'S GOING ON?
OH, RUBY!
I HEARD!
YOU GOT IN THE MIDDLE OF A FIGHT BETWEEN SOME OLDER STUDENTS, AND TOOK THEM ALL DOWN, HUH?
THIS IS GETTING RIDICULOUS!!

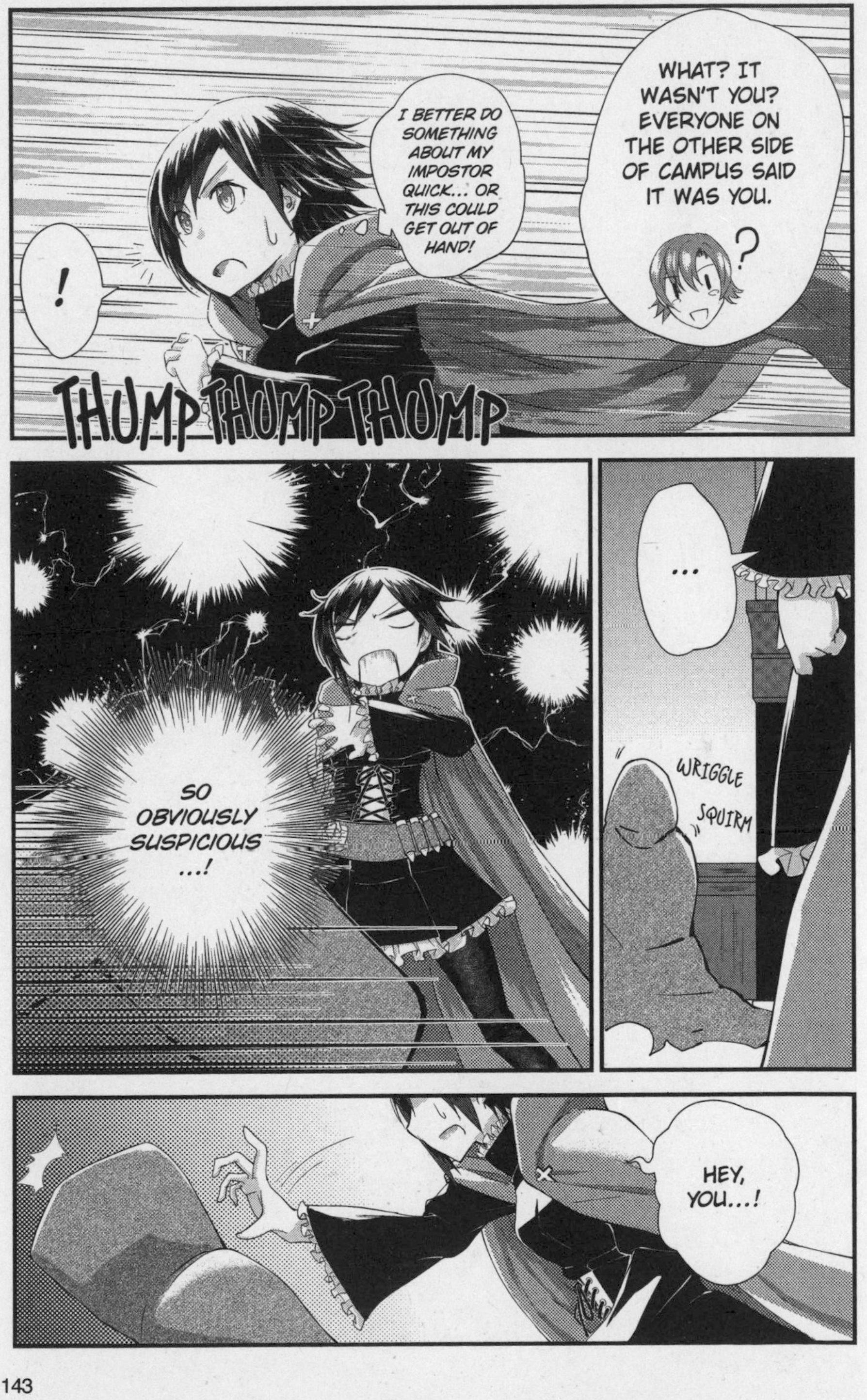
WHAT? IT WASN'T YOU? EVERYONE ON THE OTHER SIDE OF CAMPUS SAID IT WAS YOU.
?
I BETTER DO SOMETHING ABOUT MY IMPOSTOR QUICK... OR THIS COULD GET OUT OF HAND!
!
THUMP THUMP THUMP
...
WRIGGLE
SQUIRM
SO OBVIOUSLY SUSPICIOUS ...!
HEY, YOU...!

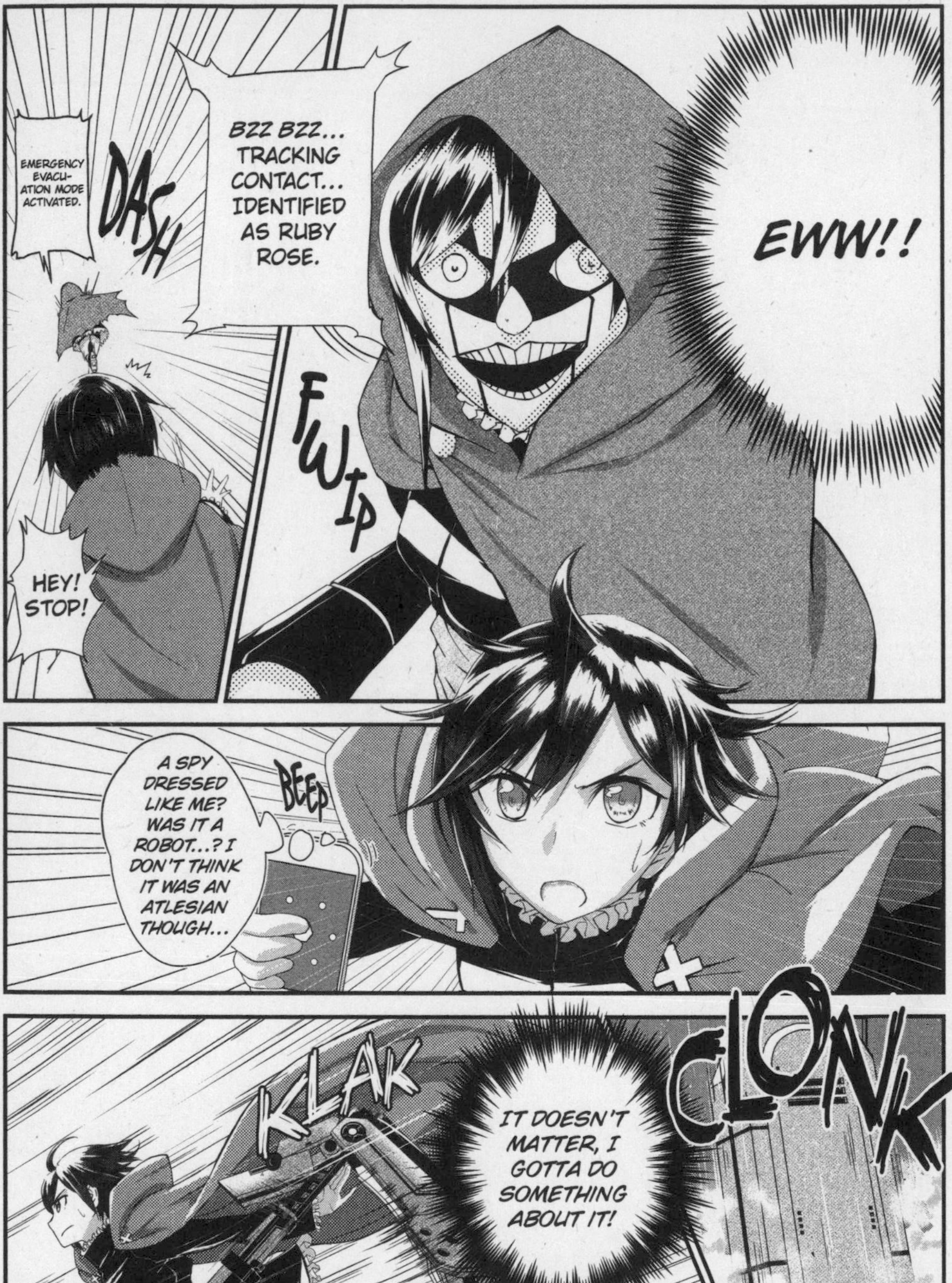
BZZ BZZ... TRACKING CONTACT... IDENTIFIED AS RUBY ROSE.
EWW!!
FWIP
EMERGENCY EVACU-ATION MODE ACTIVATED.
DASH
HEY! STOP!
BEEP
A SPY DRESSED LIKE ME? WAS IT A ROBOT...? I DON'T THINK IT WAS AN ATLESIAN THOUGH...
CLONK
KLAK
IT DOESN'T MATTER, I GOTTA DO SOMETHING ABOUT IT!

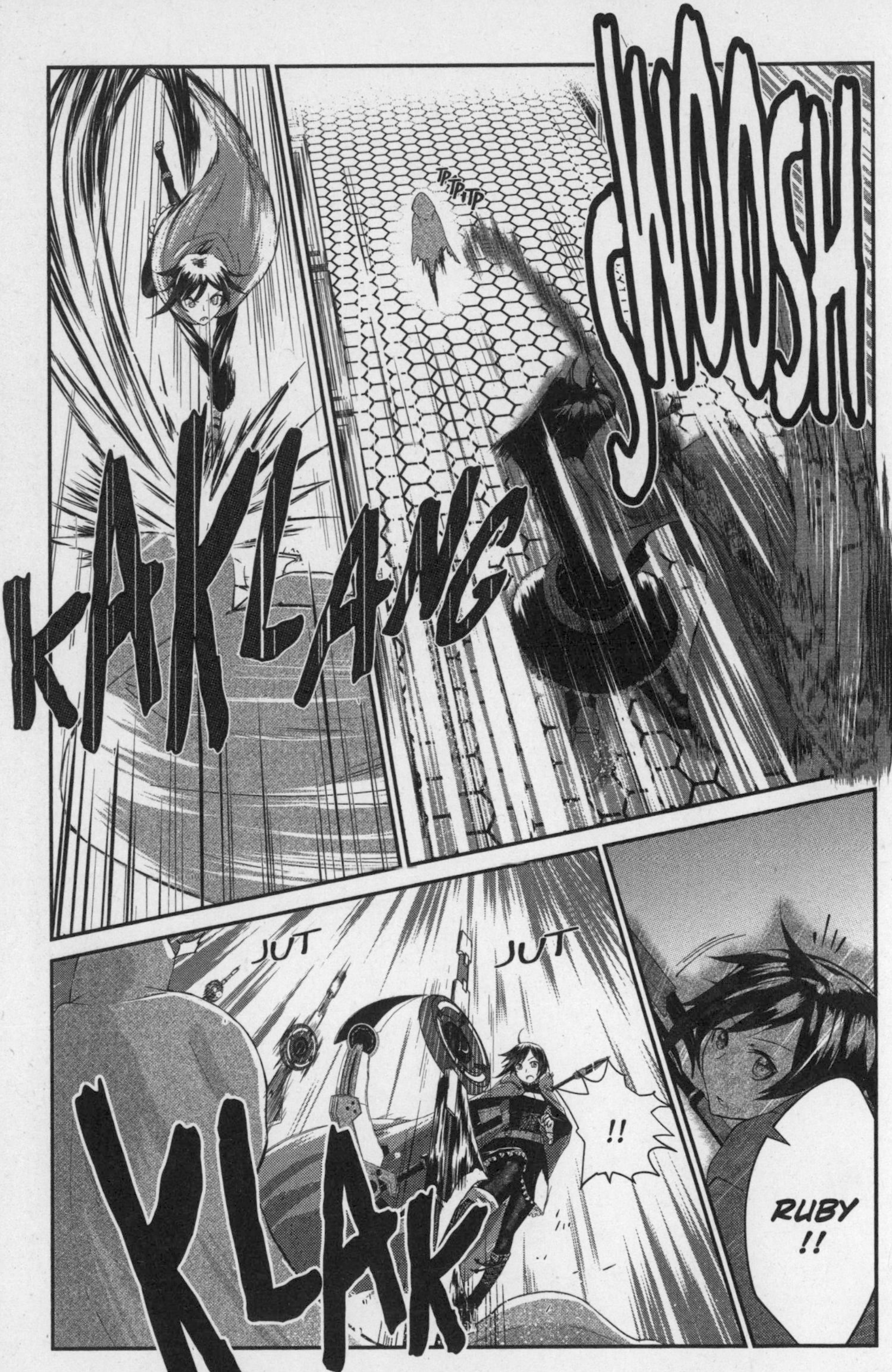
TP TP TP
WHOOSH
KAKLANG
RUBY !!
JUT
JUT
!!
KLAK

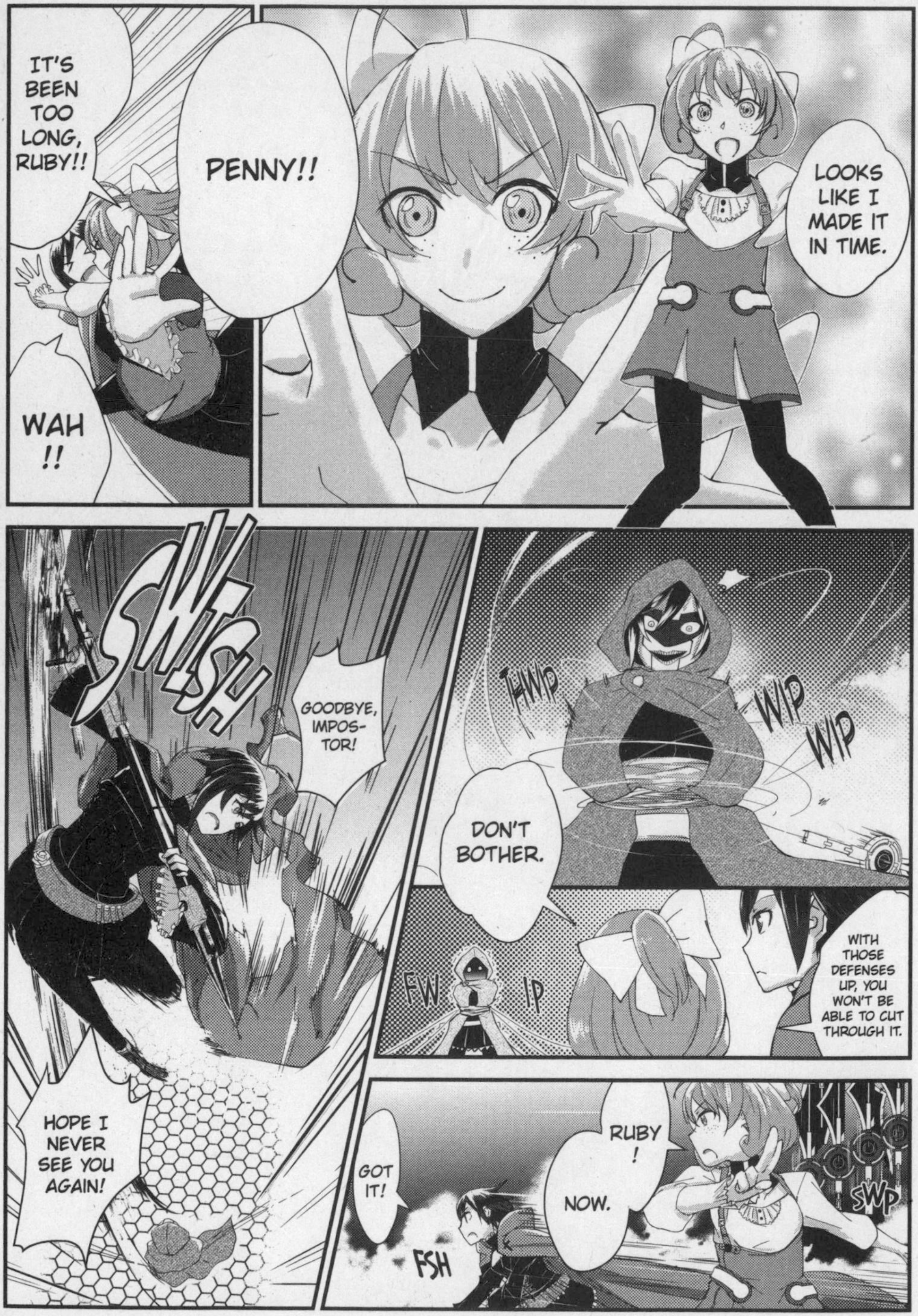
LOOKS LIKE I MADE IT IN TIME.
PENNY!!
IT'S BEEN TOO LONG, RUBY!!
WAH!!
THWP
WP WP
DON'T BOTHER.
WITH THOSE DEFENSES UP, YOU WON'T BE ABLE TO CUT THROUGH IT.
FWIP
SWP
RUBY! NOW.
GOT IT!
FSH
SWISH
GOODBYE, IMPOSTOR!
HOPE I NEVER SEE YOU AGAIN!

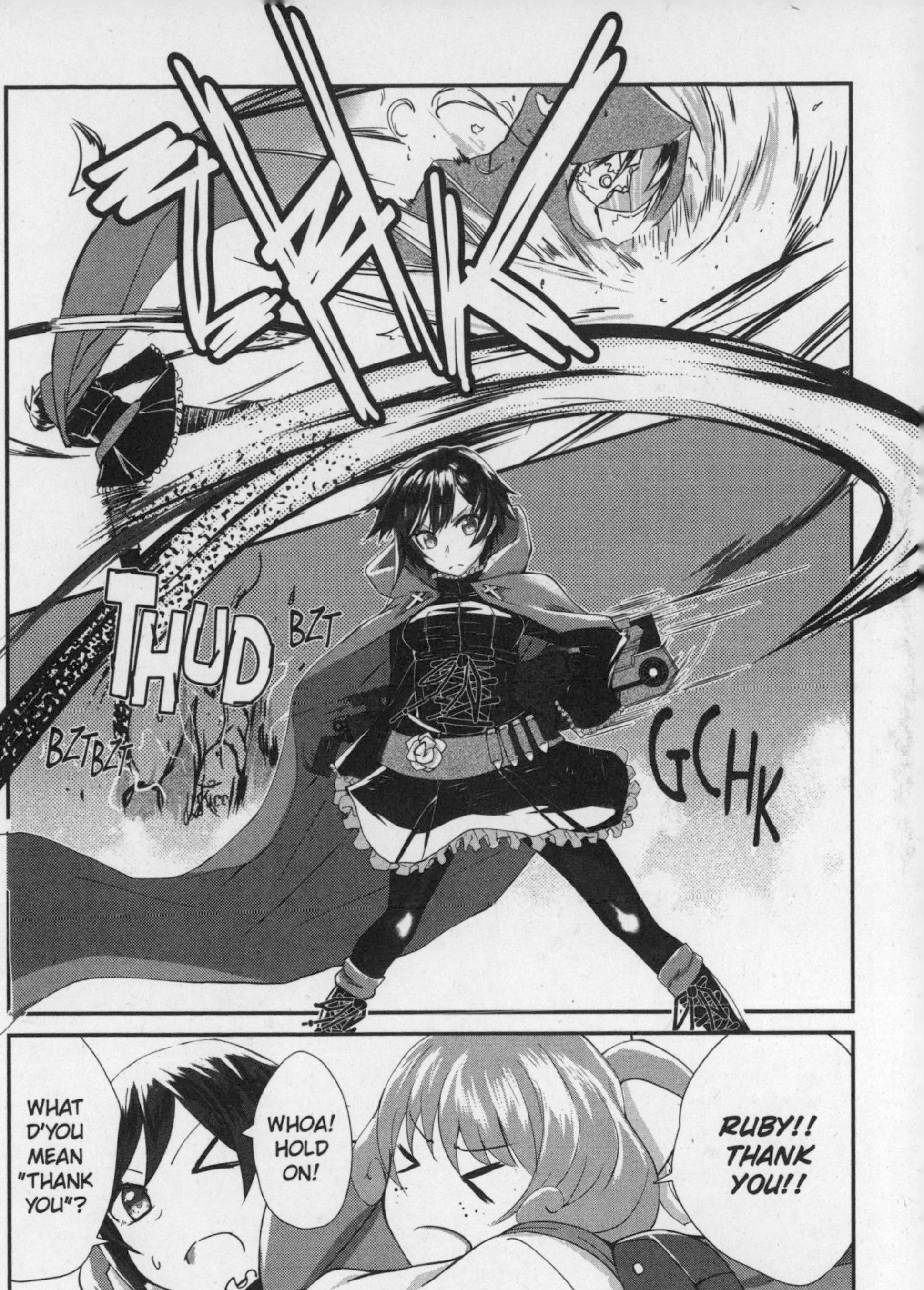
THUD
BZT
BZTBZT
GCHK
RUBY!! THANK YOU!!
WHOA! HOLD ON!
WHAT D'YOU MEAN "THANK YOU"?

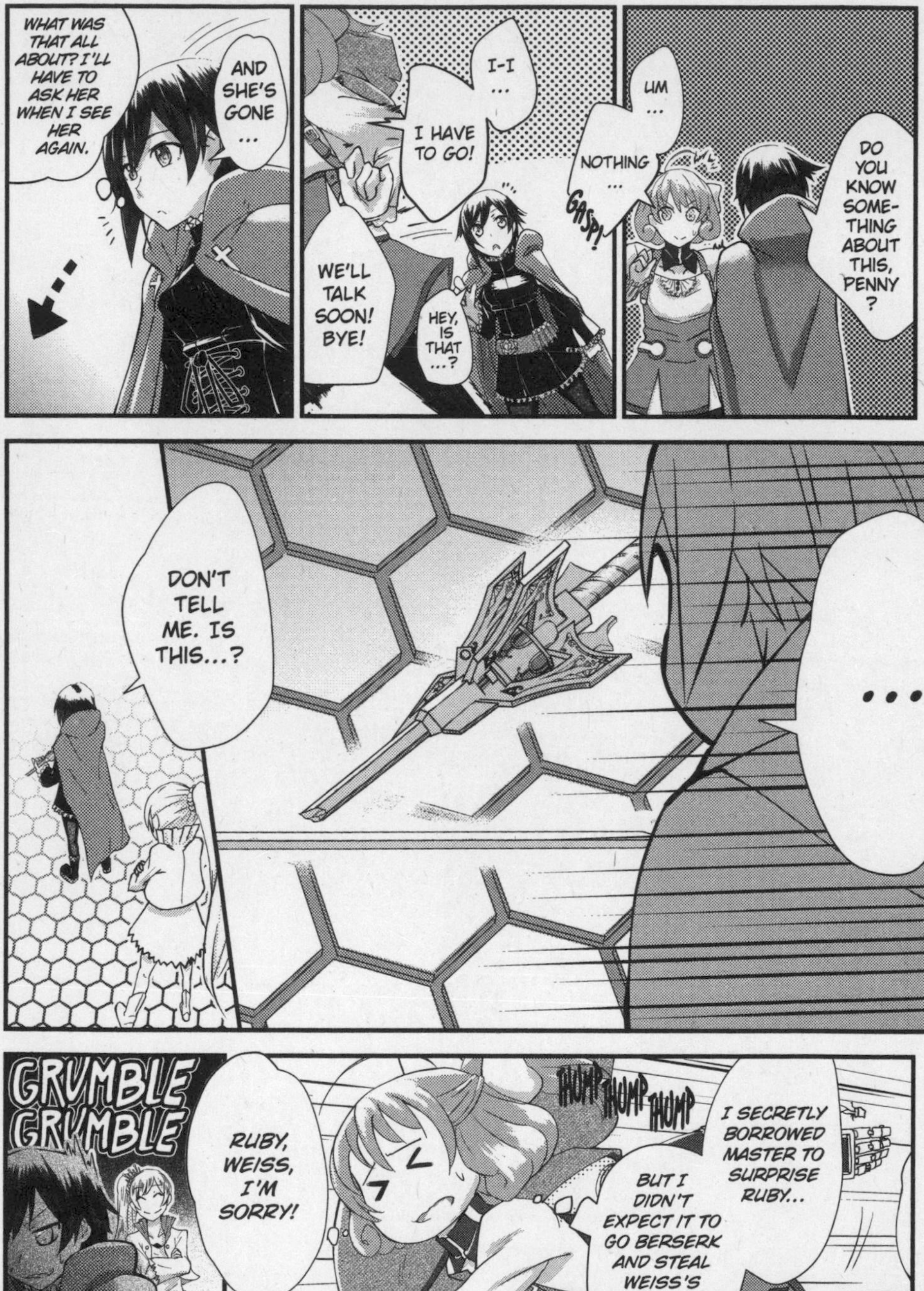
DO YOU KNOW SOMETHING ABOUT THIS, PENNY?
UM ...
NOTHING ...
GASP!
I-I ...
I HAVE TO GO!
WE'LL TALK SOON! BYE!
HEY, IS THAT ...?
AND SHE'S GONE ...
WHAT WAS THAT ALL ABOUT? I'LL HAVE TO ASK HER WHEN I SEE HER AGAIN.
...
DON'T TELL ME. IS THIS...?
THUMP THUMP THUMP
I SECRETLY BORROWED MASTER TO SURPRISE RUBY...
BUT I DIDN'T EXPECT IT TO GO BERSERK AND STEAL WEISS'S SWORD THEN BREAK UP A FIGHT...
RUBY, WEISS, I'M SORRY!
GRUMBLE GRUMBLE

RPY/END

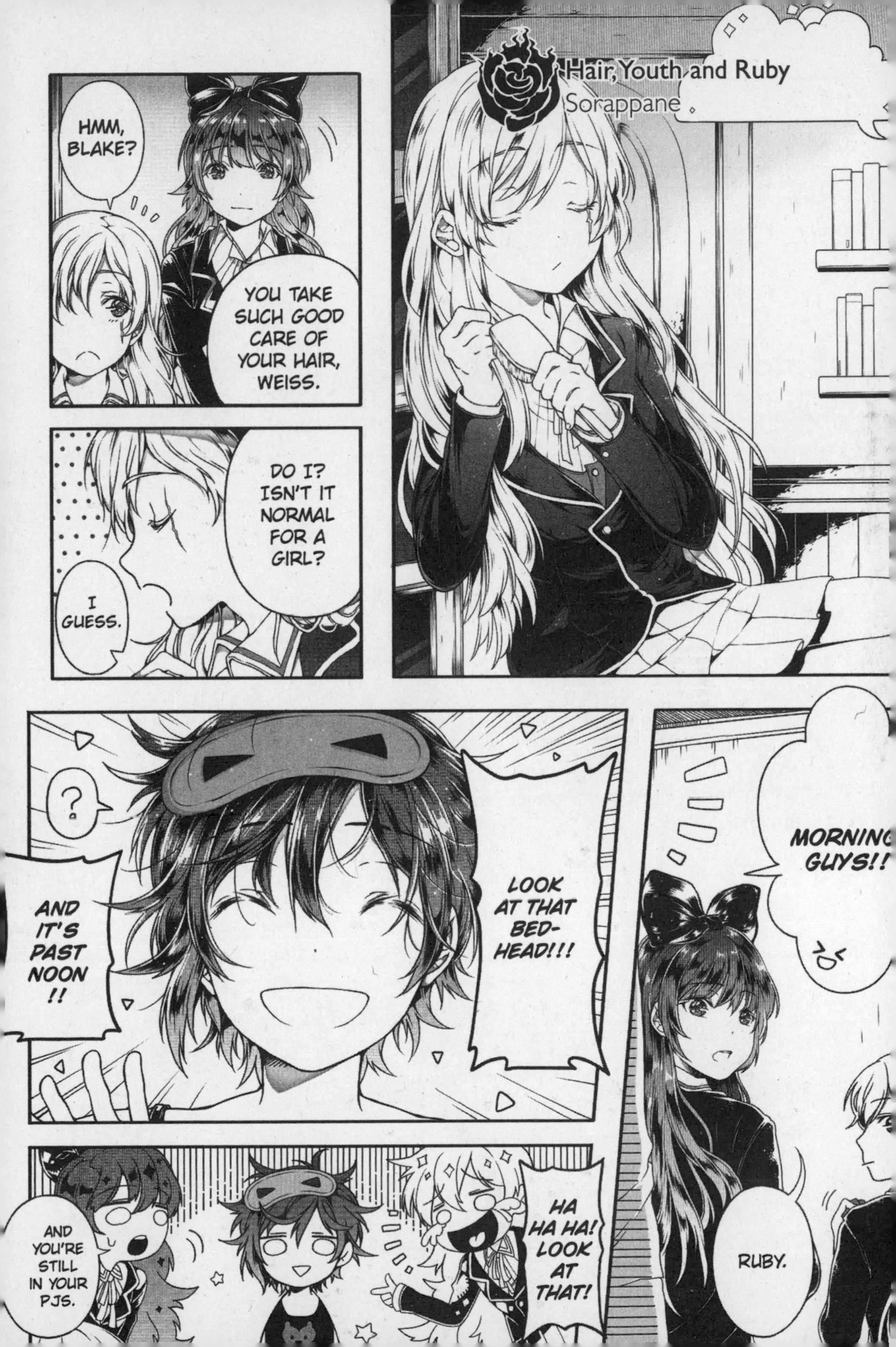
Hair, Youth and Ruby
Sorappane
HMM, BLAKE?
YOU TAKE SUCH GOOD CARE OF YOUR HAIR, WEISS.
DO I? ISN'T IT NORMAL FOR A GIRL?
I GUESS.
MORNING GUYS!!
RUBY.
?
LOOK AT THAT BED-HEAD!!!
AND IT'S PAST NOON!!
HA HA HA! LOOK AT THAT!
AND YOU'RE STILL IN YOUR PJS.

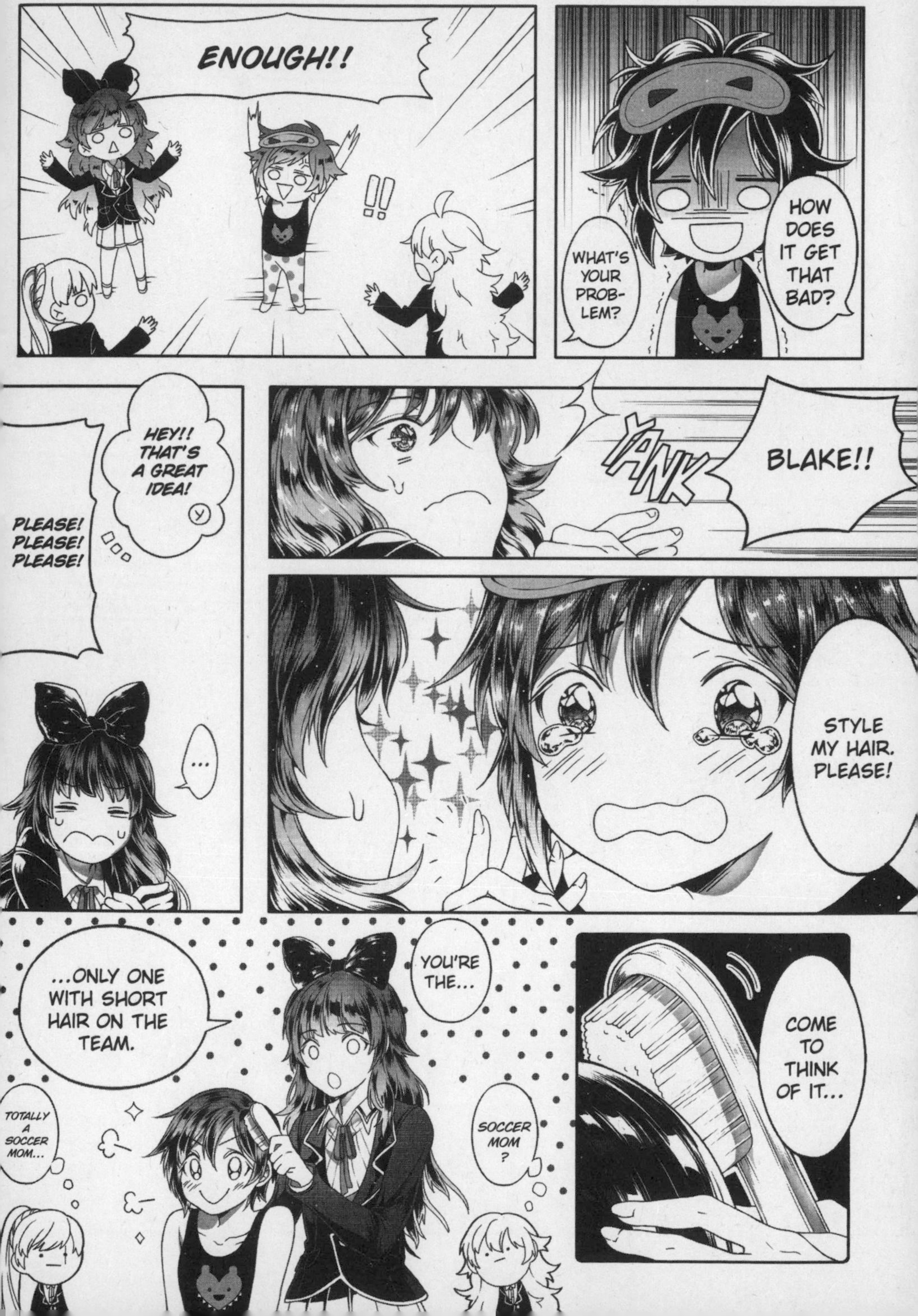
HOW DOES IT GET THAT BAD?
WHAT'S YOUR PROB-LEM?
ENOUGH!!
!!
BLAKE!!
YANK
STYLE MY HAIR. PLEASE!
HEY!! THAT'S A GREAT IDEA!
PLEASE! PLEASE! PLEASE!
...
COME TO THINK OF IT...
YOU'RE THE...
...ONLY ONE WITH SHORT HAIR ON THE TEAM.
SOCCER MOM?
TOTALLY A SOCCER MOM...

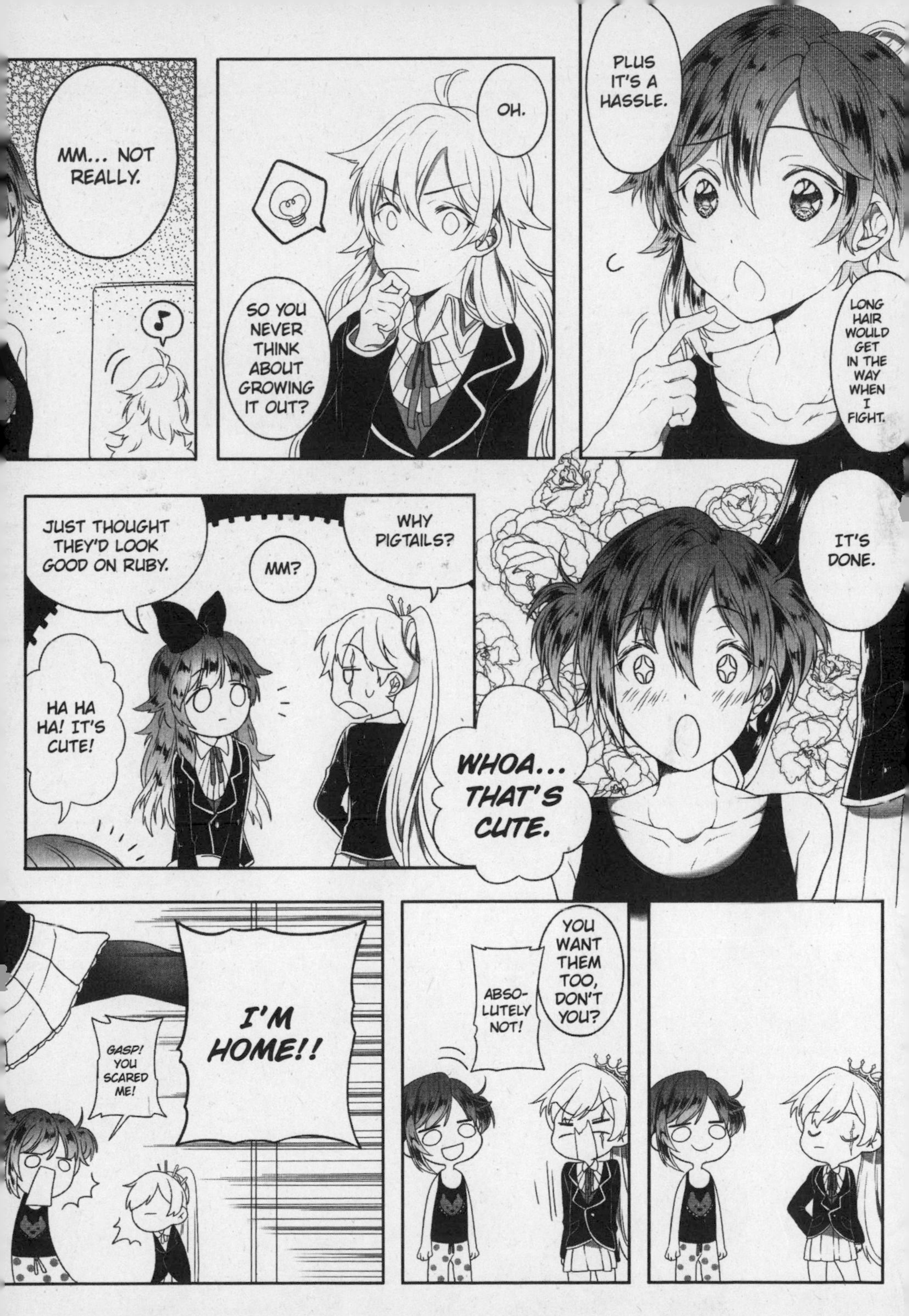
MM... NOT REALLY.
OH.
SO YOU NEVER THINK ABOUT GROWING IT OUT?
LONG HAIR WOULD GET IN THE WAY WHEN I FIGHT.
PLUS IT'S A HASSLE.
WHY PIGTAILS?
MM?
JUST THOUGHT THEY'D LOOK GOOD ON RUBY.
HA HA HA! IT'S CUTE!
IT'S DONE.
WHOA... THAT'S CUTE.
I'M HOME!!
GASP! YOU SCARED ME!
YOU WANT THEM TOO, DON'T YOU?
ABSO-LUTELY NOT!

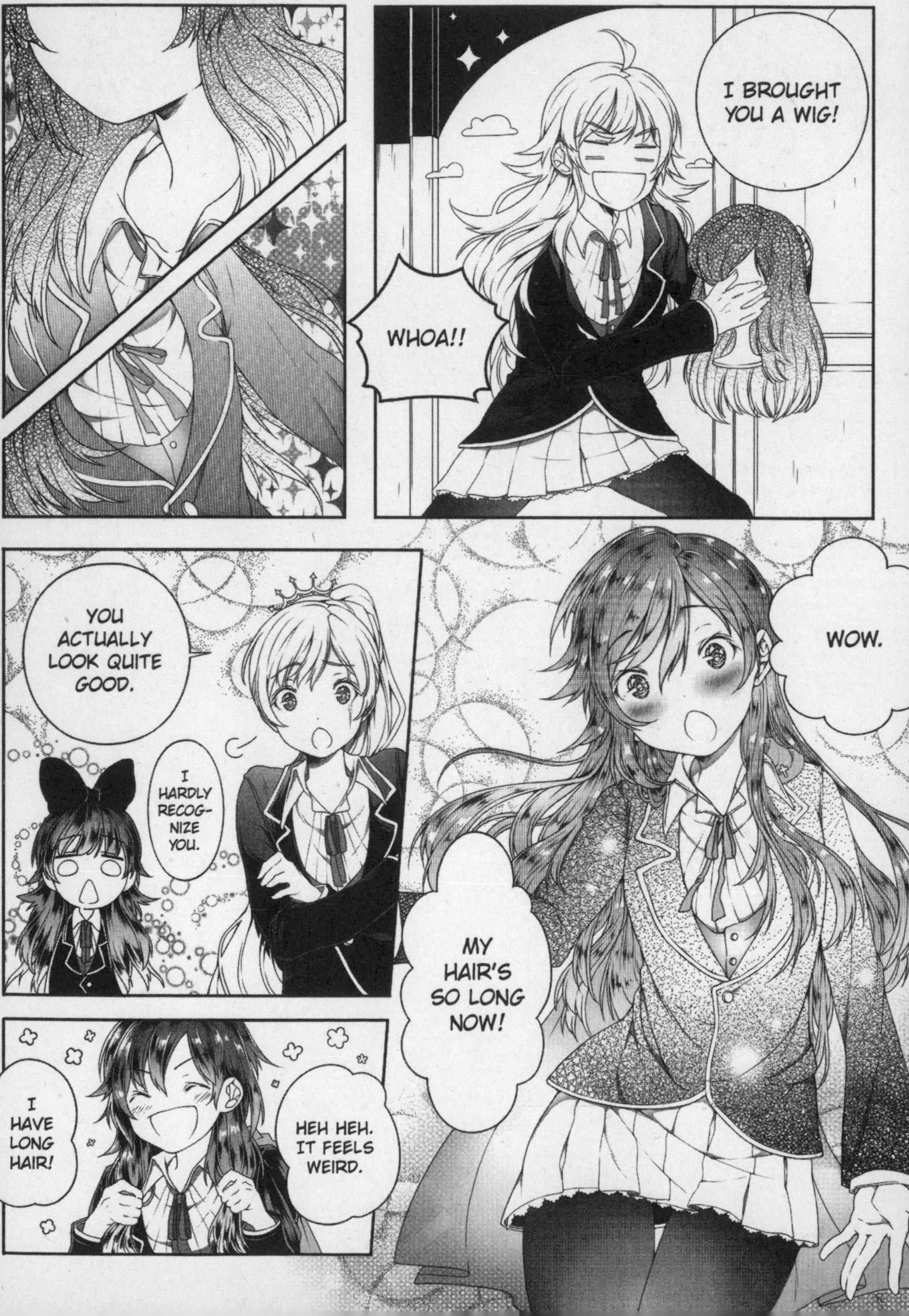
I BROUGHT YOU A WIG!
WHOA!!
WOW.
MY HAIR'S SO LONG NOW!
YOU ACTUALLY LOOK QUITE GOOD.
I HARDLY RECOG-NIZE YOU.
HEH HEH. IT FEELS WEIRD.
I HAVE LONG HAIR!

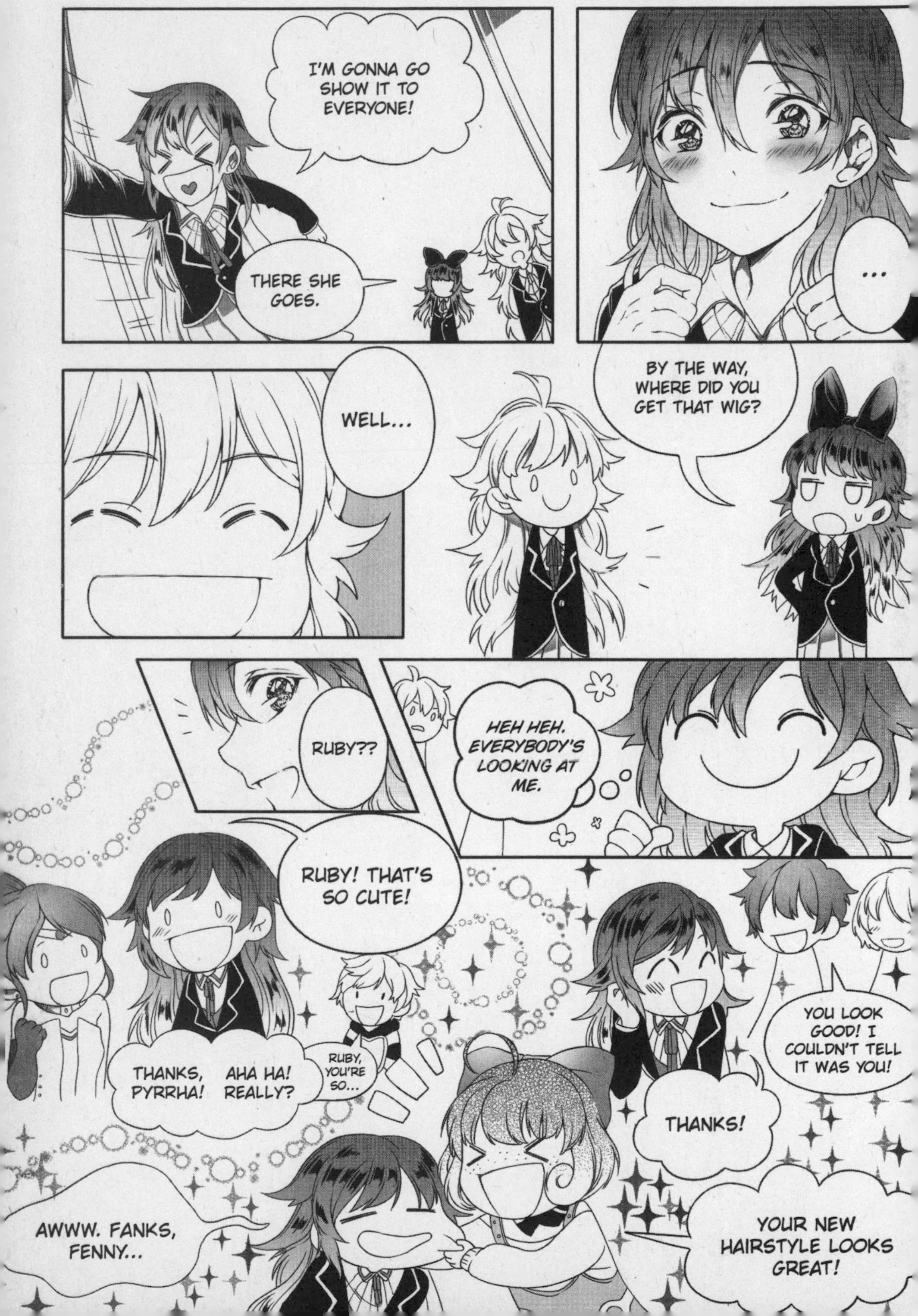
...
I'M GONNA GO SHOW IT TO EVERYONE!
THERE SHE GOES.
BY THE WAY, WHERE DID YOU GET THAT WIG?
WELL...
HEH HEH. EVERYBODY'S LOOKING AT ME.
RUBY??
RUBY! THAT'S SO CUTE!
THANKS, PYRRHA!
YOU LOOK GOOD! I COULDN'T TELL IT WAS YOU!
THANKS!
RUBY, YOU'RE SO...
AHA HA! REALLY?
YOUR NEW HAIRSTYLE LOOKS GREAT!
AWWW. FANKS, FENNY...

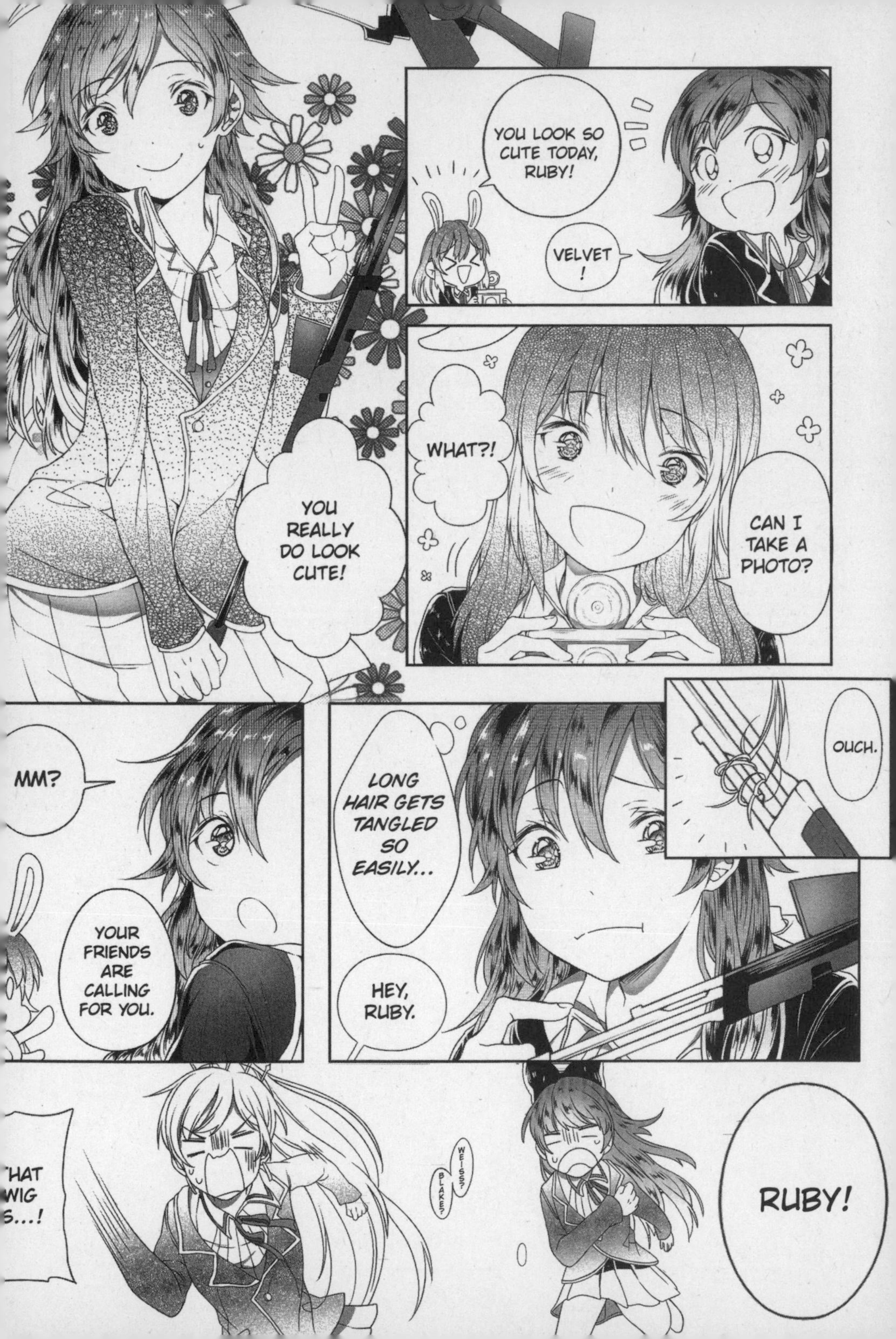
YOU LOOK SO CUTE TODAY, RUBY!
VELVET!
CAN I TAKE A PHOTO?
WHAT?!
YOU REALLY DO LOOK CUTE!
OUCH.
LONG HAIR GETS TANGLED SO EASILY...
HEY, RUBY.
MM?
YOUR FRIENDS ARE CALLING FOR YOU.
RUBY!
WEISS?
BLAKE?
HAT WIG S...!

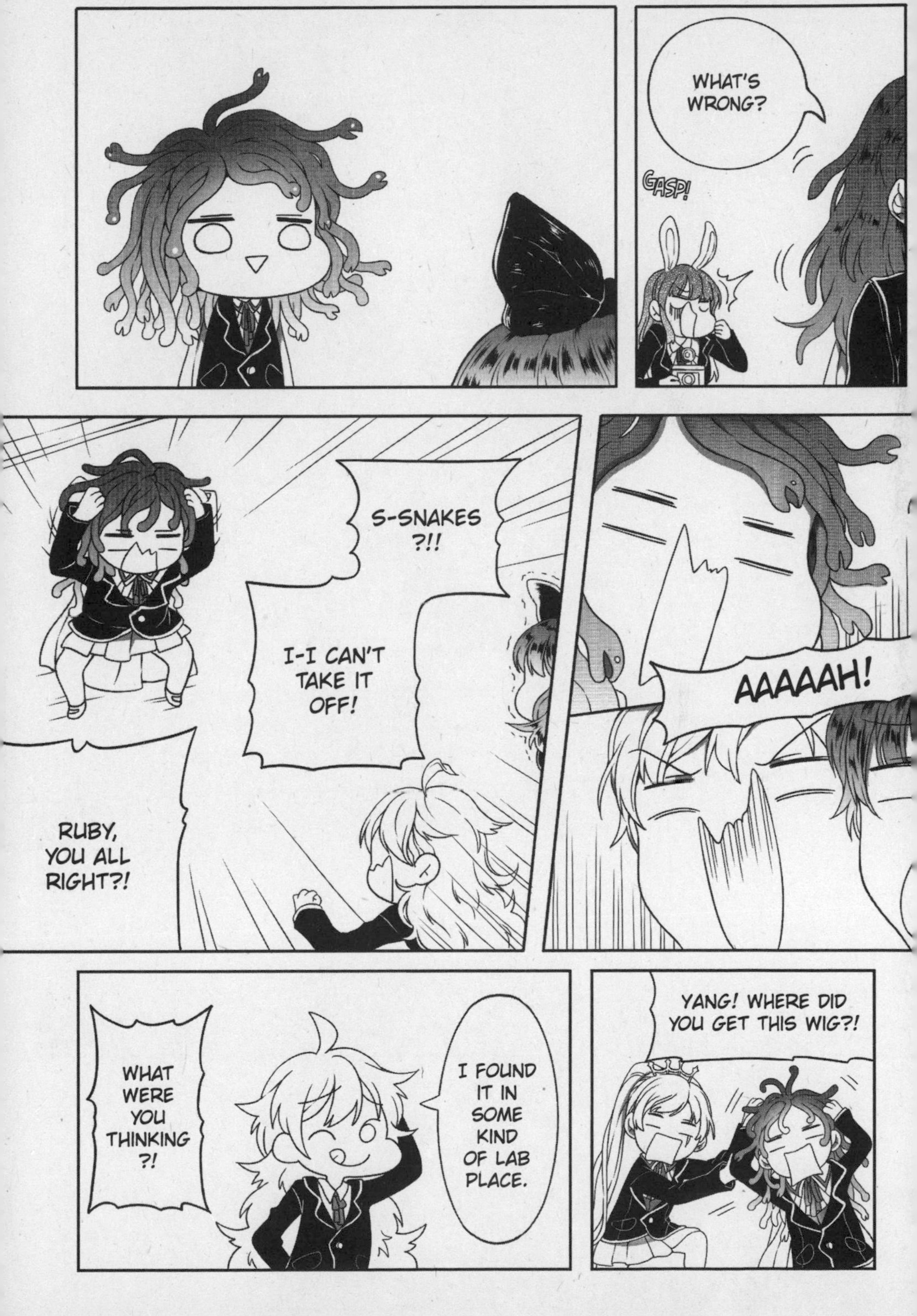
WHAT'S WRONG?
GASP!
AAAAAH!
S-SNAKES ?!!
I-I CAN'T TAKE IT OFF!
RUBY, YOU ALL RIGHT?!
YANG! WHERE DID YOU GET THIS WIG?!
I FOUND IT IN SOME KIND OF LAB PLACE.
WHAT WERE YOU THINKING ?!

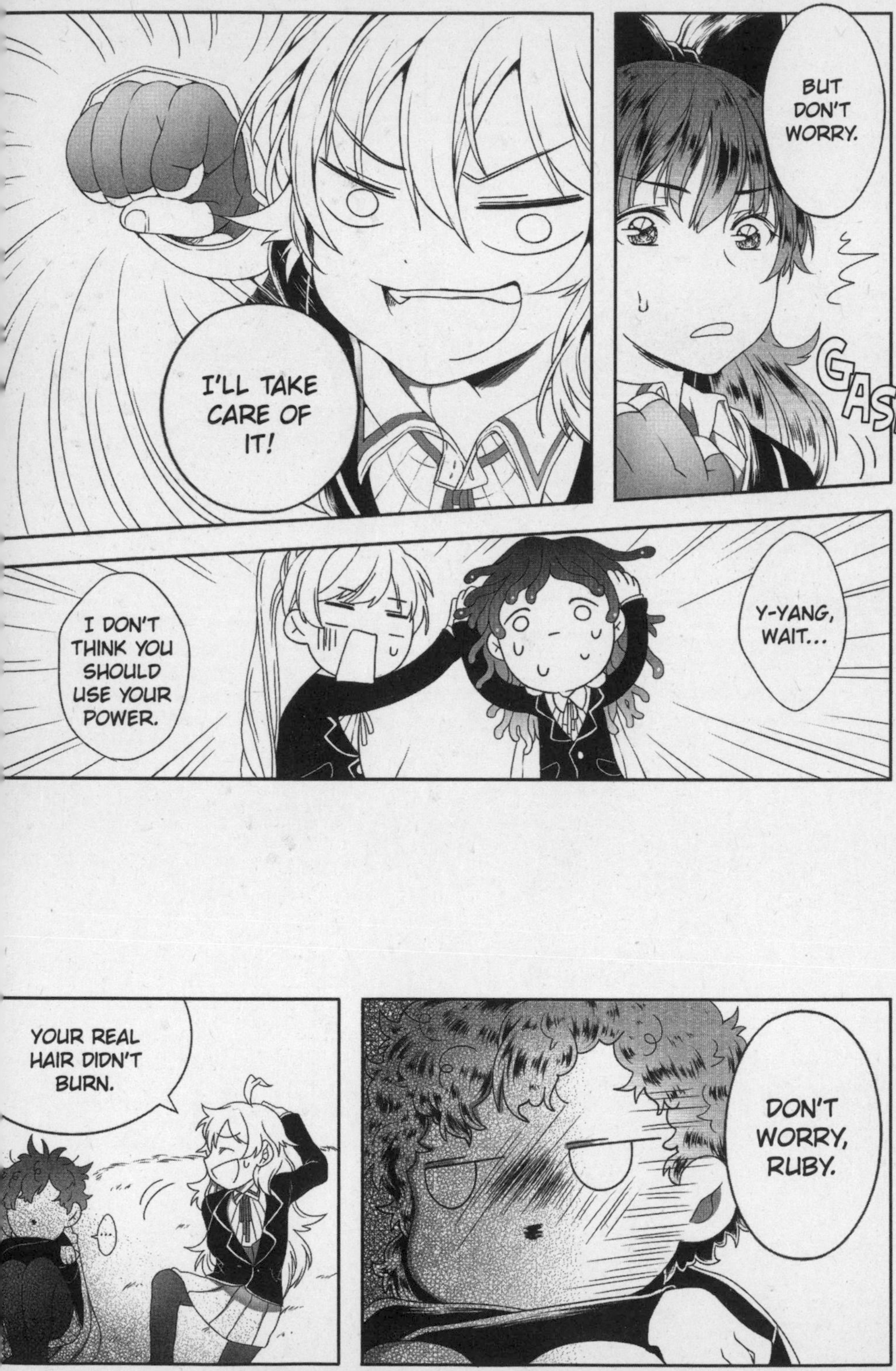
BUT DON'T WORRY.
GASP
I'LL TAKE CARE OF IT!
Y-YANG, WAIT...
I DON'T THINK YOU SHOULD USE YOUR POWER.
DON'T WORRY, RUBY.
YOUR REAL HAIR DIDN'T BURN.
...

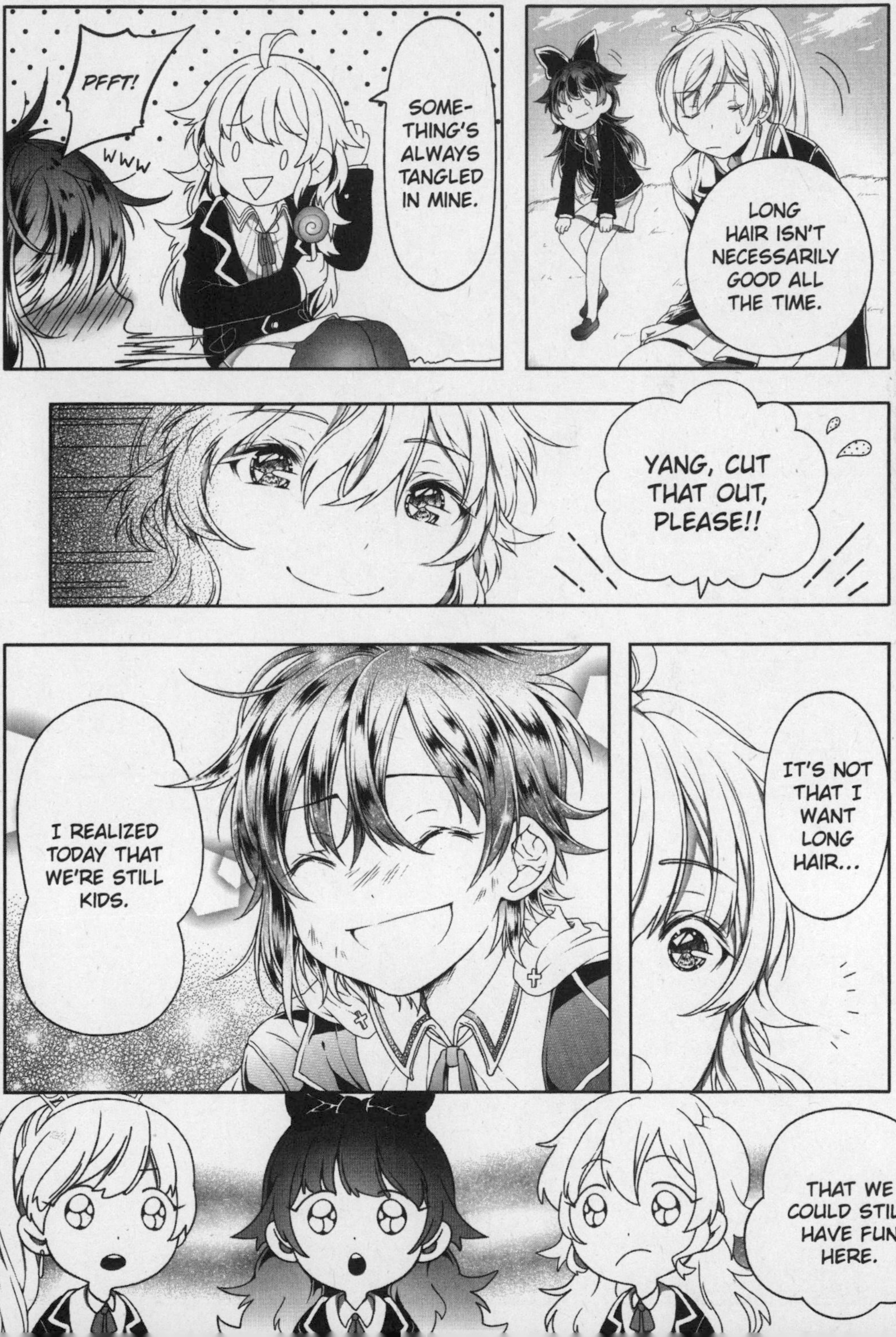
LONG HAIR ISN'T NECESSARILY GOOD ALL THE TIME.
SOME-THING'S ALWAYS TANGLED IN MINE.
PFFT!
WWW
YANG, CUT THAT OUT, PLEASE!!
IT'S NOT THAT I WANT LONG HAIR...
I REALIZED TODAY THAT WE'RE STILL KIDS.
THAT WE COULD STILL HAVE FUN HERE.

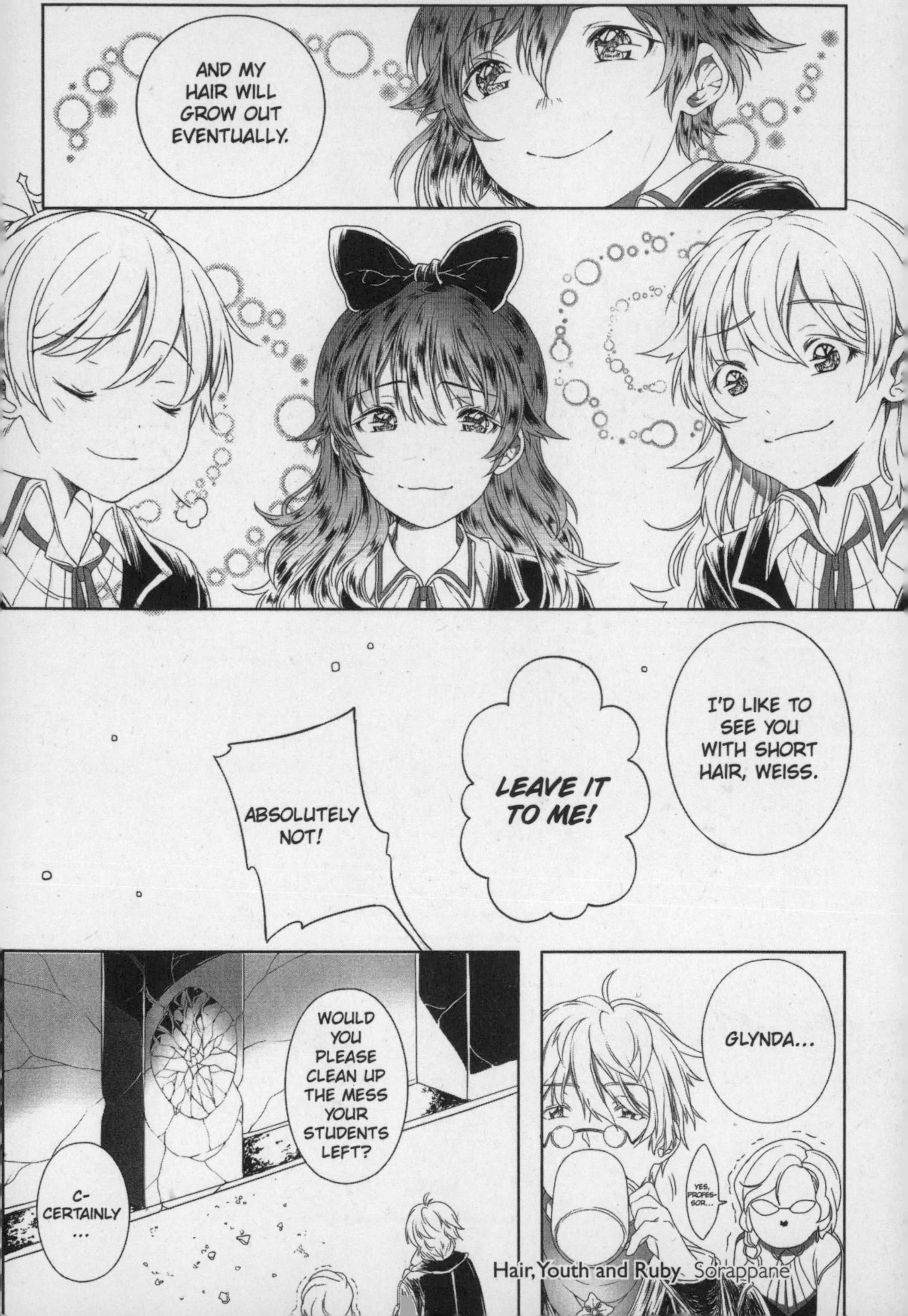
AND MY HAIR WILL GROW OUT EVENTUALLY.
I'D LIKE TO SEE YOU WITH SHORT HAIR, WEISS.
LEAVE IT TO ME!
ABSOLUTELY NOT!
GLYNDA...
YES, PROFES-SOR...
WOULD YOU PLEASE CLEAN UP THE MESS YOUR STUDENTS LEFT?
C-CERTAINLY...

Hair, Youth and Ruby Sorappane

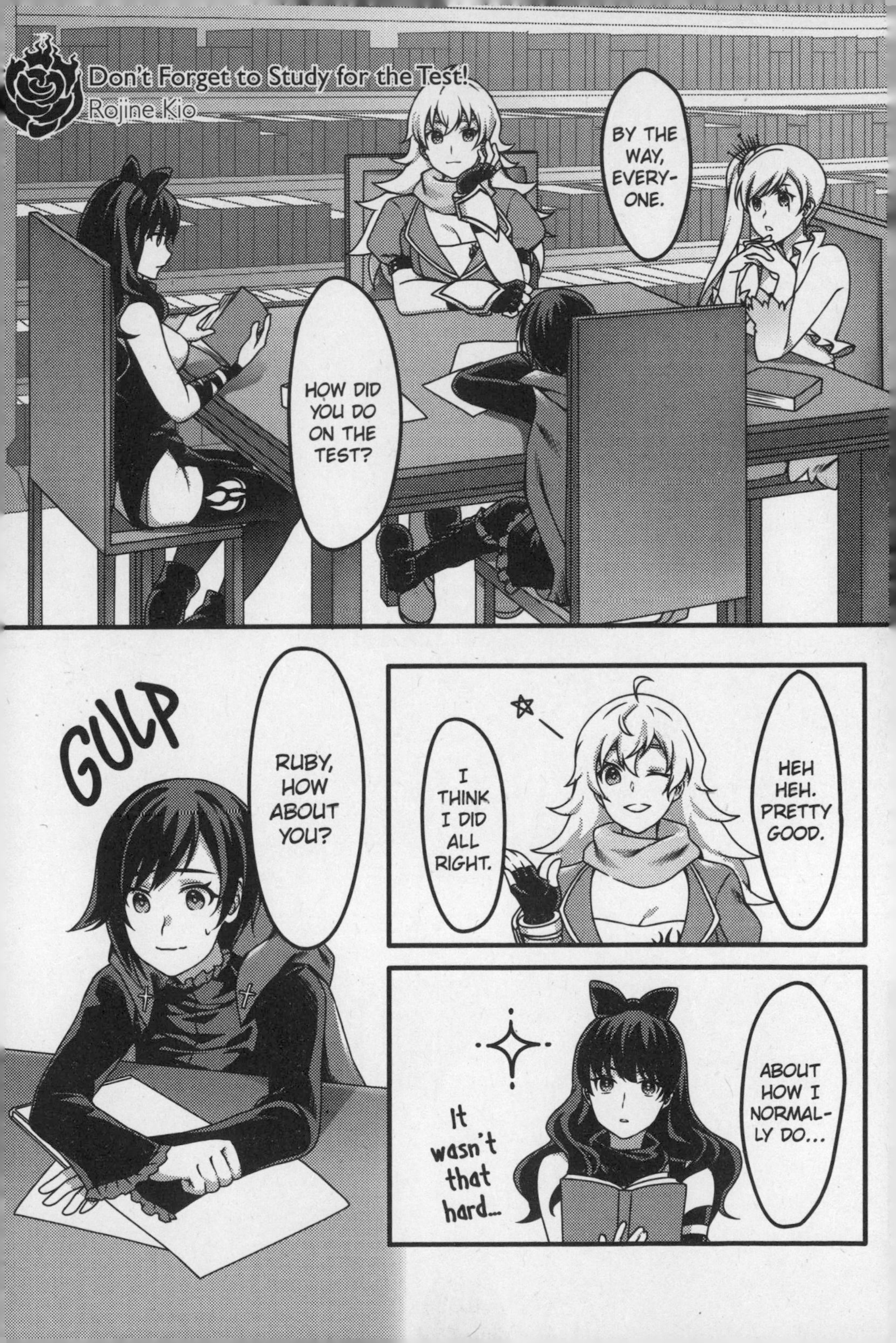
Don't Forget to Study for the Test!
Rojine Kio
BY THE WAY, EVERYONE.
HOW DID YOU DO ON THE TEST?
HEH HEH. PRETTY GOOD.
I THINK I DID ALL RIGHT.
ABOUT HOW I NORMALLY DO...
It wasn't that hard...
RUBY, HOW ABOUT YOU?
GULP

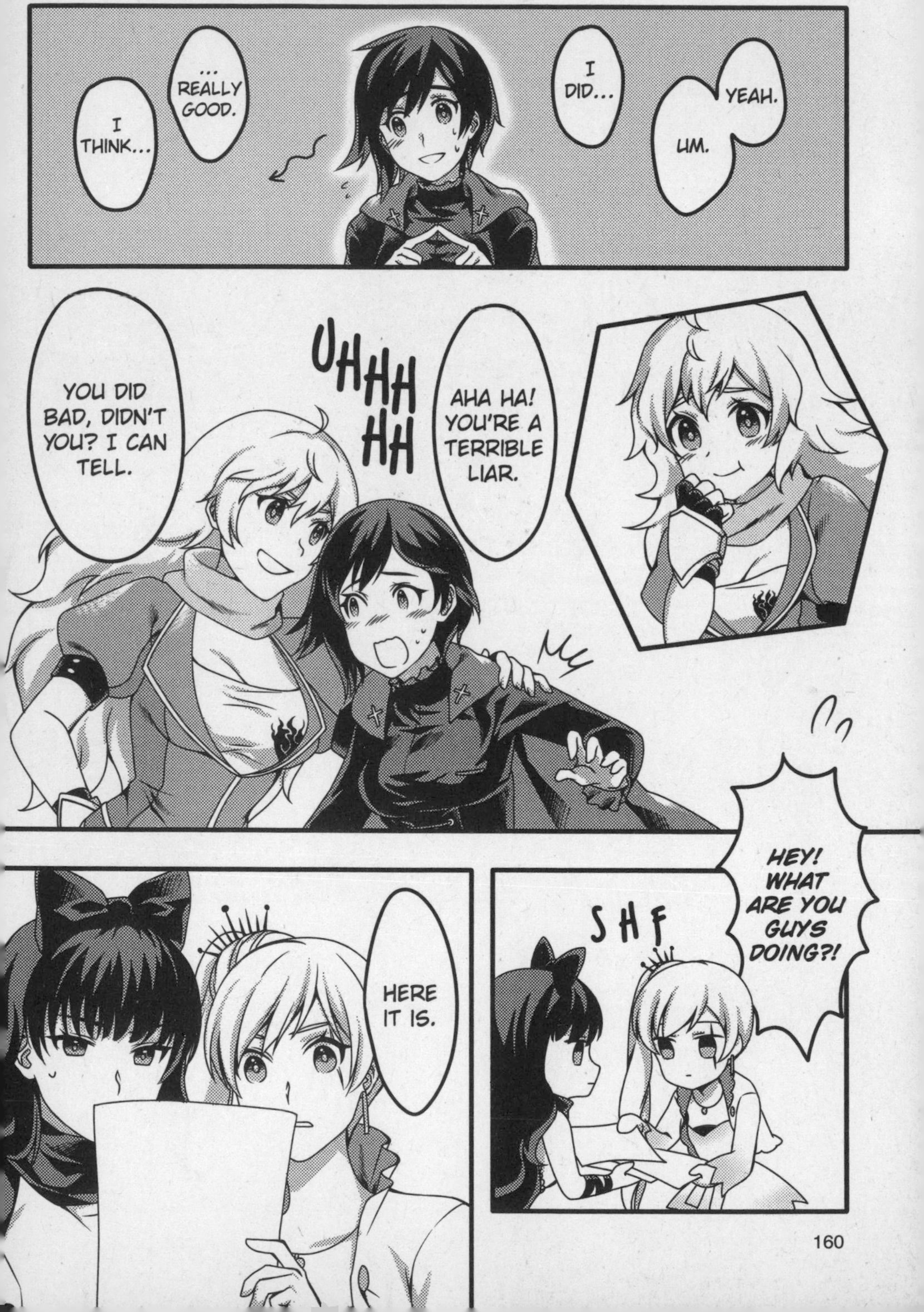
UM. YEAH.
I DID...
... REALLY GOOD.
I THINK...
AHA HA! YOU'RE A TERRIBLE LIAR.
UHHHHH
YOU DID BAD, DIDN'T YOU? I CAN TELL.
HEY! WHAT ARE YOU GUYS DOING?!
SHF
HERE IT IS.

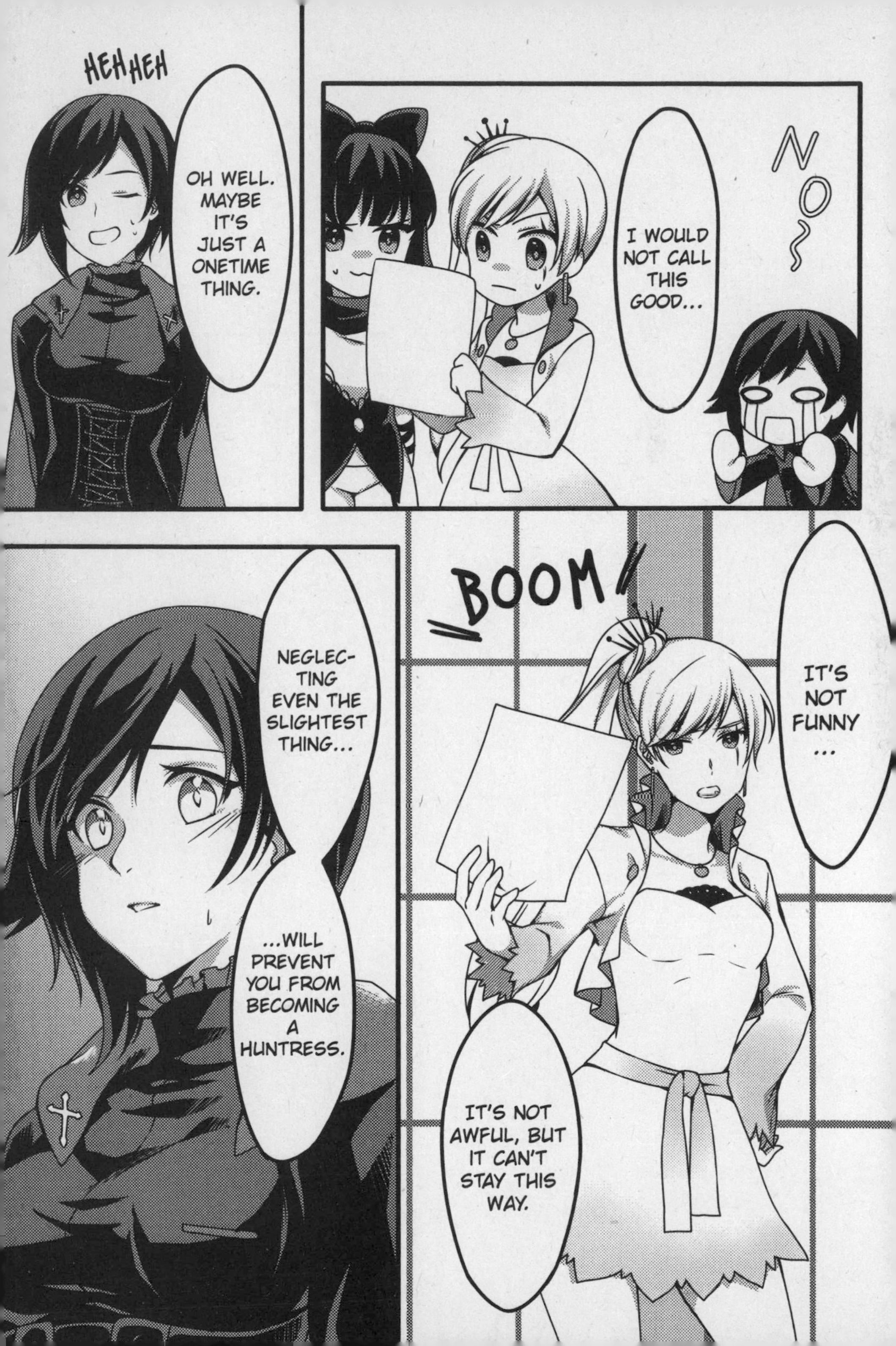
NO~
I WOULD NOT CALL THIS GOOD...
HEH HEH
OH WELL. MAYBE IT'S JUST A ONETIME THING.
BOOM
IT'S NOT FUNNY...
IT'S NOT AWFUL, BUT IT CAN'T STAY THIS WAY.
NEGLEC-TING EVEN THE SLIGHTEST THING...
...WILL PREVENT YOU FROM BECOMING A HUNTRESS.

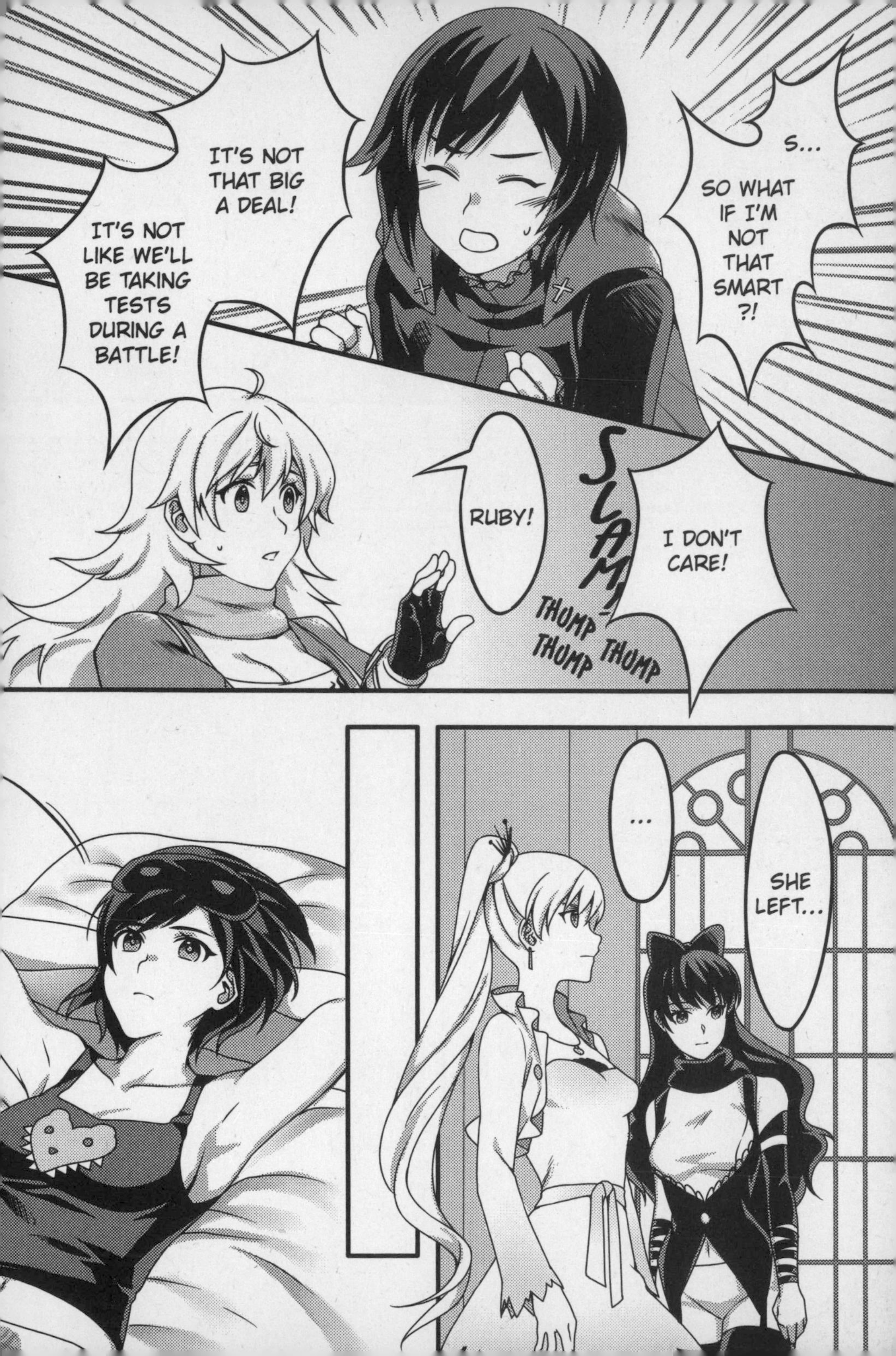
S...
SO WHAT IF I'M NOT THAT SMART?!
IT'S NOT THAT BIG A DEAL!
IT'S NOT LIKE WE'LL BE TAKING TESTS DURING A BATTLE!
I DON'T CARE!
SLAM!
THUMP THUMP THUMP
RUBY!
SHE LEFT...
...

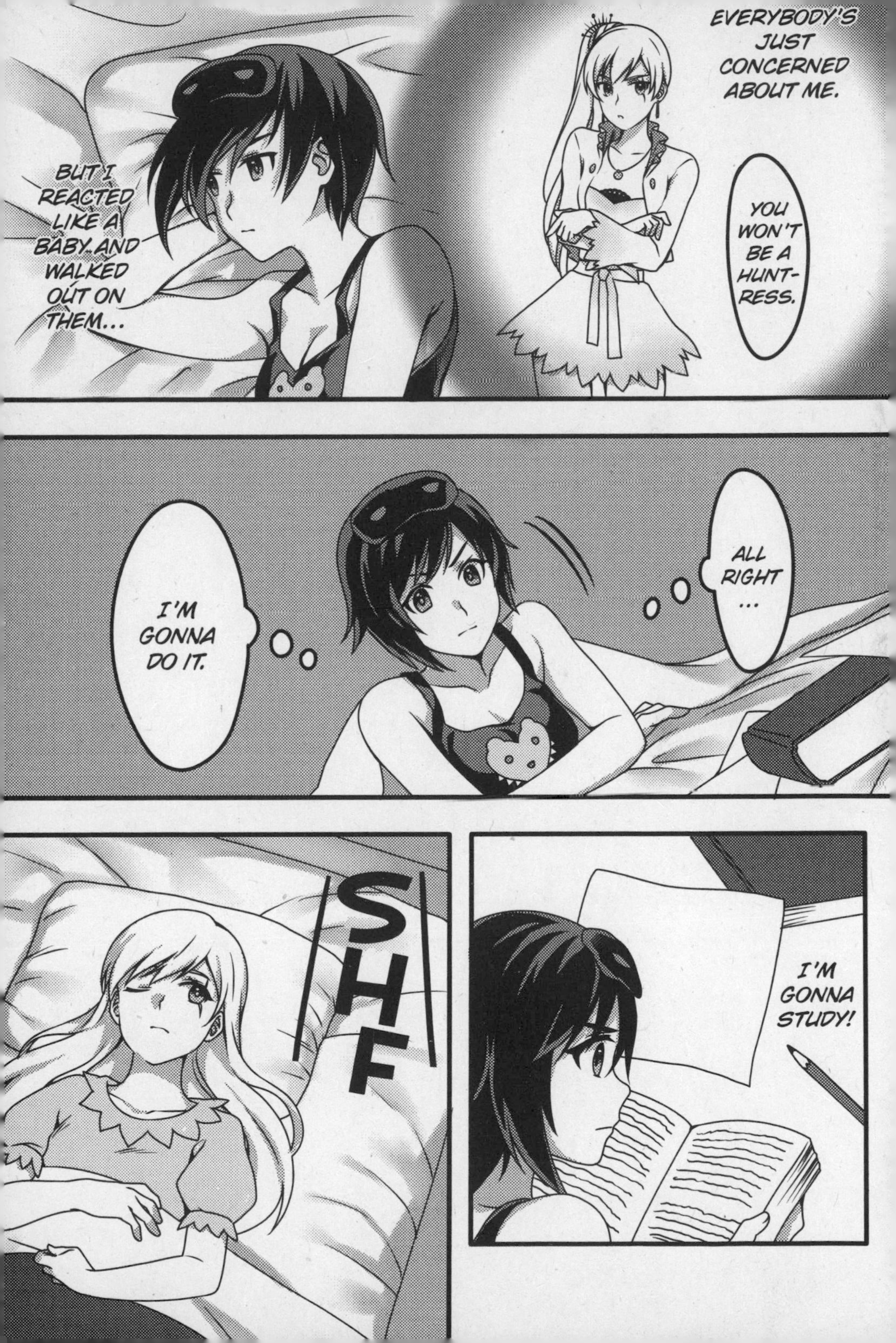
EVERYBODY'S JUST CONCERNED ABOUT ME.
YOU WON'T BE A HUNT-RESS.
BUT I REACTED LIKE A BABY AND WALKED OUT ON THEM...
ALL RIGHT...
I'M GONNA DO IT.
I'M GONNA STUDY!
SHF

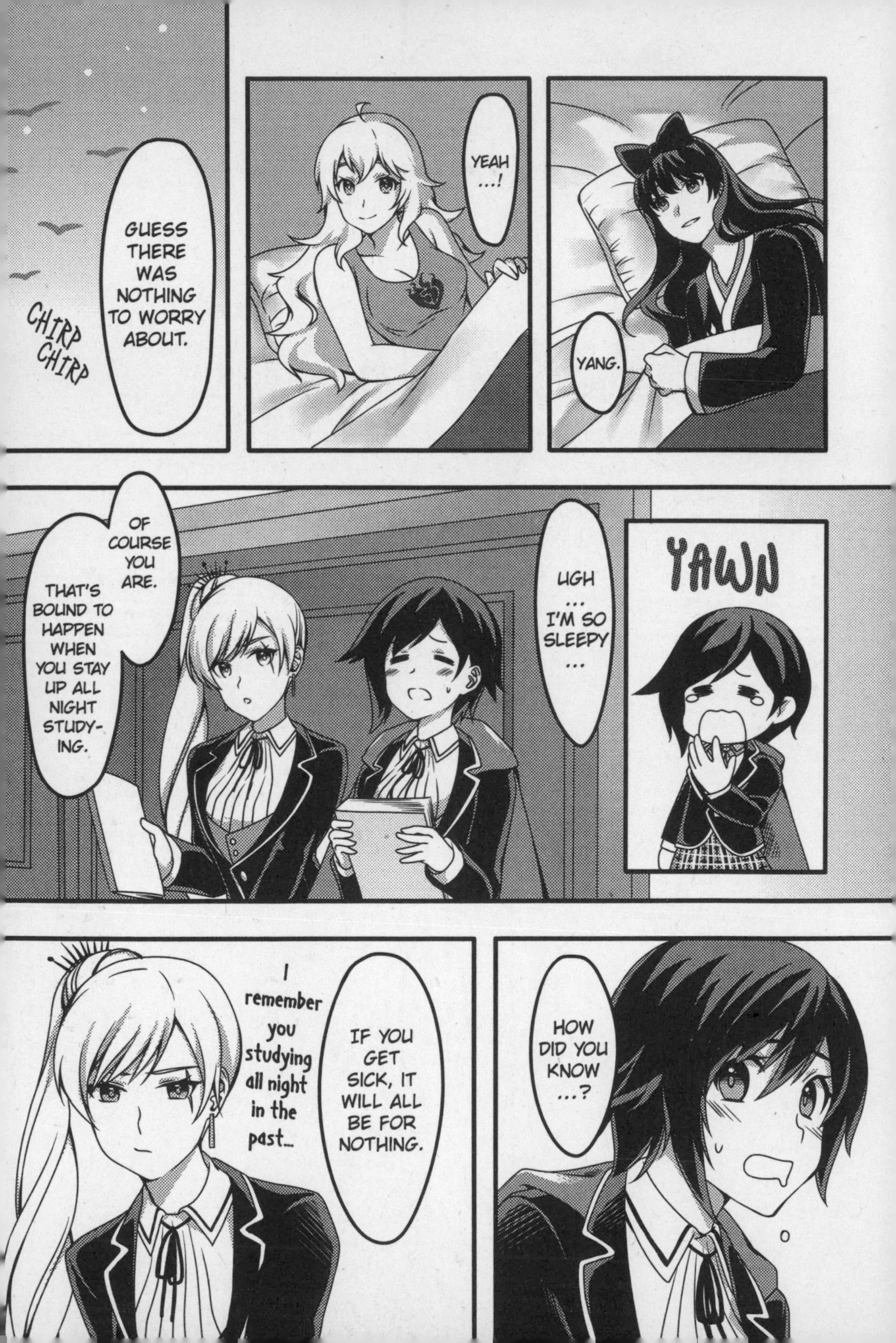
YANG.
YEAH ...!
GUESS THERE WAS NOTHING TO WORRY ABOUT.
CHIRP CHIRP
YAWN
UGH ... I'M SO SLEEPY ...
OF COURSE YOU ARE.
THAT'S BOUND TO HAPPEN WHEN YOU STAY UP ALL NIGHT STUDY-ING.
HOW DID YOU KNOW ...?
IF YOU GET SICK, IT WILL ALL BE FOR NOTHING.
I remember you studying all night in the past...

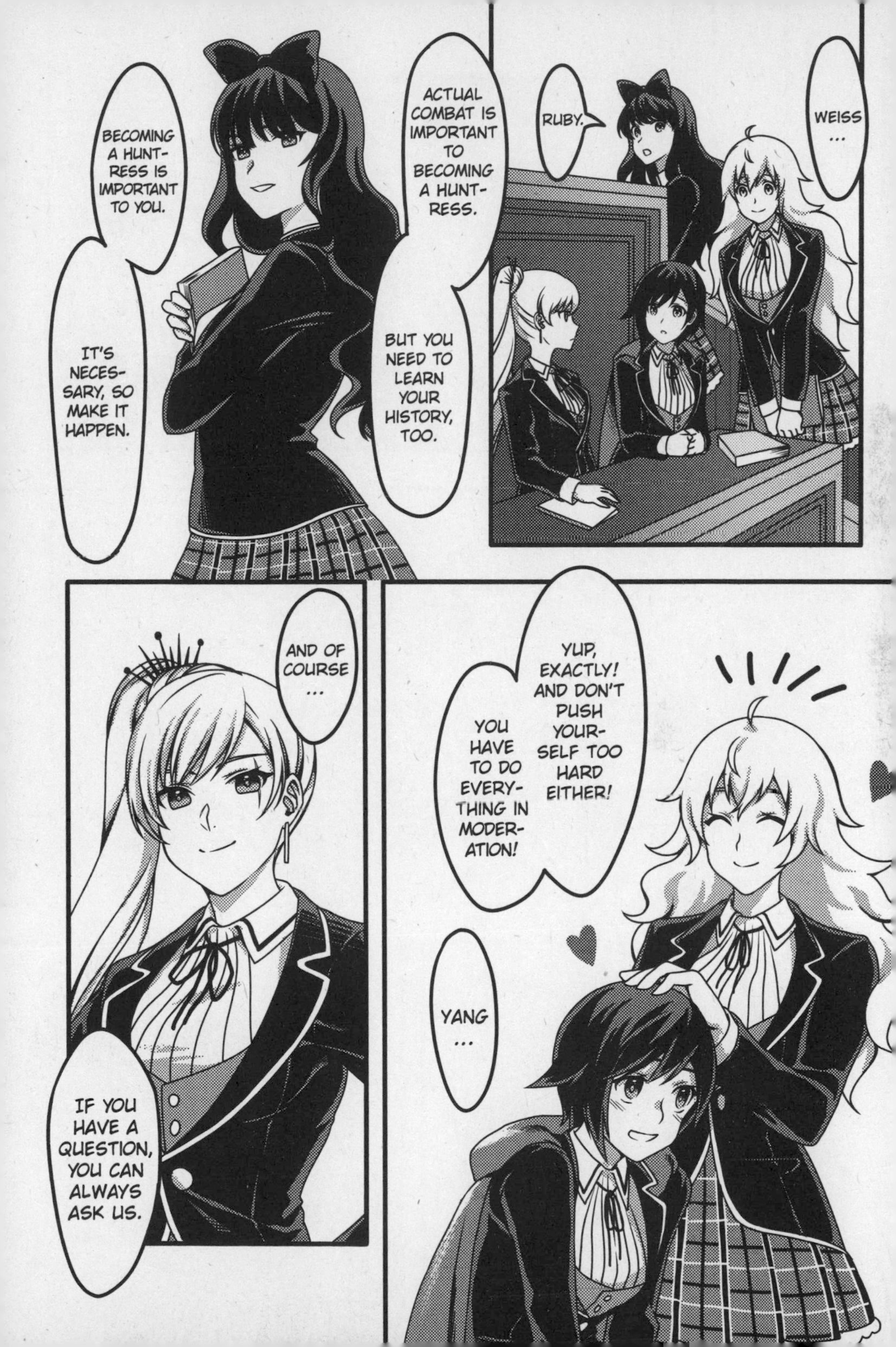
WEISS ...
RUBY.
ACTUAL COMBAT IS IMPORTANT TO BECOMING A HUNTRESS.
BECOMING A HUNTRESS IS IMPORTANT TO YOU.
BUT YOU NEED TO LEARN YOUR HISTORY, TOO.
IT'S NECESSARY, SO MAKE IT HAPPEN.
YUP, EXACTLY! AND DON'T PUSH YOURSELF TOO HARD EITHER!
YOU HAVE TO DO EVERYTHING IN MODERATION!
YANG ...
AND OF COURSE ...
IF YOU HAVE A QUESTION, YOU CAN ALWAYS ASK US.

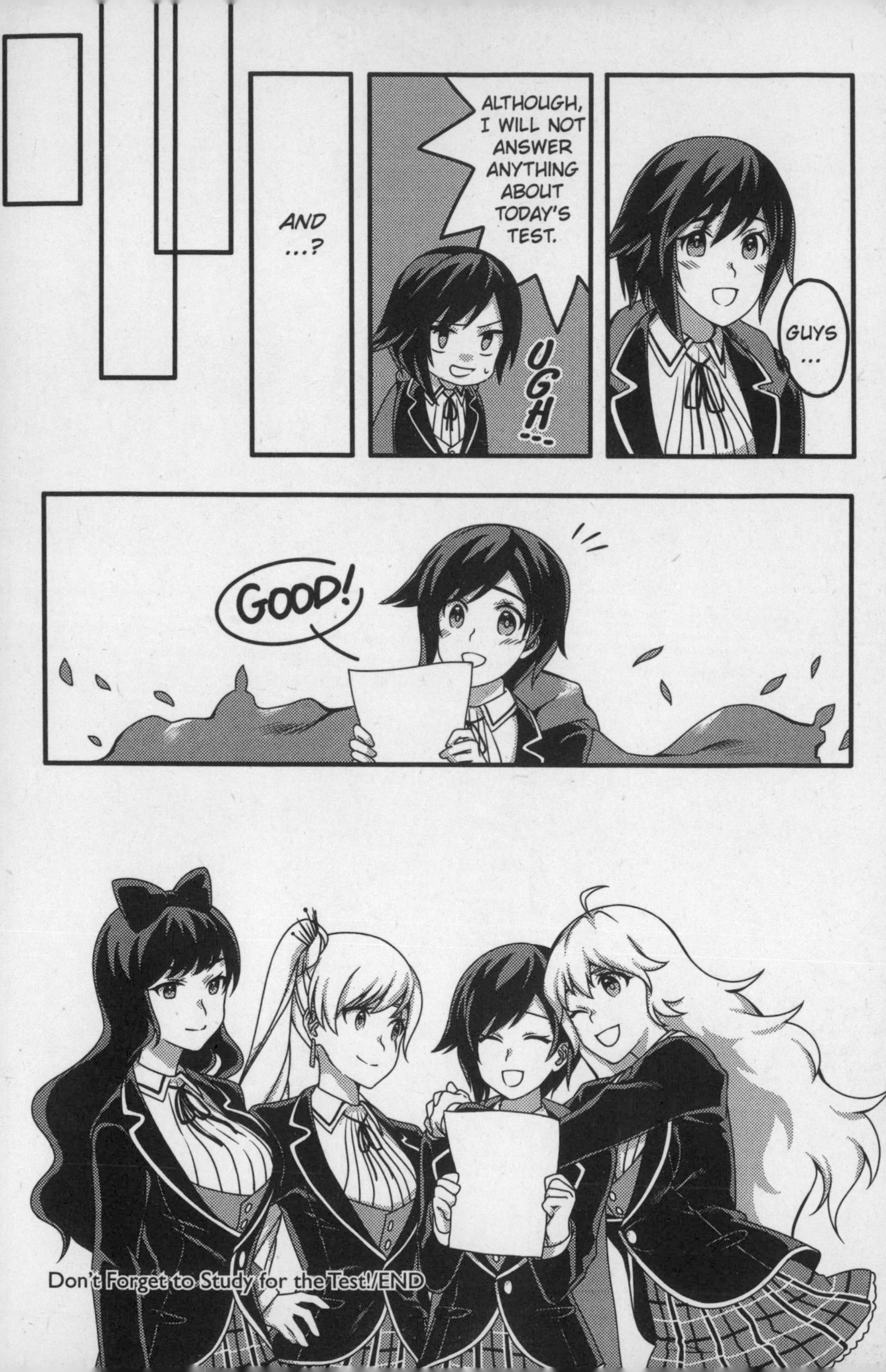
GUYS ...
ALTHOUGH, I WILL NOT ANSWER ANYTHING ABOUT TODAY'S TEST.
UGH...
AND ...?
GOOD!
Don't Forget to Study for the Test!/END

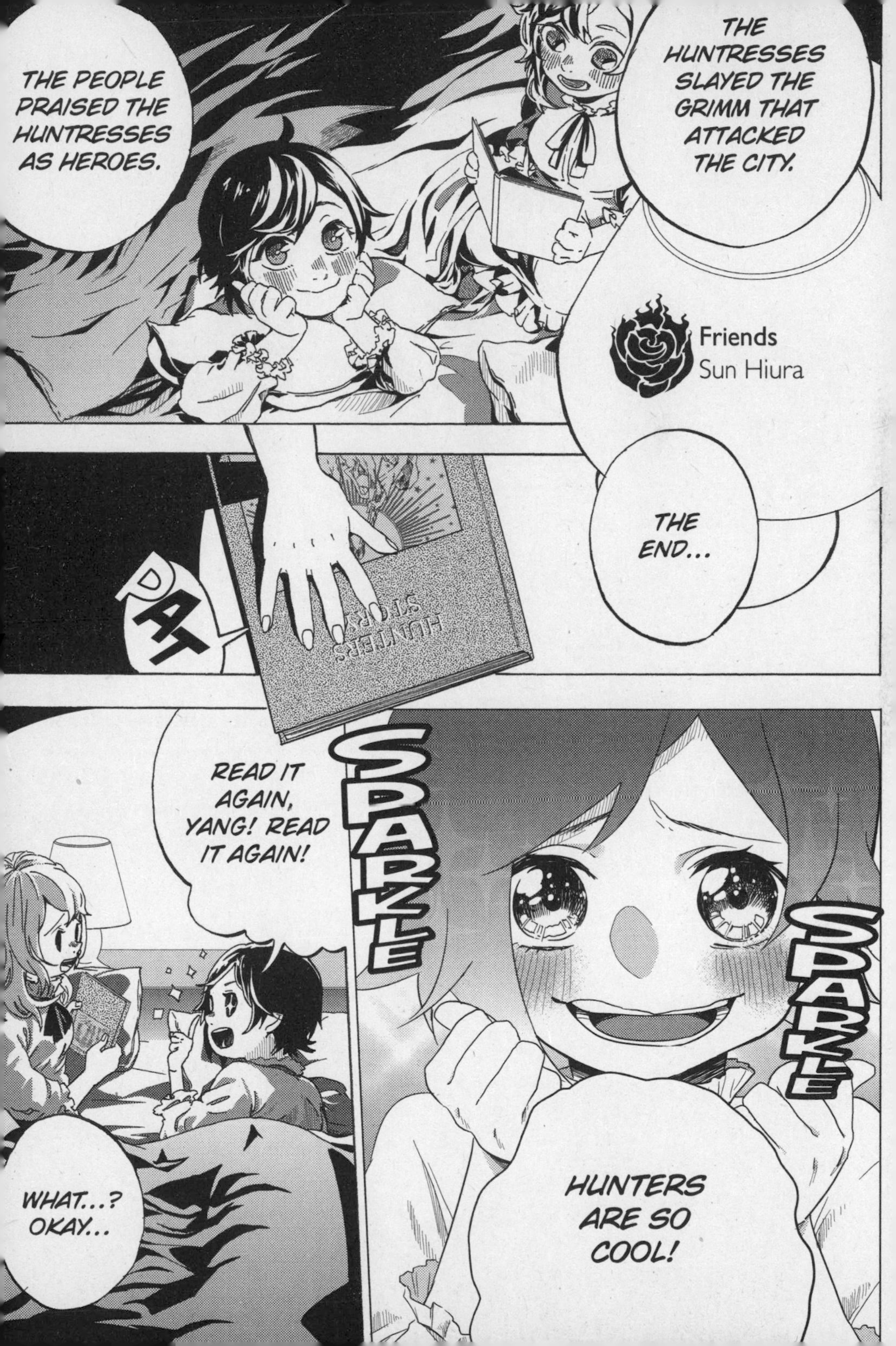
THE HUNTRESSES SLAYED THE GRIMM THAT ATTACKED THE CITY.
THE PEOPLE PRAISED THE HUNTRESSES AS HEROES.
Friends
Sun Hiura
THE END...
PAT
SPARKLE
SPARKLE
HUNTERS ARE SO COOL!
READ IT AGAIN, YANG! READ IT AGAIN!
WHAT...? OKAY...

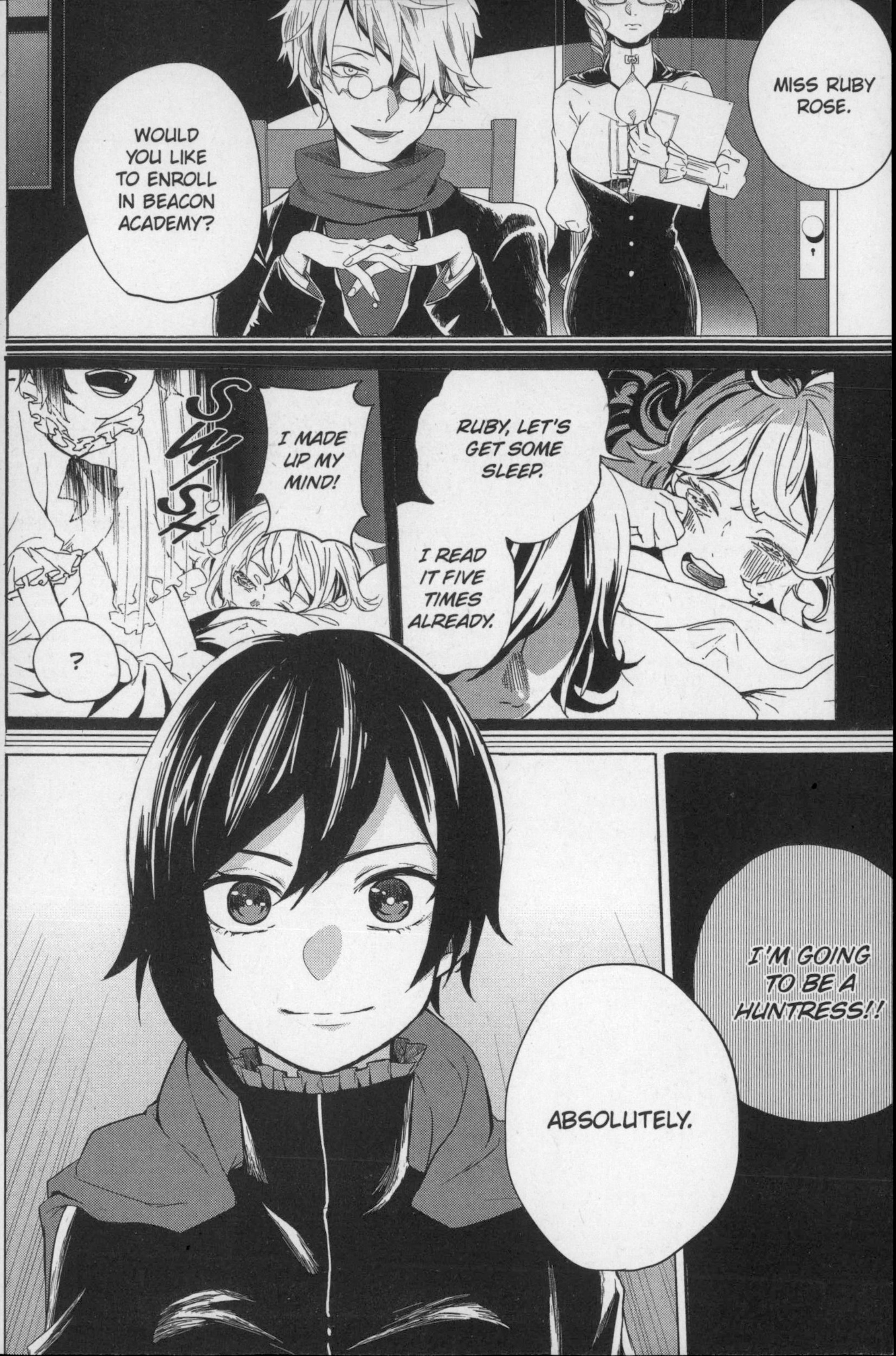

MISS RUBY ROSE.
WOULD YOU LIKE TO ENROLL IN BEACON ACADEMY?
RUBY, LET'S GET SOME SLEEP.
I READ IT FIVE TIMES ALREADY.
I MADE UP MY MIND!
SWISH
?
I'M GOING TO BE A HUNTRESS!!
ABSOLUTELY.

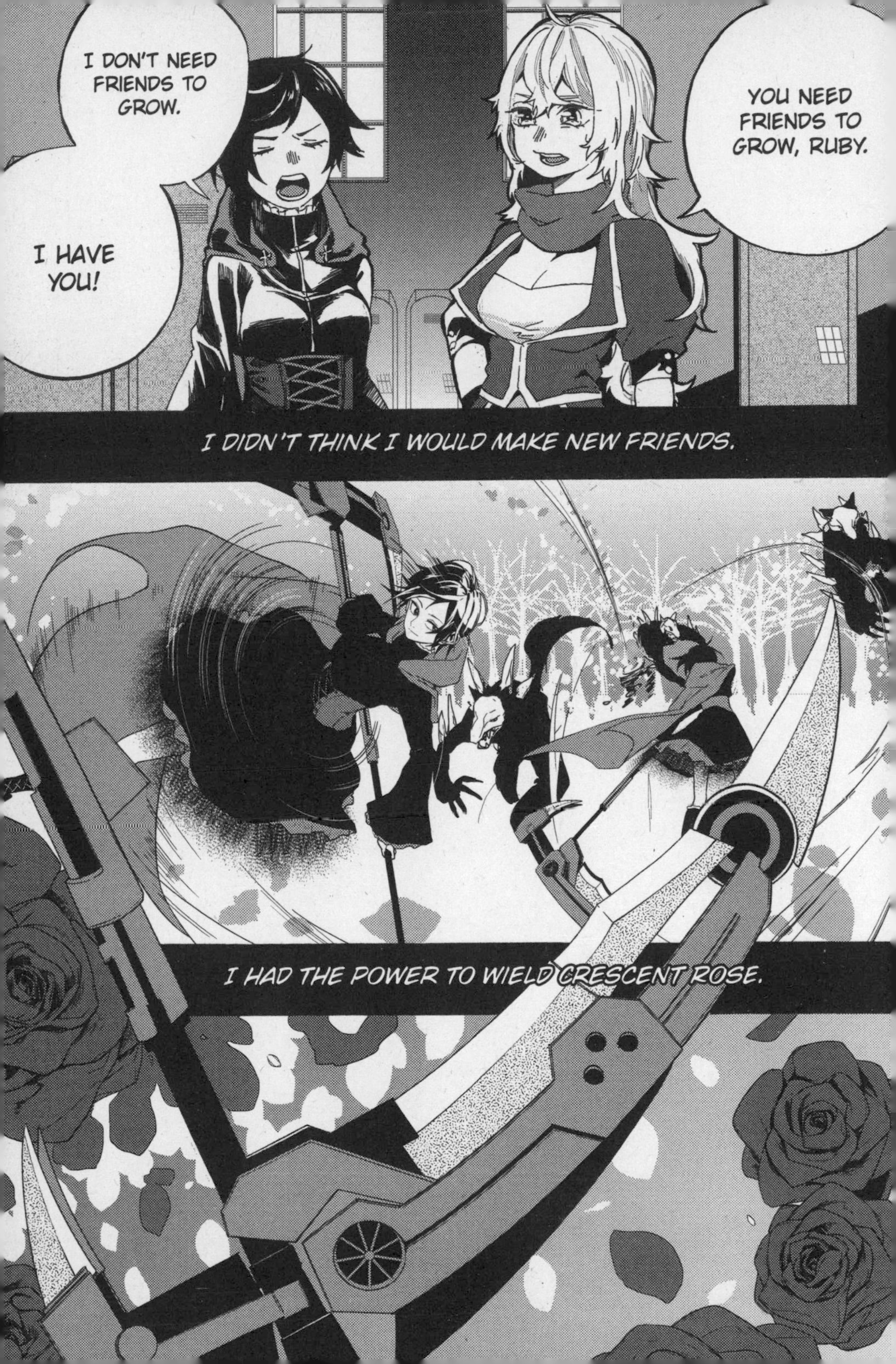
YOU NEED FRIENDS TO GROW, RUBY.
I DON'T NEED FRIENDS TO GROW.
I HAVE YOU!
I DIDN'T THINK I WOULD MAKE NEW FRIENDS.
I HAD THE POWER TO WIELD CRESCENT ROSE.

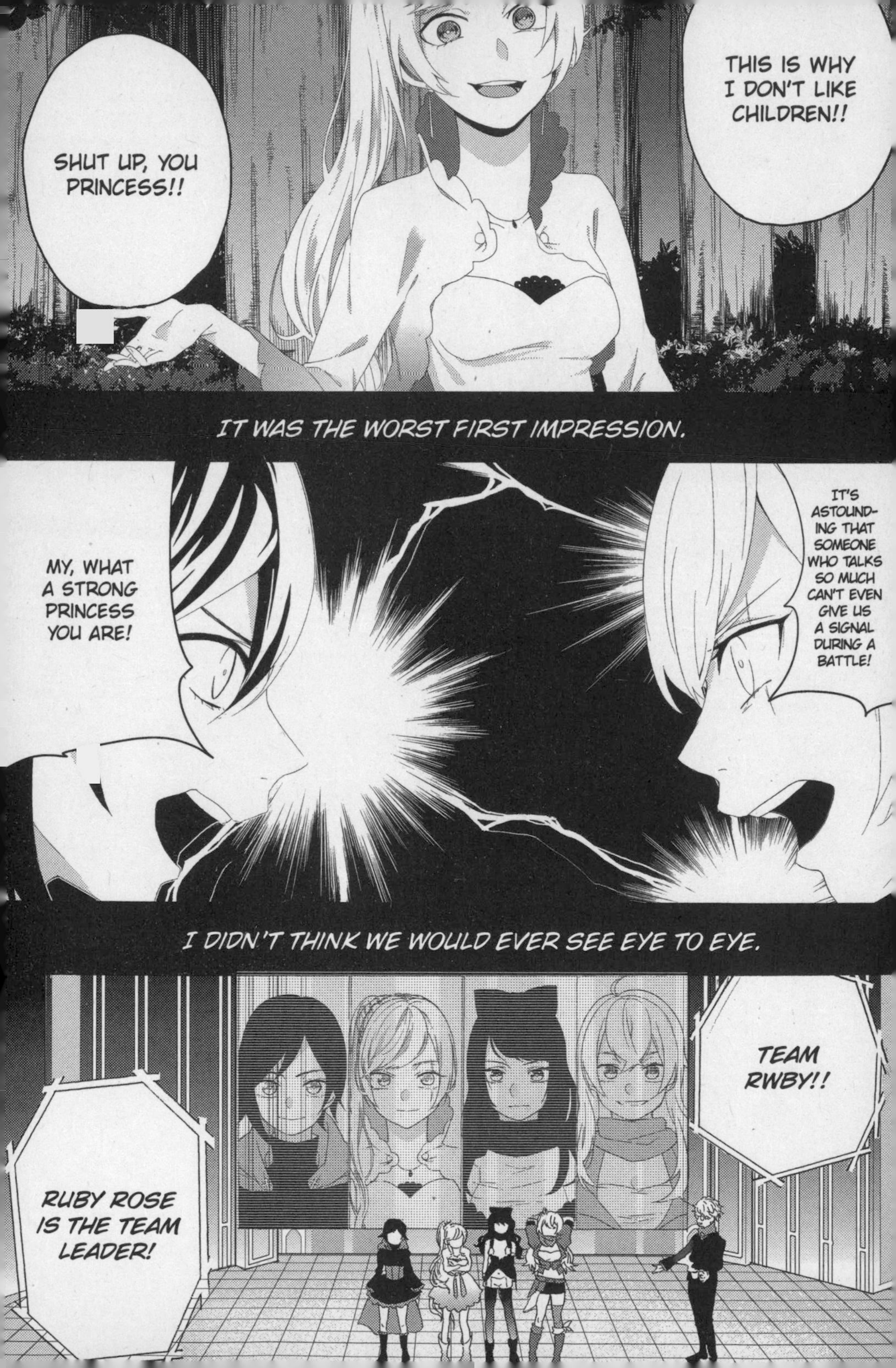
THIS IS WHY I DON'T LIKE CHILDREN!!
SHUT UP, YOU PRINCESS!!
IT WAS THE WORST FIRST IMPRESSION.
IT'S ASTOUNDING THAT SOMEONE WHO TALKS SO MUCH CAN'T EVEN GIVE US A SIGNAL DURING A BATTLE!
MY, WHAT A STRONG PRINCESS YOU ARE!
I DIDN'T THINK WE WOULD EVER SEE EYE TO EYE.
TEAM RWBY!!
RUBY ROSE IS THE TEAM LEADER!

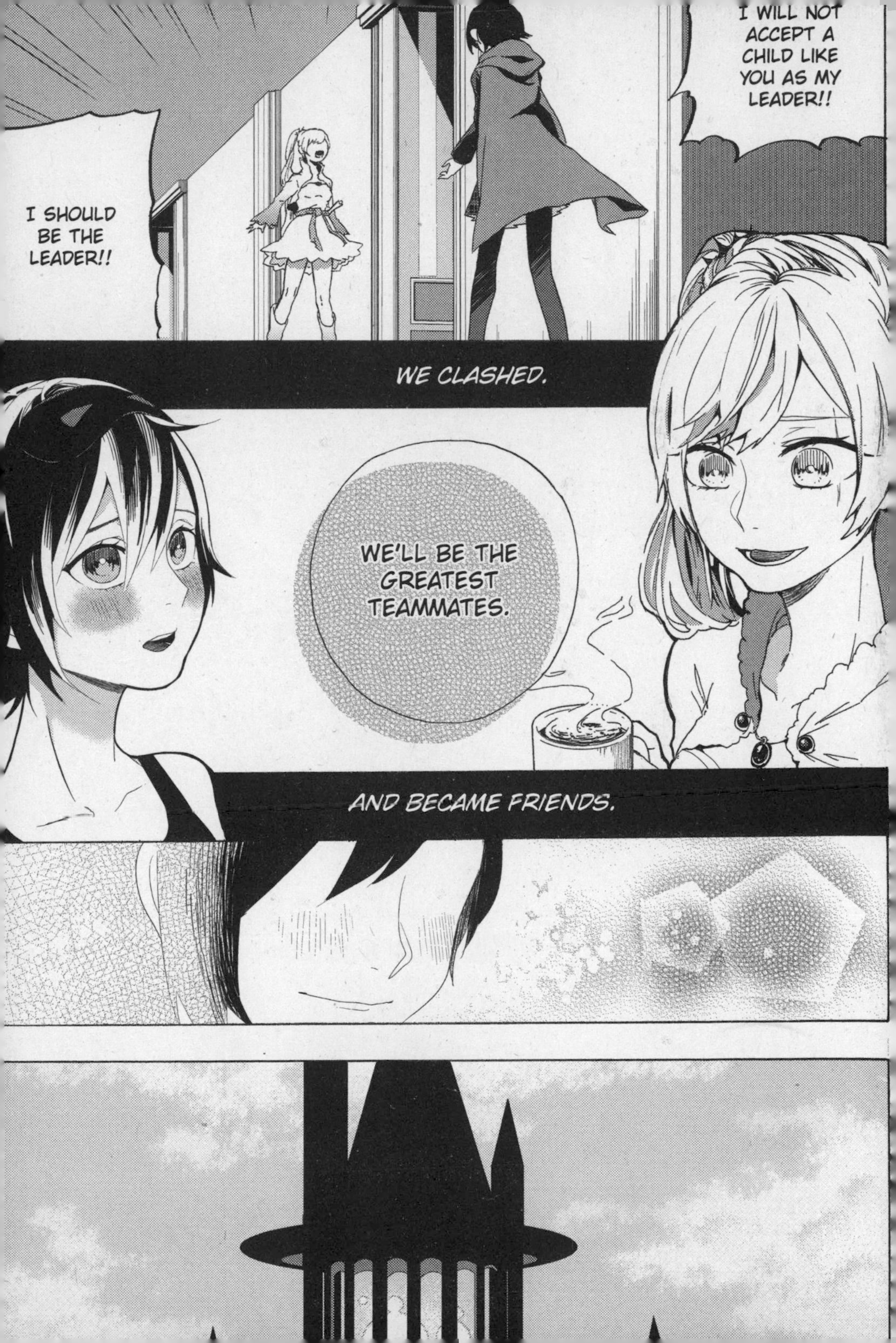
I WILL NOT ACCEPT A CHILD LIKE YOU AS MY LEADER!!
I SHOULD BE THE LEADER!!
WE CLASHED.
WE'LL BE THE GREATEST TEAMMATES.
AND BECAME FRIENDS.

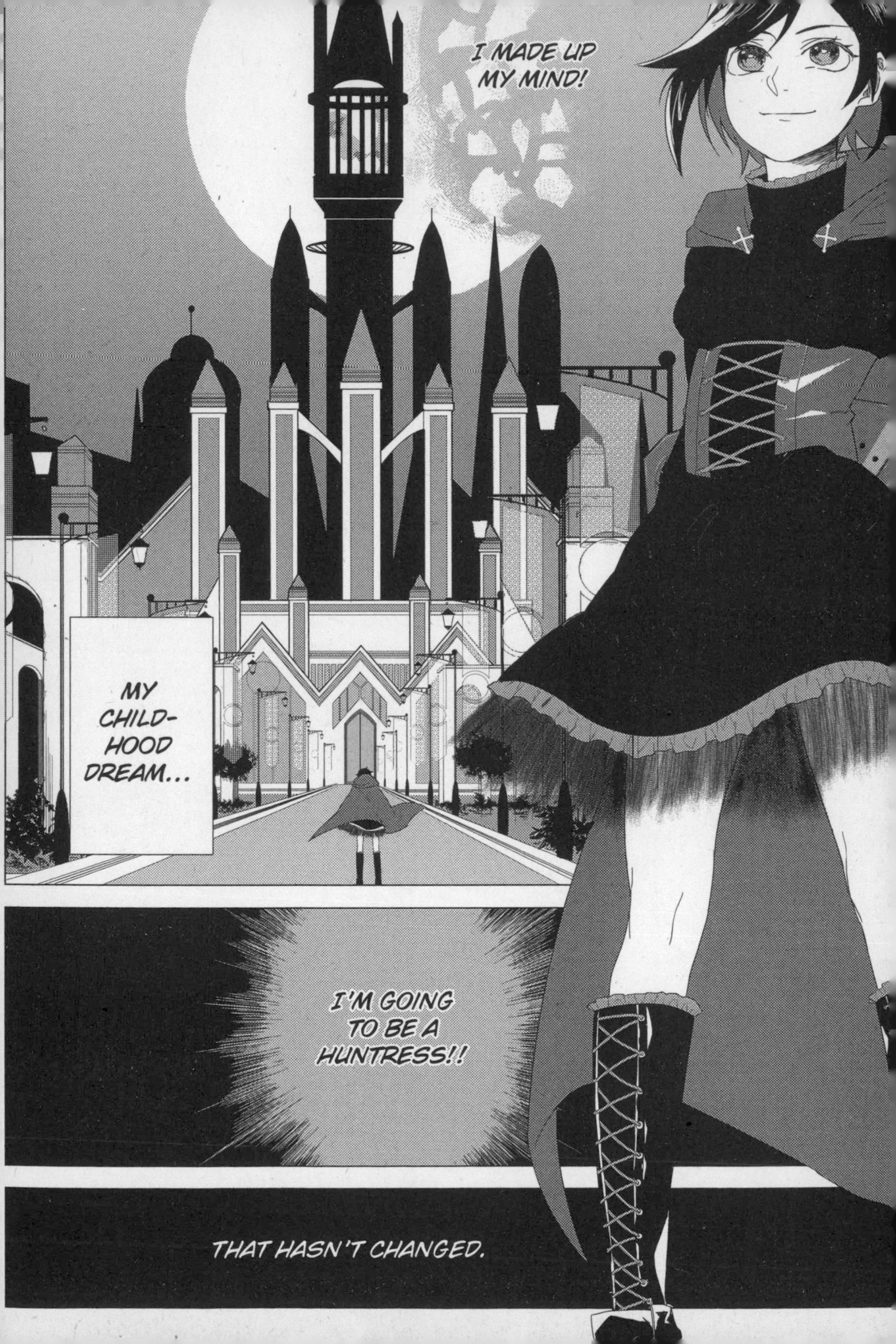
I MADE UP MY MIND!
MY CHILD-HOOD DREAM...
I'M GOING TO BE A HUNTRESS!!
THAT HASN'T CHANGED.

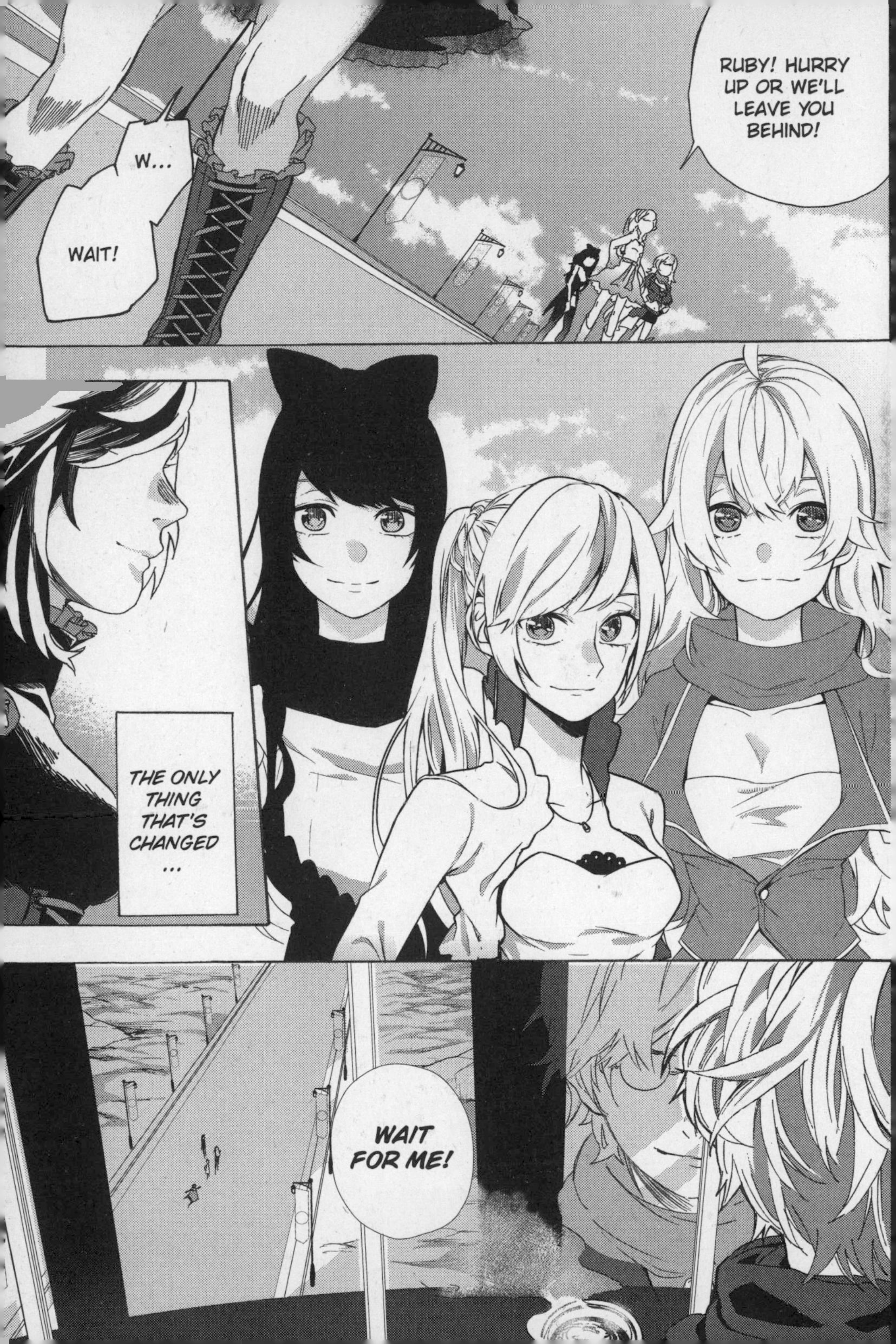
RUBY! HURRY UP OR WE'LL LEAVE YOU BEHIND!
W...
WAIT!
THE ONLY THING THAT'S CHANGED ...
WAIT FOR ME!

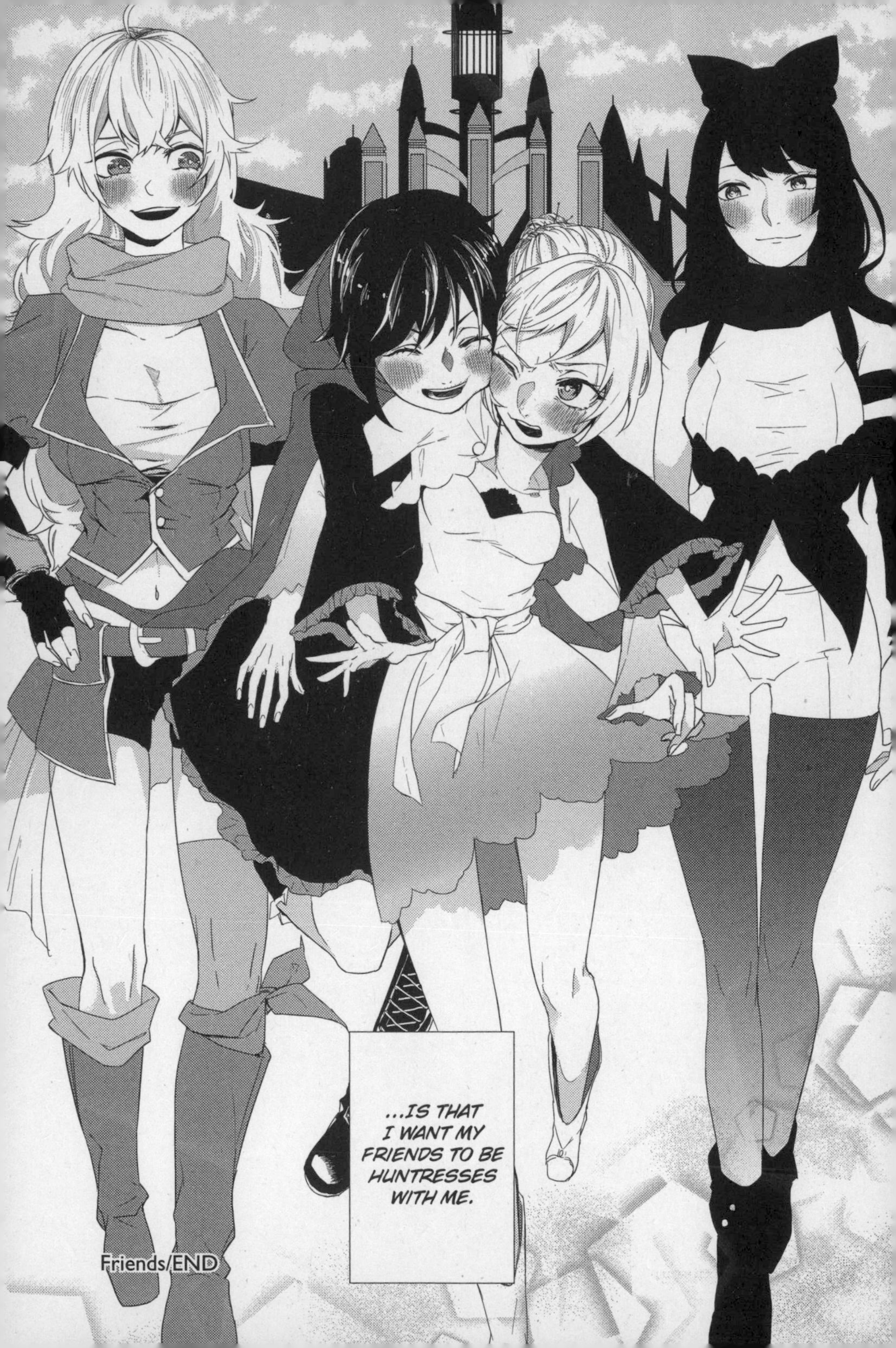
...IS THAT I WANT MY FRIENDS TO BE HUNTRESSES WITH ME.
Friends/END

Ruby Smile

RWBY No Doubt: Ruby

RWBY No Doubt: Ruby
Umiya

Scarfff

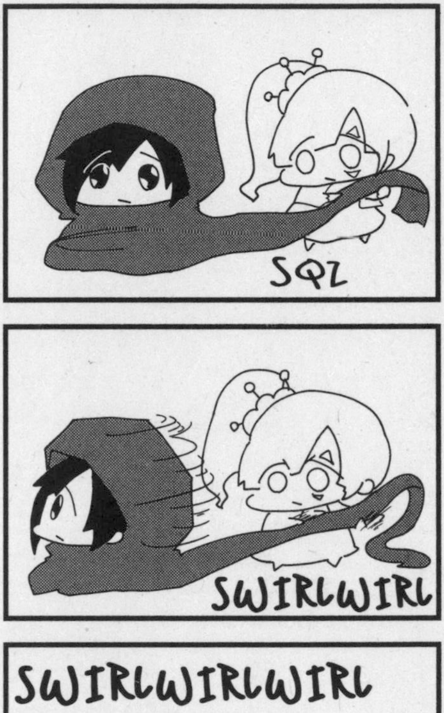
SQZ
SWIRLWIRL
SWIRLWIRLWIRL
SWIRLWIRLWIRL
SWIRLWIRLWIRLWIRL

Taking Out Bad Guys –Part I–

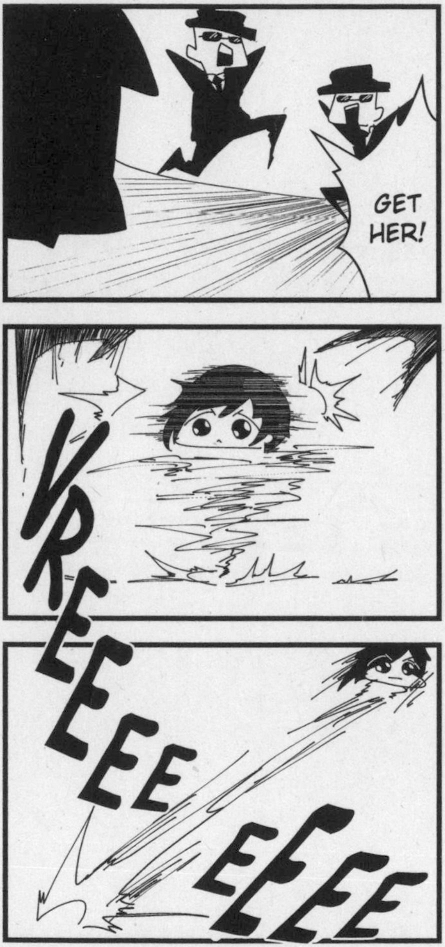
GET HER!
VREEEEEEEEE
TWINKLE

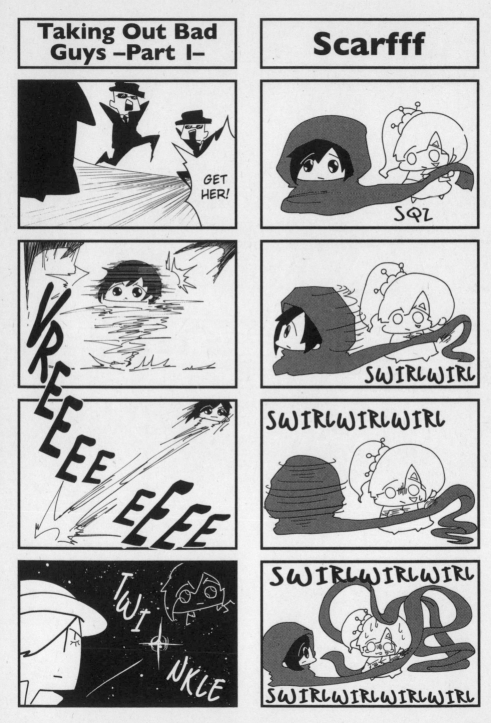

Taking Out Bad Guys –Part 2–

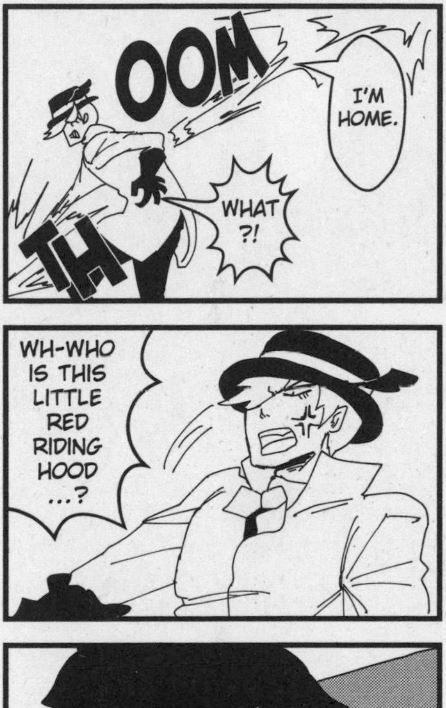
I'M HOME.
OOM
WHAT ?!
TH
WH-WHO IS THIS LITTLE RED RIDING HOOD ...?
WHOOSH
TUG

Taking Out Bad Guys –Part 3–

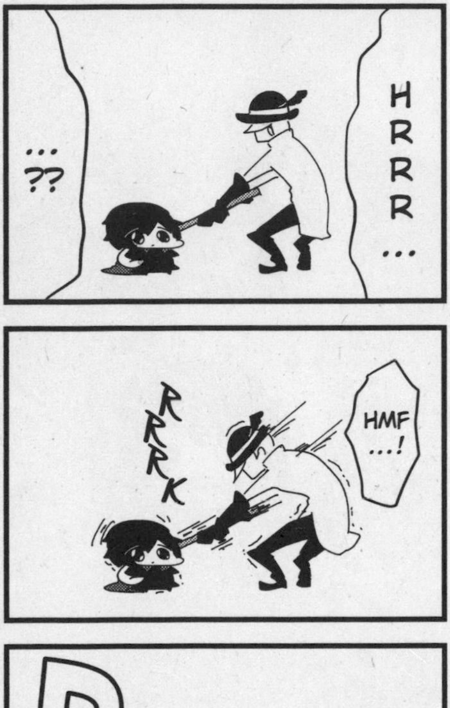
HRRR...
...??
HMF ...!
RRRK
POP
OH?

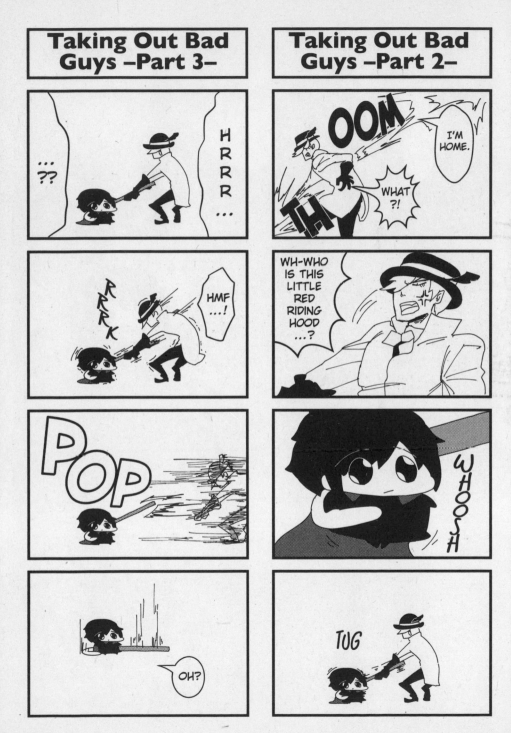

About Ruby

Ein Lee

Ruby is the main character of this story and the girl who has captured the hearts of fans all over the world. Besides some small details of her outfit, Monty, not me, was responsible for her character design. Her "modern fantasy" image was the impetus for creating the story's atmosphere and characters.

I first met Monty at RTX (the annual Rooster Teeth event held in Austin) in 2013. At the time he was wearing fingerless gloves, a white wig and punk-style clothing. I thought, "If he were a girl, Ruby's ordinary clothes would be just like that!"

Wakanabe and Kusano provided direction for the cover illustration. They wanted a white background, so instead of the usual smooth lines created using CG, I drew her using various colors and shapes. Ruby is the heroine, so I always try to express her confidence and toughness.

I had another idea for the illustration (the rough sketch on this page) where I tried going for a romantic feel instead of her standing. I drew her lying on rose petals—her symbol—and added effects to make it look like she's floating on water. I like the quiet and fragile feel of it, but it was decided that it lacked the dynamism needed for a manga cover so the standing-pose one was chosen.

Looking back now, maybe I should have included her weapon. Although I'm not sure if Crescent Rose would float on water.

Her portrait (rough sketch, below) was designed to contrast with Weiss's which you'll see on this page in volume 2. I hope you enjoy comparing them.

Hello, dear reader! You are about to embark on a journey into the world of Remnant with team *RWBY*. I hope that the twists and turns in your voyage are as exciting as the progression of *RWBY* has been, as a whole.

On behalf of the entire *RWBY* crew, I want to sincerely thank you for your overwhelming love and support. We never imagined that *RWBY* would have so many incredible, passionate, and devoted fans. With the help of fans like you, the show has redefined animation genres, reached international audiences and spread through multiple various mediums. Now you get to experience *RWBY* in a completely new way: as a manga.

I hope you enjoy the adventure that lies ahead, just beyond the next page. We will certainly enjoy the story of *RWBY* as it continues to grow and take new forms. Thanks to you.

Lindsay Jones

RWBY

OFFICIAL MANGA ANTHOLOGY 1

Red Like Roses

VIZ Signature Edition
Official Manga Anthology Vol. 1
RED LIKE ROSES
Based on the Rooster Teeth Series Created by MONTY OUM.

©2017 Rooster Teeth Productions, LLC
©2017 Warner Bros. Japan LLC All rights reserved.
©2017 Home-sha

TRANSLATION Joe Yamazaki
ENGLISH ADAPTATION Jeremy Haun & Jason A. Hurley
TOUCH-UP ART AND LETTERING Evan Waldinger
DESIGN Shawn Carrico
EDITOR Joel Enos

COVER ILLUSTRATION Ein Lee & Meteo
ORIGINAL COVER DESIGN Tsuyoshi Kusano

SPECIAL THANKS
Ken Takizawa (Home-sha)
Takanori Inoue (Home-sha)
Misato Kaneko
Yoshihiko Wakanabe (Editor/Planner of RWBY OFFICIAL MANGA ANTHOLOGY)

The stories, characters and incidents mentioned in this
publication are entirely fictional.

No portion of this book may be reproduced or transmitted in
any form or by any means without written permission from the
copyright holders.

Printed in the U.S.A.

Published by VIZ Media, LLC
P.O. Box 77010
San Francisco, CA 94107

10 9 8 7 6 5 4 3 2 1
First printing, May 2018

PARENTAL ADVISORY
RWBY is rated T for Teen and is recommended
for ages 13 and up. This volume contains violence
and peril.